Plutarch's Morals

Plutarch

PLUTARCH'S MORALS.

ON EDUCATION.

§ I. Come let us consider what one might say on the education of free children, and by what training they would become good citizens.

§ II. It is perhaps best to begin with birth: I would therefore warn those who desire to be fathers of notable sons, not to form connections with any kind of women, such as courtesans or mistresses: for those who either on the father or mother's side are ill-born have the disgrace of their origin all their life long irretrievably present with them, and offer a ready handle to abuse and vituperation. So that the poet was wise, who said, "Unless the foundation of a house be well laid, the descendants must of necessity be unfortunate."[3] Good birth indeed brings with it a store of assurance, which ought to be greatly valued by all who desire legitimate offspring. For the spirit of those who are a spurious and bastard breed is apt to be mean and abject: for as the poet truly says, "It makes a man even of noble spirit servile, when he is conscious of the ill fame of either his father or mother."[4] On the other hand the sons of illustrious parents are full of pride and arrogance. As an instance of this it is recorded of Diophantus,[5] the son of Themistocles, that he often used to say to various people "that he could do what he pleased with the Athenian people, for what he wished his mother wished, and what she wished Themistocles wished, and what Themistocles wished all the Athenians wished." All praise also ought we to bestow on the Lacedæmonians for their loftiness of soul in fining their king Archidamus for venturing to marry a small woman, for they charged him with intending to furnish them not with kings but kinglets.

§ III. Next must we mention, what was not overlooked even by those who handled this subject before us, that those who approach their wives for procreation must do so either without having drunk any wine or at least very little. For those children, that their parents begot in drink, are wont to be fond of wine and apt to turn out drunkards. And so Diogenes, seeing a youth out of his mind and crazy, said, "Young man, your father was drunk when he begot you." Let this hint serve as to procreation: now let us discuss education.

§ IV. To speak generally, what we are wont to say about the arts and sciences is also true of moral excellence, for to its perfect development three things must meet together, natural ability, theory, and practice. By theory I mean training, and by practice working at one's craft. Now the foundation must be laid in training, and practice gives facility, but perfection is attained only by the junction of all three. For if any one of these elements be wanting, excellence must be so far deficient. For natural ability without training is blind: and training without natural ability is defective, and practice without both natural ability and training is imperfect. For just as in farming the first requisite is good soil, next a good farmer, next good seed, so also here: the soil corresponds to natural ability, the training to the farmer, the seed to precepts and instruction. I should therefore maintain stoutly that these three elements were found combined in the souls of such universally famous men as Pythagoras, and Socrates, and Plato, and of all who have won undying fame. Happy at any rate and dear to the gods is he to whom any deity has vouchsafed all these elements! But if anyone thinks that those who have not good natural ability cannot to some extent make up for the deficiencies of nature by right training and practice, let such a one know that he is very wide of the mark, if not out of it altogether. For good natural parts are impaired by sloth; while inferior ability is mended by training: and while simple things escape the eyes of the careless, difficult things are reached by painstaking. The wonderful efficacy and power of long and continuous labour you may see indeed every day in the world around you.[6] Thus water continually dropping wears away rocks: and iron and steel are moulded by the hands of the artificer: and chariot wheels bent by some strain can never recover their original symmetry: and the crooked staves of actors can never be made straight. But by toil what is contrary to nature becomes stronger than even nature itself. And are these the only things that teach the power of diligence? Not so: ten thousand things teach the same truth. A soil naturally good becomes by neglect barren, and the better its original condition, the worse its ultimate state if uncared for. On the other hand a soil exceedingly rough and sterile by being farmed well produces excellent crops. And what trees do not by neglect become gnarled and unfruitful, whereas by pruning they become fruitful and productive? And what constitution so good but it is marred and impaired by sloth, luxury, and too full habit? And what weak constitution has not derived benefit from exercise and athletics? And what horses broken in young are not docile to their riders? while if they are not broken in till late they become hard-mouthed and unmanageable. And why should we be surprised at similar cases, seeing that we find many of the savagest animals docile and tame by training? Rightly answered the Thessalian, who was asked who the mildest Thessalians were, "Those who have done with fighting."[7] But why pursue the line of argument further? For the Greek name for moral virtue is only habit: and if anyone defines moral virtues as habitual virtues, he will not be beside the mark. But I will employ only one more illustration, and dwell no longer on this topic. Lycurgus, the Lacedæmonian legislator, took two puppies of the same parents, and brought them up in an entirely different way: the one he pampered and cosseted up, while he taught the other to hunt and be a retriever. Then on one occasion, when the Lacedæmonians were convened in assembly, he said, "Mighty, O Lacedæmonians, is the influence on moral excellence of habit, and education, and training, and modes of life, as I will prove to you at once." So saying he produced the two puppies, and set before them a platter and a hare: the one darted on the hare, while the other made for the platter. And when the Lacedæmonians could not guess what his meaning was, or with what intent he had produced the puppies, he said, "These puppies are of the same parents, but by virtue of a different bringing up the one is pampered, and the other a good hound." Let so much suffice for habit and modes of life.

§ V. The next point to discuss will be nutrition. In my opinion mothers ought to nurse and suckle their own children. For they will bring them up with more sympathy and care, if they love them so intimately and, as the proverb puts it, "from their first growing their nails."[8] Whereas the affection of wet or dry nurses is spurious and counterfeit, being merely for pay. And nature itself teaches that mothers ought themselves to suckle and rear those they have given birth to. And for that purpose she has supplied every female parent with milk. And providence has wisely provided women with two breasts, so that if they should bear twins, they would have a breast for each. And besides this, as is natural enough, they would feel more affection and love for their children by suckling them. For this supplying them with food is as it were a tightener of love, for even the brute creation, if taken away from their young, pine away, as we constantly see. Mothers must therefore, as I said, certainly try to suckle their own children: but if they are unable to do so either through physical weakness (for this contingency sometimes occurs), or in haste to have other children, they must select wet and dry nurses with the greatest care, and not introduce into their houses any kind of women. First and foremost they must be Greeks in their habits. For just as it is necessary immediately after birth to shapen the limbs of children, so that they may grow straight and not crooked, so from the beginning must their habits be carefully attended to. For infancy is supple and easily moulded, and what children learn sinks deeply into their souls while they are young and tender, whereas everything hard is softened only with great difficulty. For just as seals are impressed on soft wax, so instruction leaves its permanent mark on the minds of those still young. And divine Plato seems to me to give excellent advice to nurses not to tell their children any kind of fables, that their souls may not in the very dawn of existence be full of folly or corruption.[9] Phocylides the poet also seems to give admirable advice when he says, "We must teach good habits while the pupil is still a boy."

§VI. Attention also must be given to this point, that the lads that are to wait upon and be with young people must be first and foremost of good morals, and able to speak Greek distinctly and idiomatically, that they may not by contact with foreigners of loose morals contract any of their viciousness. For as those who are fond of quoting proverbs say not amiss, "If you live with a lame man, you will learn to halt."[10]

§VII. Next, when our boys are old enough to be put into the hands of tutors,[11] great care must be taken that we do not hand them over to slaves, or foreigners, or flighty persons. For what happens nowadays in many cases is highly ridiculous: good slaves are made farmers, or sailors, or merchants, or stewards, or money-lenders; but if they find a winebibbing, greedy, and utterly useless slave, to him parents commit the charge of their sons, whereas the good tutor ought to be such a one as was Phoenix, the tutor of Achilles. The point also which I am now going to speak about is of the utmost importance. The schoolmasters we ought to select for our boys should be of blameless life, of pure character, and of great experience. For a good training is the source and root of gentlemanly behaviour. And just as farmers prop up their trees, so good schoolmasters prop up the young by good advice and suggestions, that they may become upright. How one must despise, therefore, some fathers, who, whether from ignorance or inexperience, before putting the intended teachers to the test, commit their sons to the charge of untried and untested men. If they act so through inexperience it is not so ridiculous; but it is to the remotest degree absurd when, though perfectly aware of both the inexperience and worthlessness of some schoolmasters, they yet entrust their sons to them; some overcome by flattery, others to gratify friends who solicit their favours; acting just as if anybody ill in body, passing over the experienced physician, should, to gratify his friend, call him in, and so throw away his life; or as if to gratify one's friend one should reject the best pilot and choose him instead. Zeus and all the gods! can anyone bearing the sacred name of father put obliging a petitioner before obtaining the best education for his sons? Were they not then wise words that the time-honoured Socrates used to utter, and say that he would proclaim, if he could, climbing up to the highest part of the city, "Men, what can you be thinking of, who move heaven and earth to make money, while you bestow next to no attention on the sons you are going to leave that money to?"[12] I would add to this that such fathers act very similarly to a person who should be very careful about his shoe but care nothing about his foot. Many persons also are so niggardly about their children, and indifferent to their interests, that for the sake of a paltry saving, they prefer worthless teachers for their children, practising a vile economy at the expense of their children's ignorance. *Apropos* of this, Aristippus on one occasion rebuked an empty-headed parent neatly and wittily. For being asked how much money a parent ought to pay for his son's education, he answered, "A thousand drachmæ." And he replying, "Hercules, what a price! I could buy a slave for as much;" Aristippus answered, "You shall have two slaves then, your son and the slave you buy."[13] And is it not altogether strange that you accustom your son to take his food in his right hand, and chide him if he offers his left, whereas you care very little about his hearing good and sound discourses? I will tell you what happens to such admirable fathers, when they have educated and brought up their sons so badly: when the sons grow to man's estate, they disregard a sober and well-ordered life, and rush headlong into disorderly and low vices; then at the last the parents are sorry they have neglected their education, bemoaning bitterly when it is too late their sons' debasement. For some of them keep flatterers and parasites in their retinue--an accursed set of wretches, the defilers and pest of youth; others keep mistresses and common prostitutes, wanton and costly; others waste their money in eating; others come to grief through dice and revelling; some even go in for bolder profligacy, being whoremongers and defilers of the marriage bed,[14] who would madly pursue their darling vice if it cost them their lives. Had they associated with some philosopher, they would not have lowered themselves by such practices, but would have remembered the precept of Diogenes, whose advice sounds rather low, but is really of excellent moral intent,[15] "Go into a brothel, my lad, that you may see the little difference between vice and virtue."

§ VIII. I say, then, to speak comprehensively (and I might be justly considered in so saying to speak as an oracle, not to be delivering a mere precept), that a good education and sound bringing-up is of the first and middle and last importance; and I declare it to be most instrumental and conducive to virtue and happiness. For all other human blessings compared to this are petty and insignificant. For noble birth is a great honour, but it is an advantage from our forefathers. And wealth is valuable, but it is the acquisition of fortune, who has often taken it away from those who had it, and brought it to those who little expected it; and much wealth is a sort of mark for villanous slaves and informers to shoot at to fill their own purses; and, what is a most important point, even the greatest villains have money sometimes. And glory is noble, but insecure. And beauty is highly desirable, but shortlived. And health is highly valuable, but soon impaired. And strength is desirable, but illness or age soon made sad inroads into it. And generally speaking, if anyone prides himself on his bodily strength, let him know that he is deficient in judgment. For how much inferior is the strength of a man to that of animals, as elephants, bulls, and lions! But education is of all our advantages the only one immortal and divine. And two of the most powerful agencies in man's nature are mind and reason. And mind governs reason, and reason obeys mind; and mind is irremovable by fortune, cannot be taken away by informers, cannot be destroyed by disease, cannot have inroads made into it by old age. For the mind alone flourishes in age; and while time takes away everything else, it adds wisdom to old age. Even war, that sweeps away everything else like a winter torrent, cannot take away education. And Stilpo, the Megarian, seems to me to have made a memorable answer when Demetrius enslaved Megara and rased it to the ground. On his asking whether Stilpo had lost anything, he replied, "Certainly not, for war can make no havoc of virtue." Corresponding and consonant to this is the answer of Socrates, who when asked, I think by Gorgias,[16] if he had any conception as to the happiness of the King of Persia, replied, "I do not know his position in regard to virtue and education: for happiness lies in these, and not in adventitious advantages."

§ IX. And as I advise parents to think nothing more important than the education of their children, so I maintain that it must be a sound and healthy education, and that our sons must be kept as far as possible from vulgar twaddle. For what pleases the vulgar displeases the wise. I am borne out by the lines of Euripides, "Unskilled am I in the oratory that pleases the mob; but amongst the few that are my equals I am reckoned rather wise. For those who are little thought of by the wise, seem to hit the taste of the vulgar."[17] And I have myself noticed that those who practise to speak acceptably and to the gratification of the masses promiscuously, for the most part become also profligate and lovers of pleasure in their lives. Naturally enough. For if in giving pleasure to others they neglect the noble, they would be hardly likely to put the lofty and sound above a life of luxury and pleasure, and to prefer moderation to delights. Yet what better advice could we give our sons than to follow this? or to what could we better exhort them to accustom themselves? For perfection is only attained by neither speaking nor acting at random--as the proverb says, *Perfection is only attained by practice*.[18] Whereas extempore oratory is easy and facile, mere windbag, having neither beginning nor end. And besides their other shortcomings extempore speakers fall into great disproportion and repetition, whereas a well considered speech preserves its due proportions. It is recorded by tradition that Pericles, when called on by the people for a speech, frequently refused on the plea that he was unprepared. Similarly Demosthenes, his state-rival, when the Athenians called upon him for his advice, refused to give it, saying, "I am not prepared." But this you will say, perhaps, is mere tradition without authority. But in his speech against Midias he plainly sets forth the utility of preparation, for he says, "I do not deny, men of Athens, that I have prepared this speech to the best of my ability: for I should have been a poor creature if, after suffering so much at his hands, and even still suffering, I had neglected how to plead my case."[19] Not that I would altogether reject extempore oratory, or its use in critical cases, but it should be used only as one would take medicine.[20] Up, indeed, to man's estate I would have no extempore speaking, but when anyone's powers of speech are rooted and grounded, then, as emergencies call for it, I would allow his words to flow freely. For as those who have been for a long time in fetters stumble if unloosed, not being able to walk from being long used to their fetters, so those who for a long time have used compression in their words, if they are suddenly called upon to speak off-hand, retain the same character of expression. But to let mere lads speak extempore is to give rise to the acme of foolish talk. A wretched painter once showed Apelles, they say, a picture, and said, "I have just done it." Apelles replied, "Without your telling me, I should know it was painted quickly; I only wonder you haven't painted more such in the time." As then (for I now return from my digression), I advise to avoid stilted and bombastic language, so again do I urge to avoid a finical and petty style of speech; for tall talk is unpopular, and petty language makes no impression. And as the body ought to be not only sound but in good condition, so speech ought to be not only not feeble but vigorous. For a safe mediocrity is indeed praised, but a bold venturesomeness is also admired. I am also of the same opinion with regard to the disposition of the soul, which ought to be neither audacious nor timid and easily dejected: for the one ends in impudence and the other in servility; but to keep in all things the mean between extremes is artistic and proper. And, while I am still on this topic, I wish to give my opinion, that I regard a monotonous speech first as no small proof of want of taste, next as likely to generate disdain, and certain not to please long. For to harp on one string is always tiresome and brings satiety; whereas variety is pleasant always whether to the ear or eye.

§ X. Next our freeborn lad ought to go in for a course of what is called general knowledge, but a smattering of this will be sufficient, a taste as it were (for perfect knowledge of all subjects would be impossible); but he must seriously cultivate philosophy. I borrow an illustration to show my meaning: it is well to sail round many cities, but advantageous to live in the best. It was a witty remark of the philosopher Bion,[21] that, as those suitors who could not seduce Penelope took up with her maids as a *pis aller*, so those who cannot attain philosophy wear themselves out in useless pursuits. Philosophy, therefore, ought to be regarded as the most important branch of study. For as regards the cure of the body, men have found two branches, medicine and exercise: the former of which gives health, and the latter good condition of body; but philosophy is the only cure for the maladies and disorders of the soul. For with her as ruler and guide we can know what is honourable, what is disgraceful; what is just, what unjust; generally speaking, what is to be sought after, what to be avoided; how we ought to behave to the gods, to parents, to elders, to the laws, to foreigners, to rulers, to friends, to women, to children, to slaves: viz., that we ought to worship the gods, honour parents, reverence elders, obey the laws, submit ourselves to rulers, love our friends, be chaste in our relations with women, kind to our children, and not to treat our slaves badly; and, what is of the greatest importance, to be neither over elated in prosperity nor over depressed in adversity,[22] nor to be dissolute in pleasures, nor fierce and brutish in anger. These I regard as the principal blessings that philosophy teaches. For to enjoy prosperity nobly shows a man; and to enjoy it without exciting envy shows a moderate man; and to conquer the passions by reason argues a wise man; and it is not everybody who can keep his temper in control. And those who can unite political ability with philosophy I regard as perfect men, for I take them to attain two of the greatest blessings, serving the state in a public capacity, and living the calm and tranquil life of philosophy. For, as there are three kinds of life, the practical, the contemplative, and the life of enjoyment, and of these three the one devoted to enjoyment is a paltry and animal life, and the practical without philosophy an unlovely and harsh life, and the contemplative without the practical a useless life, so we must endeavour with all our power to combine public life with philosophy as far as circumstances will permit. Such was the life led by Pericles, by Archytas of Tarentum, by Dion of Syracuse, by Epaminondas the Theban, one of whom was a disciple of Plato (viz., Dion). And as to education, I do not know that I need dwell any more on it. But in addition to what I have said, it is useful, if not necessary, not to neglect to procure old books, and to make a collection of them, as is usual in agriculture. For the use of books is an instrument in education, and it is profitable in learning to go to the fountain head.

§ XI. Exercise also ought not to be neglected, but we ought to send our boys to the master of the gymnasium to train them duly, partly with a view to carrying the body well, partly with a view to strength. For good habit of body in boys is the foundation of a good old age. For as in fine weather we ought to lay up for winter, so in youth one ought to form good habits and live soberly so as to have a reserve stock of strength for old age. Yet ought we to husband the exertions of the body, so as not to be wearied out by them and rendered unfit for study. For, as Plato says,[23] excessive sleep and fatigue are enemies to learning. But why dwell on this? For I am in a hurry to pass to the most important point. Our lads must be trained for warlike encounters, making themselves efficient in hurling the javelin and darts, and in the chase. For the possessions of those who are defeated in battle belong to the conquerors as booty of war; and war is not the place for delicately brought up bodies: it is the spare warrior that makes the best combatant, who as an athlete cuts his way through the ranks of the enemies. Supposing anyone objects: "How so? As you undertook to give advice on the education of freeborn children, do you now neglect the poor and plebeian ones, and give instructions only suitable to the rich?" It is easy enough to meet such critics. I should prefer to make my teaching general and suitable to all; but if any, through their poverty, shall be unable to follow up my precepts, let them blame fortune, and not the author of these hints. We must try with all our might to procure the best education for the poor as well as the rich, but if that is impossible, then we must put up with the practicable. I inserted those matters into my discourse here, that I might hereafter confine myself to all that appertains to the right education of the young.

§ XII. And this I say that we ought to try to draw our boys to good pursuits by entreaties and exhortation, but certainly not by blows or abusive language. For that seems to be more fitting for slaves than the freeborn. For slaves try to shirk and avoid their work, partly because of the pain of blows, partly on account of being reviled. But praise or censure are far more useful than abuse to the freeborn, praise pricking them on to virtue, censure deterring them from vice. But one must censure and praise alternately: when they are too saucy we must censure them and make them ashamed of themselves, and again encourage them by praise, and imitate those nurses who, when their children sob, give them the breast to comfort them. But we must not puff them up and make them conceited with excessive praise, for that will make them vain and give themselves airs.

§ XIII. And I have ere now seen some fathers, whose excessive love for their children has turned into hatred My meaning I will endeavour to make clearer by illustration. While they are in too great a hurry to make their sons take the lead in everything, they lay too much work upon them, so that they faint under their tasks, and, being overburdened, are disinclined for learning. For just as plants grow with moderate rain, but are done for by too much rain, so the mind enlarges by a proper amount of work, but by too much is unhinged. We must therefore give our boys remission from continuous labour, bearing in mind that all our life is divided into labour and rest; thus we find not only wakefulness but sleep, not only war but peace, not only foul weather but fine also, not only working days but also festivals. And, to speak concisely, rest is the sauce of labour. And we can see this not only in the case of animate, but even inanimate things, for we make bows and lyres slack that we may be able to stretch them. And generally the body is preserved by repletion and evacuation, and the soul by rest and work. We ought also to censure some fathers who, after entrusting their sons to tutors and preceptors, neither see nor hear how the teaching is done. This is a great mistake. For they ought after a few days to test the progress of their sons, and not to base their hopes on the behaviour of a hireling; and the preceptors will take all the more pains with the boys, if they have from time to time to give an account of their progress. Hence the propriety of that remark of the groom, that nothing fats the horse so much as the king's eye.[24] And especial attention, in my opinion, must be paid to cultivating and exercising the memory of boys, for memory is, as it were, the storehouse of learning; and that was why they fabled Mnemosyne to be the mother of the Muses, hinting and insinuating that nothing so generates and contributes to the growth of learning as memory. And therefore the memory must be cultivated, whether boys have a good one by nature, or a bad one. For we shall so add to natural good parts, and make up somewhat for natural deficiencies, so that the deficient will be better than others, and the clever will outstrip themselves. For good is that remark of Hesiod, "If to a little you keep adding a little, and do so frequently, it will soon be a lot."[25] And let not fathers forget, that thus cultivating the memory is not only good for education, but is also a great aid in the business of life. For the remembrance of past actions gives a good model how to deal wisely in future ones.

§ XIV. We must also keep our sons from filthy language. For, as Democritus says, Language is the shadow of action. They must also be taught to be affable and courteous. For as want of affability is justly hateful, so boys will not be disagreeable to those they associate with, if they yield occasionally in disputes. For it is not only excellent to know how to conquer, but also to know how to be defeated, when victory would be injurious, for there is such a thing as a Cadmean victory.[26] I can cite wise Euripides as a witness of the truth of what I say, who says, "When two are talking, and one of them is in a passion, he is the wiser who first gives way."[27]

I will next state something quite as important, indeed, if anything, even more important. That is, that life must be spent without luxury, the tongue must be under control, so must the temper and the hands. All this is of extreme importance, as I will show by examples. To begin with the last case, some who have put their hands to unjust gains, have lost all the fruits of their former life, as the Lacedæmonian Gylippus,[28] who was exiled from Sparta for embezzling the public money. To be able to govern the temper also argues a wise man. For Socrates, when a very impudent and disgusting young fellow kicked him on one occasion, seeing all the rest of his class vexed and impatient, even to the point of wanting to prosecute the young man, said, "What! If a young ass kicked me would you have me kick it back?" Not that the young fellow committed this outrage on Socrates with impunity, for as all reviled him and nicknamed him the kicker, he hung himself. And when Aristophanes brought his *"Clouds"* on the stage, and bespattered Socrates with his gibes and flouts, and one of the spectators said, "Aren't you vexed, Socrates, at his exhibiting you on the stage in this comic light?" he answered, "Not I, by Zeus, for I look upon the theatre as only a large supper party."[29] Very similar to this was the behaviour of Archytas of Tarentum and Plato. The former, on his return from war, where he had been general, finding his land neglected, called his bailiff, and said to him, "You would have caught it, had I not been very angry." And Plato, very angry with a gluttonous and shameless slave, called his sister's son Speusippus, and said, "Go and beat him, for I am too angry." But someone will say, these examples are difficult and hard to follow. I know it. But we must try, as far as possible, following these examples, to avoid ungovernable and mad rage. For we cannot in other respects equal those distinguished men in their ability and virtue, nevertheless we must, like initiating priests of the gods and torchbearers of wisdom, attempt as far as possible to imitate and nibble at their practice. Then, again, if anyone thinks it a small and unimportant matter to govern the tongue, another point I promised to touch on, he is very far from the reality. For silence at the proper season is wisdom, and better than any speech. And that is, I think, the reason why the ancients instituted the mysteries that we, learning therein to be silent, might transfer our secrecy to the gods to human affairs. And no one ever yet repented of his silence, while multitudes have repented of their speaking. And what has not been said is easy to say, while what has been once said can never be recalled. I have heard of myriads who have fallen into the greatest misfortunes through inability to govern their tongues. Passing over the rest, I will mention one or two cases in point. When Ptolemy Philadelphus married his sister Arsinoe, Sotades said, "You are contracting an unholy marriage."[30] For this speech he long lingered in prison, and paid the righteous penalty for his unseasonable babbling, and had to weep a long time for making others laugh. Theocritus the Sophist similarly cracked his jokes, and had to pay even a greater penalty. For when Alexander ordered the Greeks to furnish him with purple robes to wear at the sacrifices on his triumphal return from war against the barbarians, and his subjects contributed so much per head, Theocritus said, "Before I doubted, but now I am sure, that this is the *purple death* Homer speaks of."[31] By this speech he made Alexander his enemy. The same Theocritus put Antigonus, the King of the Macedonians, a one-eyed man, into a thundering rage by alluding to his misfortune. For the King sent his chief cook, Eutropio, an important person at his court, to go and fetch Theocritus before him to confer with him, and when he had frequently requested him to come without avail, Theocritus at last said, "I know well you wish to serve me up raw to the Cyclops;" flouting the King as one-eyed and the cook with his profession. Eutropio replied, "You shall lose your head, and pay the penalty for this babbling and mad insolence;" and reported his words to the King, who sent and had his head taken off. Our boys must also be taught to speak the truth as a most sacred duty; for to lie is servile, and most hateful in all men, hardly to be pardoned even in poor slaves.

§ XV. Thus much have I said about the good conduct and self-control of boys without any doubt or hesitation: but as to what I am now going to say I am doubtful and undecided, and like a person weighed in the scales against exactly his weight, and feel great hesitation as to whether I should recommend or dissuade the practice. But I must speak out. The question is this--whether we ought to let the lovers of our boys associate and be with them, or on the contrary, debar them from their company and scare them off. For when I look at fathers self-opinionated sour and austere, who think their sons having lovers a disgrace not to be borne, I am rather afraid of recommending the practice. But when, on the other hand, I think of Socrates, Xenophon, Æschines, Cebes, and all the company of those men who have approved of male loves, and who have introduced their minions to learning, to high positions in the State, and to good morals, I change my opinion, and am moved to emulate those men. And Euripides seems to favour these views in the passage, "But there is among mortals another love, that of the righteous temperate and pure soul."[32] Nor must we omit the remark of Plato, which seems to mix seriousness with mirth, that "those who have distinguished themselves ought to be permitted to kiss any handsome boy they like."[33] Those then that seek only carnal enjoyment must be kept off, but those that love the soul must be encouraged. And while the loves common at Thebes and Elis, and the so-called rape at Crete, must be avoided, the loves of Athens and Lacedæmon should be emulated.

§ XVI. As to this matter, therefore, let every parent follow his inclination. And now, as I have spoken about the good and decent behaviour of boys, I shall change my subject and speak a little about youths. For I have often censured the introducers of bad habits, who have set over boys tutors and preceptors, but have given to youths full liberty, when they ought, on the contrary, to have watched and guarded them more than boys. For who does not know that the offences of boys are petty and easily cured, and proceed from the carelessness of tutors or want of obedience to preceptors; but the faults of young men are often grave and serious, as gluttony, and robbing their fathers, and dice, and revellings, and drinking-bouts, and deflowering of maidens, and seducing of married women. Such outbreaks ought to be carefully checked and curbed. For that prime of life is prodigal in pleasure, and frisky, and needs a bridle, so that those parents who do not strongly check that period, are foolishly, if unawares, giving their youths license for vice.[34] Sensible parents, therefore, ought during all that period to guard and watch and restrain their youths, by precepts, by threats, by entreaties, by advice, by promises, by citing examples,[35] on the one hand, of those who have come to ruin by being too fond of pleasure, on the other hand, of those who by their self-control have attained to praise and good report. For these are, as it were, the two elements of virtue, hope of honour, and fear of punishment; the former inciting to good practices, the latter deterring from bad.

§ XVII. We ought, at all hazards, to keep our boys also from association with bad men, for they will catch some of their villany. This was the meaning of Pythagoras' enigmatical precepts, which I shall quote and explain, as they give no slight momentum towards the acquisition of virtue: as, *Do not touch black tails*: that is, do not associate with bad men.[36] *Do not go beyond the balance*: that is, we must pay the greatest attention to justice and not go beyond it. *Do not sit on a measure*: that is, do not be lazy, but earn tomorrow's bread as well as to-day's. *Do not give everyone your right hand*: that is, do not be too ready to strike up a friendship. *Do not wear a tight ring*: that is, let your life be free, do not bind yourself by a chain. *Do not poke the fire with a sword*: that is, do not provoke an angry person, but yield to such. *Do not eat the heart*: do not wear away the heart by anxiety. *Abstain from beans*: that is, do not meddle in state affairs, for the voting for offices was formerly taken by beans. *Do not put your food in the chamber-pot*: that is, do not throw your pearls before swine, for words are the food of the mind, and the villany of men twist them to a corrupt meaning. *When you have come to the end of a journey do not look back*: that is, when people are going to die and see that their end is near, they ought to take it easily and not be dejected. But I will return from my digression. We must keep our boys, as I said, from association with all bad men, but especially from flatterers. For, as I have often said to parents, and still say, and will constantly affirm, there is no race more pestilential, nor more sure to ruin youths swiftly, than the race of flatterers, who destroy both parents and sons root and branch, making the old age of the one and the youth of the others miserable, holding out pleasure as a sure bait. The sons of the rich are by their fathers urged to be sober, but by them to be drunk; by their fathers to be chaste, by them to wax wanton; by their fathers to save, by them to spend; by their fathers to be industrious, by them to be lazy. For they say, "'Our life's but a span;'[37] we can only live once; why should you heed your father's threats? he's an old twaddler, he has one foot in the grave; we shall soon hoist him up and carry him off to burial." Some even pimp for them and supply them with prostitutes or even married women, and cut huge slices off the father's savings for old age, if they don't run off with them altogether. An accursed tribe, feigning friendship, knowing nothing of real freedom, flatterers of the rich, despisers of the poor, drawn to young men by a sort of natural logic,[38] showing their teeth and grinning all over when their patrons laugh,[39] misbegotten brats of fortune and bastard elements in life, living according to the nod of the rich, free in their circumstances, but slaves by inclination, when they are not insulted thinking themselves insulted, because they are parasites to no purpose. So, if any father cares for the good bringing-up of his sons, he must banish from his house this abominable race. He must also be on his guard against the viciousness of his sons' schoolfellows, for they are quite sufficient to corrupt the best morals.

§ XVIII. What I have said hitherto is *apropos* to my subject: I will now speak a word to the men. Parents must not be over harsh and rough in their natures, but must often forgive their sons' offences, remembering that they themselves were once young. And just as doctors by infusing a sweet flavour into their bitter potions find delight a passage to benefit, so fathers must temper the severity of their censure by mildness; and sometimes relax and slacken the reins of their sons' desires, and again tighten them; and must be especially easy in respect to their faults, or if they are angry must soon cool down. For it is better for a father to be hot-tempered than sullen, for to continue hostile and irreconcilable looks like hating one's son. And it is good to seem not to notice some faults, but to extend to them the weak sight and deafness of old age, so as seeing not to see, and hearing not to hear, their doings. We tolerate the faults of our friends; why should we not that of our sons? often even our slaves' drunken debauches we do not expose. Have you been rather near? spend more freely. Have you been vexed? let the matter pass. Has your son deceived you by the help of a slave? do not be angry. Did he take a yoke of oxen from the field, did he come home smelling of yesterday's debauch? wink at it. Is he scented like a perfume shop? say nothing. Thus frisky youth gets broken in.[40]

§ XIX. Those of our sons who are given to pleasure and pay little heed to rebuke, we must endeavour to marry, for marriage is the surest restraint upon youth. And we must marry our sons to wives not much richer or better born, for the proverb is a sound one, "Marry in your own walk of life."[41] For those who marry wives superior to themselves in rank are not so much the husbands of their wives as unawares slaves to their dowries.[42]

§ XX. I shall add a few remarks, and then bring my subject to a close. Before all things fathers must, by a good behaviour, set a good example to their sons, that, looking at their lives as a mirror, they may turn away from bad deeds and words. For those fathers who censure their sons' faults while they themselves commit the same, are really their own accusers, if they know it not, under their sons' name; and those who live a depraved life have no right to censure their slaves, far less their sons. And besides this they will become counsellors and teachers of their sons in wrongdoing; for where old men are shameless youths will of a certainty have no modesty. We must therefore take all pains to teach our sons self-control, emulating the conduct of Eurydice, who, though an Illyrian and more than a barbarian, to teach her sons educated herself though late in life, and her love to them is well depicted in the inscription which she offered to the Muses: "Eurydice of Hierapolis made this offering to the Muses, having conceived a vast love for knowledge. For when a mother with sons full-grown she learnt letters, the preservers of knowledge."

To carry out all these precepts would be perhaps a visionary scheme; but to attain to many, though it would need a happy disposition and much care, is a thing possible to human nature.[43]

[3] Euripides, "Here. Fur." 1261, 1262.

[4] Euripides, "Hippol." 424, 425.

[5] Cleophantus is the name given to this lad by other writers.

[6] Compare Sophocles, "Oedipus Tyrannus," 112, 113.

[7] The Thessalians were very pugnacious. Cf. Isocrates, "Oratio de Pace," p. 316. [Greek: ohi men (Thettaloi) sphisin autois haei polemousin].

[8] A proverbial expression among the ancients for earliest childhood. See Erasmus, "Adagia."

[9] Plato, "Republic," ii. p. 429, E.

[10] See Erasmus, "Adagia."

[11] It is difficult to know how to render the word [Greek: paidagôgos] in English. He was the slave who took the boy to school, and generally looked after him from his seventh year upward. Tutor or governor seems the best rendering. He had great power over the boy entrusted to him.

[12] Plato, "Clitophon," p. 255, D.

[13] Compare Diogenes Laertius, ii. 72.

[14] Reading [Greek: koitophthorountes], the excellent emendation of Wyttenbach.

[15] From the heathen standpoint of course, not from the Christian. Compare the advice of Cato in Horace's "Satires," Book i. Sat. ii. 31-35. It is a little difficult to know what Diogenes' precept really means. Is it that vice is universal? Like Shakespeare's "Measure for Measure," Act ii. Sc. ii. 5. "All sects, all ages smack of this vice."

[16] He was asked by Polus, see Plato, "Gorgias," p. 290, F.

[17] "Hippolytus," 986-989.

[18] Cf. Plato, "Cratylus," p. 257, E. [Greek: ô pai Hipponikou Hermogenes, palaia paroimia, oti chalepa ta kala estin opê echei mathein]. So Horace, "Sat." i. ix. 59, 60, "Nil sine magno Vita labore dedit mortalibus."

[19] "Midias," p. 411, C.

[20] *i.e.*, occasionally and sparingly.

[21] Diogenes Laertius assigns the remark to Aristippus, while Stobæus fathers it on Aristo.

[22] A favourite thought with the ancients. Compare Isocrates, "Admonitio ad Demonicum," p. 18; and Aristotle, "Nic. Eth.," iv. 3.

[23] "Republic," vii. p. 489, E.

[24] A famous Proverb. It is "the master's eye" generally, as in Xenophon, "Oeconom." xii. 20; and Aristotle, "Oeconom." i. 6.

[25] "Works and Days," 361, 362. The lines were favourite ones with our author. He quotes them again, § 3, of "How one may be aware of one's Progress in Virtue."

[26] See Pausanias, ix. 9. Also Erasmus, "Adagia."

[27] A fragment from the "Protesilaus" of Euripides. Our "It takes two to make a quarrel."

[28] See Plutarch's Lysander.

[29] Or *symposium*, where all sorts of liberties were taken.

[30] I have softened his phrase. His actual words were very coarse, and would naturally be resented by Ptolemy. See Athenæus, 621, A.

[31] See "Iliad," v. 83; xvi. 334; xx, 477.

[32] A fragment from the "Dictys" of Euripides.

[33] "Republ." v. 463, F. sq.

[34] Cf. Shakespeare's "Winter Tale," Act iii. sc. iii. 59-63.

[35] As Horace's father did. See "Satires," Book i. Sat. iv. 105-129.

[36] What we call *black sheep*.

[37] From Simonides. Cf. Seneca, "Epist." xlix. "Punctum est quod vivimus, et adhuc puncto minus."

[38] Reading with Wyttenbach, [Greek: hôs ek logikês technês.]

[39] Like *Carker* in Dombey.

[40] Compare the character of Micio in the "Adelphi" of Terence.

[41] This saying is assigned by Diogenes Laertius to Pittacus.

[42] Compare Plautus, "Asinaria," i. 1. 74. "Argentum accepi: dote imperum vendidi." Compare also our author, "Whether Vice is sufficient to cause Unhappiness," § i.

[43] Wyttenbach thinks this treatise is not Plutarch's. He bases his conclusion partly on external, partly on internal, grounds. It is not quoted by Stobæus, or any of the ancients, before the fourteenth century. And its style is not Plutarch's; it has many words foreign to Plutarch: it has "nescio quid novum ac peregrinum, ab illa

Plutarchea copia et gravitate diversum leve et inane." Certainly its matter is superior to its manner.

ON LOVE TO ONE'S OFFSPRING.

§ I. Appeals to foreign law-courts were first devised among the Greeks through mistrust of one another's justice, for they looked on justice as a necessity not indigenous among them. Is it not on much the same principle that the philosophers, in regard to some of their questions, owing to their variety of opinion, have appealed to the brute creation as to a strange state, and submitted the decision to their instincts and habits as not to be talked over and impartial? Or is it a general charge against human infirmity that, having different opinions on the most necessary and important things, we seek in horses and dogs and birds how to marry and beget and rear children, as though we had no means of making our own nature known, and appeal to the habits and instincts of the brute creation, and call them in to bear witness against the many deviations from nature in our lives, which from the first are confused and disorderly. For among the brutes nature remains ever the same, pure and simple, but in men, owing to reason and habit, like oil in the hands of the perfumers, being mixed up with many added opinions, it becomes various and loses its original simplicity. And let us not wonder that the brutes follow nature more closely than human beings, for in that respect even they are outstripped by inanimate things, which, being dowered neither with imagination nor any appetite or inclination contrary to nature, ever continue in the one path which nature has prescribed for them, as if they were tied and bound. But in brutes the gentleness of mood inspired by reason, the subtlety, the love of freedom, are not qualities found in excess, but they have unreasonable appetites and desires, and act in a roundabout way within certain limits, riding, as it were, at the anchor of nature, and only going straight under bit and bridle. But in man reason, which is absolute master, inventing different modes and fashions of life, has left no plain or evident trace of nature.[44]

§ II. Consider in their marriages how much the animals follow nature. For they do not wait for any legislation about bachelor or late-married, like the citizens of Lycurgus and Solon, nor do they fear penalties for childlessness, nor are they anxious for the *jus trium liberorum*,[45] like many of the Romans, who only marry and have children for the privileges it bestows, not to have heirs, but to be qualified for succeeding themselves to inheritances. Then, again, the male animal does not go with the female at all times; for its aim is not pleasure but procreation: so in the season of spring, the most appropriate time for such pairings,[46] the female being submissive and tender attracts the male by her beautiful condition of body, coming as she does from the dew and fresh pastures, and when pregnant modestly retires and takes thought for the birth and safety of her offspring. We cannot adequately describe all this, but every animal exhibits for its young affection and forethought and endurance and unselfishness. We call the bee wise, and celebrate its "making the yellow honey,"[47] flattering it for its tickling sweetness; but we neglect the wisdom and ingenuity of other creatures, both as regards the birth and bringing up of their young. For example, the kingfisher after conception weaves its nest with the thorns of the marine needle, making it round and oblong in shape like a fisherman's basket, and after deftly and closely weaving it together, subjects it to the action of the sea waves, that its surface may be rendered waterproof by this plash and cement, and it is hard for even iron or stone to break it. And what is more wonderful still, so symmetrically is the entrance of the nest adjusted to the kingfisher's shape and size, that no beast either greater or smaller can enter it, they even say that it does not admit the sea, or even the very smallest things. And cats, when they breed, very often let their kittens go out and feed, and take them back into their entrails again.[48] And the bear, a most savage and ugly beast, gives birth to its young without shape or joints, and with its tongue as with an instrument moulds its features, so that it seems to give form as well as life to its progeny. And the lion in Homer, "whom the hunters meet in the wood with its whelps, exulting in its strength, which so frowns that it hides its eyes,"[49] does it not intend to bargain with the hunters for its whelps? For universally the love of animals for their offspring makes timid ones bold, and lazy ones energetic, and greedy ones unselfish. And so the bird in Homer, feeding its young "with its beak, with whatever it has captured, even though it goes ill with itself,"[50] nourishes its young at the cost of its own hunger, and when the food is near its maw abstains from it, and holds it tightly in its mouth, that it may not gulp it down unawares. "And so a bitch bestriding her tender pups, barks at a strange man, and yearns for the fray,"[51] making her fear for them a sort of second anger. And partridges when they are pursued with their young let them fly on, and, contriving their safety, themselves fly so near the sportsmen as to be almost caught, and then wheel round, and again fly back and make the sportsmen hope to catch them, till at last, having thus provided for the safety of their young, they lead the sportsmen on a long way. As to hens, we see every day how they watch over their chicks, dropping their wings over some, and letting others climb on their backs, or anywhere about them, and clucking for joy all the time: and though they fly from dogs and dragons when only afraid for themselves, if they are afraid for their chicks they stand their ground and fight valiantly. Are we to suppose then that nature has only implanted these instincts in fowls and dogs and bears, anxious only about their offspring, to put us mortals out of countenance and to give us a bad name? considering these examples for us to follow, while disgrace justly attaches to our inhumanity, for mankind only is accused of having no disinterested affection, and of not knowing how to love except in regard to advantage. For that line is greatly admired in the theatres, "Man loves man only for reward," and is the view of Epicurus, who thinks that the father so loves his son, the mother her child, children their parents. Whereas, if the brutes could understand conversation, and if anyone were to introduce horses and cows and dogs and birds into a common theatre,[52] and were to change the sentiment into "neither do dogs love their pups, nor horses their foals, nor birds their young, out of interest, but gratuitously and by nature," it would be recognized by the affections of all of them to be a true sentiment. Why it would be disgraceful, great God, that birth and travail and procreation should be gratis and mere nature among the beasts, while among mankind they should be merely mercenary transactions!

§ III. But such a statement is not true or worthy of credit. For as nature, in wild growths, such as wild vines, wild figs, or wild olives, makes the fruit imperfect and inferior to the fruit of cultivated trees, so has she given to the brutes an imperfect affection for their kind, one neither marked by justice nor going beyond commodity: whereas to man, a logical and social animal, she has taught justice and law, and honour to the gods, and building of cities, and philanthropy, and has contributed the noble and goodly and fruitful seeds of all these in love to one's offspring, thereby following the very first elements that are found in the construction of the body. For nature is everywhere perfect and artistic and complete, and, to borrow the expression of Erasistratus, has nothing tawdry about her: but one cannot adequately describe all the processes appertaining to birth, nor would it be perhaps decent to pry too closely into such hidden matters, and to particularize too minutely all their wondrous ingenuity. But her contrivance and dispensation of milk alone is sufficient to prove nature's wonderful care and forethought. For all the superfluous blood in women, that owing to their languor and thinness of spirit floats about on the surface and oppresses them, has a safety-valve provided by nature in the menses, which relieve and cleanse the rest of the body, and fit the womb for conception in due season. But after conception nature stops the menses, and arrests the flow of the blood, using it as aliment for the babe in the womb, until the time arrives for its birth, and it requires a different kind of food. At this stage the blood is most ingeniously changed into a supply of milk, not diffused all over the body, but externally in the breasts, so that the babe can with its mouth imbibe the gentle and soothing nutriment.[53] But all these various processes of nature, all this economy, all this forethought, would be useless, had not nature also implanted in mothers love to their offspring and anxiety for their welfare.

"For of all things, that on the earth do breathe Or creep, man is by far the wretchedest."[54]

And the poet's words are especially applicable to a newborn babe. For there is nothing so imperfect, so helpless, so naked, so shapeless, so foul as a newborn babe: to whom almost alone nature has given an impure outlet to the light of day: being kneaded with blood, and full of defilement, and like one killed rather than born: which no one would touch, or lift up, or kiss, or embrace, but from natural affection. And that is why all the animals have their udders under the belly, women alone have their breasts high on their bodies, that they can lift up their babes to kiss, to dandle, and to fondle: seeing that their bearing and rearing children comes not from necessity but love.

§ IV. Refer the question to the ancient inhabitants of the earth, to the first mothers and fathers. There was no law ordering them to have families, no expectation of advantage or return to be got out of them. I should rather say that mothers would be likely to be hostile and bear malice to their babes, owing to the great danger and pains of travail. And women say the lines, "When the sharp pangs of travail seize on the pregnant woman, then come to her aid the Ilithyiæ, who help women in hard childbirth, those daughters of Hera, goddesses of travail,"[55] were not written by Homer, but by some Homerid who had been a mother, or was even then in the throes of travail, and who vividly felt the sharp pain in her womb. But the love to one's offspring implanted by nature, moves and influences the mother even then: in the very height of her throes, she neglects not nor flees from her babe, but turns to it and smiles at it, and takes it up and caresses it, though she derives no pleasure or utility from it, but with pain and sorrow receives it, "warming it and fostering it in swaddling clothes, with unintermittent assiduity both night and day."[56] What hope of gain or advantage had they in those days? nay, or even now? for the hopes of parents are uncertain, and have to be long waited for. He who plants a vine in the spring equinox, gleans its vintage in the autumnal equinox; he who sows corn when the Pleiads set, reaps it when they rise; cattle and horses and birds have produce at once fit for use; whereas man's bringing up is toilsome, his growth slow; and as excellence flowers late, most fathers die before their sons attain to fame. Neocles lived not to see Themistocles' victory at Salamis, nor Miltiades Cimon's at the Eurymedon, nor did Xanthippus hear Pericles haranguing, nor did Aristo hear Plato philosophizing, nor did their fathers know of the triumphs of Euripides and Sophocles. They heard them faltering in speech and lisping in syllables, the poor parents saw their errors in revelling and drinking and love-affairs, so that of all Evenus'[57] lines, that one alone is most remembered and quoted, "to a father a son is always a cause of fear or pain." Nevertheless, parents do not cease to bring up sons, even when they can least need them. For it is ridiculous to suppose that the rich, when they have sons, sacrifice and rejoice that they will have people to take care of them and to bury them; unless indeed they bring up sons from want of heirs; as if one could not find or fall in with anyone who would be willing to have another's property! Why, the sand on the sea shore, and the dust, and the wings of birds of varied note, are less numerous than the number of would-be heirs. For had Danaus, the father of fifty daughters, been childless, he would have had more heirs, and of a different spirit. For sons have no gratitude, nor regard, nor veneration for inheritance; but take it as a debt; whereas the voices of strangers which you hear round the childless man, are like those lines in the play, "O People, first bathe, after one decision in the courts, then eat, drink, gobble, take the three-obol-piece."[58] And what Euripides has said, "Money finds friends for men, and has the greatest power among mankind," is not merely a general truth, but is especially true in the case of the childless. For those the rich entertain to dinner, those great men pay court to, to those alone orators give their services gratis. "A mighty personage is a rich man, whose heir is unknown." It has at any rate made many much loved and honoured, whom the possession of one child would have made unloved and insignificant. Whence we see that there is no power or advantage to be got from children, but that the love of them, alike in mankind as among the animals, proceeds entirely from nature.

§ V. What if this natural affection, like many other virtues, is obscured by badness, as a wilderness chokes a garden? Are we to say that man does not love himself by nature, because many cut their throats or throw themselves down precipices? Did not Oedipus put out his eyes? And did not Hegesias by his speeches make, many of his hearers to commit suicide?[59] "Fatality has many different aspects."[60] But all these are diseases and maladies of the soul driving a man contrary to nature out of his wits: as men themselves testify even against themselves. For if a sow destroys one of its litter, or a bitch one of its pups, men are dejected and troubled, and think it an evil omen, and sacrifice to the gods to avert any bad results, on the score that it is natural to all to love and cherish their offspring, unnatural to destroy it. For just as in mines the gold is conspicuous even though mixed up with earth, so nature manifests plainly love to offspring even in instances of faulty habits and affections. For when the poor do not rear their children, it is from fear that if reared to man's estate they would be more than ought to be the case servile, and have little culture, and be debarred of all advantages: so, thinking poverty the worst of all evils, they cannot bear to give it their children, any more than they would some bad disease.[61]

[44] Much of this is very corrupt in the Greek. I have tried to get the best sense I could; but it is very obscure. Certainly Plutarch's style is often very harsh and crabbed.

[45] The *jus trium liberorum* assigned certain privileges to the father of three children, under the Roman

Emperors. Frequent allusions are made to this law by the ancient writers.

[46] Compare Lucretius, i. 10-20.

[47] A quotation from Simonides.

[48] We are not bound to swallow all the ancients tell us. Credat Judæus Apella!

[49] "Iliad," xvii. 134-136.

[50] "Iliad," ix. 324. Quoted again in "How one may be aware of one's Progress in Virtue," § 8.

[51] "Odyssey," xx. 14, 15.

[52] A theatre, that is, in which animals and birds and human beings should meet in common.

[53] All that is said here about the milk, the menses, and the blood, I have been obliged somewhat to condense and paraphrase. The ancients sometimes speak more plainly than we can. Ever and anon one must pare down a phrase or word in translating an ancient author. It is inevitable. *Verbum sat sapienti.*

[54] Homer, "Iliad," xvii. 446, 447.

[55] Ibid. xi. 269-271.

[56] A fragment from Euripides, according to Xylander.

[57] Evenus of Paros was an Elegiac Poet.

[58] Aristophanes, "Equites," 50, 51.

[59] See Cicero "Tuscul." i. 34.

[60] Euripides, "Alcestis," 1159; "Helena," 1688; "Andromache," 1284; "Bacchæ," 1388.

[61] The discourse breaks off abruptly. It is directed against the Epicureans. It throws ridicule on appealing to the affection of brutes for their offspring instead of appealing to human nature.

ON LOVE.

FLAVIANUS AND AUTOBULUS, THE OPENERS OF THE DIALOGUE, ARE BROTHERS. THE OTHER SPEAKERS ARE THEIR FATHER, DAPHNÆUS, PROTOGENES, PISIAS, AND OTHERS.

1. *Flavianus.*--You say that it was on Mount Helicon, Autobulus, that those conversations took place about Love, which you are now about to narrate to us at our request, as you either wrote them down, or at least remember them from frequently asking our father about them.

Autobulus.--It was on Mount Helicon among the Muses, Flavianus, when the people of Thespiæ were celebrating their Festival to the God of Love, which they celebrate very magnificently and splendidly every five years to that God, as also to the Muses.

Flavianus.--Do you know what all of us who have come to this audience intend to ask of you?

Autobulus.--No, but I shall know if you tell me.

Flavianus.--Remove from your discourse for this once the poet's meadows and shades, and talk about ivy and yews, and all other commonplaces of that kind that writers love to introduce, with more zeal than discretion, in imitation of Plato's Ilissus and the famous willow and the gentle slope of grass.[62]

Autobulus.--My dear Flavianus, my narrative needs not any such exordium. The occasion that caused the conversation simply demands a chorus for the action and a stage, nothing else is wanting to the drama, let us only pray to the Mother of the Muses to be propitious, and give me memory for my narrative.

§ II. Long ago our father, before we were born, having lately married our mother, had gone to sacrifice to the God of Love, in consequence of a dispute and variance that broke out among their parents, and took our mother to the Festival, for she also had her part in the vow and sacrifice. Some of their intimate friends journeyed with them from the town where they lived, and when they got to Thespiæ they found there Daphnæus the son of Archidamus, a lover of Lysandra the daughter of Simo, and of all her suitors the one who stood highest in her favour, and Soclarus the son of Aristio, who had come from Tithorea. And there were there also Protogenes of Tarsus, and Zeuxippus from Sparta, strangers, and my father said most of the most notable Boeotians were there also. For two or three days they went about the town in one another's company, as it was likely they would do, quietly carrying on philosophical discussions in the wrestling-schools and theatres: after that, to avoid a wearisome contest of harpers, decided beforehand by canvassing and cabal, most broke up their camp as if they had been in a hostile country, and removed to Mount Helicon, and bivouacked there with the Muses. In the morning they were visited by Anthemion and Pisias, both men of good repute, and very great friends of Baccho, who was surnamed the Handsome, and also rivals of one another somewhat through their affection for him. Now you must know that there was at Thespiæ a lady called Ismenodora, famous for her wealth and good family, and of uncommon good repute for her virtuous life: for she had been a widow some time without a breath of slander lighting upon her, though she was young and good-looking. As Baccho was the son of a friend and crony of hers, she had tried to bring about a marriage between him and a maiden who was her own relation, but by frequently being in his company and talking to him she had got rather smitten with him herself. And hearing much in his favour, and often talking about him, and seeing that many noble young men were in love with him, she fell violently in love with him, and, being resolved to do nothing unbecoming to her fair fame, determined to marry and live openly with him. And the matter seeming in itself rather odd, Baccho's mother looked rather askance at the proposed matrimonial alliance as being too high and splendid for her son, while some of his companions who used to go out hunting with him, frightening him and flouting him with Ismenodora's being rather too old for him, really did more to break off the match than those who seriously opposed it. And Baccho, being only a youth, somehow felt a little ashamed at the idea of marrying a widow, but, neglecting the opinions of everybody else, he submitted the decision as to the expediency of the marriage to Pisias and Anthemion, the latter being his cousin, though older than him, and the former the gravest[63] of his lovers. Pisias objected to the marriage, and upbraided Anthemion with throwing the youth away on Ismenodora. Anthemion replied that it was not well in Pisias, being a good fellow in other respects, to imitate depraved lovers by shutting out his friend from house and marriage and wealth, merely that he might enjoy the sight of him as long as possible naked and in all his virgin bloom at the wrestling-schools.

§ III. To avoid getting estranged by provoking one another on the question, they came and chose our father and his companions as umpires on the matter. And of the other friends, as if by concerted arrangement, Daphnæus espoused the view of Anthemion, and Protogenes the view of Pisias. And Protogenes inveighing somewhat too freely against Ismenodora, Daphnæus took him up and said, "Hercules, what are we not to expect, if Protogenes is going to be hostile to love? he whose whole life, whether in work or at play, has been devoted to love, in forgetfulness of letters, in forgetfulness of his country, not like Laius, away from his country only five days, his was only a torpid and land love: whereas your love 'unfolding its swift wings,' flew over the sea from Cilicia to Athens, merely to gaze at and saunter about with handsome boys. For that was the original reason, doubtless, of Protogenes' journey abroad."

§ IV. And some laughter ensuing, Protogenes replied, "Do I really seem to you now to be hostile to love, and not to be fighting for love against ungovernable lust, which with most disgraceful acts and emotions assumes the most honourable of titles?" Whereupon Daphnæus, "Do you call the marriage and union of man and woman most disgraceful, than which no holier tie exists nor ever did?" Protogenes replied, "Why, as all this is necessary for the human race to continue, our legislators do not act amiss in crying up marriage and eulogizing it to the masses, but of genuine love there is not a particle in the woman's side of a house;[64] and I also say that you who are sweet on women and girls only love them as flies love milk, and bees the honey-comb, and butchers and cooks calves and birds, fattening them up in darkness.[65] But as nature leads one to eat and drink moderately and sufficiently, and excess in this is called gluttony and gormandizing, so the mutual desires between men and women are natural; but that headlong, violent, and uncontrollable passion for the sex is not rightly called love. For love, when it seizes a noble and young soul, ends in virtue through friendship; but these violent passions for women, at the best, aim only at carnal enjoyment and reaping the harvest of a beauteous prime, as Aristippus showed in his answer to one who told him Lais loved him not, 'No more,' he said, 'do meat and wine love me, but I gladly enjoy both.'[66] For the end of passion is pleasure and fruition: but love, when it has once lost the promise of friendship, will not remain and continue to cherish merely for beauty that which gives it pain, where it gives no return of friendship and virtue. You remember the husband in the play saying to his wife, 'Do you hate me? I can bear that hatred very easily, since of my dishonour I make money.' Not a whit more really in love than this husband is the one, who, not for gain but merely for the sexual appetite, puts up with a peevish and unsympathetic wife, as Philippides, the comic poet, ridiculed the orator, Stratocles, 'You scarce can kiss her if she turns her back on you.' If, however, we ought to give the name of love to this passion, then is it an effeminate and bastard love, and like at Cynosarges,[67] taking us to the woman's side of the house: or rather as they say there is a genuine mountain eagle, which Homer called 'black, and a bird of prey,' and there are other kinds of spurious eagles, which catch fish and lazy birds in marshes, and often in want of food emit an hungry wail: so the genuine love is the love of boys, a love not 'flashing with desire,' as Anacreon said the love of maidens was, nor 'redolent of ointment and sprightly,' but you will see it plain and without airs in the schools of the philosophers, or perhaps in the gymnasiums and wrestling-schools, keenly and nobly pursuing youths, and urging on to virtue those who are well worthy of attention: but that soft and stay-at-home love, spending all its time in women's bosoms and beds, always pursuing effeminate delights, and enervated by unmanly, unfriendly, and unimpassioned pleasures, we ought to condemn as Solon condemned it: for he forbade slaves to love boys or to anoint them with oil, while he allowed them to associate with women. For friendship is noble and refined, whereas pleasure is vulgar and illiberal. Therefore, for a slave to love boys is neither liberal or refined: for it is merely the love of copulation, as the love of women."

§ V. Protogenes was intending to go on at greater length, when Daphnæus stopped him and said, "You do well, by Zeus, to mention Solon, and we too may use him as the test of an amorous man. Does he not define such a one in the lines, 'As long as you love boys in the glorious flower of their youth for their kisses and embraces.' And add to Solon the lines of Æschylus, 'You did not disdain the honour of the thighs, O thankless one after all my frequent kisses.'[68] For some laugh at them if they bid lovers, like sacrificing priests and seers, to inspect thighs and loins; but I think this a mighty argument in behalf of the love of women. For if the unnatural commerce with males does not take away or mar the amorous propensity, much more likely is it that the natural love of women will end in friendship after the favour. For, Protogenes, the yielding of the female to the male was called by the ancients the favour. Thus Pindar says Hephæstus was the son of Hera 'without any favours':[69] and Sappho, addressing a girl not yet ripe for marriage, says to her, 'You seemed to me a little girl, too young for the favour.' And someone asks Hercules, 'Did you obtain the girl's favour by force or by persuasion?' But the love of males for males, whether rape or voluntary--pathicks effeminately submitting, to use Plato's words, 'to be treated bestially'--is altogether a foul and unlovely favour. And so I think Solon wrote the lines quoted above 'in his hot youth,' as Plato puts it; but when he became older wrote these other lines, 'Now I delight in Cyprus-born Aphrodite, and in Dionysus, and in the Muses: all these give joys to men': as if, after the heat and tempest of his boyish loves, he had got into a quiet haven of marriage and philosophy. But indeed, Protogenes, if we look at the real facts of the case, the love for boys and women is really one and the same passion: but if you wish in a disputatious spirit to make any distinction, you will find that this boy-love goes beyond all bounds, and, like some late-born and ill-begotten bastard brat, seeks to expel its legitimate brother the older love, the love of women. For indeed, friend, it is only yesterday or the day before, since the strippings and exposures of the youths in the gymnasiums, that this boy-love crept in, and gently insinuated itself and got a footing, and at last in a little time got fully-fledged in the wrestling-schools, and has now got fairly unbearable, and insults and tramples on conjugal love, that love that gives immortality to our mortal race, when our nature has been extinguished by death, kindling it again by new births. And this boy-love denies that pleasure is its aim: for it is ashamed and afraid to confess the truth: but it needs some specious excuse for the liberties it takes with handsome boys in their prime: the pretext is friendship and virtue. So your boy-lover wallows in the dust, bathes in cold water, raises his eyebrows, gives himself out for a philosopher, and lives chaste abroad because of the law: but in the stillness of night

'Sweet is the ripe fruit when the guard's withdrawn.'[70]

But if, as Protogenes says, there is no carnal intercourse in these boy-familiarities, how is it Love, if Aphrodite is not present, whom it is the destiny of Love to cherish and pay court to, and to partake of just as much honour and power as she assigns to him? But if there is any Love without Aphrodite, as there is drunkenness without wine in drinks made from figs and barley, the disturbing it will be fruitless and without effect, and surfeiting and disgusting."

§ VI. At the conclusion of this speech, it was clear that Pisias was vexed and indignant with Daphnæus; and after a moment's silence he began: "O Hercules! what levity and audacity for men to state that they are tied to women as dogs to bitches, and to banish the god of Love from the gymnasiums and public walks, and light of day and open intercourse, and to restrict him to brothels[71] and philtres and incantations of wanton women: for to chaste women, I am sure, it belongs not either to love or be loved." At this point our father told me he interposed, and took Protogenes by the hand, and said to him:

"'This word of yours rouses the Argive host,'

and of a verity Pisias makes us to side with Daphnæus by his extravagant language, charging marriage with being a loveless intercourse, and one that has no participation in divine friendship, although we can see that it is an intercourse, if erotic persuasion and favour fail, that cannot be restrained by shame and fear as by bit and bridle." Thereupon Pisias said, "I care little about his arguments; but I see that Daphnæus is in the same condition as brass: for, just as it is not worked upon so much by the agency of fire as by the molten and liquid brass fused with it, so is he not so much captivated by the beauty of Lysandra as by his association with one who is the victim of the gentle passion; and it is plain that, if he doesn't take refuge with us, he will soon melt away in the flame altogether. But I see, what Anthemion would very much like, that I am offending the Court, so I stop." "You amuse us," said Anthemion: "but you ought from the first to have spoken to the point."

§ VII. "I say then," continued Pisias, "and give it out boldly, as far as I am concerned, let every woman have a lover; but we ought to guard against giving the wealth of Ismenodora to Baccho, lest, if we involve him in so much grandeur and magnificence, we unwittingly lose him in it, as tin is lost in brass. For if the lad were to marry quite a plain and insignificant woman, it would be great odds whether he would keep the upper hand, as wine mixed with water; and Ismenodora seems already marked out for sway and command; for otherwise she would not have rejected such illustrious and wealthy suitors to woo a lad hardly yet arrived at man's estate, and almost requiring a tutor still. And therefore men of sense prune the excessive wealth of their wives, as if it had wings that required clipping; for this same wealth implants in them luxury, caprice, and vanity, by which they are often elated and fly away altogether: but if they remain, it would be better to be bound by golden fetters, as in Ethiopia, than to a woman's wealth."

§ VIII. Here Protogenes put in, "You say nothing about the risk we run of unseasonably and ridiculously reversing the well-known advice of Hesiod:

'If seasonable marriage you would make, Let about thirty be the bridegroom's age, The bride be in the fifth year of her womanhood:'[72]

if we thus marry a lad hardly old enough for marriage to a woman so many years older, than himself, as dates and figs are forced. You will say she loves him passionately: who prevents her, then, from serenading at his doors, singing her amorous ditty, putting garlands on his statues, and wrestling and boxing with her rivals in his affections? For all these are what people in love do. And let her lower her eyebrows, and give up the airs of a coquette, and assume the appearance of those that are deeply smitten. But if she is modest and chaste, let her decorously stay at home and await there her lovers and sweethearts; for any sensible man would be disgusted and flee from a woman who took the initiative in love, far less would he be likely to marry her after such a barefaced wooing."

§ IX. When Protogenes had done speaking, my father said, "Do you see, Anthemion, that they force us to intervene again, who have no objection to dance in the retinue of conjugal Love?" "I do," said Anthemion, "but pray defend Love at some length, as you are on his side, and moreover come to the rescue of wealth,[73] with which Pisias seeks to scare us." Thereupon my father began, "What on earth will not be brought as a charge against a woman, if we are to reject Ismenodora because she is in love and has money? Granted she loves sway and is rich? What then, if she is young and handsome? And what if she plumes herself somewhat on the lustre of her race? Have not chaste women often something of the morose and peevish in their character almost past bearing? Do they not sometimes get called waspish and shrewish by virtue of their very chastity? Would it be best then to marry off the street some Thracian Abrotonus, or some Milesian Bacchis, and seal the bargain by the present of a handful of nuts? But we have known even such turn out intolerable tyrants, Syrian flute-girls and ballet-dancers, as Aristonica, and Oenanthe with her tambourine, and Agathoclea, who have lorded it over kings' diadems.[74] Why Syrian Semiramis was only the servant and concubine of one of king Ninus's slaves, till Ninus the great king seeing and falling in love with her, she got such power over him that she thought so cheap of him, that she asked to be allowed one day to sit on the royal throne, with the royal diadem on her head, and to transact state affairs. And Ninus having granted her permission, and having ordered all his subjects to obey her as himself, she first gave several very moderate orders to make trial of the guards; but when she saw that they obeyed her without the slightest hesitation, she ordered them to seize Ninus and put him in fetters, and at last put him to death; and all her commands being obeyed, she ruled over Asia for a long time with great lustre. And was not Belestiche a foreign woman off the streets, although at Alexandria she has shrines and temples, with an inscription as Aphrodite Belestiche, which she owes to the king's love? And she who has in this very town[75] a temple and rites in common with Eros, and at Delphi stands in gold among kings and queens, by what dowry got she her lovers? But just as the lovers of Semiramis, Belestiche, and Phryne, became their prey unconsciously through their weakness and effeminacy, so on the other hand poor and obscure men, having contracted alliances with rich women of rank, have not been thereby spoilt nor merged their personality, but have lived with their wives on a footing of kindness, yet still kept their position as heads of the house. But he that abases his wife and makes her small, like one who tightens the ring on a finger too small for it fearing it will come off,[76] is like those who cut their mares' tails off and then take them to a river or pond to drink, when they say that sorrowfully discerning their loss of beauty these mares lose their self-respect and allow themselves to be covered by asses.[77] To select a wife for wealth rather than for her excellence or family is dishonourable and illiberal; but it is silly to reject wealth when it is accompanied by excellence and family. Antigonus indeed wrote to his officer who had garrisoned Munychia[78] to make not only the collar strong but the dog lean, that he might undermine the strength of the Athenians; but it becomes not the husband of a rich or handsome woman to make his wife poor or ugly, but by his self-control and good sense, and by not too extravagantly showing his admiration for her, to exhibit himself as her equal not her slave, and (to borrow an illustration from the scales) to add just so much weight to his character as shall over-balance her, yet only just. Moreover, both Ismenodora and Baccho are of a suitable age for marriage and procreation of children; Ismenodora, I hear, is still in her prime, and" (here my father smiled slily at Pisias) "she is certainly not a bit older than her rivals, and has no grey hairs, as some of those who consort with Baccho have. And if their union is seasonable, who knows but that she may be a better partner for him than any young woman? For young couples do not blend and mix well together, and it takes a long time and is not an easy process for them to divest themselves of their pride and spirit, and at first there's a good deal of dirty weather and they don't pull well together, and this is oftenest the case when there's love on both sides, and, just as a storm wrecks the ship if no pilot is on board, so their marriage is trouble and confusion, neither party knowing how either to rule or to give way properly. And if the baby is under the nurse, and the boy under the master, and the lad under the master of the gymnasium, and the youth under his lover, and the full-grown man under the law and magistrate, and no one is his own master and exempt from obedience to someone, what wonder would it be if a sensible woman rather older than her husband would direct well the life of a young man, being useful to him by reason of her superior wisdom, and acceptable to him for her sweetness and gentleness? And to sum up the whole matter," said he, "we Boeotians ought to revere Hercules, and so find no fault in any inequality of age in marriages, seeing that he gave his own wife Megara in marriage to Iolaus, though he was only sixteen and she three-and-thirty."[79]

§ X. As the conversation was going on, our father said that a friend of Pisias came galloping up from the town to report an act of marvellous audacity. Ismenodora, it appears, thinking Baccho had no personal dislike to the match, but only stood in awe of his friends who tried to dissuade him from it, determined that she would not let the young fellow slip through her fingers. Accordingly, she sent for the most active and intimate[80] of her male friends, and for some of her female cronies, and instructed them as to what part they should play, and waited the hour when Baccho was accustomed regularly to pass by her house on his way to the wrestling-school. And as he passed by on this occasion with two or three of his companions, anointed for the exercise, Ismenodora met him at the door and just touched his cloak, and her friends rushed out all together and prettily seized the pretty fellow as he was in his cloak and jersey,[81] and hurried him into the house and at once locked the doors. And the women inside at once divested him of his cloak and put on him a bridal robe; and the servants ran about the town and put olive wreaths and laurel garlands at the doors of Baccho's house as well as Ismenodora's, and a flute-girl went up and down the street playing and singing the wedding-song. And some of the inhabitants of Thespiæ and the strangers laughed, others were indignant and tried to make the superintendents of the gymnasium move in the matter, for they have great power in Thespiæ over the youths, and pay great attention to their actions. And now there was no more talk about the sports, but everyone left the theatre for the neighbourhood of Ismenodora's house, and there stood in groups talking and disputing about what had happened.

§ XI. Now when Pisias' friend had come up like an *aide-de-camp* in war, "bloody with spurring, fiery red with haste," to report this news that Ismenodora had seized Baccho, my father said that Zeuxippus smiled, and being a great lover of Euripides repeated the line,

"Lady, though rich, thou hast thy sex's feelings."

But Pisias jumped up and cried out, "Ye gods, what will be the end of license like this which will overthrow our town? Already we are fast tending to lawlessness through our independence. And yet it is perhaps ridiculous to be indignant about law and justice, when nature itself is trampled upon by being thus subjected to women? Saw even Lemnos ever the like of this?[82] Let us go," he continued, "let us go and hand over to the women the gymnasium and council-hall, if the townsmen have lost all their nerve." Pisias then left the company, and Protogenes went with him, partly sympathizing with his indignation, but still endeavouring to cool him. And Anthemion said, "'Twas a bold deed and certainly does savour somewhat of Lemnos--I own it now we are alone--this Ismenodora must be most violently in love." Hereupon Soclarus said, with a sly smile, "You don't think then that this rape and detention was an excuse and stratagem on the part of a wily young man to escape from the clutches of his lovers, and fly of his own volition to the arms of a rich and handsome widow?" "Pray don't say so, Soclarus," said Anthemion, "pray don't entertain any such suspicions of Baccho, for even if he were not by nature most simple and naïve, he would not have concealed the matter from me to whom he divulges all his secrets, especially as he knows that I have always been very anxious he should marry Ismenodora. But as Heraclitus says truly, It is more difficult to control love than anger; for whatever love has a fancy to, it will buy even at the cost of life, money, and reputation. Who lives a more quiet life in our town than Ismenodora? When did ever any ugly rumour attach itself to her? When did ever any breath of suspicion sully her house? Some divine inspiration, beyond human calculation, seems now to have possessed her."

§ XII. Then Pemptides laughed and said, "Of course you know that there is a certain disease of the body called the sacred disease.[83] It is no wonder, therefore, if some call the greatest and most insane passion of the soul sacred and divine. However, as in Egypt I once saw two neighbours disputing when a serpent passed by them on the road, both calling it a good omen, but each claiming the blessing as his alone; so seeing lately that some of you drag Love to the men's apartments, while others confine it to the women's side of the house, while all of you regard it as a divine and superlative blessing, I do not wonder, since it is a passion that has such power and honour, that those who ought to banish it from every quarter and clip its wings do themselves add to its influence and power. And hitherto I held my peace, for I saw that the discussion turned rather on private than public interests, but now that we have got rid of Pisias, I would gladly hear from you to what they had an eye who first called Love a god."

§ XIII. Just as Pemptides had left off, and our father was about to answer his question, another messenger came from the town, sent by Ismenodora to summon Anthemion, for the tumult had increased, and there was a difference of opinion between the superintendents of the gymnasium, one thinking they ought to demand the liberation of Baccho, the other thinking they ought not to interfere. Anthemion got up at once and went off. And our father, addressing Pemptides especially, said, "You seem to me, my dear Pemptides, to be handling a great and bold matter, or rather to be discussing things that ought not to be discussed, in asking for a reason in each case for our opinion about the gods. Our ancient and hereditary faith is sufficient, a better argument than which we cannot either utter or find,

'Not e'en if wisdom in our brains resides;'[84]

but if this common foundation and basis of all piety be disturbed, and its stability and time-honoured ideas be unsettled, it becomes undermined and is suspected by everybody. You have heard, of course, what hot water Euripides got into, when he wrote at the beginning of his 'Melanippe,'

'Zeus, whosoe'er he is, I do not know Except by hearsay,'[85]

but if he changed the opening line, he had confidence, it seems, that his play would go down with the public uncommonly well,[86] so he altered it into

'Zeus the divine, as he is truly called.'[87]

And what difference is there between calling in question the received opinion about Zeus or Athene, and that about Love? For it is not now for the first time that Love asks for an altar and sacrifices, nor is he a strange god introduced by foreign superstition, as some Attis or Adonis, furtively smuggled in by hermaphrodites and women, and secretly receiving honours not his own, to avoid an indictment among the gods for coming among them under false pretences. And when, my friend, you hear the words of Empedocles,

'Friendship is there too, of same length and breadth, But with the mind's eye only can you see it, Till with the sight your very soul is thralled,'

you must suppose that they refer to Love. For this god is invisible, but to be extolled by us as one of the very oldest gods. And if you demand proofs about every one of the gods, laying a profane hand on every temple, and bringing a learned doubt to every altar, you will scrutinize and pry into everything. But we need not go far to find Love's pedigree.

'See you how great a goddess Aphrodite is? She 'tis that gave us and engendered Love, Whereof come all that on the earth do live.'[88]

And so Empedocles calls Aphrodite *Life-giving*,[89] and Sophocles calls her *Fruitful*, both very appropriate epithets. And though the wonderful act of generation belongs to Aphrodite only, and Love is only present in it as a subordinate, yet if he be absent the whole affair becomes undesirable, and low, and tame. For a loveless coition brings only satiety, as the satisfaction of hunger and thirst, and has nothing noble resulting from it, whereas by Love Aphrodite removes the cloying element in pleasure, and produces harmonious friendship. And so Parmenides declares Love to be the oldest of the creations of Aphrodite, writing in his Cosmogony,

'Of all the gods first Love she did contrive.'

But Hesiod, more naturally in my opinion, makes Love the most ancient of all, so that all things derive their existence from him.[90] If we then deprive Love of his ancient honours, those of Aphrodite will be lost also. For we cannot argue that, while some revile Love, all spare Aphrodite, for on the same stage we hear of Love,

'Love is an idle thing and for the idle:'[91]

and again of Aphrodite,

'Cypris, my boys, is not her only name, For many names has she. She is a hell, A power remorseless, nay a raging madness.'[92]

Just as in the case of the other gods there is hardly one that has not been reviled, or escaped the scurrility of ignorance. Look, for example, at Ares, who may be considered as it were the counterpart of Love, what honours he has received from men, and again what abuse, as

'Ares is blind, ye women, has no eyes, And with his pig's snout roots up all good things.'[93]

And Homer calls him 'blood-stained' and 'fickle.'[94] And Chrysippus brings a grievous charge against him, in defining his name to mean destroyer,[95] thereby giving a handle to those who think that Ares is only the fighting, wrangling, and quarrelsome instinct among mankind. Others again will tell us that Aphrodite is simply desire, and Hermes eloquence, and the Muses the arts and sciences, and Athene wisdom. You see what an abyss of impiety opens up before us, if we describe each of the gods, as only a passion, a power, or a virtue!"

§ XIV. "I see it," said Pemptides, "and it is impious either to make the gods passions, or to do just the contrary, and make the passions gods." "What then?" said my father, "do you consider Ares a god, or only a human passion?" And Pemptides, answering that he looked on Ares as god of the passionate and manly element in mankind, "What," cried my father, "shall the passionate and warlike and antagonistic instincts in man have a god, but the affectionate and social and clubable have none? Shall Ares, under his names of Enyalius and Stratius, preside over arms and war and sieges and sacks of cities, and shall there be no god to witness and preside over, to direct and guide, conjugal affection, that friendship of closest union and communion? Why even those who hunt gazelles and hares and deer have a silvan deity who harks and halloos them on, for to Aristæus[96] they pay their vows when in pitfalls and snares they trap wolves and bears,

'For Aristæus first set traps for animals.'

And Hercules invoked another god, when he was about to shoot at the bird, as the line of Æschylus shows,

'Hunter Apollo, make my bolt go straight!'[97]

And shall no god or good genius assist and prosper the man who hunts in the best chase of all, the chase of friendship? For I cannot for my part, my dear Daphnæus, consider man a less beautiful or important plant than the oak, or sacred olive, or the vine which Homer glorifies,[98] seeing that man too has his growth and glorious prime alike of soul and body."

§ XV. Then said Daphnæus, "In the name of the gods, who thinks differently?" "All those certainly must," answered my father, "who think that the gods care only about ploughing and planting and sowing. Have they not Nymphs attending upon them, called Dryads, 'whose age is coeval with the trees they live in: and Dionysus the mirth-giving does he not increase the yield of the trees, the sacred splendour of Autumn,' as Pindar says?[99] And if they care about all this, is there no god or genius who is interested in the nurture and growth of boys and youths in all their glorious flower? is there no one that cares that the growing man may be upright and virtuous, and that the nobility of his nature may not be warped and corrupted, either through want of a guardian or by the depravity of those he associates with? Is it not monstrous and thankless to say so, seeing that we enjoy the divine bounty, which is dealt out to us richly, and never abandons us in our straits? And yet some of these same straits have more necessity than beauty. For example, our birth, in spite of the unpleasant circumstances attending it, is witnessed by the divine Ilithyia and Artemis: and it would be better not to be born at all than to become bad through want of a good guardian and guide. Moreover in sickness the god who is over that province does not desert us, nor even in death: for even then there is a conductor and guide for the departed, to lay them to sleep, and convey their souls to Hades,[100] as the poet says,

'Night bore me not to be lord of the lyre, Nor to be seer, or healer of diseases, But to conduct the souls of the departed.'

And yet these duties involve much unpleasantness, whereas we cannot mention a holier work, nor any struggle or contest more fitting for a god to attend and play the umpire in, than the guidance of the young and beautiful in the prosecution of their love-affairs. For there is here nothing of an unpleasant nature, no compulsion of any kind, but persuasion and grace, truly making toil sweet and labour delightful, lead the way to virtue and friendship, and do not arrive at that desired goal without the deity, for they have as their leader and lord no other god than Love, the companion of the Muses and Graces and Aphrodite. For Love 'sowing in the heart of man the sweet harvest of desire,' to borrow the language of Melanippides, mixes the sweetest and most beautiful things together. But perhaps you are of a different opinion, Zeuxippus."

§ XVI. "Not I, by Zeus," replied Zeuxippus. "To have a different opinion would be ridiculous." "Then," continued my father, "is it not also ridiculous, if there are four kinds of friendship, for so the ancients distinguished, the natural first, the second that to one's kindred, the third that to one's companions, the fourth the friendship of love, and each of the first three have a god as patron, either a god of friendship, or a god of hospitality, or a god of the family, or a god of the race,[101] whereas the friendship of love only, as something altogether unholy, is left without any patron god, and that, too, when it needs most of all attentive direction?" "It is," said Zeuxippus, "highly ridiculous." My father continued, "The language of Plato is very suggestive here, to make a slight digression. One kind of madness (he says) is conveyed to the soul from the body through certain bad temperaments or mixtures, or through the prevalence of some noxious spirit, and is harsh, difficult to cure, and baneful. Another kind of madness is not uninspired or from within, but an afflatus from without, a deviation from sober reason, originated and set in motion by some higher power, the ordinary characteristic of which is called enthusiasm. For, as one full of breath is called [Greek: empnoos], and as one full of sense is called [Greek: emphrôn], so the name enthusiasm is given to the commotion of the soul caused by some Divine agency.[102] Thus there is the prophetic enthusiasm which proceeds from Apollo, and the Bacchic enthusiasm which comes from Dionysus, to which Sophocles alludes where he says, 'Dance with the Corybantes;' for the rites of Cybele and Pan have great affinities to the orgies of Bacchus. And the third madness proceeds from the Muses, and possesses an impressionable and pure soul, and stirs up the poetry and music in a man. As to the martial and warlike madness, it is well known from what god it proceeds, namely, Ares, 'kindling tearful war, that puts an end to the dance and the song, and exciting civic strife.'[103] There remains, Daphnæus, one more kind of madness in man, neither obscure nor tranquil, as to which I should like to ask Pemptides here,

'What god it is that shakes the fruitful thyrsus?'

I refer to that love-fury for modest boys and chaste women, which is far the keenest and fiercest passion of all. For have you not observed how the soldier, when he lays aside his arms, ceases from his warlike fury, as the poet says,

'Then from him Right gladly did his squires remove the armour,'[104]

and sits down a peaceful spectator of others?[105] The Bacchic and Corybantic dances one can also modulate and quell, by changing the metre from the trochaic and the measure from the Phrygian. Similarly, too, the Pythian priestess, when she descends from her tripod, possesses her soul in peace. Whereas the love-fury, when once it has really seized on a man and inflamed him, can be laid by no Muse, no charm or incantation, no change of place; but present they burn, absent they desire, by day they follow their loves about, by night they serenade them, sober call for them, and drunken sing about them. And he who said that poetic fancies, owing to their vividness, were dreams of people awake, would have more truly spoken so of the fancies of lovers, who, as if their loves were present, converse with them, greet them, chide them. For sight seems to paint all other fancies on a wet ground, so soon do they fade and recede from the memory, but the images of lovers, painted by the fancy as it were on encaustic tiles, leave impressions on the memory, that move, and live, and speak, and are permanent for all time. The Roman Cato, indeed, said that the soul of the lover resided in the soul of the loved one, and I should extend the remark to the appearance, the character, the life, and the actions, conducted by which he travels a long journey in a short time, as the Cynics say they have found a short cut and, as it were, forced march to virtue, for there is also a short cut to friendship and love when the god is propitious. To sum up, the enthusiasm of lovers is not a thing uninspired, and the god that guides and governs it is none other than the god whose festival we are now keeping, and to whom we are now sacrificing. Nevertheless, as we judge of a god mainly from his power and usefulness (as among human advantages we reckon and call these two the most divine, dominion and virtue), it is high time to consider, before we proceed any further, whether Love yields to any of the gods in power. Certainly, as Sophocles says, 'Wonderful is the power which the Cyprian Queen exerts so as always to win the victory:'[106] great also is the might of Ares; and in some sort we see the power of all the other gods divided among these two; for Aphrodite has most intimate connection with the beautiful, and Ares is in our souls from the first to combat against the sordid, to borrow the idea of Plato. Let us consider, then, to begin with, that the venereal delight can be purchased for six obols, and that no one ever yet put himself into any trouble or danger about it, unless he was in love. And not to mention here such famous courtesans as Phryne or Lais, Gnathænium, 'kindling her lamp at evening time,' on the look-out for lovers and inviting them, is often passed by; 'yet, if some sudden whiff arise' of mighty love and desire, it makes this very delight seem equal to the fabled wealth of Tantalus and his domains. So feeble and cloying is the venereal indulgence, if Love inspires it not. And you will see this more plainly still from the following consideration. Many have allowed others to share in their venereal enjoyments, prostituting not only their mistresses but their wives, like that Roman Galba, who used to ask Mæcenas to dinner, and when he saw from his nods and winks that he had a mind to do with his wife, turned his head gently aside as if asleep; but when one of his slaves came up to the table and stole some wine, his eyes were wide open enough, and he said, 'Villain, don't you know that I am asleep only for Mæcenas?'[107] But this is not perhaps so strange, considering Galba was a buffoon. But at Argos Nicostratus and Phayllus were great political rivals: so when King Philip visited that city, Phayllus thought if he prostituted his wife, who was very handsome, to the King, he would get from him some important office or place. And Nicostratus getting wind of this, and walking about the doors of Phayllus' house with some of his servants on the *qui vive*, Phayllus made his wife put on men's boots, and a military cloak, and a Macedonian broad-brimmed hat, and so smuggled her into the King, without being detected, as one of the King's young men. But, of all the multitude of lovers, did you ever hear of one that prostituted his boy-love even for the honours of Zeus? I think not. Why, though no one will generally either speak or act against tyrants, many will who find them their rivals and are jealous about their handsome minions. You must have heard how Aristogiton of Athens, and Antileon of Metapontum, and Melanippus of Agrigentum, rose not against tyrants, although they saw how badly they managed affairs, and what drunken tricks they played, yet, when they attempted the chastity of their boy-loves, they retaliated on them, jeoparding their lives, as if they were defending the inviolability of temples and sanctuaries. It is also recorded that Alexander wrote to Theodoras, the brother of Proteas, 'Send me your singing-girl, unless you love her yourself, and I will give you ten talents;' and when Antipatridas, one of his companions, came to revel with him, bringing with him a female harper, he fancied the girl not a little, and asked Antipatridas if he cared very much about her. And when he replied that he did immensely, Alexander said, 'Plague take you,' but nevertheless abstained from touching the girl.

§ XVII. "Consider also how Love excels in warlike feats, and is by no means idle, as Euripides called him,[108] nor a carpet-knight, nor 'sleeping on a maiden's soft cheeks.'[109] For a man inspired by Love needs not Ares to help him when he goes out as a warrior against the enemy, but at the bidding of his own god is 'ready' for his friend 'to go through fire and water and whirlwinds.' And in Sophocles' play,[110] when the sons of Niobe are being shot at and dying, one of them calls out for no helper or assister but his lover. And you know of course how it was that Cleomachus the Pharsalian fell in battle?" "We certainly don't," said Pemptides and those near him, "but we should very much like to." "Well," said my father, "the tale's worth hearing. When the war between the Eretrians and Chalcidians was at its height, Cleomachus had come to aid the latter with a Thessalian force; and the Chalcidian infantry seemed strong enough, but they had great difficulty in repelling the enemy's cavalry. So they begged that high-souled hero Cleomachus to charge the Eretrian cavalry first. And he asked his boy-love, who was by, if he would be a spectator of the fight, and he saying he would, and affectionately kissing him and putting his helmet on his head, Cleomachus with a proud joy put himself at the head of the bravest of the Thessalians, and charged the enemy's cavalry with such impetuosity that he threw them into disorder and routed them; and the Eretrian infantry also fleeing in consequence, the Chalcidians won a splendid victory. However, Cleomachus got killed, and they show his tomb in the market-place at Chalcis, over which a huge pillar stands to this day, and whereas before that the people of Chalcis had censured boy-loves, from that time forward they preferred that kind of love to the normal love. Aristotle gives a slightly different account, namely, that this Cleomachus came not from Thessaly, but from Chalcis in Thrace, to the help of the Chalcidians in Euboea; and that that was the origin of the song in vogue among the Chalcidians,

'Ye boys, who come of noble sires and beauteous are in face, Grudge not to give to valiant men the joy of your embrace: For Love that does the limbs relax combined with bravery In the Chalcidian cities has fame that ne'er shall die.'

But according to the account of the poet Dionysius, in his 'Causes,'[111] the name of the lover was Anton, and that of the boy-love was Philistus. And among you Thebans, Pemptides, is it not usual for the lover to give his boy-love a complete suit of armour when he is enrolled among the men? And did not the erotic Pammenes change the disposition of the heavy-armed infantry, censuring Homer as knowing nothing about love, because he drew up the Achæans in order of battle in tribes and clans, and did not put lover and love together, that so

'Spear should be next to spear, helmet to helmet,'[112]

seeing that Love is the only invincible general.[113] For men in battle will leave in the lurch clansmen and friends, aye, and parents and sons, but what warrior ever broke through or charged through lover and love, seeing that even when there is no necessity lovers frequently display their bravery and contempt of life. As Thero the Thessalian, who put his left hand on a wall, and drew his sword, and chopped off his thumb, and challenged his rival to do the same. And another in battle falling on his face, as his enemy was about to give him the *coup-de-grace*, begged him to wait a little till he could turn round, that his love should not see him with a wound in his back. And not only are the most warlike nations most amorous, as the Boeotians the Lacedæmonians and the Cretans, but also of the old heroes, who were more amorous than Meleager, Achilles, Aristomenes, Cimon, and Epaminondas. Why, Epaminondas had as his boy-loves Asopichus and Cephisodorus, the latter of whom fell with him at Mantinea, and is buried near him. As to ..., who was most formidable and a source of terror to the enemy, Eucnamus of Amphissa, who first stood up against him and smote him, received hero honours from the Phocians for his exploit. And as to all the loves of Hercules, it would take up too much time to enumerate them, but those who think that Iolaus was one of them do up to this day worship and honour him, and make their loves swear fidelity at his tomb. Hercules is also said, having understood the art of healing, to have preserved the life of Alcestis, when she was given up by the doctors, to gratify Admetus, who passionately loved his wife, and was Hercules' minion. They say also in legend that Apollo was enamoured of Admetus,

'And was his hired slave for one long year.'

It was a happy thought our remembering Alcestis, for though women have not much of Ares in them, yet when possessed by Love they are bold even to the death, beyond what one would expect from their nature. For if we may credit legendary lore, the stories about Alcestis, and Protesilaus, and Eurydice the wife of Orpheus, show that the only one of the gods that Hades pays attention to is Love; although to everybody else, as Sophocles says, "he knows of no forbearance or favour, or anything but strict justice;" yet before lovers his genius stands rebuked, and they alone find him neither implacable nor relentless. Wherefore although, my friend, it is an excellent thing to be initiated in the Eleusinian mysteries, yet I see that the votaries and initiated of Love have a better time of it in Hades than they have, * *[114] though in regard to legendary lore I stand in the position of one who neither altogether believes nor altogether disbelieves. For legendary lore speaks well, and by a certain wonderful good fortune lights upon the truth, in saying that lovers have a return from Hades to the light of day, but it knows not by what way or how, having as it were got benighted on the road which Plato first discovered by philosophy. There are, indeed, some slender and obscure particles of truth scattered about in the mythology of the Egyptians, but they require a clever man to hunt them out, a man capable of getting great results from small data. Wherefore let that matter pass. And now next to the mighty power of Love let us consider its good will and favour to mankind, I do not mean as to whether it bestows many gifts on its votaries--that is palpable to all--but whether they derive any further advantage from it. For Euripides, though very amorous, admired a very small matter, when he wrote the line--

'Love teaches letters to a man unlearn'd.'[115]

For it makes one previously sluggish quick and intelligent, and, as has been said before, it makes the coward brave, as people harden wood in the fire and make it strong from being weak. And every lover becomes liberal and genuine and generous, even if he was mean before, his littleness and miserliness melting away like iron in the fire, so that they rejoice to give to their loves more than they do to receive themselves from others. You know of course that Anytus, the son of Anthemion, was in love with Alcibiades, and was on one occasion sumptuously entertaining several of his friends, when Alcibiades broke in and took from the table half the cups and went away again; and when some of the guests were indignant and said, 'The stripling has used you most insolently and contemptuously,' Anytus replied, 'Nay, rather, he has dealt kindly with me, for when he might have taken all he has left me half.'"

§ XVIII. Zeuxippus was pleased with this story, and said, "O Hercules, you have been within an ace of making me forget my hereditary hatred to Anytus for his behaviour to Socrates and philosophy,[116] since he was so mild and noble to his love." "Be it so," said my father, "Love also makes peevish and gloomy persons kind and agreeable to those they live with; for as 'when the fire blazes the house looks brighter,'[117] so man, it seems, becomes more cheerful through the heat of love. But most people are affected rather curiously; if they see by night a light in a house, they look on it with admiration and wonder; but if they see a little, mean, and ignoble soul suddenly filled with noble-mindedness, freedom, dignity, grace, and liberality, they do not feel constrained to say with Telemachus, 'Surely, some god is there within.'[118] And is it not wonderful, Daphnæus," continued my father,[119] "in the name of the Graces, that the lover who cares about hardly anything, either his companions and friends, or even the laws and magistrates and kings, who fears nothing, admires nothing, courts nothing, but can even endure to gaze on 'the forked lightning,'[120] yet directly he looks on his love 'he crouches like a cock with drooping feathers,' and his boldness is broken and his pride is cowed. And among the Muses it would not be amiss to mention Sappho; for as the Romans say Cacus the son of Hephæstus vomited out of his mouth fire and flames, so she really speaks words that burn like fire, and in her songs shows the warmth of her heart, as Philoxenus puts it, 'by euphonious songs assuaging the pains of love.' And if you have not in your love for Lysandra forgot all your old love-songs, do repeat to us,

Daphnæus, the lines in which beautiful Sappho says that 'when her love appeared her voice failed and her body burned, and she was seized with paleness and trembling and vertigo.'" And when Daphnæus had repeated the lines, my father resumed, "In the name of Zeus, is not this plainly a divine seizure? Is not this a wonderful commotion of soul? Why, the Pythian priestess on the tripod is not moved so much as this! Who of those inspired by Cybele are made beside themselves to this extent by the flute and the kettledrum? Moreover, while many see the same body and the same beauty, only the lover is taken by it. Why is this the case? We get no light on it from Menander's words, 'Love is opportunity; and he that is smitten is the only one wounded.' But the god is the cause of it, striking one and letting another go scot-free. But I will not pass over now, 'since it has come into my mouth,' as Æschylus says, what perhaps would have been better spoken before, for it is a very important point. Perhaps, my friend, of all other things which we do not perceive through the senses, some got believed through legend, some through the law, some through reason; whereas we owe our conception of the gods altogether to the poets and legislators and philosophers: all alike teaching the existence of gods, but greatly differing as to their number and order, nature and power. For the gods of the philosophers 'know nothing of disease or old age or pain, and have not to cross the resounding Acheron;' nor do the philosophers accept as gods Strifes, or Prayers, which are found in poetry;[121] nor will they admit Terror and Fear as gods or as the sons of Ares. And on many points also they are at variance with the legislators, as Xenophanes bade the Egyptians, if they regarded Osiris as mortal, not to honour him as a god; but if they thought him a god not to mourn for him. And, again, the poets and legislators will not listen to, nor can they understand, the philosophers who make gods of ideas and numbers and units and spirits. And their views generally are very different. As there were formerly three parties at Athens, the Parali, the Epacrii, and the Pediei, all at variance with one another, yet all agreed to vote for Solon, and chose him with one accord as their mediator and ruler and lawgiver, as he seemed indisputably to hold the first place in merit; so the three parties that entertain different views about the gods are all unanimous on one point, for poets legislators and philosophers all alike register Love as one of the gods, 'loudly singing his praises with one voice,' as Alcæus says the people of Mitylene chose Pittacus as their monarch. But our king and ruler and governor, Love, is brought down crowned from Helicon to the Academy by Hesiod and Plato and Solon, and in royal apparel rides in a chariot drawn by friendship and intimacy (not such as Euripides speaks of in the line, 'he has been bound in fetters not of brass,'[122] shamefully throwing round him cold and heavy necessity), and soars aloft to the most beautiful and divine things, about which others have spoken better than I can."

§ XIX. When my father had spoken thus much, Soclarus began, "Do you see that a second time you have committed the same fault, not cancelling your debts as you ought to do--for I must speak my mind--but evading them on purpose, and not delivering to us your promised ideas on a sacred subject? For as some little time back you only just touched on Plato and the Egyptians as if unwilling to enter on the subject more fully, so now you are doing again. However, as to what has been 'eloquently told'[123] by Plato, or rather by the Muses through Plato's mouth, do not tell us that, my good friend, even if we ask for it; but as to your hint that the Egyptian legend about Love corresponded with Plato's views, you need not discuss it fully and minutely, we shall be satisfied if we hear a little of such mighty matters." And as the rest of the company made the same request, my father said, "The Egyptians, (like the Greeks) recognize two Loves, the Pandemian and the Celestial, to which they add the Sun, they also highly venerate Aphrodite. We also see much similarity between Love and the Sun, for neither is a fire, as some think, but a sweet and productive radiance and warmth, the Sun bringing to the body nourishment and light and growth, and Love doing the same to the soul. And as the heat of the Sun is more powerful when it emerges from clouds and after mist, so Love is sweeter and hotter after a jealous tiff with the loved one,[124] and moreover, as some think the Sun is kindled and extinguished, so also do people conceive of Love as mortal and uncertain. Moreover, just as without training the body cannot easily bear the heat of the Sun, so neither can the untrained soul easily bear the yoke of Love, but both are equally out of tune and suffer, for which they blame the deity and not their own weakness. But in this respect they seem to differ, in that the Sun exhibits to the eye things beautiful and ugly alike, whereas Love throws its light only on beautiful things, and persuades lovers to concentrate their attention on these, and to neglect all other things. As to those that call Aphrodite the Moon, they, too, find some points in common between them; for the Moon is divine and heavenly and a sort of halfway-house between mortal and immortal, but inactive in itself and dark without the presence of the Sun, as is the case with Aphrodite in the absence of

Love. So we may say that Aphrodite resembles the Moon, and Love the Sun, more than any other deities, yet are not Love and the Sun altogether the same, for just as body and soul are not the same, but something different, so is it with the Sun and Love, the former can be seen, the latter only felt. And if it should not seem too harsh a saying, one might argue that the Sun acts entirely opposite to Love, for it turns the mind away from the world of fancy to the world of reality, beguiling us by its grace and splendid appearance, and persuading us to seek for truth and everything else in and round it and nowhere else. For as Euripides says,

'Too passionately do we love the Sun, Because it always shines upon the earth, From inexperience of another life,'[125]

or rather from forgetfulness of those things which Love brings to our remembrance. For as when we are woke by a great and bright light, everything that the soul has seen in dreams is vanished and fled, so the Sun is wont to banish the remembrance of past changes and chances, and to bewitch the intelligence, pleasure and admiration causing this forgetfulness. And though reality is really there, yet the soul cleaves to dreams and is dazzled by what is most beautiful and divine. 'For round the soul are poured sweet yet deceiving dreams,' so that the soul thinks everything here good and valuable, unless it obtain divine and chaste Love as its physician and preserver. For Love brings the soul through the body to truth and the region of truth, where pure and guileless beauty is to be found, kindly befriending its votaries like an initiator at the mysteries. And it associates with the soul only through the body. And as geometricians, in the case of boys who cannot yet be initiated into the perception of incorporeal and impassive substance, convey their ideas through the medium of spheres, cubes, and dodecahedrons, so celestial Love has contrived beautiful mirrors of beautiful things, and exhibits them to us glittering in the shapes colours and appearances of youths in all their flower, and calmly stirs the memory which is inflamed first by these. Consequently some, through the stupidity of their friends and intimates, who have endeavoured by force and against reason to extinguish the flame, have got no advantage from it, but filled themselves with smoke and confusion, or have rushed into secret and lawless pleasures and ingloriously wasted their prime. But as many as by sober reason and modesty have abated the extravagance of the passion, and left in the soul only a bright glow--not exciting a tornado of passion, but a wonderful and productive diffusion, as in a growing plant, opening the pores of complaisance and friendliness--these in no long time cease to regard the personal charms of those they love, and study their inward characters, and gaze at one another with unveiled eyes, and associate with one another in words and actions, if they find in their minds any fragment or image of the beautiful; and if not they bid them farewell and turn to others, like bees that only go to those flowers from which they can get honey. But wherever they find any trace or emanation or pleasing resemblance of the divine, in an ecstasy of pleasure and delight they indulge their memory, and revive to whatever is truly lovely and felicitous and admired by everybody."

§ XX. "The poets indeed seem for the most part to have written and sung about Love in a playful and merry manner, but have sometimes spoken seriously about him, whether out of their own mind, or the god helping them to truth. Among these are the lines about his birth, 'Well-sandalled Iris bare the most powerful of the gods to golden-haired Zephyr.'[126] But perhaps the learned have persuaded you that these lines are only a fanciful illustration of the variety and beauty of love." "Certainly," said Daphnæus, "what else could they mean?" "Hear me," said my father, "for the heavenly phenomenon compels us so to speak. The rainbow[127] is, I suppose, a reflection caused by the sun's rays falling on a moist cloud, making us think the appearance is in the cloud. Similarly erotic fancy in the case of noble souls causes a reflection of the memory, from things which here appear and are called beautiful, to what is really divine and lovely and felicitous and wonderful. But most lovers pursuing and groping after the semblance of beauty in boys and women, as in mirrors,[128] can derive nothing more certain than pleasure mixed with pain. And this seems the love-delirium of Ixion, who instead of the joy he desired embraced only a cloud, as children who desire to take the rainbow into their hands, clutching at whatever they see. But different is the behaviour of the noble and chaste lover: for he reflects on the divine beauty that can only be felt, while he uses the beauty of the visible body only as an organ of the memory, though he embraces it and loves it, and associating with it is still more inflamed in mind. And so neither in the body do they sit ever gazing at and desiring this light, nor after death do they return to this world again, and skulk and loiter about the doors and bedchambers of newly-married people, disagreeable ghosts of pleasure-loving and sensual men and women, who do not rightly deserve the name of lovers. For the true lover, when he has got into the other world and associated with beauties as much as is lawful, has wings and is initiated and passes his time above in the presence of his Deity, dancing and waiting upon him, until he goes back to the meadows of the Moon and Aphrodite, and sleeping there commences a new existence. But this is a subject too high for the present occasion. However, it is with Love as with the other gods, to borrow the words of Euripides, 'he rejoices in being honoured by mankind,'[129] and *vice versa*, for he is most propitious to those that receive him properly, but visits his displeasure on those that affront him. For neither does Zeus as god of Hospitality punish and avenge any outrages on strangers or suppliants, nor as god of the family fulfil the curses of parents, as quickly as Love hearkens to lovers unfairly treated, being the chastiser of boorish and haughty persons. Why need I mention the story of Euxynthetus and Leucomantis, the latter of whom is called The Peeping Girl to this day in Cyprus? But perhaps you have not heard of the punishment of the Cretan Gorgo, a somewhat similar case to that of Leucomantis, except that she was turned into stone as she peeped out of window to see her lover carried out to burial. For this Gorgo had a lover called Asander, a proper young man and of a good family, but reduced in fortune, though he thought himself worthy to mate with anybody. So he wooed Gorgo, being a relation of hers, and though he had many rivals, as she was much run after for her wealth belike, yet he had won the esteem of all the guardians and relations of the young girl.[130] * * * *

§ XXI. * * * Now the origins and causes of Love are not peculiar to either sex, but common to both. For those attractions that make men amorous may as well proceed from women as from boys.[131] And as to those beautiful and holy reminiscences and invitations to the divine and genuine and Olympian beauty, by which the soul soars aloft, what hinders but that they may come either from boys or lads, maidens or grown women, whenever a chaste and orderly nature and beauteous prime are associated together (just as a neat shoe exhibits the shapeliness of the foot, to borrow the illustration of Aristo), whenever connoisseurs of beauty descry in beautiful forms and pure bodies clear traces of an upright and unenervated soul.[132] For if[133] the man of pleasure, who was asked whether "he was most given to the love of women or boys," and answered, "I care not which so beauty be but there," is considered to have given an appropriate answer as to his erotic desires, shall the noble lover of beauty neglect beauty and nobility of nature, and make love only with an eye to the sexual parts? Why, the lover of horses will take just as much pleasure in the good points of Podargus, as in those of Æthe, Agamemnon's mare,[134] and the sportsman rejoices not only in dogs, but also rears Cretan and Spartan bitches,[135] and shall the lover of the beautiful and of humanity be unfair and deal unequally with either sex, and think that the difference between the loves of boys and women is only their different dress? And yet they say that beauty is a flower of virtue; and it is ridiculous to assert that the female sex never blossoms nor make a goodly show of virtue, for as Æschylus truly says,

'I never can mistake the burning eye Of the young woman that has once known man.'[136]

Shall the indications then of a forward wanton and corrupt character be found in the faces of women, and shall there be no gleam of chastity and modesty in their appearance? Nay, there are many such, and shall they not move and provoke love? To doubt it would be neither sensible nor in accordance with the facts, for generally speaking, as has been pointed out, all these attractions are the same in both sexes.... But, Daphnæus, let us combat those views which Zeuxippus lately advanced, making Love to be only irregular desire carrying the soul away to licentiousness, not that this was so much his own view as what he had often heard from morose men who knew nothing of love: some of whom marry unfortunate women for their dowries, and force on them economy and illiberal saving, and quarrel with them every day of their lives: while others, more desirous of children than wives, when they have made those women they come across mothers, bid farewell to marriage, or regard it not at all, and neither care to love nor be loved. Now the fact that the word for conjugal love differs only by one letter from the word for endurance, the one being [Greek: stergein] the other [Greek: stegein], seems to emphasize the conjugal kindness mixed by time and intimacy with necessity. But that marriage which Love has inspired will in the first place, as in Plato's Republic, know nothing of *Meum* and *Tuum*, for the proverb, 'whatever belongs to a friend is common property,'[137] is especially true of married persons who, though disunited in body, are perforce one in soul, neither wishing to be two, nor thinking themselves so. In the second place there will be mutual respect, which is a vital necessity in marriage. For as to that external respect which has in it more of compulsion than choice, being forced by the law and shame and fear,

"Those needful bits and curbs to headstrong weeds,"[138]

that will always exist in wedlock. But in Love there is such self-control and decorum and constancy, that if the god but once enter the soul of a licentious man, he makes him give up all his amours, abates his pride, and breaks down his haughtiness and dissoluteness, putting in their place modesty and silence and tranquillity and decorum, and makes him constant to one. You have heard of course of the famous courtesan Lais,[139] how she set all Greece on fire with her charms, or rather was contended for by two seas,[140] and how, when she fell in love with Hippolochus the Thessalian, 'she left Acro-Corinthus washed by the green sea,'[141] and deserted all her other lovers, that great army, and went off to Thessaly and lived faithful to Hippolochus. But the women there, envious and jealous of her for her surpassing beauty, dragged her into the temple of Aphrodite, and there stoned her to death, for which reason probably it is called to this day the temple of Aphrodite the Murderess.[142] We have also heard of servant girls who have refused the embraces of their masters, and of private individuals who have scorned an amour with queens, when Love has had dominion in their hearts. For as in Rome, when a dictator is proclaimed, all other magistrates lay down their offices, so those over whom Love is lord are free henceforward from all other lords and masters, and pass the rest of their lives dedicate to the god and slaves in his temple. For a noble woman united by Love to her lawful husband would prefer the embraces of bears and dragons to those of any other man."

§ XXII. "Although there are plenty of examples of this virtue of constancy, yet to you, that are the festive votaries of the god,[143] it will not be amiss to relate the story of the Galatian Camma. She was a woman of most remarkable beauty, and the wife of the tetrarch Sinatus, whom Sinorix, one of the most influential men in Galatia, and desperately in love with Camma, murdered, as he could neither get her by force or persuasion in the lifetime of her husband. And Camma found a refuge and comfort in her grief in discharging the functions of hereditary priestess to Artemis, and most of her time she spent in her temple, and, though many kings and potentates wooed her, she refused them all. But when Sinorix boldly proposed marriage to her, she declined not his offer, nor blamed him for what he had done, as though she thought he had only murdered Sinatus out of excessive love for her, and not in sheer villany. He came, therefore, with confidence, and asked her hand, and she met him and greeted him and led him to the altar of the goddess, and pledged him in a cup of poisoned mead, drinking half of it herself and giving him the rest. And when she saw that he had drunk it up, she shouted aloud for joy, and calling upon the name of her dead husband, said, 'Till this day, dearest husband, I have lived, deprived of you, a life of sorrow: but now take me to yourself with joy, for I have avenged you on the worst of men, as glad to share death with him as life with you.' Then Sinorix was removed out of the temple on a litter, and soon after gave up the ghost, and Camma lived the rest of that day and following night, and is said to have died with a good courage and even with gaiety."[144]

§ XXIII. "As many similar examples might be adduced, both among ourselves and foreigners, who can feel any patience with those that reproach Aphrodite with hindering friendship when she associates herself with Love as a partner? Whereas any reflecting person would call the love of boys wanton and gross lasciviousness, and say with the poet:

'This is an outrage, not an act of love.'

All willing pathics, therefore, we consider the vilest of mankind, and credit them with neither fidelity, nor modesty, nor friendship, for as Sophocles says:

'Those who shall lose such friends may well be glad, And those who have such pray that they may lose them,'[145]

But as for those who, not being by nature vicious, have been seduced or forced, they are apt all their life to despise and hate their seducers, and when an opportunity has presented itself to take fierce vengeance. As Crateus, who murdered Archelaus, and Pytholaus, who murdered Alexander of Pheræ. And Periander, the tyrant of the Ambraciotes, having asked a most insulting question of his minion, was murdered by him, so exasperated was he. But with women and wives all this is the beginning of friendship, and as it were an initiation into the sacred mysteries. And pleasure plays a very small part in this, but the esteem and favour and mutual love and constancy that result from it, proves that the Delphians did not talk nonsense in giving the name of Arma[146] to Aphrodite, nor Homer in giving the name of friendship[147] to sexual love, and testifies to the fact that Solon was a most experienced legislator in conjugal matters, seeing that he ordered husbands not less than thrice a month to associate with their wives, not for pleasure, but as states at certain intervals renew their treaties with one another, so he wished that by such friendliness marriage should, as it were, be renewed after any intervening tiffs and differences. But you will tell me there is much folly and even madness in the love of women. Is there not more extravagance in the love of boys?

'Seeing my many rivals I grow faint. The lad is beardless, smooth and soft and handsome, O that I might in his embraces die, And have the fact recorded on my tomb.'

Such extravagant language as this is madness not love. And it is absurd to detract from woman's various excellence. Look at their self-restraint and intelligence, their fidelity and uprightness, and that bravery courage and magnanimity so conspicuous in many! And to say that they have a natural aptitude for all other virtues, but are deficient as regards friendship alone, is monstrous. For they are fond of their children and husbands, and generally speaking the natural affection in them is not only, like a fruitful soil, capable of friendship, but is also accompanied by persuasion and other graces. And as poetry gives to words a kind of relish by melody and metre and rhythm, making instruction thereby more interesting, but what is injurious more insidious, so nature, investing woman with beautiful appearance and attractive voice and bewitching figure, does much for a licentious woman in making her wiles more formidable, but makes a modest one more apt thereby to win the goodwill and friendship of her husband. And as Plato advised Xenocrates, a great and noble man in all other respects, but too austere in his temperament, to sacrifice to the Graces, so one might recommend a good and modest woman to sacrifice to Love, that her husband might be a mild and agreeable partner, and not run after any other woman, so as to be compelled to say like the fellow in the comedy, 'What a wretch I am to ill-treat such a woman!' For to love in marriage is far better than to be loved, for it prevents many, nay all, of those offences which spoil and mar marriage.

§ XXIV. As to the passionate affection in the early days of marriage,[148] my dear Zeuxippus, do not fear that it will leave any sore or irritation, though it is not wonderful that there should be some friction at the commencement of union with a virtuous woman, just as at the grafting of trees, as there is also pain at the beginning of conception, for there can be no complete union without some suffering. Learning puts boys out somewhat when they first go to school, as philosophy does young men at a later day, but the ill effects are not lasting, either in their cases or in the case of lovers. As in the fusion of two liquors, love does indeed at first cause a simmering and commotion, but eventually cools down and settles and becomes tranquil. For the union of lovers is indeed a complete union, whereas the union of those that live together without love resembles only the friction and concussion of Epicurus' atoms in collision and recoil, forming no such union as Love makes, when he presides over the conjugal state. For nothing else produces so much pleasure, or such lasting advantages, or such beautiful remarkable and desirable friendship,

'As when husband and wife live in one house, Two souls beating as one.'[149]

And the law gives its countenance, and nature shows that even the gods themselves require love for the production of everything. Thus the poets tell us that 'the earth loves a shower, and heaven loves the earth,' and the natural philosophers tell us that the sun is in love with the moon, and that they are husband and wife, and that the earth is the mother of man and beast and the producer of all plants. Would not the world itself then of necessity come to an end, if the great god Love and the desires implanted by the god should leave matter, and matter should cease to yearn for and pursue its lead? But not to seem to wander too far away and altogether to trifle, you know that many censure boy-loves for their instability, and jeeringly say that that intimacy like an egg is destroyed by a hair,[150] for that boy-lovers like Nomads, spending the summer in a blooming and flowery country, at once decamp then as from an enemy's territory. And still more vulgarly Bion the Sophist called the sprouting beards of beautiful boys Harmodiuses and Aristogitons,[151] inasmuch as lovers were delivered by them from a pleasant tyranny. But this charge cannot justly be brought against genuine lovers, and it was prettily said by Euripides, as he embraced and kissed handsome Agatho whose beard was just sprouting, that the Autumn of beautiful youths was lovely as well as the Spring. And I maintain that the love of beautiful and chaste wives flourishes not only in old age amid grey hairs and wrinkles, but even in the grave and monument. And while there are few such long unions in the case of boy-loves, one might enumerate ten thousand such instances of the love of women, who have kept their fidelity to the end of their lives. One such case I will relate, which happened in my time in the reign of the Emperor Vespasian.

§ XXV. Julius, who stirred up a revolt in Galatia, among several other confederates had one Sabinus, a young man of good family, and for wealth and renown the most conspicuous of all the men in those parts. But having attempted what was too much for them they were foiled, and expecting to pay the penalty, some committed suicide, others fled and were captured. Now Sabinus himself could easily have got out of the way and made his escape to the barbarians, but he had married a most excellent wife, whose name in that part of the world was Empone, but in Greek would be Herois, and he could neither leave her behind nor take her with him. As he had in the country some underground caves, known only to two of his freedmen, where he used to stow away things, he dismissed all the rest of his slaves, as if he intended to poison himself, and taking with him these two trusty freedmen he descended with them into those underground caves, and sent one of them, Martialis, to tell his wife that he had poisoned himself, and that his body was burnt in the flames of his country-house, for he wanted his wife's genuine sorrow to lend credit to the report of his death. And so it happened. For she, throwing herself on to the ground, groaned and wailed for three days and nights, and took no food. And Sabinus, being informed of this, and fearing that she would die of grief, told Martialis to inform her secretly that he was alive and well and in hiding, and to beg her not to relax her show of grief, but to keep up the farce. And she did so with the genius of a professional actress, but yearning to see her husband she visited him by night, and returned without being noticed, and for six or seven months she lived with him this underground life. And she disguised him by changing his dress, and cutting off his beard, and re-arranging his hair, so that he should not be known, and took him to Rome, having some hopes of obtaining his pardon. But being unsuccessful in this she returned to her own country, and spent most of her time with her husband underground, but from time to time visited the town, and showed herself to some ladies who were her friends and relations. But what is most astonishing of all is that, though she bathed with them, she concealed her pregnancy from them. For the dye which women use to make their hair a golden auburn, has a tendency to produce corpulence and flesh and a full habit, and she rubbed this abundantly over all parts of her body, and so concealed her pregnancy. And she bare the pangs of travail by herself, as a lioness bears her whelps, having hid herself in the cave with her husband, and there she gave birth to two boys, one of whom died in Egypt, the other, whose name was Sabinus, was among us only the other day at Delphi. Vespasian eventually put her to death, but paid the penalty for it, his whole progeny in a short time being wiped off the face of the earth.[152] For during the whole of his reign he did no more savage act, nor could gods or demons have turned away their eyes from a crueller sight. And yet her courage and bold language abated the pity of the spectators, though it exasperated Vespasian, for, despairing of her safety, she bade them go and tell the Emperor, 'that it was sweeter to live in darkness and underground than to wear his crown.'"[153]

§ XXVI Here my father said that the conversation about Love which took place at Thespiæ ended. And at this moment Diogenes, one of Pisias' companions, was noticed coming up at a faster pace than walking. And while he was yet a little way off, Soclarus hailed him with, "You don't announce war, Diogenes," and he replied, "Hush! it is a marriage; come with me quickly, for the sacrifice only waits for you." All were delighted, and Zeuxippus asked if Pisias was still against the marriage. "As he was first to oppose it," said Diogenes, "so he was first to yield the victory to Ismenodora, and he has now put on a crown and robed himself in white, so as to take his place at the head of the procession to the god through the market-place."

"Come," said my father, "in Heaven's name, let us go and laugh at him, and worship the god; for it is clear that the god has taken delight in what has happened, and been propitious."

[62] The allusion is to Plato's "Phædrus," p. 230, B. Much, indeed, of the subject-matter here is, we shall find, somewhat similar to that of the Phædrus.

[63] It is difficult to know what the best English word here is. From the sly thrust in § ix. Pisias was evidently grey. I have therefore selected the word *gravest*. But *the most austere, the most sensible, the most solid, the most sedate*, all might express the Greek word also. Let the reader take which he likes best.

[64] In a Greek house the women and men had each their own separate apartments. This must be borne in mind here to explain the allusion.

[65] That is, from interested and selfish motives.

[66] On Lais and Aristippus see Cicero, "Ad. Fam.," ix. 26.

[67] Pausanias, i. 19, shows us that there was at Athens a Temple of Hercules called Cynosarges. But the matter is obscure. What the exact allusion is I cannot say.

[68] Fragment of Æschylus. See Athenæus, xiii. p. 602, E, which explains the otherwise obscure allusion.

[69] That is the son of Hera alone, who was unwilling to be outdone by Zeus, who had given birth to Pallas Athene alone. Hesiod has the same view, "Theog." 927.

[70] [Greek: opôra] is so used also in Æsch. "Suppl.," 998, 1015. See also "Athenæus," 608, F. Daphnæus implies these very nice gentlemen, like the same class described by Juvenal, "Curios simulant et Bacchanalia vivunt."

[71] I omit [Greek: kai kopidas] as a gloss or explanation of the old reading [Greek: makeleia] instead of [Greek: matruleia]. Nothing can be made of [Greek: kai kopidas] in the context.

[72] "Works and Days," 606-608.

[73] I follow here the reading of Wyttenbach. Through the whole of this essay the reading is very uncertain frequently. My text in it has been formed from a careful collation of Wyttenbach, Reiske, and Dübner. I mention this here once for all, for it is unnecessary in a translation to minutely specify the various readings on every occasion. I am not editing the "Moralia."

[74] "De Oenantha et Agathoclea, v. Polyb. excerpt, l. xv."--*Reiske*.

[75] Thespiæ. The allusion is to Phryne. See Pausanias, ix. 27; x. 15.

[76] Reading with Wyttenbach, [Greek: hôsper daktylion ischnou, hô mê perirrhuê dediôs.]

[77] Perhaps *cur* = coward, was originally *cur-tail*.

[78] One of the three ports at Athens. See Pausanias, i. 1.

[79] Iolaus was the nephew of Hercules, and was associated with him in many of his Labours. See Pausanias, i. 19; vii. 2; viii. 14, 45.

[80] I read [Greek: synoarizontas]. The general reading [Greek: synerôntas] will hardly do here. Wyttenbach suggests [Greek: synearizontas].

[81] What the [Greek: dibolia] was is not quite clear. I have supposed a jersey.

[82] The women of Lemnos were very masterful. On one memorable occasion they killed all their husbands in one night. Thus the line of Ovid has almost a proverbial force, "Lemniadesque viros nimium quoque vincere norunt."--*Heroides*, vi. 53. Siebelis in his Preface to Pausanias, p. xxi, gives from an old Scholia a sort of excuse for the action of the women of Lemnos.

[83] Probably the epilepsy. See Herodotus, iii. 33.

[84] Euripides, "Bacchae," 203.

[85] Euripides, Fragment of the "Melanippe."

[86] I take Wyttenbach's suggestion as to the reading here.

[87] This line is taken bodily by Aristophanes in his "Frogs," 1244.

[88] The first line is the first line of a passage from Euripides, consisting of thirteen lines, containing similar sentiments to this. See Athenæus, xiii. p. 599, F. The last two lines are from Euripides, "Hippolytus," 449, 450.

[89] Compare Lucretius, i. 1-5.

[90] Hesiod, "Theogony," 116-120.

[91] Euripides, "Danae," Frag. Compare Ovid, "Cedit amor rebus: res age, tutus eris."

[92] Sophocles, Fragm. 678, Dindorf. Compare a remark of Sophocles, recorded by Cicero, "De Senectute," ch. xiv.

[93] Sophocles, Fragm. 720. Reading [Greek: kala] with Reiske.

[94] Iliad, v. 831.

[95] Connecting [Greek: Arês] with [Greek: anairein].

[96] The *Saint Hubert* of the Middle Ages.

[97] Æschylus, Frag. 1911. Dindorf.

[98] Odyssey, v. 69.

[99] Fragm. 146, 125.

[100] Hermes is alluded to.

[101] All these four were titles of *Zeus*. They are very difficult to put into English so as to convey any distinctive and definite idea to an English reader.

[102] Enthusiasm is the being [Greek: entheos], or inspired by some god.

[103] From Æschylus, "Supplices," 681, 682.

[104] "Iliad," vii. 121, 122.

[105] Like the character described in Lucretius, ii. 1-6.

[106] Sophocles, "Trachiniae," 497. The Cyprian Queen is, of course, Aphrodite.

[107] Hence the famous Proverb, "Non omnibus dormio." See Cic. "Ad. Fam." vii. 24.

[108] Above, in § xiii.

[109] See Sophocles, "Antigone," 783, 784. And compare Horace, "Odes," Book iv. Ode xiii. 6-8, "Ille virentis et Doctæ psallere Chiæ *Pulchris excubat in genis.*"

[110] The "Niobe," which exists only in a few fragments.

[111] This was the name of Dionysius' Poem. He was a Corinthian poet.

[112] "Iliad," xiii. 131.

[113] Reading according to the conjecture of Wyttenbach, [Greek: hôs ton Erôta uonon aêttêton onta tôn stratêgôn].

[114] Something has probably dropped out here, as Dübner suspects.

[115] Fragment from the "Stheneboea" of Euripides.

[116] Anytus was one of the accusers of Socrates, and so one of the causers of his death. So Horace calls Socrates "Anyti reum," "Sat." ii. 4, 3.

[117] Homeric Epigrammata, xiii. 5. Quoted also in "On Virtue and Vice," § 1.

[118] Odyssey, xix. 40.

[119] I adopt the suggestion of Wyttenbach, [Greek: eipen, ô Daphnaie].

[120] Pinder, "Pyth." i. 8.

[121] See for example Homer, Iliad, xi. 3, 73; ix. 502.

[122] Euripides, "Pirithous," Fragm. 591. Dindorf.

[123] An allusion to Homer, "Odyssey," xii. 453.

[124] So Terence, "Andria," 555. "Amantium iræ amoris integratiost."

[125] Euripides, "Hippolytus," 194-196.

[126] The lines are from Alcæus. Thus Love was the child of the Rainbow and the West Wind. A pretty

conceit.

[127] Greek *iris*.

[128] The mirrors of the ancients were of course not like our mirrors. They were only burnished bronze. Hence the view in them would be at best somewhat obscure. This explains 1 Cor. xiii. 12; 2 Cor. iii. 18; James i. 23.

[129] See Euripides, "Hippolytus," 7, 8.

[130] Here the story unfortunately ends, and for all time we shall know no more of it. Reiske somewhat forcibly says, "Vel lippus videat Gorgus historiam non esse finitam, et multa, ut et alias, periisse."

[131] Like Reiske we condense here a little.

[132] Reading with Reiske [Greek: orthês kai athruptou.]

[133] I read [Greek: ei gar].

[134] See "Iliad," xxiii. 295. Podargus was an entire horse.

[135] See Ovid, "Metamorph." iii. 206-208.

[136] Æschylus, "Toxotides," Fragm. 224.

[137] A very favourite proverb among the ancients. See Plat. "Phaedr." fin. Martial, ii. 43.

[138] Soph. Fragm. 712.

[139] On Laïs, see Pausanias, ii. 2. Her Thessalian lover is there called Hippostratus. Her favours were so costly that the famous proverb is said to owe its origin to her, "Non cuivis homini contingit adire Corinthum."

[140] The Ægean and Ionian. Cf. Horace, "Odes," i. 7, 2.

[141] On Acro-Corinthus, see Pausanias, ii. 4. The words in inverted commas are from Euripides, Fragm. 921.

[142] On Laïs generally, and her end, see Athenæus, xiii. 54, 55.

[143] See § I. The Festival of Love was being kept at this very time.

[144] This story is also told by Plutarch, "De Mulierum Virtutibus," § xx.

[145] Sophocles, Fragm. 741. Quoted again in "On Abundance of Friends," § iii.

[146] A Delphic word for love. Can it be connected with [Greek: arma]?

[147] Very frequent in Homer, *e.g.*, "Iliad," ii. 232; vi. 165; xiii. 636: xiv. 353, etc.

[148] See Lucretius, iv. 1105-1114. I tone down the original here a little.

[149] Homer, "Odyssey," vi. 183, 184. Cf. Eurip. "Medea," 14, 15.

[150] This means when the moustache and beard and whiskers begin to grow.

[151] The whole story about Harmodius and Aristogiton and how they killed Hipparchus is told by Thucydides, vi. 54-59. Bion therefore practically called these sprouting beards *tyrant-killers, tyrannicides.*

[152] "Scriptus igitur hic libellus est post caedem Domitiani."--*Reiske.*

[153] Vespasian certainly was not cruel generally. "Non temere quis punitus insons reperietur, nisi absente eo et ignaro aut certe invito atque decepto..... Sola est, in qua merito culpetur, pecuniæ cupiditas."--Suetonius, "Divus Vespasianus," 15, 16.

CONJUGAL PRECEPTS.

PLUTARCH SENDS GREETING TO POLLIANUS AND EURYDICE.

After the customary marriage rites, by which, the Priestess of Demeter has united you together, I think that to make an appropriate discourse, and one that will chime in with the occasion, will be useful to you and agreeable to the law. For in music one of the tunes played on the flute is called Hippothorus,[154] which is a tune that excites fierce desire in stallions to cover mares; and though in philosophy there are many goodly subjects, yet is there none more worthy of attention than that of marriage, on which subject philosophy spreads a charm over those who are to pass life together, and makes them gentle and mild to one another. I send therefore as a gift to both of you a summary of what you have often heard, as you are both well versed in philosophy, arranging my matter in a series of short observations that it may be the more easily remembered, and I pray that the Muses will assist and co-operate with Aphrodite, so that no lyre or lute could be more harmonious or in tune than your married life, as the result of philosophy and concord. And thus the ancients set up near Aphrodite statues of Hermes, to show that conversation was one of the great charms of marriage, and also statues of Peitho[155] and the Graces, to teach married people to gain their way with one another by persuasion, and not by wrangling or contention.

§ I. Solon bade the bride eat a quince the first night of marriage, intimating thereby, it seems, that the bridegroom, was to expect his first pleasure from the bride's mouth and conversation.

§ II. In Boeotia they dress up the bride with a chaplet of asparagus, for as the asparagus gives most excellent fruit from a thorny stalk, so the bride, by not being too reluctant and coy in the first approaches, will make the married state more agreeable and pleasant. But those husbands who cannot put up with the early peevishness of their brides, are not a whit wiser than those persons who pluck unripe grapes and leave the ripe grapes for others.[156] On the other hand, many brides, being at first disgusted with their husbands, are like those that stand the bee's sting but neglect the honey.

§ III. Married people should especially at the outset beware of the first quarrel and collision, observing that vessels when first fabricated are easily broken up into their component parts, but in process of time, getting compact and firmly welded together, are proof against either fire or steel.

§ IV. As fire gets kindled easily in chaff or in a wick or in the fur of hares, but is easily extinguished again, if it find no material to keep it in and feed it, so we must not consider that the love of newly-married people, that blazes out so fiercely in consequence of the attractions of youth and beauty, will be durable and lasting, unless it be fixed in the character, and occupy the mind, and make a living impression.[157]

§ V. As catching fish by drugged bait is easy, but makes the fish poor to eat and insipid, so those wives that lay traps for their husbands by philtres and charms, and become their masters by pleasure, have stupid senseless and spoiled husbands to live with. For those that were bewitched by Circe did her no good, nor could she make any use of them when they were turned into swine and asses, but she was greatly in love with the prudent Odysseus who dwelt with her sensibly.

§ VI. Those women who would rather lord it over fools than obey sensible men, resemble those people who would rather lead the blind on a road, and not people who have eyesight and know how to follow.

§ VII. Women disbelieve that Pasiphäe, a king's wife, was enamoured of a bull, although they see some of their sex despising grave and sober men, and preferring to associate with men who are the slaves of intemperance and pleasure, and like dogs and he-goats.

§ VIII. Men who through weakness or effeminacy cannot vault upon their horses' backs, teach them to kneel and so receive their riders. Similarly, some men that marry noble or rich wives, instead of making themselves better humble their wives, thinking to rule them easier by lowering them. But one ought to govern with an eye to the merit of a woman, as much as to the size of a horse.

§ IX. We see that the moon when it is far from the sun is bright and glorious, but pales and hides its light when it is near. A modest wife on the contrary ought to be seen chiefly with her husband, and to stay at home and in retirement in his absence.

§ X. It is not a true observation of Herodotus, that a woman puts off her modesty with her shift.[158] On the contrary, the modest woman puts on her modesty instead, and great modesty is a sign of great conjugal love.

§ XI. As where two voices are in unison the loudest prevails; so in a well-managed household everything is done by mutual consent, but the husband's supremacy is exhibited, and his wishes are consulted.

§ XII. The Sun beat the North Wind.[159] For when it blew a strong and terrible blast, and tried to make the man remove his cloak, he only drew it round him more closely, but when the Sun came out with its warm rays, at first warmed and afterwards scorched, he stripped himself of coat as well as cloak. Most woman act similarly: if their husbands try to curtail by force their luxury and extravagance, they are vexed and fight for their rights, but if they are convinced by reason, they quietly drop their expensive habits, and keep within bounds.

§ XIII. Cato turned out of the Senate a man who kissed his own wife in the presence of his daughter. This was perhaps too strong a step, but if it is unseemly, as indeed it is, for husband and wife in the presence of others to fondle and kiss and embrace one another, is it not far more unseemly in the presence of others to quarrel and jangle? Just as conjugal caresses and endearments ought to be private, so ought admonition and scolding and plain speaking.

§ XIV. Just as there is little use in a mirror adorned with gold or precious stones, unless it conveys a true likeness, so there is no advantage in a rich wife, unless she conforms her life and habits to her husband's position. For if when a man is joyful the mirror makes him look sad, and when he is put out and sad it makes him look gay and smiling from ear to ear, the mirror is plainly faulty. So the wife is faulty and devoid of tact, who frowns when her husband is in the vein for mirth and jollity, and who jokes and laughs when he is serious: the former conduct is disagreeable, the latter contemptuous.[160] And, just as geometricians say lines and surfaces do not move of themselves, but only in connection with bodies, so the wife ought to have no private emotions of her own, but share in her husband's gravity or mirth, anxiety or gaiety.

§ XV. As those husbands who do not like to see their wives eating and drinking in their company only teach them to take their food on the sly, so those husbands who are not gay and jolly with their wives, and never joke or smile with them, only teach them to seek their pleasures out of their company.

§ XVI. The kings of Persia have their wedded wives at their side at banquets and entertainments; but when they have a mind for a drunken debauch they send them away,[161] and call for singing-girls and concubines, rightly so doing, for so they do not mix up their wives with licentiousness and drunkenness. Similarly, if a private individual, lustful and dissolute, goes astray with a courtesan or maid-servant, the wife should not be vexed or impatient, but consider that it is out of respect to her that he bestows upon another all his wanton depravity.

§ XVII. As kings make[162] if fond of music many musicians, if lovers of learning many men of letters, and many athletes if fond of gymnastics, so the man who has an eye for female charms teaches his wife to dress well, the man of pleasure teaches his meretricious tricks and wantonness, while the true gentleman makes his virtuous and decorous.

§ XVIII. A Lacedæmonian maiden, when someone asked her if she had yet had dealings with a man, replied, "No, but he has with me." This methinks is the line of conduct a matron should pursue, neither to decline the embraces of a husband when he takes the initiative, nor to provoke them herself, for the one is forward and savours of the courtesan, the other is haughty and unnatural.

§ XIX. The wife ought not to have her own private friends, but cultivate only those of the husband. Now the gods are our first and greatest friends, so the wife ought only to worship and recognize her husband's gods, and the door ought to be shut on all superfluous worship and strange superstitions, for none of the gods are pleased with stealthy and secret sacrifices on the part of a wife.

§ XX. Plato says that is a happy and fortunate state, where the words *Meum* and *Tuum* are least heard,[163] because the citizens regard the common interest in all matters of importance. Far more essential is it in marriage that the words should have no place. For, as the doctors say, that blows on the left shoulders are also felt on the right,[164] so is it good[165] for husband and wife to mutually sympathize with one another, that, just as the strength of ropes comes from the twining and interlacing of fibres together, so the marriage knot may be confirmed and strengthened by the interchange of mutual affection and kindness. Nature itself teaches this by the birth of children, which are so much a joint result, that neither husband nor wife can discriminate or discern which part of the child is theirs. So, too, it is well for married persons to have one purse, and to throw all their property into one common stock, that here also there may be no *Meum* and *Tuum*. And just as we call the mixture of water and wine by the name of wine, even though the water should preponderate,[166] so we say that the house and property belongs to the man, even though the wife contribute most of the money.

§ XXI. Helen was fond of wealth, Paris of pleasure, whereas Odysseus was prudent, Penelope chaste. So the marriage of the last two was happy and enviable, while that of the former two brought an Iliad of woe on Greeks and barbarians alike.

§ XXII. The Roman who was taken to task by his friends for repudiating a chaste wealthy and handsome wife, showed them his shoe and said, "Although this is new and handsome, none of you know where it pinches me."[167] A wife ought not therefore to put her trust in her dowry, or family, or beauty, but in matters that more vitally concern her husband, namely, in her disposition and companionableness and complaisance with him, not to make every-day life vexatious or annoying, but harmonious and cheerful and agreeable. For as doctors are more afraid of fevers that are generated from uncertain causes, and from a complication of ailments, than of those that have a clear and adequate cause, so the small and continual and daily matters of offence between husband and wife, that the world knows nothing about, set the household most at variance, and do it the greatest injury.

§ XXIII. King Philip was desperately enamoured of a Thessalian woman,[168] who was accused of bewitching him; his wife Olympias therefore wished to get this woman into her power. But when she came before her, and was evidently very handsome, and talked to her in a noble and sensible manner, Olympias said, "Farewell to calumny! Your charms lie in yourself."[169] So invincible are the charms of a lawful wife to win her husband's affection by her virtuous character, bringing to him in herself dowry, and family, and philtres, and even Aphrodite's cestus.[170]

§ XXIV. Olympias, on another occasion, when a young courtier had married a wife who was very handsome, but whose reputation was not very good, remarked, "This fellow has no sense, or he would not have married with his eyes." We ought neither to marry with our eyes, nor with our fingers, as some do, who reckon up on their fingers what dowry the wife will bring, not what sort of partner she will make.

§ XXV. It was advice of Socrates, that when young men looked at themselves in the mirror, those who were not handsome should become so through virtue, and those who were so should not by vice deform their beauty. Good also is it for the matron, when she has the mirror in her hands, if not handsome to say to herself, "What should I be, if I were not virtuous?" and if handsome to say to herself, "How good it were to add virtue to beauty!" for it is a feather in the cap of a woman not handsome to be loved for herself and not for good looks.

§ XXVI. Dionysius, the tyrant of Sicily, sent some costly dresses and necklaces to the daughters of Lysander, but he would not receive them, and said, "These presents will bring my daughters more shame than adornment." And Sophocles said still earlier than Lysander, "Your madness of mind will not appear handsome, wretch, but most unhandsome." For, as Crates says, "that is adornment which adorns," and that adorns a woman that makes her more comely; and it is not gold or diamonds or scarlet robes that make her so, but her dignity, her correct conduct, and her modesty.

§ XXVII. Those who sacrifice to Hera as goddess of marriage,[171] do not burn the gall with the other parts of the victim, but when they have drawn it throw it away beside the altar: the lawgiver thus hinting that gall and rage have no place in marriage. For the austerity of a matron should be, like that of wine, wholesome and pleasant, not bitter as aloes, or like a drug.

§ XXVIII. Plato advised Xenocrates, a man rather austere but in all other respects a fine fellow, to sacrifice to the Graces. I think also that a chaste wife needs the graces with her husband that, as Metrodorus said, "she may live agreeably with him, and not be bad-tempered because she is chaste." For neither should the frugal wife neglect neatness, nor the virtuous one neglect to make herself attractive, for peevishness makes a wife's good conduct disagreeable, as untidiness makes one disgusted with simplicity.

§ XXIX. The wife who is afraid to laugh and jest with her husband, lest she should appear bold and wanton, resembles one that will not anoint herself with oil lest she should be thought to use cosmetics, and will not wash her face lest she should be thought to paint. We see also in the case of those poets and orators, that avoid a popular illiberal and affected style, that they artificially endeavour to move and sway their audience by the facts, and by a skilful arrangement of them, and by their gestures. Consequently a matron will do well to avoid and repudiate over-preciseness meretriciousness and pomposity, and to use tact in her dealings with her husband in every-day life, accustoming him to a combination of pleasure and decorum. But if a wife be by nature austere and apathetic, and no lover of pleasure, the husband must make the best of it, for, as Phocion said, when Antipater enjoined on him an action neither honourable nor becoming, "You cannot have me as a friend and flatterer both," so he must say to himself about his strict and austere wife, "I cannot have in the same woman wife and mistress."

§ XXX. It was a custom among the Egyptian ladies not to wear shoes, that they might stay at home all day and not go abroad. But most of our women will only stay at home if you strip them of their golden shoes, and bracelets, and shoe-buckles, and purple robes, and pearls.

§ XXXI. Theano, as she was putting on her shawl, displayed her arm, and somebody observing, "What a handsome arm!" she replied, "But not common." So ought not even the speech, any more than the arm, of a chaste woman, to be common, for speech must be considered as it were the exposing of the mind, especially in the presence of strangers. For in words are seen the state of mind and character and disposition of the speaker.

§ XXXII. Phidias made a statue of Aphrodite at Elis, with one foot on a tortoise,[172] as a symbol that women should stay at home and be silent. For the wife ought only to speak either to her husband, or by her husband, not being vexed if, like a flute-player, she speaks more decorously by another mouth-piece.

§ XXXIII. When rich men and kings honour philosophers, they really pay homage to themselves as well; but when philosophers pay court to the rich, they lower themselves without advancing their patrons. The same is the case with women. If they submit themselves to their husbands they receive praise, but if they desire to rule, they get less credit even than the husbands who submit to their rule. But the husband ought to rule his wife, not as a master does a chattel, but as the soul governs the body, by sympathy and goodwill. As he ought to govern the body by not being a slave to its pleasures and desires, so he ought to rule his wife by cheerfulness and complaisance.

§ XXXIV. The philosophers tell us that some bodies are composed of distinct parts, as a fleet or army; others of connected parts, as a house or ship; others united and growing together, as every animal is. The marriage of lovers is like this last class, that of those who marry for dowry or children is like the second class, and that of those who only sleep together is like the first class, who may be said to live in the same house, but in no other sense to live together. But, just as doctors tell us that liquids are the only things that thoroughly mix, so in married people there must be a complete union of bodies, wealth, friends, and relations. And thus the Roman legislator forbade married people to exchange presents with one another, not that they should not go shares with one another, but that they should consider everything as common property.

§ XXXV. At Leptis, a town in Libya, it is the custom for the bride the day after marriage to send to her mother-in-law's house for a pipkin, who does not lend her one, but says she has not got one, that from the first the daughter-in-law may know her mother-in-law's stepmotherly mind,[173] that if afterwards she should be harsher still, she should be prepared for it and not take it ill. Knowing this the wife ought to guard against any cause of offence, for the bridegroom's mother is jealous of his affection to his wife. But there is one cure for this condition of mind, to conciliate privately the husband's affection, and not to divert or diminish his love for his mother.

§ XXXVI. Mothers seem to love their sons best as able to help them, and fathers their daughters as needing their help; perhaps also it is in compliment to one another, that each prefers the other sex in their children, and openly favours it. This, however, is a matter perhaps of little importance. But it looks very nice in the wife to show greater respect to her husband's parents than to her own, and if anything unpleasant has happened to confide it to them rather than to her own people. For trust begets trust,[174] and love love.

§ XXXVII. The generals of the Greeks in Cyrus's army ordered their men to receive the enemy silently if they came up shouting, but if they came up silently to rush out to meet them with a shout. So sensible wives, in their husband's tantrums, are quiet when they storm, but if they are silent and sullen talk them round and appease them.

§ XXXVIII. Rightly does Euripides[175] censure those who introduce the lyre at wine-parties, for music ought to be called in to assuage anger and grief, rather than to enervate the voluptuous still more than before. Think, therefore, those in error who sleep together for pleasure, but when they have any little difference with one another sleep apart, and do not then more than at any other time invoke Aphrodite, who is the best physician in such cases, as the poet, I ween, teaches us, where he introduces Hera, saying:

"Their long-continued strife I now will end, For to the bed of love I will them send."[176]

§ XXXIX. Everywhere and at all times should husband and wife avoid giving one another cause of offence, but most especially when they are in bed together. The woman who was in labour and had a bad time said to those that urged her to go to bed, "How shall the bed cure me, which was the very cause of this trouble?"[177] And those differences and quarrels which the bed generates will not easily be put an end to at any other time or place.

§ XL. Hermione seems to speak the truth where she says:

"The visits of bad women ruined me."[178]

But this case does not happen naturally, but only when dissension and jealousy has made wives open not only their doors but their ears to such women. But that is the very time when a sensible wife will shut her ears more than at any other time, and be especially on her guard against whisperers, that fire may not be added to fire,[179] and remember the remark of Philip, who, when his friends tried to excite him against the Greeks, on the ground that they were treated well and yet reviled him, answered, "What will they do then, if I treat them ill?" Whenever, then, calumniating women come and say to a wife, "How badly your husband treats you, though a chaste and loving wife!" let her answer, "How would he act then, if I were to begin to hate him and injure him?"

§ XLI. The master who saw his runaway slave a long time after he had run away, and chased him, and came up with him just as he had got to the mill, said to him, "In what more appropriate place could I have wished to find you?"[180] So let the wife, who is jealous of her husband, and on the point of writing a bill of divorce in her anger, say to herself, "In what state would my rival be better pleased to see me in than this, vexed and at variance with my husband, and on the point of abandoning his house and bed?"

§ XLII. The Athenians have three sacred seedtimes: the first at Scirus, as a remembrance of the original sowing of corn, the second at Rharia, the third under Pelis, which is called Buzygium.[181] But a more sacred seedtime than all these is the procreation of children, and therefore Sophocles did well to call Aphrodite "fruitful Cytherea." Wherefore it behoves both husband and wife to be most careful over this business, and to abstain from lawless and unholy breaches of the marriage vow, and from sowing in quarters where they desire no produce, or where, if any produce should come, they would be ashamed of it and desire to conceal it.[182]

§ XLIII. When Gorgias the Rhetorician recited his speech at Olympia recommending harmony to the Greeks, Melanthius cried out, "He recommend harmony to us! Why, he can't persuade his wife and maid to live in harmony, though there are only three of them in the house!" Gorgias belike had an intrigue with the maid, and his wife was jealous. He then must have his own house in good order who undertakes to order the affairs of his friends and the public, for any ill-doings on the part of husbands to their wives is far more likely to come out and be known to the public than the ill-doings of wives to their husbands.

§ XLIV. They say the cat is driven mad by the smell of perfumes. If it happens that wives are equally affected by perfumes, it is monstrous that their husbands should not abstain from using perfumes, rather than for so small a pleasure to incommode so grievously their wives. And since they suffer quite as much when their husbands go with other women, it is unjust for a small pleasure to pain and grieve wives, and not to abstain from connection with other women, when even bee-keepers will do as much, because bees are supposed to dislike and sting those that have had dealings with women.

§ XLV. Those that approach elephants do not dress in white, nor those that approach bulls in red, for these colours render those animals savage; and tigers they say at the beating of drums go quite wild, and tear themselves in their rage. Similarly, as some men cannot bear to see scarlet and purple dresses, and others are put out by cymbals and drums,[183] what harm would it do wives to abstain from these things, and not to vex or provoke husbands, but to live with them quietly and meekly?

§ XLVI. A woman said to Philip, who against her will was pulling her about, "Let me go, all women are alike when the lamp is put out."[184] A good remark to adulterers and debauchees. But the married woman ought to show when the light is put out that she is not like all other women, for then, when her body is not visible, she ought to exhibit her chastity and modesty as well as her personal affection to her husband.

§ XLVII. Plato[185] recommended old men to act with decorum especially before young men, that they too might show respect to them; for where the old behave shamelessly, no modesty or reverence will be exhibited by the young. The husband ought to remember this, and show no one more respect than his wife, knowing that the bridal chamber will be to her either a school of virtue or of vice. And he who enjoys pleasures that he forbids his wife, is like a man that orders his wife to go on fighting against an enemy to whom he has himself surrendered.

§ XLVIII. As to love of show, Eurydice, read and try to remember what was written by Timoxena to Aristylla: and do you, Pollianus, not suppose that your wife will abstain from extravagance and expense, if she sees that you do not despise such vanities in others, but delight in gilt cups, and pictures in houses, and trappings for mules, and ornaments for horses. For it is not possible to banish extravagance from the women's side of the house if it is always to be seen in the men's apartments. Moreover, Pollianus, as you are already old enough for the study of philosophy, adorn your character by its teaching, whether it consists of demonstration or constructive reasoning, by associating and conversing with those that can profit you. And for your wife gather honey from every quarter, as the bees do, and whatever knowledge you have yourself acquired impart to her, and converse with her, making the best arguments well known and familiar to her. For now

"Father thou art to her, and mother dear, And brother too."[186]

And no less decorous is it to hear the wife say, "Husband, you are my teacher and philosopher and guide in the most beautiful and divine subjects." For such teaching in the first place detaches women from absurdities: for the woman who has learnt geometry will be ashamed to dance, nor will she believe in incantations and spells, if she has been charmed by the discourses of Plato and Xenophon; and if anyone should undertake to draw the moon down from the sky, she will laugh at the ignorance and stupidity of women that credit such nonsense, well understanding geometry, and having heard how Aglaonice, the daughter of the Thessalian Hegetor, having a thorough knowledge of the eclipses of the moon, and being aware beforehand of the exact time when the moon would be in eclipse, cheated the women, and persuaded them that she herself had drawn it down from the sky. For no woman was ever yet credited with having had a child without intercourse with a man, for those shapeless embryos and gobbets of flesh that take form from corruption are called moles. We must guard against such false conceptions as these arising in the minds of women, for if they are not well informed by good precepts, and share in the teaching that men get, they generate among themselves many foolish and absurd ideas and states of mind. But do you, Eurydice, study to make yourself acquainted with the sayings of wise and good women, and ever have on your tongue those sentiments which as a girl you learnt with us, that so you may make your husband's heart glad, and be admired by all other women, being in yourself so wonderfully and splendidly adorned. For one cannot take or put on, except at great expense, the jewels of this or that rich woman, or the silk dresses of this or that foreign woman, but the virtues that adorned Theano,[187] and Cleobuline, and Gorgo the wife of Leonidas, and Timoclea the sister of Theagenes, and the ancient Claudia,[188] and Cornelia the sister of Scipio,[189] and all other such noble and famous women, these one may array oneself in without money and without price, and so adorned lead a happy and famous life. For if Sappho plumed herself so much on the beauty of her lyrical poetry as to write to a certain rich woman, "You shall lie down in your tomb, nor shall there be any remembrance of you, for you have no part in the roses of Pieria," how shall you not have a greater right to plume yourself on having a part not in the roses but in the fruits which the Muses bring, and which they freely bestow on those that admire learning and philosophy?[190]

[154] This tune is again alluded to by Plutarch in "Quæstion. Convival.", p. 704, F. See also Clemens Alexandrinus, "Pædagog." ii. p. 164, [Greek: A tais de hippois mignumenais oion hymenaios epauleitai nomos aulôdias hippothoron touton keklêkasin oi Mousikoi.]

[155] Peitho means Persuasion, and is represented as one of the Graces by Hermes anax. See Pausanias, ix. 35.

[156] Compare the Proverb [Greek: Eikelos omphakizetai], and Tibullus, iii. 5, 19: "Quid fraudare juvat vitem crescentibus uvis?"

[157] Cf. Shakspere, "Romeo and Juliet," A. ii. Sc. vi. 9-15.

[158] Herodotus, i. 8.

[159] An allusion to the well-known Fable of Æsop, No. 82 in Halm's edition.

[160] This comparison of the mirror is beautifully used by Keble in his "Christian Year:" "Without a hope on earth to find A mirror in an answering mind." *Wednesday before Easter.*

[161] Does this throw light on Esther, i. 10-12?

[162] By their patronage.

[163] "Republic," v. p. 462, C.

[164] By the power of sympathy. This is especially true of eyes. Wyttenbach compares the Epigram in the Anthology, i. 46. 9. [Greek: Kai gar dexion omma kakoumenon ommati laiô Pollaki tous idious antididôsi ponous.]

[165] Reading [Greek: kalon] with Hercher.

[166] The ancients hardly ever drank wine neat. Hence the allusion. The symposiarch, or arbiter bibendi, settled the proportions to be used.

[167] Compare the French proverb, "Le beau soulier blesse souvent le pied."

[168] Thessaly was considered by the ancients famous for enchantments and spells. So Juvenal, vi. 610, speaks of "Thessala philtia," and see Horace, "Odes," i. 27. 21, 22; "Epodes," v. 45.

[169] Wyttenbach well compares the lines of Menander:--

[Greek: enest alêthes philtron eugnômôn tropos, toutô katakratein andros eiôthen gunê.]

[170] An allusion to Homer, "Iliad," xiv. 214-217.

[171] Called by the Romans "pronuba Juno." See Verg. "Æneid," iv. 166; Ovid, "Heroides," vi. 43.

[172] See Pausanias, vi. 25. The statue was made of ivory and gold.

[173] Compare Terence, "Hecyra," 201. "Uno animo omnes socrus oderunt nurus." As to stepmotherly feelings, the "injusta noverca" has passed into a proverb with all nations. See for example Hesiod, "Works and Days," 823, [Greek: allote mêtruiê pelei hêmerê, allote mêtêr].

[174] Wyttenbach compares Seneca's "Fidelem si putaveris facies." "Ep." iii. p. 6.

[175] Euripides, "Medea," 190-198.

[176] Homer, "Iliad," xiv. 205, 209.

[177] See Mulier Parturiens, Phaedrus' "Fables," i. 18.

[178] Euripides, "Andromache," 930.

[179] Proverb. Cf. Horace, "Oleum adde camino," ii. "Sat." iii. 321.

[180] See Æsop's Fables, No. 121. Halme. [Greek: Drapetês] is the title. All readers of Plautus and Terence know what a bugbear to slaves the threat of being sent to the mill was. They would have to turn it instead of horses, or other cattle.

[181] That is, *Yoking oxen for the plough*.

[182] Procreation of children was among the ancients frequently called *Ploughing* and *Sowing*. Hence the allusions in this paragraph. So, too, Shakspere, "Measure for Measure," Act i. Sc. iv. 41-44.

[183] The reference is to the rites of Cybele. See Lucretius, ii. 618.

[184] See Erasmus, "Adagia." The French proverb is "La nuit tous les chats sont gris."

[185] "Laws," p. 729, C.

[186] From the words of Andromache to Hector, "Iliad," vi. 429, 430.

[187] Theano was the wife of Pythagoras.

[188] See Livy, xxix. 14. Propertius, v. 11. 51, 52. Ovid, "Fasti," iv. 305 sq.

[189] And mother of the Gracchi.

[190] Jeremy Taylor, in his beautiful sermon on "The Marriage Ring," has borrowed not a few hints from this treatise of Plutarch, as usual investing with a new beauty whatever he borrows, from whatever source. He had the classics at his fingers' end, and much of his unique charm he owes to them. But he read them as a philosopher, and not as a grammarian.

CONSOLATORY LETTER TO HIS WIFE.

§ I. Plutarch to his wife sends greeting. The messenger that you sent to me to announce the death of our little girl seems to have missed his way *en route* for Athens; but when I got to Tanagra I heard the news from my niece. I suppose the funeral has already taken place, and I hope everything went off so as to give you least sorrow both now and hereafter. But if you left undone anything you wished to do, waiting for my opinion, and thinking your grief would then be lighter, be it without ceremoniousness or superstition, both which things are indeed foreign to your character.

§ II. Only, my dear wife, let us both be patient at this calamity. I know and can see very clearly how great it is, but should I find your grief too excessive, it would trouble me even more than the event itself. And yet I have not a heart hard as heart of oak or flintstone, as you yourself know very well, who have shared with me in the bringing up of so many children, as they have all been educated at home by ourselves. And this one I know was more especially beloved by you, as she was the first daughter after four sons, when you longed for a daughter, and so I gave her your name.[191] And as you are very fond of children your grief must have a peculiar bitterness when you call to mind her pure and simple gaiety, which was without a tincture of passion or querulousness. For she had from nature a wonderful contentedness of mind and meekness, and her affectionateness and winning ways not only pleased one but also afforded a means of observing her kindliness of heart, for she used to bid her nurse[192] give the teat not only to other children but even to her favourite playthings, and so invited them as it were to her table in kindliness of heart, and gave them a share of her good things, and provided the best entertainment for those that pleased her.

§ III. But I see no reason, my dear wife, why these and similar traits in her character, that gave us delight in her lifetime, should now, when recalled to the memory, grieve and trouble us. Though, on the other hand, I fear that if we cease to grieve we may also cease to remember her, like Clymene, who says in the Play[193]--

"I hate the supple bow of cornel-wood, And would put down athletics,"

because she ever avoided and trembled at anything that reminded her of her son, for it brought grief with it, and it is natural to avoid everything that gives us pain. But as she gave us the greatest pleasure in embracing her and even in seeing and hearing her, so ought her memory living and dwelling with us to give us more, aye, many times more, joy than grief, since those arguments that we have often used to others ought to be profitable to us in the present conjuncture, nor should we sit down and rail against fortune, opposing to those joys many more griefs.

§ IV. Those who were present at the funeral tell me with evident surprise that you put on no mourning, and that you bedizened up neither yourself nor your maids with the trappings of woe, and that there was no ostentatious expenditure of money at the funeral, but that everything was done orderly and silently in the presence of our relations. I am not myself surprised that you, who never made a display either at the theatre or on any other public occasion, and thought extravagance useless even in the case of pleasure, should have been frugal in your grief. For not only ought the chaste woman to remain uncorrupt in Bacchanalian revels,[194] but she ought to consider her self-control not a whit less necessary in the surges of sorrow and emotion of grief, contending not (as most people think) against natural affection, but against the extravagant wishes of the soul. For we are indulgent to natural affection in the regret, and honour, and memory that it pays to the dead: but the insatiable desire for a passionate display of funeral grief, coming to the climax in coronachs and beatings of the breast, is not less unseemly than intemperance in pleasure and is unreasonably[195] forgiven only because pain and grief instead of delight are elements in the unseemly exhibition. For what is more unreasonable than to curtail excessive laughter or any other demonstration of joy, and to allow a free vent to copious lamentation and wailing that come from the same source? And how unreasonable is it, as some husbands do, to quarrel with their wives about perfume and purple robes, while they allow them to shear their heads in mourning, and to dress in black, and to sit in idle grief, and to lie down in weariness! And what is worst of all, how unreasonable is it for husbands to interfere if their wives chastise the domestics and maids immoderately or without sufficient cause, yet allow them to ill-treat themselves cruelly in cases and conjunctures that require repose and kindness!

§ V. But between us, my dear wife, there never was any occasion for such a contest, nor do I think there ever will be. For as to your economy in dress and simple way of living, there is no philosopher with whom you are acquainted whom you did not amaze, nor is there any citizen who has not observed[196] how plainly you dressed at sacred rites, and sacrifices, and theatres. You have also already on similar painful occasions exhibited great fortitude, as when you lost your eldest son, and again when our handsome Chæron died. For when I was informed of his death, I well remember some guests from the sea were coming home with me to my house as well as some others, but when they saw the great quiet and tranquillity of the household, they thought, as they afterwards told some other people, that no such disaster had really happened, but that the news was untrue. So well had you ordered everything in the house, at a time when there would have been great excuse for disorder. And yet you had suckled that son, though your breast had had to be lanced owing to a contusion. This was noble conduct and showed your great natural affection.

§ VI. But most mothers we see, when their children are brought to them clean and tidy, take them into their hands as playthings, and when they die burst out into idle and unthankful grief, not so much out of affection--for affection is thoughtful and noble--but a great yearning for vain glory[197] mixed with a little natural affection makes their grief fierce and vehement and hard to appease. And this does not seem to have escaped Æsop's notice, for he says that when Zeus assigned their honours to various gods, Grief also claimed his. And Zeus granted his wish, with this limitation that only those who chose and wished need pay him honour.[198] It is thus with grief at the outset, everyone welcomes it at first, but after it has got by process of time settled, and become an inmate of the house, it is with difficulty dislodged again, however much people may wish to dislodge it. Wherefore we ought to keep it out of doors, and not let it approach the garrison by wearing mourning or shearing the hair, or by any similar outward sign of sorrow. For these things occurring daily and being importunate make the mind little, and narrow, and unsocial, and harsh, and timid, so that, being besieged and taken in hand by grief, it can no longer laugh, and shuns daylight, and avoids society. This evil will be followed by neglect of the body, and dislike to anointing and the bath and the other usual modes of life: whereas the very opposite ought to be the case, for the mind ill at ease especially requires that the body should be in a sound and healthy condition. For much of grief is blunted and relaxed when the body is permeated by calm, like the sea in fine weather. But if the body get into a dry and parched condition from a low diet, and gives no proper nutriment to the soul, but only feeds it with sorrow and grief, as it were with bitter and injurious exhalations, it cannot easily recover its tone however people may wish it should. Such is the state of the soul that has been so ill-treated.

§ VII. Moreover, I should not hesitate to assert[199] that the most formidable peril in connection with this is "the visits of bad women,"[200] and their chatter, and joint lamentation, all which things fan the fire of sorrow and aggravate it, and suffer it not to be extinguished either by others or by itself. I am not ignorant what a time of it you had lately, when you went to the aid of Theon's sister, and fought against the women who came on a visit of condolence and rushed up with lamentation and wailing, adding fuel as it were to her fire of grief in their simplicity. For when people see their friends' houses on fire they put it out as quickly and energetically as they can, but when their souls are on fire they themselves bring fuel. And if anybody has anything the matter with his eyes they will not let him put his hands to them, however much he wish, nor do they themselves touch the inflamed part; but a person in grief sits down and gives himself up to every chance comer, like a river [that all make use of], to stir up and aggravate the sore, so that from a little tickling and discomfort it grows into a great and terrible disease. However, as to all this I know you will be on your guard.

§ VIII. Try also often to carry yourself back in memory to that time when, this little girl not having been then born, we had nothing to charge Fortune with, and to compare that time and this together, as if our circumstances had gone back to what they were then. Otherwise, my dear wife, we shall seem discontented at the birth of our little daughter, if we consider our position before her birth as more perfect. But we ought not to erase from our memory the two years of her life, but to consider them as a time of pleasure giving us gratification and enjoyment, and not to deem the shortness of the blessing as a great evil, nor to be unthankful for what was given us, because Fortune did not give us a longer tenure as we wished. For ever to be careful what we say about the gods, and to be cheerful and not rail against Fortune, brings a sweet and goodly profit; and he who in such conjunctures as ours mostly tries to remember his blessings, and turns and diverts his mind from the dark and disturbing things in life to the bright and radiant, either altogether extinguishes his grief or makes it small and dim from a comparison with his comforts. For as perfume gives pleasure to the nose, and is a remedy against disagreeable smells, so the remembrance of past happiness in present trouble gives all the relief they require to those who do not shut out of their memory the blessings of the past, or always and everywhere rail against Fortune. And this certainly ought not to be our case, that we should slander all our past life because, like a book, it has one erasure in it, when all the other pages have been bright and clean.

§ IX. You have often heard that happiness consists in right calculations resulting in a healthy state of mind, and that the changes which Fortune brings about need not upset it, and introduce confusion into our life. But if we too must, like most people, be governed by external events, and make an inventory of the dealings of Fortune, and constitute other people the judges of our felicity, do not now regard the tears and lamentations of those who visit you, which by a faulty custom are lavished on everybody, but consider rather how happy you are still esteemed by them for your family, your house, and life. For it would be monstrous, if others would gladly prefer your destiny to theirs, even taking into account our present sorrow, that you should rail against and be impatient at our present lot, and in consequence of our bitter grief not reflect how much comfort is still left to us. But like those who quote imperfect verses of Homer[201] and neglect the finest passages of his writings, to enumerate and complain of the trials of life, while you pay no attention to its blessings, is to resemble those stingy misers, who heap up riches and make no use of them when they have them, but lament and are impatient if they are lost. And if you grieve over her dying unmarried and childless, you can comfort yourself with the thought that you have had both those advantages. For they should not be reckoned as great blessings in the case of those who do not enjoy them, and small blessings in the case of those who do. And that she has gone to a place where she is out of pain ought not to pain us, for what evil can we mourn for on her account if her pains are over? For even the loss of important things does not grieve us when we have no need of them. But it was only little things that your Timoxena was deprived of, little things only she knew, and in little things only did she rejoice; and how can one be said to be deprived of things of which one had no conception, nor experience, nor even desire for?

§ X. As to what you hear from some people, who get many to credit their notion, that the dead suffer no evil or pain, I know that you are prevented from believing that by the tradition of our fathers and by the mystic symbols of the mysteries of Dionysus, for we are both initiated. Consider then that the soul, being incorruptible, is in the same condition after death as birds that have been caught. For if it has been a long time in the body, and during this mortal life has become tame by many affairs and long habit, it swoops down again and a second time enters the body, and does not cease to be involved in the changes and chances of this life that result from birth. For do not suppose that old age is abused and ill-spoken of only for its wrinkles and white hair and weakness of body, but this is the worst feature about it, that it makes the soul feeble in its remembrance of things in the other world, and strong in its attachment to things in this world, and bends and presses it, if it retain the form which it had in the body from its experience. But that soul, which does indeed enter the body, but remains only a short time in it, being liberated from it by the higher powers, rears as it were at a damp and soft turning post in the race of life, and hastens on to its destined goal. For just as if anyone put out a fire, and light it again at once, it is soon rekindled, and burns up again quickly, but if it has been out a long time, to light it again will be a far more difficult and irksome task, so the soul that has sojourned only a short time in this dark and mortal life, quickly recovers the light and blaze of its former bright life, whereas for those who have not had the good fortune very early, to use the language of the poet, "to pass the gates of Hades,"[202] nothing remains but a great passion for the things of this life, and a softening of the soul through contact with the body, and a melting away of it as if by the agency of drugs.[203]

§ XI. And the truth of this is rendered more apparent in our hereditary and time-honoured customs and laws. For when infants die no libations are poured out for them, nor are any other rites performed for them, such as are always performed for adults. For they have no share in the earth or in things of the earth, nor do parents haunt their tombs or monuments, or sit by their bodies when they are laid out. For the laws do not allow us to mourn for such, seeing that it is an impious thing to do so in the case of persons who have departed into a better and more divine place and sphere. I know that doubts are entertained about this, but since to doubt is harder for them than to believe, let us do externally as the laws enjoin, and internally let us be more holy and pure and chaste.[204]

[191] Timoxena, as we see later on, § ix.

[192] Adopting Reiske's reading, [Greek: maston keleuousa, proekaleito kathaper].

[193] Euripides' "Phaethon," which exists only in fragments. Clymene was the daughter of Oceanus, and mother of Phaethon.

[194] An allusion to Euripides, "Bacchæ," 317, 318.

[195] Reading with Reiske [Greek: oudeni logô de], or [Greek: alogôs de]. Some such reading seems necessary to comport with the [Greek: ti gar alogôteron] two lines later.

[196] Reading [Greek: pareiches] with Xylander.

[197] A great craving for sympathy would be the modern way of putting it.

[198] See the Fable of Æsop, entitled [Greek: Penthous geras], No. 355. Halme. See also Plutarch's "Consolation to Apollonius," § xix., where the Fable is told at some length.

[199] Reading with Reiske [Greek: ouk an eipein phobêtheiên].

[200] An allusion to Euripides, "Andromache," 930. See Plutarch's "Conjugal Precepts," § xl.

[201] The whole subject is discussed in full by Athenæus, p. 632, F. F. A false quantity we see was a bugbear even before the days of Universities.

[202] Homer, "Iliad," v. 646; xxiii. 71.

[203] This section is dreadfully corrupt. I have adopted, it will be seen, the suggestions of Wyttenbach.

[204] This Consolatory Letter ends rather abruptly. It is probable that there was more of it.

THAT VIRTUE MAY BE TAUGHT.

§ I. As to virtue we deliberate and dispute whether good sense, and justice, and rectitude can be taught: and then we are not surprised that, while the works of orators, and pilots, and musicians, and house-builders, and farmers, are innumerable, good men are only a name and expression, like Centaurs and Giants and Cyclopes, and that it is impossible to find any virtuous action without alloy of base motives, or any character free from vice: but if nature produces spontaneously anything good, it is marred by much that is alien to it, as fruit choked by weeds. Men learn to play on the harp, and to dance, and to read, and to farm, and to ride on horseback: they learn how to put on their shoes and clothes generally: people teach how to pour out wine, how to cook; and all these things cannot be properly performed, without being learned. The art of good living alone, though all those things I have mentioned only exist on its account, is untaught, unmethodical, inartistic, and supposed to come by the light of nature!

§ II. O sirs, by asserting that virtue is not a thing to be taught, why are we making it unreal? For if teaching produces it, the deprivation of teaching prevents it. And yet, as Plato says, a discord and false note on the lyre makes not brother go to war with brother, nor sets friends at variance, nor makes states hostile to one another, so as to do and suffer at one another's hands the most dreadful things:[205] nor can anyone say that there was ever a dissension in any city as to the pronunciation of Telchines: nor in a private house any difference between man and wife as to woof and warp. And yet no one without learning would undertake to ply the loom, or write a book, or play on the lyre, though he would thereby do no great harm, but he fears making himself ridiculous, for as Heraclitus says, "It is better to hide one's ignorance," yet everyone thinks himself competent to manage a house and wife and the state and hold any magisterial office. On one occasion, when a boy was eating rather greedily, Diogenes gave the lad's tutor a blow with his fist, ascribing the fault not to the boy, who had not learnt how to eat properly, but to the tutor who had not taught him. And can one not properly handle a dish or a cup, unless one has learnt from a boy, as Aristophanes bids us, "not to giggle, nor eat too fast, nor cross our legs,"[206] and yet be perfectly fit to manage a family and city, and wife, and live well, and hold office, when one has not learnt how one should behave in the conduct of life? When Aristippus was asked by someone, "Are you everywhere then?" he smiled and said, "If I am everywhere, I lose my passage money."[207] Why should not you also say, "If men are not better for learning, the money paid to tutors is also lost?" For just as nurses mould with their hands the child's body, so tutors, receiving it immediately it is weaned, mould its soul, teaching it by habit the first vestiges of virtue. And the Lacedæmonian, who was asked, what good he did as a tutor, replied, "I make what is good pleasant to boys." Moreover tutors teach boys to walk in the streets with their heads down,[208] to touch salt fish with one finger only, other fish bread and meat with two, to scratch themselves in such a way, and in such a way to put on their cloak.[209]

§ III. What then? He that says that the doctor's skill is wanted in the case of a slight skin-eruption or whitlow, but is not needed in the case of pleurisy, fever, or lunacy, in what respect does he differ from the man that says that schools and teaching and precepts are only for small and boyish duties, while great and important matters are to be left to mere routine and accident? For, as the man is ridiculous who says we ought to learn to row but not to steer, so he who allows all other arts to be learnt, but not virtue, seems to act altogether contrary to the Scythians. For they, as Herodotus tells us,[210] blind their slaves that they may remain with them, but such an one puts the eye of reason into slavish and servile arts, and takes it away from virtue. And the general Iphicrates well answered Callias, the son of Chabrias, who asked him, "What are you? an archer? a targeteer? cavalry, or infantry?" "None of these," said he, "but the commander of them all." Ridiculous therefore is he who says that the use of the bow and other arms and the sling and riding are to be taught, but that strategy and how to command an army comes by the light of nature. Still more ridiculous is he who asserts that good sense alone need not be taught, without which all other arts are useless and profitless, seeing that she is the mistress and orderer and arranger of all of them, and puts each of them to their proper use. For example, what grace would there be in a banquet, though the servants had been well-trained, and had learnt how to dress and cook the meat and pour out the wine,[211] unless there was good order and method among the waiters?[212]

[205] Plato, "Clitophon," p. 407, C.

[206] Aristophanes, "Clouds," 983.

[207] Does Juvenal allude to this, viii. 97?

[208] So as to look modest and be "Ingenui vultus pueri, ingenuique pudoris."

[209] Reading with Salmasius, [Greek: anabalein].

[210] Herodotus, iv. 2. The historian, however, assigns other reasons for blinding them.

[211] A line from "Odyssey," xv. 323.

[212] "Malim [Greek: daitumonas]." Wyttenbach, who remarks generally on this short treatise, "Non integra videtur esse nec continua disputatio, sed disputationis, Plutarcheæ tamen, excerptum compendium."

ON VIRTUE AND VICE.

§ I. Clothes seem to warm a man, not by throwing out heat themselves (for in itself every garment is cold, whence in great heat or in fevers people frequently change and shift them), but the heat which a man throws out from his own body is retained and wrapped in by a dress fitting close to the body, which does not admit of the heat being dissipated when once it has got firm hold. A somewhat similar case is the idea that deceives the mass of mankind, that if they could live in big houses, and get together a quantity of slaves and money, they would have a happy life. But a happy and cheerful life is not from without, on the contrary, a man adds the pleasure and gratification to the things that surround him, his temperament being as it were the source of his feelings.[213]

"But when the fire blazes the house is brighter to look at."[214]

So, too, wealth is pleasanter, and fame and power more splendid, when a man has joy in his heart, seeing that men can bear easily and quietly poverty and exile and old age if their character is a contented and mild one.

§ II. For as perfumes make threadbare coats and rags to smell sweet, while the body of Anchises sent forth a fetid discharge, "distilling from his back on to his linen robe," so every kind of life with virtue is painless and pleasurable, whereas vice if infused into it makes splendour and wealth and magnificence painful, and sickening, and unwelcome to its possessors.

"He is deemed happy in the market-place, But when he gets him home, thrice miserable, His wife rules all, quarrels, and domineers."[215]

And yet there would be no great difficulty in getting rid of a bad wife, if one was a man and not a slave. But a man cannot by writing a bill of divorce to his vice get rid of all trouble at once, and enjoy tranquillity by living apart: for it is ever present in his vitals, and sticks to him night and day, "and burns without a torch, and consigns him to gloomy old age,"[216] being a disagreeable fellow-traveller owing to its arrogance, and a costly companion at table owing to its daintiness, and an unpleasant bed-fellow, disturbing and marring sleep by anxiety and care and envy. For during such a one's sleep the body indeed gets rest, but the mind has terrors, and dreams, and perturbations, owing to superstition,

"For when my trouble catches me asleep, I am undone by the most fearful dreams,"

as one says. For thus envy, and fear, and anger, and lust affect one. During the daytime, indeed, vice looks abroad and imitates the behaviour of others, is shy and conceals its evil desires, and does not altogether give way to its propensities, but often even resists and fights stoutly against them; but in sleep it escapes the observation of people and the law, and, being as far as possible removed from fear or modesty, gives every passion play, and excites its depravity and licentiousness, for, to borrow Plato's expression,[217] "it attempts incest with its mother, and procures for itself unlawful meats, and abstains from no action whatever," and enjoys lawlessness as far as is practicable in visions and phantasies, that end in no complete pleasure or satisfaction, but can only stir up and inflame the passions and morbid emotions.

§ III. Where then is the pleasure of vice, if there is nowhere in it freedom from anxiety and pain, or independence, or tranquillity, or rest?[218] A healthy and sound constitution does indeed augment the pleasures of the body, but for the soul there can be no lasting joy or gratification, unless cheerfulness and fearlessness and courage supply a calm serenity free from storms; for otherwise, even if hope or delight smile on the soul, it is soon confused and disturbed by care lifting up its head again, so that it is but the calm of a sunken rock.

§ IV. Pile up gold, heap up silver, build covered walks, fill your house with slaves and the town with debtors, unless you lay to rest the passions of the soul, and put a curb on your insatiable desires, and rid yourself of fear and anxiety, you are but pouring out wine for a man in a fever, and giving honey to a man who is bilious, and laying out a sumptuous banquet for people who are suffering from dysentery, and can neither retain their food nor get any benefit from it, but are made even worse by it. Have you never observed how sick persons turn against and spit out and refuse the daintiest and most costly viands, though people offer them and almost force them down their throats, but on another occasion, when their condition is different, their respiration good, their blood in a healthy state, and their natural warmth restored, they get up, and enjoy and make a good meal of simple bread and cheese and cress? Such, also, is the effect of reason on the mind. You will be contented, if you have learned what is good and honourable. You will live daintily and be a king in poverty, and enjoy a quiet and private life as much as the public life of general or statesman. By the aid of philosophy you will live not unpleasantly, for you will learn to extract pleasure from all places and things: wealth will make you happy, because it will enable you to benefit many; and poverty, as you will not then have many anxieties; and glory, for it will make you honoured; and obscurity, for you will then be safe from envy.

[213] Happiness comes from within, not from without. The true seat of happiness is the mind. Compare Milton, "Paradise Lost," Book i. 254, 255:--

"The mind is its own place, and in itself Can make a Heaven of Hell, a Hell of Heaven."

[214] Homeric Epigrammata, xiii. 5.

[215] Wyttenbach thinks these lines are by Menander. Plutarch quotes them again "On Contentedness of Mind," § xi.

[216] Hesiod, "Works and Days," 705.

[217] Plato, "Republic," ix. p. 571, D. Quoted again, "How one may be aware of one's Progress in Virtue," § xii.

[218] And so Dr. Young truly says,--

"A man of pleasure is a man of pains."

Night Thoughts.

ON MORAL VIRTUE.

§ I. I propose to discuss what is called and appears to be moral virtue (which differs mainly from contemplative virtue in that it has emotion for its matter, and reason for its form), what its nature is, and how it subsists, and whether that part of the soul which takes it in is furnished with reason of its own, or participates in something foreign, and if the latter, whether as things that are mixed with something better than themselves, or rather as that which is subject to superintendence and command, and may be said to share in the power of that which commands. For I think it is clear that virtue can exist and continue altogether free from matter and mixture. My best course will be to run briefly over the views of others, not so much to display my research as because, when their ideas have been set forth, mine will become more clear and be on a firmer basis.

§ II. Menedemus of Eretria took away the number and differences of virtues, on the ground that virtue was one though it had many names; for that just as mortal is synonymous with man, so temperance and bravery and justice were the same thing. And Aristo of Chios also made virtue one in substance, and called it soundness of mind: its diversities and varieties only existing in certain relations, as if one called our sight when it took in white objects white-sight, and when it took in black objects black-sight, and so on. For virtue, when it considers what it ought to do and what it ought not to do, is called prudence; and when it curbs passion, and sets a fit and proper limit to pleasure, it is called self-control; and when it is associated with our dealings and covenants with one another, it is called justice; just as a knife is one article, though at different times it cuts different things in half: and so, too, fire acts on different matter though it has but one property. And Zeno of Cittium seems to incline somewhat to the same view, as he defines prudence in distribution as justice, in choice as self-control, in endurance as fortitude: and those who defend these views maintain that by the term prudence Zeno means knowledge. But Chrysippus, thinking each particular virtue should be arranged under its particular quality, unwittingly stirred up, to use Plato's language, "a whole swarm of virtues,"[219] unusual and unknown. For as from brave we get bravery, and from mild mildness, and from just justice, so from acceptable he got acceptableness, and from good goodness, and from great greatness, and from the honourable honourableness, and he made virtues of many other such clevernesses, affabilities, and versatilities, and filled philosophy, which did not at all require it, with many strange names.

§ III. Now all these agree in supposing virtue to be a disposition and faculty of the governing part of the soul set in motion by reason, or rather to be reason itself conformable and firm and immutable. They think further that the emotional and unreasoning part of the soul is not by any natural difference distinct from the reasoning part, but that that same part of the soul, which they call intellect and the leading principle of action, being altogether diverted and changed by the passions, and by the alterations which habit or disposition have brought about, becomes either vice or virtue, without having in itself any unreasoning element, but that it is called unreasoning when, by the strong and overpowering force of appetite, it launches out into excesses contrary to the direction of reason. For passion, according to them, is only vicious and intemperate reason, getting its strength and power from bad and faulty judgement. But all of those philosophers seem to have been ignorant that we are all in reality two-fold and composite, though they did not recognize it, and only saw the more evident mixture of soul and body. And yet that there is in the soul itself something composite and two-fold and dissimilar (the unreasoning part of it, as if another body, being by necessity and nature mixed up with and united to reason), seems not to have escaped the notice even of Pythagoras, as we infer from his zeal for music, which he introduced to calm and soothe the soul, as knowing that it was not altogether amenable to precept and instruction, or redeemable from vice only by reason, but that it needed some other persuasion and moulding and softening influence to co-operate with reason, unless it were to be altogether intractable and refractory to philosophy. And Plato saw very plainly and confidently and decidedly that the soul of this universe is not simple or uncomposite or uniform, but is made up of forces that work uniformly and differently, in the one case it is ever marshalled in the same order and moves about in one fixed orbit, in the other case it is divided into motions and orbits contrary to each other and changing about, and thus generates differences in things. So, too, the soul of man, being a part or portion of the soul of the universe, and compounded upon similar principles and proportions, is not simple or entirely uniform, but has one part intelligent and reasoning, which is intended by nature to rule and dominate in man, and another part unreasoning, and subject to passion and caprice, and disorderly, and in need of direction. And this last again is divided into two parts, one of which, being most closely connected with the body, is called desire, and the other, sometimes taking part with the body, sometimes with reason, lending its influence against the body, is called anger. And the difference between reason and sense on the one hand, and anger and desire on the other, is shown by their antipathy to one another, so that they are often at variance with one another as to what is best.[220] These were at first[221] the views of Aristotle, as is clear from his writings, though afterwards he joined anger to desire, as if anger were nothing but a desire and passion for revenge. However, he always considered the emotional and unreasoning part of the soul as distinct from the reasoning, not that it is altogether unreasoning as the perceptive, or nutritive, or vegetative portions of the soul, for these are always deaf and disobedient to reason, and in a certain sense are off-shoots from the flesh, and altogether attached to the body; but the emotional, though it is destitute of any reason of its own, yet is naturally inclined to listen to reason and sense, and turn and submit and mould itself accordingly, unless it be entirely corrupted by brute pleasure and a life of indulgence.

§ IV. As for those who wonder that what is unreasoning should obey reason, they do not seem to me to recognize the power of reason, how great it is, and how far-reaching its dominion is--a power not gained by harsh and repelling methods, but by attractive ones, as mild persuasion which always accomplishes more than compulsion or violence. For even the spirit and nerves and bones, and other parts of the body, though devoid of reason, yet at any instigation of reason, when she shakes as it were the reins, are all on the alert and compliant and obedient, the feet to run, and the hands to throw or lift, at her bidding. Right excellently has the poet set forth in the following lines the sympathy and accordance between the unreasoning and reason:--

"Thus were her beauteous cheeks diffused with tears, Weeping her husband really present then. But though Odysseus pitied her in heart, His eyes like horn or steel impassive stood Within their lids, and craft his tears repressed."[222]

So completely under the control of judgement did he keep his spirit and blood and tears. The same is shown by the subsidence of our passions, which are laid to rest in the presence of handsome women or boys, whom reason and the law forbid us to touch; a case which most frequently happens to lovers, when they hear that they have unwittingly fallen in love with a sister or daughter. For at once passion is laid at the voice of reason, and the body exhibits its members as subservient to decorum. And frequently in the case of dainty food, people very much attracted by it, if they find out at the time or learn afterwards that they have eaten what is unclean or unlawful, not only suffer distress and grief in their imagination, but even their very body is upset by the notion, and violent retchings and vomitings follow.[223] I fear I should seem to be introducing merely novel and enticing arguments, if I were to enumerate stringed instruments and lyres, and harps and flutes, and other harmonious musical instruments, which, although inanimate, yet speak to man's passions, rejoicing with him, and mourning with him, and chiming in with him, and rioting with him,--in a word, falling in with the vein and emotions and characters of those that play on them. And they say that Zeno on one occasion, going into the theatre when Amoebeus[224] was playing on the harp, said to the pupils, "Let us go and learn what music can be produced by guts and nerves and wood and bones, when they preserve proportion and time and order." But passing these things over, I would gladly learn from them, if, when they see dogs and horses and birds domesticated, and by habit and training uttering sounds that can be understood, and making obedient movements and gestures, and acting quietly and usefully to us, and when they notice that Achilles in Homer cheers on horses as well as men to the fight,[225] they still wonder and doubt, whether the passionate and emotional and painful and pleasurable elements in us are by nature obedient to the voice of reason, and influenced and affected by it, seeing that those elements are not apart from us or detached from us, or formed from outside, or hammered into us by force, but are innate in us, and ever associate with us, and are nourished within us, and abound in us through habit. Accordingly moral character is well called by the Greeks [Greek: êthos], for it is, to speak generally, a quality of the unreasoning element in man, and is called [Greek: êthos] because the unreasoning element moulded by reason receives this quality and difference by habit, which is called [Greek: ethos].[226] Not that reason wishes to expel passion altogether (that is neither possible, nor advisable), but only to keep it within bounds and order, and to engender the moral virtues, which are not apathetic, but hold the due proportion and mean in regard to passion. And this she does by reducing the power of passion to a good habit. For there are said to be three things existing in the soul, power, passion, and habit. Power is the principle or matter of passion, as power to be angry, ashamed, or confident: and passion is the actual setting in motion of that power, being itself anger, confidence, or shame; and habit is the strong formation of power in the unreasoning element engendered by use, being vice if the passions are badly tutored by reason, virtue if they are well tutored.

§ V. But since they do not regard every virtue as a mean, nor call it moral, we must discuss this difference by approaching the matter more from first principles. Some things in the world exist absolutely, as the earth, the sky, the stars, and the sea; others have relation to us, as good and evil, as what is desirable or to be avoided, as pleasant and painful: and since reason has an eye to both of these classes, when it considers the former it is scientific and contemplative, when it considers the latter it is deliberative and practical. And prudence is the virtue in the latter case, as knowledge in the former. And there is this difference between prudence and knowledge, prudence consists in applying the contemplative to the practical and emotional so as to make reason paramount. On which account it often needs the help of fortune; whereas knowledge needs neither the help of fortune nor deliberation to gain its ends: for it considers only things which are always the same. And as the geometrician does not deliberate about the triangle, as to whether its interior angles are together equal to two right angles, for he knows it as a fact--and deliberation only takes place in the case of things which differ at different times, not in the case of things which are certain and unchangeable--so the contemplative mind having its scope in first principles, and things that are fixed, and that ever have one nature which does not admit of change, has no need for deliberation. But prudence, which has to enter into matters full of obscurity and confusion, frequently has to take its chance, and to deliberate about things which are uncertain, and, in carrying the deliberation into practice, has to co-operate with the unreasoning element, which comes to its help, and is involved in its decisions, for they need an impetus. Now this impetus is given to passion by the moral character, an impetus requiring reason to regulate it, that it may render moderate and not excessive help, and at the seasonable time. For the emotional and unreasoning elements are subject to motions sometimes too quick and vehement, at other times too remiss and slow. And so everything we do may be a success from one point of view, but a failure from many points of view; as to hit the mark one thing only is requisite, but one may miss it in various ways, as one may shoot beyond or too short. This then is the function of practical reason following nature, to prevent our passions going either too far or too short. For where from weakness and want of strength, or from fear and hesitation, the impetus gives in and abandons what is good, there reason is by to stir it up and rekindle it; and where on the other hand it goes ahead too fast and in disorder, there it represses and checks its zeal. And thus setting bounds to the emotional motions, it engenders in the unreasoning part of the soul moral virtues, which are the mean between excess and deficiency. Not that we can say that all virtue exists in the mean, but knowledge and prudence being in no need of the unreasoning element, and being situated in the pure and unemotional part of the soul, is a complete perfection and power of reason, whereby we get the most divine and happy fruit of understanding. But that virtue which is necessary because of the body, and needs the help of the passions as an instrument towards the practical, not destroying or doing away with but ordering and regulating the unreasoning part of the soul, is perfection as regards its power and quality, but in quantity it is a mean correcting both excess and deficiency.

§ VI. But since the word mean has a variety of meanings--for there is one kind of mean compounded of two simple extremes, as grey is the mean between white and black; and there is another kind of mean, where that which contains and is contained is the mean between the containing and contained, as eight is the mean between twelve and four; and there is a third kind of mean which has part in neither extreme, as the indifferent is the mean between good and bad,--virtue cannot be a mean in any of these ways. For neither is it a mixture of vices, nor containing that which is defective is it contained by that which is excessive, nor is it again altogether free from, emotional storms of passion, wherein are excess and deficiency. But it is, and is commonly so called, a mean like that in music and harmony. For as in music there is a middle note between the highest and lowest in the scale, which being perfectly in tune avoids the sharpness of the one and the flatness of the other; so virtue, being a motion and power in the unreasoning part of the soul, takes away the remissness and strain, and generally speaking the excess and defect of the appetite, by reducing each of the passions to a state of mean and rectitude. For example, they tell us that bravery is the mean between cowardice and foolhardiness, whereof the former is a defect, the latter an excess of anger: and that liberality is the mean between stinginess and prodigality: and that meekness is the mean between insensibility and savageness: and so of temperance and justice, that the latter, being concerned with contracts, is to assign neither too much nor too little to litigants, and that the former ever reduces the passions to the proper mean between apathy (or insensibility) and gross intemperance. This last illustration serves excellently to show us the radical difference between the unreasoning and reasoning parts of the soul, and to prove to us that passion and reason are wide as the poles asunder. For the difference would not be discernible between temperance and continence, nor between intemperance and incontinence, in pleasure and desires, if the appetite and judgement were in the same portion of the soul. Now temperance is a state, wherein reason holds the reins, and manages the passions as a quiet and well-broken-in animal, finding them obedient and submissive to the reins and masters over their desires.[227] Continence on the other hand is not driven by reason without some trouble, not being docile but jibbing and kicking, like an animal compelled by bit and bridle and whip and backing, being in itself full of struggles and commotion. Plato explains this by his simile of the chariot-horses of the soul, the worse one of which ever kicking against the other and disturbing the charioteer, he is obliged ever to hold them in with all his might, and to tighten the reins, lest, to borrow the language of Simonides, "he should drop from his hands the purple reins." And so they do not consider continence to be an absolute virtue, but something less than a virtue; for no mean arises from the concord of the worse with the better, nor is the excess of the passion curtailed, nor does the appetite obey or act in unison with reason, but it both gives and suffers trouble, and is constrained by force, and is as it were an enemy in a town given up to faction.

"The town is full of incense, and at once Resounds with triumph-songs and bitter wailing."[228]

Such is the state of soul of the continent person owing to his conflicting condition. On the same grounds they consider incontinence to be something less than vice, but intemperance to be a complete vice. For it, having both its appetite and reason depraved, is by the one carried away to desire disgraceful things,[229] by the other, through bad judgement consenting to desire, loses even the perception of wrongdoing. But incontinence keeps its judgement sound through reason, but is carried away against its judgement by passion which is too strong for reason, whence it differs from intemperance. For in the one case reason is mastered by passion, in the other it does not even make a fight against it, in the one case it opposes its desires even when it follows them, in the other it is their advocate and even leader, in the one case it gladly participates in what is wrong, in the other sorrowfully, in the one case it willingly rushes into what is disgraceful, in the other it abandons the honourable unwillingly. And as there is a difference in their deeds, so no less manifest is the difference in their language. For these are the expressions of the intemperate. "What grace or pleasure in life is there without golden Aphrodite? May I die, when I care no longer for these things!" And another says, "To eat, to drink, to enjoy the gifts of Aphrodite is everything, for all other things I look upon as supplementary," as if from the bottom of his soul he gave himself up to pleasures, and was completely subverted by them. And not less so he who said, "Let me be ruined, it is best for me," had his judgement diseased through his passion. But the sayings of incontinence are quite different, as

"My nature forces me against my judgement,"[230]

and

"Alas! it is poor mortals' plague and bane, To know the good, yet not the good pursue."[231]

And again--

"My anger draws me on, has no control, 'Tis but a sandy hook against a tempest."

Here he compares not badly to a sandy hook, a sorry kind of anchor, the soul that is unsettled and has no steady reason, but surrenders judgment through flabbiness and feebleness. And not unlike this image are the lines,

"As some ship moored and fastened to the shore, If the wind blows, the cables cannot hold it."

By cables he means the judgement which resists what is disgraceful, though sometimes it gives way under a tremendous storm of passion. For indeed it is with full sail that the intemperate man is borne on to pleasure by his desires, and surrenders himself to them, and even plays the part of pilot to the vessel; whereas the incontinent man is dragged sidelong into the disgraceful, and is its victim, as it were, while he desires eagerly to resist and overcome his passion, as Timon bantered Anaxarchus: "The recklessness and frantic energy of Anaxarchus to rush anywhere seemed like a dog's courage, but he being aware of it was miserable, so people said, but his voluptuous nature ever plunged him into excesses again, nature which even most sophists are afraid of." For neither is the wise man continent but temperate, nor the fool incontinent but intemperate; for the one delights in what is good, and the other is not vexed at what is bad. Incontinence, therefore, is a mark of a sophistical soul, endued with reason which cannot abide by what it knows to be right.

§ VII. Such, then, are the differences between incontinence and intemperance, and continence and temperance have their counterpart and analogous differences; for remorse and trouble and annoyance are companions of continence, whereas in the soul of the temperate person there is everywhere such equability and calm and soundness, by which the unreasoning is adjusted and harmonized to reason, being adorned with obedience and wonderful mildness, that looking at it you would say with the poet, "At once the wind was laid, and a wondrous calm ensued, for the god allayed the fury of the waves,"[232] reason having extinguished the vehement and furious and frantic motions of the desires, and making those which nature necessarily requires sympathetic and obedient and friendly and co-operative in carrying purposes out in action, so that they do not outrun or come short of reason, or behave disorderly and disobediently, but that every appetite is tractable, "as sucking foal runs by the side of its dam."[233] And this confirms the saying of Xenocrates about true philosophers, that they alone do willingly what all others do unwillingly at the compulsion of the law, as dogs are turned away from their pleasures by a blow, or cats by a noise, looking at nothing but their danger. It is clear then that there is in the soul a perception of such a generic and specific difference in relation to the desires, as of something fighting against and opposing them. But some say that there is no radical distinction difference or variance between reason and passion, but that there is a shifting of one and the same reason from one to the other, which escapes our notice owing to the sharpness and quickness of the change, so that we do not see at a glance that desire and repentance, anger and fear, giving way to what is disgraceful through passion, and recovery from the same, are the same natural property of the soul. For desire and fear and anger and the like they consider only depraved opinions and judgements, not in one portion of the soul only but in all its leading principles, inclinations and yieldings, and assents and impulses, and generally speaking in its energies soon changed, like the sallies of children, whose fury and excessive violence is unstable by reason of their weakness. But these views are, in the first place, contrary to evidence and observation; for no one observes in himself a change from passion to judgement, and from judgement back to passion; nor does anyone cease from loving when he reflects that it would be well to break the affair off and strive with all his might against it; nor again, does he put on one side reflection and judgement, when he gives way and is overcome by desire. Moreover, when he resists passion by reason, he does not escape passion altogether; nor again, when he is mastered by passion does he fail to discern his fault through reason: so that neither by passion does he abolish reason, nor does he by reason get rid of passion, but is tossed about to and fro alternately between passion and reason. And those who suppose that the leading principle in the soul is at one time desire, and at another time reason in opposition to desire, are not unlike people who would make the hunter and the animal he hunts one and the same person, but alternately changing from hunter to animal, from animal to hunter. As their eyesight is plainly deficient, so these are faulty in regard to their perceptions, seeing that they must perceive in themselves not a change of one and the same thing, but a difference and struggle between two opposing elements. "What then," say they, "does not the deliberative element in a man often hold different views, and is it not swayed to different opinions as to expediency, and yet it is one and the same thing?" Certainly, I reply; but the case is not similar. For the rational part of the soul does not fight against itself, but though it has only one faculty, it makes use of different reasonings; or rather the reasoning is one, but employs itself in different subjects as on different matter. And so there is neither pain in reasonings without passion, nor are men compelled, as it were, to choose something contrary to their judgement, unless indeed some passion, as in a balance, secretly predominates in the scale. For this often happens, reason not opposing reason, but ambition, or contention, or favour, or jealousy, or fear opposing reason, that we do but think there is a difference between two reasons, as in the line, "They were ashamed to refuse, and feared to accept,"[234] or, "To die in battle is dreadful but glorious; but not to die, though cowardly, is more pleasant." Moreover, in judgements about contracts passions come in and cause the greatest delay; and in the councils of kings those who speak to ingratiate themselves do not favour either of the two cases, but give themselves up to passion without regard to what is expedient; and so those that rule in aristocracies do not allow orators to be pathetic in their pleadings. For reasoning without passion has a direct tendency to justice, while if passion is infused, a contest and difference is excited between pleasure and pain on the one hand, and judgement and justice on the other. For otherwise how is it that in philosophical speculations people are with little pain frequently induced by others to change their opinions, and even Aristotle himself and Democritus and Chrysippus have rejected without trouble or pain, and even with pleasure, some of the opinions which they formerly advocated? For no passion stands in the way in the theoretic and scientific part of the soul, and the unreasoning element is quiet and gives no trouble therein. And so reason gladly inclines to the truth, when it is evident, and abandons error; for in it, and not in passion, lies a willingness to listen to conviction and to change one's opinions on conviction. But the deliberations and judgements and arbitrations of most people as to matters of fact being mixed up with passion, give reason no easy or pleasant access, as she is held fast and incommoded by the unreasonable, which assails her through pleasure, or fear, or pain, or desire. And the decision in these cases lies with sense which has dealings with both passion and reason, for if one gets the better of the other the other is not destroyed, but only dragged along by force in spite of its resistance. For he who is dissatisfied with himself for falling in love calls in reason to his aid to overcome his passion, for both reason and passion are in his soul, and he perceives they are contrary one to the other, and violently represses the inflammatory one of the two. On the other hand, in deliberations and speculations without passion (such as the contemplative part of the soul is most conversant with), if they are evenly balanced no decision takes place, but the matter is left in doubt, which is a sort of stationary position of the mind in conflicting arguments. But should there be any inclination to one of the two sides, the most powerful opinion carries the day, yet without giving pain or creating hostility. And, generally speaking, when reason seems opposed to reason, there is no perception of two distinct things, but only of one under different phases, whereas when the unreasoning has a controversy with reason, since there can be no victory or defeat without pain, forthwith they tear the soul in two,[235] and make the difference between them apparent.

§ VIII. And not only from their contest, but quite as much from their agreement, can we see that the source of the passions is something quite distinct from that of reason. For since[236] one may love either a good and excellent child or a bad and vicious one, and be unreasonably angry with one's children or parents, yet in behalf of them show a just anger against enemies or tyrants; as in the one case there is the perception of a difference and struggle between passion and reason, so in the other there is a perception of persuasion and agreement inclining, as it were, the scale, and giving their help. Moreover a good man marrying a wife according to the laws is minded to associate and live with her justly and soberly, but as time goes on, his intercourse with her having engendered a strong passion for her, he perceives that his love and affection are increased by reason. Just so, again, young fellows falling in with kindly teachers at first submit themselves to them out of necessity and emulation for learning, but end by loving them, and instead of being their pupils and scholars become and get the title of their lovers. The same is the case in cities in respect to good magistrates, and neighbours, and connections by marriage; for beginning at first to associate with one another from necessity and propriety, they afterwards go on to love almost insensibly, reason drawing over and persuading the emotional element. And he who said--

"There are two kinds of shame, the one not bad, The other a sad burden to a family,"[237]

is it not clear that he felt this emotion in himself often contrary to reason and detrimental by hesitation and delay to opportunities and actions?

§ IX. In a certain sense yielding to the force of these arguments, they call shame modesty, pleasure joy, and timidity caution; nor would anyone blame them for this euphemism, if they only gave those specious names to the emotions that are consistent with reason, while they gave other kinds of names to those emotions that resist and do violence to reason. But whenever, though convicted by their tears and tremblings and changes of colour, they avoid the terms pain and fear, and speak of bitings and states of excitement, and gloss over the passions by calling them inclinations, they seem to contrive evasions and flights from facts by names sophistical, and not philosophical. And yet again they seem to use words rightly when they call those joys and wishes and cautions not apathies but good conditions of the mind. For it is a happy disposition of the soul when reason does not annihilate passion, but orders and arranges it in the case of temperate persons. But what is the condition of worthless and incontinent persons, who, when they judge they ought to love their father and mother better than some boy or girl they are enamoured of, yet cannot, and yet at once love their mistress or flatterer, when they judge they ought to hate them? For if passion and judgement were the same thing, love and hate would immediately follow the judging it right to love and hate, whereas the contrary happens, passion following some judgements, but declining to follow others. Wherefore they acknowledge, the facts compelling them to do so, that every judgement is not passion, but only that judgement that is provocative of violent and excessive impulse: admitting that judgement and passion in us are something different, as what moves is different from what is moved. Even Chrysippus himself, by his defining in many places endurance and continence to be habits that follow the lead of reason, proves that he is compelled by the facts to admit, that that element in us which follows absolutely is something different from that which follows when persuaded, but resists when not persuaded.

§ X. Now as to those who make all sins and offences equal, it is not now the occasion to discuss if in other respects they deviate from truth: but as regards the passions[238] they seem to go clean contrary to reason and evidence. For according to them every passion is a sin, and everyone who grieves, or fears, or desires, commits sin. But in good truth it is evident that there are great differences between passions, according as one is more or less affected by them. For who would say that the craven fear of Dolon[239] was not something very different from the fear of Ajax, "who retreated with his face to the enemy and at a foot's pace, drawing back slowly knee after knee"?[240] Or who would say that the grief of Plato at the death of Socrates was identical with the grief of Alexander at the death of Clitus, when he attempted to lay violent hands on himself? For grief is beyond measure intensified by falling out against expectation: and the calamity that comes unlooked for is more painful than that we may reasonably fear: as if when expecting to see one's friend basking in prosperity and admiration, one should hear that he had been put to the torture, as Parmenio heard about Philotas. And who would say that the anger of Magas against Philemon was equal to that of Nicocreon against Anaxarchus? Both Magas and Nicocreon had been insulted, but whereas Nicocreon brayed Anaxarchus to death with iron pestles and made mincemeat of him, Magas contented himself with bidding the executioner lay his naked sword on Philemon's neck, and then let him go.[241] And so Plato called anger the nerves of the mind, since it can be both intensified by bitterness, and slackened by mildness. To evade these and similar arguments, they deny that intensity and excess of passion are according to judgement, wherein is the propensity to fault, but maintain that they are bites and contractions and diffusings capable of increase or diminution through the unreasoning element. And yet it is evident that there are differences as regards judgements; for some judge poverty to be no evil, while others judge it to be a great evil, and others again the very greatest evil, insomuch that they even throw themselves headlong down rocks and into the sea on account of it. Again as to death, some think it an evil only in depriving us of good things, whereas others think it so in regard to eternal punishments and awful torments in the world below. Health again is valued by some as natural and advantageous, while to others it seems the greatest blessing of life, in comparison with which they reckon little either of wealth or children or "royal power that makes one equal to the gods," and at last come to think even virtue useless and unprofitable, if health be absent. Thus it is clear that even with regard to judgements themselves some err more, some less. But I shall bring no further proof of this now, but this one may assume therefrom, that they themselves concede that the unreasoning element is something different from judgement, in that they allow that by it passion becomes greater and more violent, and while they quarrel about the name and word they give up the thing itself to those who maintain that the emotional and unreasoning part of the soul is distinct from the reasoning and judging element. And in his treatise on Anomaly,[242] Chrysippus, after telling us that anger is blind, and frequently does not let one see what is obvious, frequently also obscures what we do get a sight of, goes on to say, "The encroachment of the passions blots out reason, and makes things look different to what they should look, violently forcing people on unreasonable acts." And he quotes as witness Menander, who says, "Alas! poor me, wherever were my brains in my body at the time when I chose that line of conduct, and not this?" And Chrysippus proceeds, "Though every living creature endowed with reason is naturally inclined to use reason and to be governed by it on every occasion, yet often do we reject it, being borne away by a more violent impulse;" thus admitting what results from the difference between passion and reason. For otherwise it is ridiculous, as Plato says, to argue that a man is sometimes better than himself, sometimes worse, sometimes master of himself, sometimes not master of himself.

§ XI. For how is it possible that the same person can be both better and worse than himself, both master of himself and not master, unless everyone is in some way twofold, having in himself both a better and worse self? For so he that makes the baser element subject to the better has self-control and is a superior man, whereas he who allows the nobler element of the soul to follow and be subservient to the incorrigible and unreasoning element, is inferior to what he might be, and is called incontinent, and is in an unnatural condition. For by nature it appertains to reason, which is divine, to rule and govern the unreasoning element, which has its origin from the body, which it also naturally resembles and participates in its passions, being placed in it and mixed up with it, as is proved by the impulses to bodily delights, which are always fierce or languid according to the changes of the body. And so it is that young men are keen and vehement in their desires, being red hot and raging from their fulness of blood and animal heat, whereas with old men the liver, which is the seat of desire, is dried up and weak and feeble, and reason has more power with them than passion which decays with the body. This principle also no doubt characterizes the nature of animals as regards the sexual appetite. For it is not of course from any fitness or unfitness of opinions, that some animals are so bold and resolute in the presence of danger, while others are helpless and full of fear and trembling; but this difference of emotion is produced by the workings of the blood and spirit and body, the emotional part growing out of the flesh, as from a root, and carrying along with it its quality and temperament. And that the body of man sympathizes with and is affected by the emotional impulses is proved by pallors, and blushings, and tremblings, and palpitations of the heart, as on the other hand by an all-pervading joy in the hope and expectation of pleasures. But whenever the mind is by itself and unmoved by passion, the body is in repose and at rest, having no participation or share in the working of the intellect, unless it involve the emotional, or the unreasoning element call it in. So that it is clear that there are two distinct parts of the soul differing from one another in their faculties.

§ XII. And generally speaking of all existing things, as they themselves admit and is clear, some are governed by nature, some by habit, some by an unreasoning soul, some by a soul that has reason and intelligence. Man too participates in all this, and is subject to all those differences here mentioned, for he is affected by habit, and nourished by nature, and uses reason and intelligence. He has also a share of the unreasoning element, and has the principle of passion innate in him, not as a mere episode in his life but as a necessity, which ought not therefore to be entirely rooted out, but requires care and attention. For the function of reason is no Thracian or Lycurgean one to root up and destroy all the good elements in passion indiscriminately with the bad, but, as some genial and mild god, to prune what is wild, and to correct disproportion, and after that to train and cultivate the useful part. For as those who are afraid to get drunk do not pour on the ground their wine, *but mix it with water*, so those who are afraid of the disturbing element in passion do not eradicate passion altogether but temper it. Similarly with oxen and horses people try to restrain their mad bounds and restiveness, not their movements and powers of work, and so reason makes use of the passions when they have become tame and docile, not by cutting out the sinews or altogether mutilating the serviceable part of the soul. For as Pindar says, "The horse to the chariot, and the ox to the plough, while he that meditates destruction for the boar must find a staunch hound."[243] But much more useful than these are the whole tribe of passions when they wait on reason and run parallel to virtue. Thus moderate anger is useful to courage, and hatred of evil to uprightness, and righteous indignation against those who are fortunate beyond their deserts, when they are inflamed in their souls with folly and insolence and need a check. And no one if they wished could pluck away or sever[244] natural affection from friendship, or pity from philanthropy, or sympathy both in joy and grief from genuine goodwill. And if those err who wish to banish love because of erotic madness, neither are they right who blame all desire because of love of money, but they act like people who refuse to run because they might stumble, or to throw because they might throw wide of the mark, or object to sing altogether because they might make a false note. For as in sounds music does not create melody by the banishment of sharps and flats, and as in bodies the art of the physician procures health not by the doing away of cold and heat but by their being blended in due proportions and quantities, so is victory won in the soul by the powers and motions of the passions being reduced by reason to moderation and due proportion. For excessive grief or fear or joy in the soul (I speak not of mere joy grief or fear), resembles a body swollen or inflamed. And Homer when he says excellently,

"The brave man's colour never changes, nor Is he much frightened,"[245]

does not take away all fear but only excessive fear, that bravery may not become recklessness, nor confidence foolhardiness. So also in regard to pleasure we must do away with excessive desire, and in regard to vengeance with excessive hatred of evil. For so in the former case one will not be apathetic but temperate, and in the latter one will not be savage or cruel but just. But if the passions were entirely removed, supposing that to be possible, reason would become in many duller and blunter, like the pilot in the absence of a storm. And no doubt it is from having noticed this that legislators try to excite in states ambition and emulation among their townsmen, and stir up and increase their courage and pugnacity against enemies by the sound of trumpets and flutes. For it is not only in poems, as Plato says, that he that is inspired by the Muses, and as it were possessed by them, will laugh to shame the plodding artist, but also in fighting battles passion and enthusiasm will be irresistible and invincible, such as Homer makes the gods inspire men with, as in the line,

"Thus speaking he infused great might in Hector, The shepherd of the people."[246]

and,

"He is not mad like this without the god,"[247]

as if the god had added passion to reason as an incitement and spur. And you may see those very persons, whose opinions I am combating, frequently urging on the young by praises, and frequently checking them by rebukes, though pleasure follows the one, pain the other. For rebukes and censure produce repentance and shame, the one bringing grief, the other fear, and these they mostly make use of for purposes of correction. And so Diogenes, when Plato was being praised, said, "What has he to vaunt of, who has been a philosopher so long, and yet never gave pain to anyone?" For one could not say, to use the words of Xenocrates, that the mathematics are such handles to philosophy as are the emotions of young men, such as shame, desire, repentance, pleasure, pain, ambition, whereon reason and the law laying a suitable grip succeed in putting the young man on the right road. So that it was no bad remark of the Lacedæmonian tutor, that he would make the boy entrusted to his charge pleased with what was good and displeased with what was bad,[248] for a higher or nobler aim cannot be proposed in the education fit for a freeborn lad.

[219] See "Meno," p. 72, A.

[220] Omitting [Greek: hetera], which Reiske justly suspects.

[221] Reading [Greek: prôton] with Wyttenbach.

[222] Homer, "Odyssey," xix. 208-212.

[223] As in the story in "Gil Blas" of the person who, after eating a ragout of rabbit, was told it was a ragout of cat.--Book X. chapter xii.

[224] As to Amoebeus, see Athenæus, p. 623. D.

[225] "Iliad," xvi. 167.

[226] Generally speaking [Greek: ethos] is the habit, [Greek: êthos] the moral character generated by habit. The former is Aristotle's [Greek: energeia], the latter his [Greek: hexis].

[227] I have adopted, it will be seen, the suggestion of Wyttenbach, "[Greek: tô logismô] mutandum videtur in [Greek: ton chalinon]."

[228] Sophocles, "Oedipus Tyrannus," 4, 5. Quoted by our author again "On Abundance of Friends," § vi.

[229] Reading with "Reiske," [Greek: exagetai pros to epithymein ta aischra].

[230] In the "Chrysippus" of Euripides, Fragm.

[231] Compare Romans viii. 19.

[232] "Odyssey," xii. 168, 169.

[233] This line is from Simonides, and is quoted again in "How one may be aware of one's Progress in Virtue," § xiv.

[234] "Iliad," vii. 93.

[235] Reading with Reiske, [Greek: eis duo].

[236] Reading [Greek: etei] with Reiske and Wyttenbach.

[237] Euripides, "Hippolytus" 385, 386.

[238] Reading with Reiske [Greek: pathesi] for [Greek: pleiosi].

[239] See "Iliad," x. 374, sq.

[240] "Iliad," xi. 547.

[241] "De Anaxarchi supplicio nota res. v. Menage ad Diog. Läert. 9, 59. De Magae, reguli Cyrenarum, adversus Philemonem lenitate v. De Cohibenda Ira, § ix."--*Reiske*.

[242] "Celebres fuere quondam Chrysippi sex libri [Greek: peri tês kata tas lézeis anômalias], in quibus auctore Varrone, *propositum habuit ostendere, similes res dissimilibus verbis et similibus dissimiles esse notatas vocabulis.* v. Menage ad Diog. Läert. 7, 192."--*Reiske*.

[243] Compare "On Contentedness of Mind," § xiii.

[244] Reading with *Reiske*, [Greek: aporrêzeien].

[245] "Iliad," xiii. 284, 285.

[246] "Iliad," xv. 262.

[247] "Iliad," v. 185.

[248] Compare "That Virtue may be Taught," § ii.

HOW ONE MAY BE AWARE OF ONE'S PROGRESS IN VIRTUE.

§ I. What amount of argument, Sossius Senecio, will make a man know that he is improving in respect to virtue, if his advances in it do not bring about some diminution in folly, but vice, weighing equally with all his good intentions, "acts like the lead that makes the net go down?"[249] For neither in music nor grammatical knowledge could anyone recognize any improvement, if he remained as unskilful in them as before, and had not lost some of his old ignorance. Nor in the case of anyone ill would medical treatment, if it brought no relief or ease, by the disease somewhat yielding and abating, give any perception of improvement of health, till the opposite condition was completely brought about by the body recovering its full strength. But just as in these cases there is no improvement unless, by the abatement of what weighs them down till they rise in the opposite scale, they recognize a change, so in the case of those who profess philosophy no improvement or sign of improvement can be supposed, unless the soul lay aside and purge itself of some of its imperfection, and if it continue altogether bad until it become absolutely good and perfect. For indeed a wise man cannot in a moment of time change from absolute badness to perfect goodness, and suddenly abandon for ever all that vice, of which he could not during a long period of time divest himself of any portion. And yet you know, of course, that those who maintain these views frequently give themselves much trouble and bewilderment about the difficulty, that a wise man does not perceive that he has become wise, but is ignorant and doubtful that in a long period of time by little and little, by removing some things and adding others, there will be a secret and quiet improvement, and as it were passage to virtue. But if the change were so great and sudden that the worst man in the morning could become the best man at night, or should the change so happen that he went to bed vicious and woke up in the morning wise, and, having dismissed from his mind all yesterday's follies and errors, should say,

"False dreams, away, you had no meaning then!"[250]

who on earth could be ignorant of so great a change happening to himself, of virtue blazing forth so completely all at once? I myself am of opinion that anyone, like Caeneus,[251] who, according to his prayer, got changed from a woman into a man, would sooner be ignorant of the transformation, than that a man should become at once, from a cowardly and senseless person with no powers of self-control, brave and sensible and perfect master of himself, and should in a moment change from a brutish life to a divine without being aware of it.

§ II. That was an excellent observation, Measure the stone by the mason's rule, not the rule by the stone.[252] But the Stoics, not applying dogmas to facts but facts to their own preconceived opinions, and forcing things to agree that do not by nature, have filled philosophy with many difficulties, the greatest of which is that all men but the perfect man are equally vicious, which has produced the enigma called progress, one little short of extreme folly, since it makes those who have not at once under its guidance given up all passions and disorders equally unfortunate as those who have not got rid of a single vile propensity. However they are their own confuters, for while they lay down in the schools that Aristides was as unjust as Phalaris, and Brasidas as great a craven as Dolon, and Plato actually as senseless as Meletus, in life and its affairs they turn away from and avoid one class as implacable, while they make use of the others and trust them in most important matters as most worthy people.

§ III. But we who see that in every kind of evil, but especially in a disordered and unsettled state of mind, there are degrees of more and less (so that the progress made differs in different cases, badness abating, as a shadow flees away, under the influence of reason, which calmly illuminates and cleanses the soul), cannot consider it unreasonable to think that the change will be perceived, as people who come up out of some ravine can take note of the progress they make upwards. Look at the case from the following point of view first. Just as mariners sailing with full sail over the gaping[253] ocean measure the course they have made by the time they have taken and the force of the wind, and compute their progress accordingly, so anyone can compute his progress in philosophy by his continuous and unceasing course, by his not making many halts on the road, and then again advancing by leaps and bounds, but by his quiet and even and steady march forward guided by reason. For the words of the poet, "If to a little you keep adding a little, and do so frequently, *it will soon be a lot*,"[254] are not only true of the increase of money, but are universally applicable, and especially to increase in virtue, since reason invokes to her aid the enormous force of habit. On the other hand the inconsistencies and dulnesses of some philosophers not only check advance, as it were, on the road, but even break up the journey altogether, since vice always attacks at its leisure and forces back whatever yields to it.[255] The mathematicians tell us that planets, after completing their course, become stationary; but in philosophy there is no such intermission or stationary position from the cessation of progress, for its nature is ever to be moving and, as it were, to be weighed in the scales, sometimes being overweighted by the good preponderating, sometimes by the bad. If, therefore, imitating the oracle given to the Amphictyones by the god, "to fight against the people of Cirrha every day and every night,"[256] you are conscious that night and day you ever maintain a fierce fight against vice, not often relaxing your vigilance, or long off your guard, or receiving as heralds to treat of peace[257] the pleasures, or idleness, or stress of business, you may reasonably go forward to the future courageously and confidently.

§ IV. Moreover, if there be any intermissions in philosophy, and yet your later studies are firmer and more continuous than your former ones, it is no bad indication that your sloth has been expelled by labour and exercise; for the contrary is a bad sign, when after a short time your lapses from zeal become many and continuous, as if your zeal were dying away. For as in the growth of a reed, which shoots up from the ground finely and beautifully to an even and continuous height, though at first from its great intervals it is hindered and baffled in its growth, and afterwards through its weakness is discouraged by any breath of air, and though strengthened by many and frequent joints, yet a violent wind gives it commotion and trembling, so those who at first make great launches out into philosophy, and afterwards find that they are continually hindered and baffled, and cannot perceive that they make any progress, finally get tired of it and cry off. "But he who is as it were winged,"[258] is by his simplicity borne along to his end, and by his zeal and energy cuts through impediments to his progress, as merely obstacles on the road. As it is a sign of the growth of violent love, not so much to rejoice in the presence of the loved one, for everyone does that, as to be distressed and grieved at his absence,[259] so many feel a liking for philosophy and seem to take a wonderful interest in the study, but if they are diverted by other matters and business their passion evaporates and they take it very easily. "But whoever is strongly smitten with love for his darling"[260] will show his mildness and agreeableness in the presence of and joint pursuit of wisdom with the loved one, but if he is drawn away from him and is not in his company you will see him in a stew and ill at ease and peevish whether at work or leisure, and unreasonably forgetful of his friends, and wholly impelled by his passion for philosophy. For we ought not to rejoice at discourses only when we hear them, as people like perfumes only when they smell them, and not to seek or care about them in their absence, but in the same condition as people who are hungry and thirsty are in if torn away from food and drink, we ought to follow after true proficiency in philosophy, whether marriage, or wealth, or friendship, or military service, strike in and produce a separation. For just as more is to be got from philosophy, so much the more does what we fail to obtain trouble us.

§ V. Either precisely the same as this or very similar is Hesiod's[261] very ancient definition of progress in virtue, namely, that the road is no longer very steep or arduous, but easy and smooth and level, its roughness being toned down by exercise, and casting the bright light of philosophy on doubt and error and regrets, such as trouble those who give themselves to philosophy at the outset, like people who leave a land they know, and do not yet descry the land they are sailing to. For by abandoning the common and familiar, before they know and apprehend what is better, they frequently flounder about in the middle and are fain to return. As they say the Roman Sextius, giving up for philosophy all his honours and offices in Rome, being afterwards discontented with philosophy from the difficulties he met with in it at first, very nearly threw himself out of window. Similarly they relate of Diogenes of Sinope,[262] when he began to be a philosopher, that the Athenians were celebrating a festival, and there were public banquets and shows and mutual festivities, and drinking and revelling all night, and he, coiled up in a corner of the market-place intending to sleep, fell into a train of thought likely seriously to turn him from his purpose and shake his resolution, for he reflected that he had adopted without any necessity a toilsome and unusual kind of life, and by his own fault sat there debarred of all the good things. At that moment, however, they say a mouse stole up and began to munch some of the crumbs of his barley-cake, and he plucked up his courage and said to himself, in a railing and chiding fashion, "What say you, Diogenes? Do your leavings give this mouse a sumptuous meal, while you, the gentleman, wail and lament because you are not getting drunk yonder and reclining on soft and luxurious couches?" Whenever such depressions of mind are not frequent, and the mind when they take place quickly recovers from them, after having put them to flight as it were, and when such annoyance and distraction is easily got rid of, then one may consider one's progress in virtue as a certainty.

§ VI. And since not only the things that in themselves shake and turn them in the opposite direction are more powerful in the case of weak philosophers, but also the serious advice of friends, and the playful and jeering objections of adversaries bend and soften people, and have ere now shaken some out of philosophy altogether, it will be no slight indication of one's progress in virtue if one takes all this very calmly, and is neither disturbed nor aggravated by people who tell us and mention to us that some of our former comrades are flourishing in kings' courts, or have married wives with dowries, or are attended by a crowd of friends when they come down to the forum to solicit some office or advocateship. He that is not moved or affected by all this is already plainly one upon whom philosophy has got a right hold; for it is impossible that we should cease to be envious of what most people admire, unless the admiration of virtue was strongly implanted in us. For over-confidence may be generated in some by anger and folly, but to despise what men admire is not possible without a true and steady elevation of mind. And so people in such a condition of mind, comparing it with that of others, pride themselves on it, and say with Solon, "We would not change virtue for wealth, for while virtue abides, wealth changes hands, and now one man, now another, has it."[263] And Diogenes compared his shifting about from Corinth to Athens, and again from Thebes to Corinth, to the different residences of the King of Persia, as his spring residence at Susa, his winter residence at Babylon, and his summer residence in Media. And Agesilaus said of the great king, "How is he better than me, if he is not more upright?" And Aristotle, writing to Antipater about Alexander, said, "that he ought not to think highly of himself because he had many subjects, for anyone who had right notions about the gods was entitled to think quite as highly of himself." And Zeno, observing that Theophrastus was admired for the number of his pupils,[264] said, "His choir is, I admit, larger than mine, but mine is more harmonious."

§ VII. Whenever then, by thus comparing the advantages of virtue with external things, you get rid of envies and jealousies and those things which fret and depress the minds of many who are novices in philosophy, this also is a great indication of your progress in virtue. Another and no slight indication is a change in the style of your discourses. For generally speaking all novices in philosophy adopt most such as tend to their own glorification; some, like birds, in their levity and ambition soaring to the height and brightness of physical things; others like young puppies, as Plato[265] says, rejoicing in tearing and biting, betake themselves to strifes and questions and sophisms; but most plunging themselves into dialectics immediately store themselves for sophistry; and some collect sentences[266] and histories and go about (as Anacharsis said he saw the Greeks used money for no other purpose but to count it up), merely piling up and comparing them, but making no practical use of them. Applicable here is that saying of Antiphanes, which someone applied to Plato's pupils. Antiphanes said playfully that in a certain city words were frozen directly they were spoken, owing to the great cold, and were thawed again in the summer, so that one could then hear what had been said in the winter. So he said of the words which were spoken by Plato to young men, that most of them only understood them late in life when they were become old men. And this is the condition people are in in respect to all philosophy, until the judgement gets into a sound and healthy state, and begins to adapt itself to those things which can produce character and greatness of mind, and to seek discourses whose footsteps turn inwards rather than outwards, to borrow the language of Æsop.[267] For as Sophocles said he had first toned down the pompous style of Æschylus, then his harsh and over-artificial method, and had in the third place changed his manner of diction, a most important point and one that is most intimately connected with the character, so those who go in for philosophy, when they have passed from flattering and artificial discourses to such as deal with character and emotion, are beginning to make genuine and modest progress in virtue.

§ VIII. Furthermore, take care, in reading the writings of philosophers or hearing their speeches, that you do not attend to words more than things, nor get attracted more by what is difficult and curious than by what is serviceable and solid and useful. And also, in studying poems or history, let nothing escape you of what is said to the point, which is likely either to correct the character or to calm the passions. For as Simonides says the bee hovers among the flowers "making the yellow honey,"[268] while others value and pluck flowers only for their beauty and fragrance, so of all that read poems for pleasure and amusement he alone that finds and gathers what is valuable seems capable of knowledge from his acquaintance with and friendship for what is noble and good.[269] For those who study Plato and Xenophon only for their style, and cull out only what is pure and Attic, and as it were the dew and the bloom, do they not resemble people who love drugs for their smell and colour, but care not for them as anodynes or purges, and are not aware of those properties? Whereas those who have more proficiency can derive benefit not from discourses only, but from sights and actions, and cull what is good and useful, as is recorded of Æschylus and other similar kind of men. As to Æschylus, when he was watching a contest in boxing at the Isthmus, and the whole theatre cried out upon one of the boxers being beaten, he nudged with his elbow Ion of Chios, and said, "Do you observe the power of training? The beaten man holds his peace, while the spectators cry out." And Brasidas having caught hold of a mouse among some figs, being bitten by it let it go, and said to himself, "Hercules, there is no creature so small or weak that it will not fight for its life!" And Diogenes, seeing a lad drinking water out of the palm of his hand, threw away the cup which he kept in his wallet. So much does attention and assiduous practice make people perceptive and receptive of what contributes to virtue from any source. And this is the case still more with those who mix discourses with actions, who not only, to use the language of Thucydides,[270] "exercise themselves in the presence of danger," but also in regard to pleasures and strifes, and judgements, and advocateships, and magistrateships make a display of their opinions, or rather form their opinions by their practice. For we can no more think those philosophers who are ever learning and busy and investigating what they have got from philosophy, and then straightway publish it in the market-place or in the haunt of young men, or at a royal supper-party, any more than we give the name of physicians to those who sell drugs and mixtures. Nay rather such a sophist differs very little at all from the bird described in Homer,[271] offering his scholars like it whatever he has got, and as it feeds its callow young from its own mouth, "though it goes ill with itself," so he gets no advantage or food from what he has got for himself.

§ IX. We must therefore see to it that our discourse be serviceable to ourselves, and that it may not appear to others to be vain-glorious or ambitious, and we must show that we are as willing to listen as to teach, and especially must we lay aside all disputatiousness and love of strife in controversy, and cease bandying fierce words with one another as if we were contending with one another at boxing, and leave off rejoicing more in smiting and knocking down one another than in learning and teaching. For in such cases moderation and mildness, and to commence arguing without quarrelsomeness and to finish without getting into a rage, and neither to be insolent if you come off best in the argument, nor dejected if you come off worst, is a sufficient sign of progress in virtue. Aristippus was an excellent example of this, when overcome in argument by the sophistry of a man, who had plenty of assurance, but was generally speaking mad or half-witted. Observing that he was in great joy and very puffed up at his victory, he said, "I who have been vanquished in the argument shall have a better night's rest than my victor." We can also test ourselves in regard to public speaking, if we are not timid and do not shrink from speaking when a large audience has unexpectedly been got together, nor dejected when we have only a small one to harangue to, and if we do not, when we have to speak to the people or before some magistrate, miss the opportunity through want of proper preparation; for these things are recorded both of Demosthenes and Alcibiades. As for Alcibiades, though he possessed a most excellent understanding, yet from want of confidence in speaking he often broke down, and in trying to recall a word or thought that slipped his memory had to stop short.[272] And Homer did not deny that his first line was unmetrical,[273] though he had sufficient confidence to follow it up by so many other lines, so great was his genius. Much more then ought those who aim at virtue and what is noble to lose no opportunity of public speaking, paying very little attention to either uproar or applause at their speeches.

§ X. And not only ought each to see to his discourses but also to his actions whether he regards utility more than show, and truth more than display. For if a genuine love for youth or maiden seeks no witnesses, but is content to enjoy its delights privately, far more does it become the philosopher and lover of the beautiful, who is conversant with virtue through his actions, to pride himself on his silence, and not to need people to praise or listen to him. As that man who called his maid in the house, and cried out to her, "See, Dionysia, I am angry no longer,"[274] so he that does anything agreeable and polite, and then goes and spreads it about the town, plainly shows that he looks for public applause and has a strong propensity to vain-glory, and as yet has no acquaintance with virtue as a reality but only as a dream, restlessly roving about amid phantoms and shadows, and making a display of whatever he does as painters display a picture. It is therefore a sign of progress in virtue not merely to have given to a friend or done a good turn to an acquaintance without mentioning it to other people, but also to have given an honest vote among many unjust ones, and to have withstood the dishonourable request of some rich man or of some man in office, and to have been above taking bribes, and, by Zeus, to have been thirsty all night and not to have drunk, or, like Agesilaus,[275] to have resisted, though strongly tempted, the kiss of a handsome youth or maiden, and to have kept the fact to oneself and been silent about it. For one's being satisfied with one's own good opinion[276] and not despising it, but rejoicing in it and acquiescing in it as competent to see and decide on what is honourable, proves that reason is rooted and grounded within one, and that, to borrow the language of Democritus, one is accustomed to draw one's delights from oneself. And just as farmers behold with greater pleasure those ears of corn which bend and bow down to the ground, while they look upon those that from their lightness stand straight upright as empty pretenders, so also among those young men who wish to be philosophers those that are most empty and without any solidity show the greatest amount of assurance in their appearance and walk, and a face full of haughtiness and contempt that looks down on everybody, but when they begin to grow full and get some fruit from study they lay aside their proud and vain[277] bearing. And just as in vessels that contain water the air is excluded, so with men that are full of solid merit their pride abates, and their estimate of themselves becomes a lower one, and they cease to plume themselves on a long beard and threadbare cloak,[278] and transfer their training to the mind, and are most severe and austere to themselves, while they are milder in their intercourse with everybody else; and they do not as before eagerly snatch at the name and reputation of philosopher, nor do they write themselves down as such, but even if he were addressed by that title by anyone else, an ingenuous young man would say, smiling and blushing, "I am not a god: why do you liken me to the immortals?"[279] For as Æschylus says,

"I never can mistake the burning eye Of the young woman that has once known man,"[280]

so to the young man who has tasted of true progress in philosophy the following lines of Sappho are applicable, "My tongue cleaves to the roof of my mouth, and a fire courses all over my lean body," and his eye will be gentle and mild, and you would desire to hear him speak. For as those who are initiated come together at first with confusion and noise and jostle one another, but when the mysteries are being performed and exhibited, they give their attention with awe and silence, so also at the commencement of philosophy you will see round its doors much confusion and assurance and prating, some rudely and violently jostling their way to reputation, but he who once enters in, and sees the great light, as when shrines are open to view, assumes another air and is silent and awe-struck, and in humility and decorum follows reason as if she were a god. And the playful remark of Menedemus seems to suit these very well. He said that the majority of those who went to school at Athens became first wise, and then philosophers, after that orators, and as time went on became ordinary kind of people, the more they had to do with learning, so much the more laying aside their pride and high estimate of themselves.

§ XI. Of people that need the help of the physician some, if their tooth ache or even finger smart, run at once to the doctor, others if they are feverish send for one and implore his assistance at their own home, others who are melancholy or crazy or delirious will not sometimes even see the doctor if he comes to their house, but drive him away, or avoid him, ignorant through their grievous disease that they are diseased at all. Similarly of those who have done what is wrong some are incorrigible, being hostile and indignant and furious at those who reprove and admonish them, while others are meeker and bear and allow reproof. Now, when one has done what is wrong, to offer oneself for reproof, to expose the case and reveal one's wrongdoing, and not to rejoice if it lies hid, or be satisfied if it is not known, but to make confession of it and ask for interference and admonishment, is no small indication of progress in virtue. And so Diogenes said that one who wished to do what was right ought to seek either a good friend or red-hot enemy, that either by rebuke or mild entreaty he might flee from vice. But as long as anyone, making a display of dirt or stains on his clothes, or a torn shoe, prides himself to outsiders on his freedom from arrogance, and, by Zeus, thinks himself doing something very smart if he jeers at himself as a dwarf or hunchback, but wraps up and conceals as if they were ulcers the inner vileness of his soul and the deformities of his life, as his envy, his malignity, his littleness, his love of pleasure, and will not let anyone touch or look at them from fear of disgrace, such a one has made little progress in virtue, yea rather none. But he that joins issue with his vices, and shows that he himself is even more pained and grieved about them than anyone else, or, what is next best, is able and willing to listen patiently to the reproof of another and to correct his life accordingly, he seems truly to be disgusted at his depravity and resolute to divest himself of it. We ought certainly to be ashamed and shun every appearance of vice, but he who is more put about by his vice itself than by the bad reputation that ensues upon it, will not mind either hearing it spoken against or even speaking against it himself if it make him a better man. That was a witty remark of Diogenes to a young man, who when seen in a tavern retired into the kitchen: "The more," said he, "you retire, the more are you in the tavern."[281] Even so the more a vicious man denies his vice, the more does it insinuate itself and master him: as those people really poor who pretend to be rich get still more poor from their false display. But he who is really making progress in virtue imitates Hippocrates, who confessed publicly and put into black and white that he had made a mistake about the sutures of the skull,[282] for he will think it monstrous, if that great man declared his mistake, that others might not fall into the same error, and yet he himself for his own deliverance from vice cannot bear to be shown he is in the wrong, and to confess his stupidity and ignorance. Moreover the sayings of Bion and Pyrrho will test not so much one's progress as a greater and more perfect habit of virtue. Bion maintained that his friends might think they had made progress, when they could listen as patiently to abuse as to such language as the following, "Stranger, you look not like a bad or foolish person,"[283] "Health and joy go with you, may the gods give you happiness!"[284] While as to Pyrrho they say, when he was at sea and in peril from a storm, that he pointed out a little pig that was quietly enjoying some grain that had been scattered about, and said to his companions that the man who did not wish to be disturbed by the changes and chances of life should attain a similar composedness of mind through reason and philosophy.

§ XII. Look also at the opinion of Zeno, who thought that everybody might gauge his progress in virtue by his dreams, if he saw himself in his dreams pleasing himself with nothing disgraceful, and neither doing nor wishing to do anything dreadful or unjust, but that, as in the clear depths of a calm and tranquil sea, his fancy and passions were plainly shown to be under the control of reason. And this had not escaped the notice of Plato,[285] it seems, who had earlier expressed in form and outline the part that fancy and unreason played in sleep in the soul that was by nature tyrannical, "for it attempts incest," he says, "with its mother, and procures for itself unlawful meats, and gives itself up to the most abandoned desires, such as in daytime the law through shame and fear debars people from." As then beasts of burden that have been well-trained do not, even if their driver let go the reins, attempt to turn aside and leave the proper road, but go forward orderly as usual, pursuing their way without stumbling, so those whose unreason has become obedient and mild and tempered by reason, will not easily wish, either in dreams or in illnesses, to deal insolently or lawlessly through their desires, but will keep to their usual habits, which acquire their power and force by attention. For if the body can by training make itself and its members so subject to control, that the eyes in sorrow can refrain from tears, and the heart from palpitating in fear, and the passions can be calm in the presence of beautiful youths and maidens, is it not far more likely that the training of the passions and emotions of the soul will allay, tame down, and mould their propensities even in dreams? A story is told about the philosopher Stilpo,[286] that he thought he saw in a dream Poseidon angry with him because he had not sacrificed an ox to him, as was usual among the Megarians:[287] and that he, not a bit frightened, said, "What are you talking about, Poseidon? Do you come here as a peevish boy, because I have not with borrowed money filled the town with the smell of sacrifice, and have only sacrificed to you out of what I had at home on a modest scale?" Then he thought that Poseidon smiled at him, and held out his right hand, and said that for his sake he would give the Megarians a large shoal of anchovies. Those, then, that have such pleasant, clear, and painless dreams, and no frightful, or harsh, or malignant, or untoward apparition, may be said to have reflections of their progress in virtue; whereas agitation and panics and ignoble flights, and boyish delights, and lamentations in the case of sad and strange dreams, are like the waves that break on the coast, the soul not having yet got its proper composure, but being still in course of being moulded by opinions and laws, from which it escapes in dreams as far as possible, so that it is once again set free and open to the passions. Do you investigate all these points too, as to whether they are signs of progress in virtue, or of some habit which has already a settled constancy and strength through reason.

§ XIII. Now since entire freedom from the passions is a great and divine thing, and progress in virtue seems, as we say, to consist in a certain remissness and mildness of the passions, we must observe the passions both in themselves and in reference to one another to gauge the difference: in themselves as to whether desire, and fear, and rage are less strong in us now than formerly, through our quickly extinguishing their violence and heat by reason; and in reference to one another as to whether we are animated now by modesty more than by fear, and by emulation more than by envy, and by love of glory rather than by love of riches, and generally speaking whether--to use the language of musicians--it is in the Dorian more than in the Lydian measures that we err either by excess or deficiency,[288] whether we are plainer in our manner of living or more luxurious, whether we are slower in action or quicker, whether we admire men and their discourses more than we should or despise them. For as it is a good sign in diseases if they turn aside from vital parts of the body, so in the case of people who are making progress in virtue, when vice seems to shift to milder passions, it is a sign it will soon die out. When Phrynis added to the seven chords two chords more, the Ephors asked him which he preferred to let them cut off, the upper or lower ones;[289] so we must cut off both above and below, if we mean to attain, to the mean and to due proportion: for progress in virtue first diminishes the excess and sharpness of the passions,

"That sharpness for which madmen are so vehement,"

as Sophocles says.

§ XIV. I have already said that it is a very great indication of progress in virtue to transfer our judgement to action, and not to let our words remain merely words, but to make deeds of them. A manifestation of this is in the first place emulation as regards what we praise, and a zeal to do what we admire, and an unwillingness either to do or allow what we censure. To illustrate my meaning by an example, it is probable that all Athenians praised the daring and bravery of Miltiades; but Themistocles alone said that the trophy of Miltiades would not let him sleep, but woke him up of a night, and not only praised and admired him, but manifestly emulated and imitated his glorious actions. Small, therefore, can we think the progress we have made, as long as our admiration for those who have done noble things is barren, and does not of itself incite us to imitate them. For as there is no strong love without jealousy, so there is no ardent and energetic praise of virtue, which does not prick and goad one on, and make one not envious but emulous of what is noble, and desirous to do something similar. For not only at the discourses of a philosopher ought we, as Alcibiades said,[290] to be moved in heart and shed tears, but the true proficient in virtue, comparing his own deeds and actions with those of the good and perfect man, and grieved at the same time at the knowledge of his own deficiency, yet rejoicing in hope and desire, and full of impulses that will not let him rest, is, as Simonides says,

"Like sucking foal running by side of dam,"[291]

being desirous all but to coalesce with the good man. For it is a special sign of true progress in virtue to love and admire the disposition of those whose deeds we emulate, and to resemble them with a goodwill that ever assigns due honour and praise to them. But whoever is steeped in contentiousness and envy against his betters, let him know that he may be pricked on by a jealous desire for glory or power, but that he neither honours nor admires virtue.

§ XV. Whenever, then, we begin so much to love good men that we deem happy, "not only," as Plato[292] says, "the temperate man himself, but also the man who hears the words that flow from his wise lips," and even admire and are pleased with his figure and walk and look and smile, and desire to adapt ourselves to his model and to stick closely to him, then may we think that we are making genuine progress. Still more will this be the case, if we admire the good not only in prosperity, but like lovers who admire even the lispings and paleness of those in their flower,[293] as the tears and dejection of Panthea in her grief and affliction won the affections of Araspes,[294] so we fear neither the exile of Aristides, nor the prison of Anaxagoras, nor the poverty of Socrates, nor the condemnation of Phocion, but think virtue worthy our love even under such trials, and join her, ever chanting that line of Euripides,

"Unto the noble everything is good."[295]

For the enthusiasm that can go so far as not to be discouraged at the sure prospect of trouble, but admires and emulates what is good even so, could never be turned away from what is noble by anybody. Such men ever, whether they have some business to transact, or have taken upon them some office, or are in some critical conjuncture, put before their eyes the example of noble men, and consider what Plato would have done on the occasion, what Epaminondas would have said, how Lycurgus or Agesilaus would have dealt; that so, adjusting and re-modelling themselves, as it were, at their mirrors, they may correct any ignoble expression, and repress any ignoble passion. For as those that have learnt the names of the Idæan Dactyli[296] make use of them to banish their fear by quietly repeating them over, so the bearing in mind and remembering good men, which soon suggests itself forcibly to those who have made some progress in virtue in all their emotions and difficulties, keeps them upright and not liable to fall. Let this also then be a sign to you of progress in virtue.

§ XVI. In addition to this, not to be too much disturbed, nor to blush, nor to try and conceal oneself, or make any change in one's dress, on the sudden appearance of a man of distinction and virtue, but to feel confident and go and meet such a one, is the confirmation of a good conscience. It is reported that Alexander, seeing a messenger running up to him full of joy and holding out his right hand, said, "My good friend, what are you going to tell me? Has Homer come to life again?" For he thought that his own exploits required nothing but posthumous fame.[297] And a young man improving in character instinctively loves nothing better than to take pride and pleasure in the company of good and noble men, and to display his house, his table, his wife, his amusements, his serious pursuits, his spoken or written discourses; insomuch that he is grieved when he remembers that his father or guardian died without seeing him in that condition in life, and would pray for nothing from the gods so much, as that they could come to life again, and be spectators of his life and actions; as, on the contrary, those that have neglected their affairs, and come to ruin, cannot look upon their relatives even in dreams without fear and trembling.

§ XVII. Add, if you please, to what I have already said, as no small indication of progress in virtue, the thinking no wrong-doing small, but being on your guard and heed against all. For as people who despair of ever being rich make no account of small expenses, thinking they will never make much by adding little to little,[298] but when hope is nearer fruition, then with wealth increases the love of it,[299] so in things that have respect to virtue, not he that generally assents to such sayings as "Why trouble about hereafter?" "If things are bad now, they will some day be better,"[300] but the man who pays heed to everything, and is vexed and concerned if vice gets pardon, when it lapses into even the most trifling wrongdoing, plainly shows that he has already attained to some degree of purity, and deigns not to contract defilement from anything whatever. For the idea that we have nothing of any importance to bring disgrace upon, makes people inclined to what is little and careless.[301] To those who are building a stone wall or coping it matters not if they lay on any chance wood or common stone, or some tombstone that has fallen down, as bad workmen do, heaping and piling up pell-mell every kind of material; but those who have made some progress in virtue, whose life "has been wrought on a golden base,"[302] like the foundation of some holy or royal building, undertake nothing carelessly, but lay and adjust everything by the line and level of reason, thinking the remark of Polycletus superlatively good, that that work is most excellent, where the model stands the test of the nail.[303]

[249] See Erasmus, Adagia, "Eadem pensari trutina."

[250] Euripides, "Iphigenia in Tauris," 569.

[251] See Ovid, "Metamorphoses," xii. 189, sq.

[252] See Erasmus, "Adagia," p. 1103.

[253] Compare Shakspere, "Tempest," A. i. Sc. i. 63, "And gape at widest to glut him."

[254] Hesiod, "Works and Days," 361, 362. Quoted again by our author, "On Education," § 13. [255]

"In via ad virtutem qui non progreditur, is non stat et manet, sed regreditur."--*Wyttenbach.* [256]

Adopting the reading of Hercher. See Pausanias, x. 37, where the oracle is somewhat different. [257]

For the town which parleys surrenders.

[258] From Homer, "Iliad," xix. 386.

[259] Compare Aristotle, *Rhetoric*, i. 11. [Greek: kai archê de tou erôtos gignetai autê pasin, otan mê monon parontos chairôsin, alla kai apontos memnêmenoi erôsin.]

[260] The line is a Fragment of Sophocles.

[261] See Hesiod, "Works and Days," 289-292.

[262] The well-known Cynic philosopher.

[263] Bergk. fr. 15. Compare Homer, "Iliad," vi. 339. [Greek: nikê d' epameibetai andras].

[264] We are told by Diogenes Läertius, v. 37, that Theophrastus had 2000 hearers sometimes at once.

[265] "Republic," vii. p. 539, B.

[266] Sentences borrowed from some author or other, such, as we still possess from the hands of Hermogenes and Aphthonius; compare the collection of bon-mots of Greek courtesans in Athenæus.

[267] A reference to Æsop's Fable, [Greek: Leôn kai Halôpêz]. Cf. Horace, "Epistles," i. i. 73-75.

[268] This passage is alluded to also in "On Love to one's Offspring." § ii.

[269] Madvig's text.

[270] Thucydides, i. 18.

[271] Homer, "Iliad," ix. 323, 324. Quoted also in "On Love to One's Offspring," § ii.

[272] The remark about Demosthenes has somehow slipped out, as Wyttenbach has suggested.

[273] Does this refer to [Greek: Pêlêiadeô] before [Greek: Hachilêos] in "Iliad," i. 1?

[274] An allusion to some passage in a Play that has not come down to us.

[275] Compare our Author, *De Audiendis Poetis*, § xi. [Greek: hôsper ho Agêsilaos ouk hypemeinen hypo tou kalou philêthênai prosiontos].

[276] Reading with Madvig and Hercher, [Greek: to gar auton], sq.

[277] Literally *cork-like*, so vain, empty. So Horace, "levior cortice," "Odes," iii. 9, 22.

[278] Marks of a philosopher among the ancients. Compare our Author, "How one may discern a flatterer from a friend," § vii.

[279] "Odyssey," xvi. 187.

[280] Æschylus, "Toxotides," Fragm. 224. Quoted again by our author, "On Love," § xxi.

[281] "Turpe habitum fuisse in caupona conspici, et hoc exemplo apparet, et alia sunt indicia. Isocrates Orat. Areopagitica laudans antiquorum Atheniensium mores, p. 257: [Greek: en kapêleiô de phagein ê piein oudeis han oiketês epieikês etolmêse]: quem locum citans Athenæus alia etiam adfert xiii. p. 566, F."--*Wyttenbach*.

[282] Wyttenbach compares Quintilian, "Institut. Orat." iii. 6, p. 255: "Nam et Hippocrates clarus arte medicinæ videtur honestissime fecisse, qui quosdam errores suos, ne posteri errarent, confessus est."

[283] Homer, "Odyssey," vi. 187.

[284] Homer, "Odyssey," xxiv. 402.

[285] Plato, "Republic," ix. p. 571, D.

[286] A somewhat similar story about Stilpo is told in Athenæus, x. p. 423, D.

[287] So Haupt and Herscher very ingeniously for [Greek: hiereusin].

[288] Adopting the suggestion of Wyttenbach as to the reading. The Dorian measure was grave and severe, the Lydian soft and effeminate.

[289] See our author, "Apophthegmata Laconica," p. 220 C.

[290] Plato, "Symposium," p. 25, E.

[291] This line is quoted again by our author, "On Moral Virtue," § vii.

[292] Plato, "Laws," iv. p. 711, E.

[293] See those splendid lines of Lucretius, iv. 1155-1169.

[294] "Res valde celebrata ex Institutione Cyri Xenophontea, v. 1, 2; vi. 1, 17."--*Wyttenbach.*

[295] This line is very like a Fragment in the "Danae" of Euripides. Dind. (328).

[296] On these see Pausanias, v. 7.

[297] Such as Homer could have brought. Compare Horace, "Odes," iv. ix. 25-28; and Cicero, "pro Archia," x. "Magnus ille Alexander--cum in Sigeo ad Achillis tumulum adstitisset, O fortunate, inquit, adolescens, qui tuæ virtutis Homerum præconem inveneris."

[298] Contrary to Hesiod's saw, "Works and Days," 361, 362.

[299] So Juvenal, xiv. 138-140.

[300] Like Horace's "Non si male nunc, et olim Sic erit." "Odes," ii. x. 16, 17.

[301] *Noblesse oblige* in fact.

[302] Pindar, Frag. 206.

[303] Like Horace's *factus ad unguem,* because the sculptor tries its polish and the niceness of the joints by drawing his nail over the surface. Casaub. Pers. i. 64; Horace, "Sat." i. v. 32, 33; A. P. 294; Erasmus, "Adagia," p. 507.

WHETHER VICE IS SUFFICIENT TO CAUSE UNHAPPINESS.[304]

§ I. ... He who gets a dowry with his wife sells himself for it, as Euripides says,[305] but his gains are few and uncertain; but he who does not go all on fire through many a funeral pile, but through a regal pyre, full of panting and fear and sweat got from travelling over the sea as a merchant, has the wealth of Tantalus, but cannot enjoy it owing to his want of leisure. For that Sicyonian horse-breeder was wise, who gave Agamemnon as a present a swift mare, "that he should not follow him to wind-swept Ilium, but delight himself at home,"[306] in the quiet enjoyment of his abundant riches and painless leisure. But nowadays courtiers, and people who think they have a turn for affairs, thrust themselves forward of their own accord uninvited into courts and toilsome escorts and bivouacs, that they may get a horse, or brooch, or some such piece of good luck. "But his wife is left behind in Phylace, and tears her cheeks in her sorrow, and his house is only half complete without him,"[307] while he is dragged about, and wanders about, and wastes his time in idle hopes, and has to put up with much insult. And even if he gets any of those things he desires, giddy and dizzy at Fortune's rope-dance, he seeks retirement, and deems those happy who live obscure and in security, while they again look up admiringly at him who soars so high above their heads.[308]

§ II. Vice has universally an ill effect on everybody, being in itself a sufficient producer of infelicity, needing no instruments nor ministers. For tyrants, anxious to make those whom they punish wretched, keep executioners and torturers, and contrive branding-irons and other instruments of torture to inspire fear[309] in the brute soul, whereas vice attacks the soul without any such apparatus, and crushes and dejects it, and fills a man with sorrow, and lamentation, and melancholy, and remorse. Here is a proof of what I say. Many are silent under mutilation, and endure scourging or torture at the hand of despots or tyrants without uttering a word, whenever their soul, abating the pain by reason, forcibly as it were checks and represses them: but you can never quiet anger or smother grief, or persuade a timid person not to run away, or one suffering from remorse not to cry out, nor tear his hair, nor smite his thigh. Thus vice is stronger than fire and sword.

§ III. You know of course that cities, when they desire to publicly contract for the building of temples or colossuses, listen to the estimates of the contractors who compete for the job, and bring their plans and charges, and finally select the contractor who will do the work at least expense, and best, and quickest. Let us suppose then that we publicly contract to make the life of man miserable, and take the estimates of Fortune and Vice for this object. Fortune shall come forward, provided with all sorts of instruments and costly apparatus to make life miserable and wretched. She shall come with robberies and wars, and the blood-guiltiness of tyrants, and storms at sea, and lightning drawn down from the sky, she shall compound hemlock, she shall bring swords, she shall levy an army of informers, she shall cause fevers to break out, she shall rattle fetters and build prisons. It is true that most of these things are owing to Vice rather than Fortune, but let us suppose them all to come from Fortune. And let Vice stand by naked, without any external things against man, and let her ask Fortune how she will make man unhappy and dejected. Fortune, dost thou threaten poverty? Metrocles laughs at thee, who sleeps during winter among the sheep, in summer in the vestibules of temples, and challenges the king of the Persians,[310] who winters at Babylon, and summers in Media, to vie with him in happiness. Dost thou bring slavery, and bondage, and sale? Diogenes despises thee, who cried out, as he was being sold by some robbers, "Who will buy a master?" Dost thou mix a cup of poison? Didst not thou offer such a one to Socrates? And cheerfully, and mildly, without fear, without changing colour or countenance, he calmly drank it up: and when he was dead, all who survived deemed him happy, as sure to have a divine lot in Hades. And as to thy fire, did not Decius, the general of the Romans, anticipate it for himself, having piled a funeral pyre between the two armies, and sacrificed himself to Cronos, dedicating himself for the supremacy of his country? And the chaste and loving wives of the Indians strive and contend with one another for the fire, and she that wins the day and gets burnt with the body of her husband, is pronounced happy by the rest, and her praises sung. And of the wise men in that part of the world no one is esteemed or pronounced happy, who does not in his lifetime, in good health and in full possession of all his faculties, separate soul from body by fire, and emerge pure from flesh, having purged away his mortal part. Or wilt thou reduce a man from a splendid property, and house, and table, and sumptuous living, to a threadbare coat and wallet, and begging of daily bread? Such was the beginning of happiness to Diogenes, of freedom and glory to Crates. Or wilt thou nail a man on a cross, or impale him on a stake? What cares Theodorus whether he rots above ground or below? Such was the happy mode of burial amongst the Scythians,[311] and among the Hyrcanians dogs, among the Bactrians birds, devour according to the laws the dead bodies of those who have made a happy end.

§ IV. Who then are made unhappy by these things? Those who have no manliness or reason, the enervated and untrained, who retain the opinions they had as children. Fortune therefore does not produce perfect infelicity, unless Vice co-operate. For as a thread saws through a bone that has been soaked in ashes and vinegar, and as people bend and fashion ivory only when it has been made soft and supple by beer, and cannot under any other circumstances, so Fortune, lighting upon what is in itself faulty and soft through Vice, hollows it out and wounds it. And as the Parthian juice, though hurtful to no one else nor injurious to those who touch it or carry it about, yet if it be communicated to a wounded man straightway kills him through his previous susceptibility to receive its essence, so he who will be upset in soul by Fortune must have some secret internal ulcer or sore to make external things so piteous and lamentable.

§ V. Does then Vice need Fortune to bring about infelicity? By no means. She lashes not up the rough and stormy sea, she girds not lonely mountain passes with robbers lying in wait by the way, she makes not clouds of hail to burst on the fruitful plains, she suborns not Meletus or Anytus or Callixenus as accusers, she takes not away wealth, excludes not people from the prætorship to make them wretched; but she scares the rich, the well-to-do, and great heirs; by land and sea she insinuates herself and sticks to people, infusing lust, inflaming with anger, afflicting them with superstitious fears, tearing them in pieces with envy.

[304] The beginning of this short Treatise is lost. Nor is the first paragraph at all clear. We have to guess somewhat at the meaning.

[305] In a fragment of the "Phaethon." Compare also "On Education," § 19.

[306] "Iliad," xxiii. 297, 298.

[307] "Iliad," ii. 700, 701.

[308] 'Tis ever so. Compare Horace, "Sat." i. i. 1-14.

[309] Adopting Reiske's reading.

[310] Proverbial for extreme good fortune. Cf. Horace, "Odes," iii. ix. 4, "Persarum vigui rege beatior."

[311] See Herodotus, iv. 72.

WHETHER THE DISORDERS OF MIND OR BODY ARE WORSE.

§ I. Homer, looking at the mortality of all living creatures, and comparing them with one another in their lives and habits, gave vent to his thoughts in the words,

"Of all the things that on the earth do breathe, Or creep, man is by far the wretchedest;"[312]

assigning to man an unhappy pre-eminence in extreme misfortune. But let us, assuming that man is, as thus publicly declared, supreme in infelicity and the most wretched of all living creatures, compare him with himself, in the estimate of his misery dividing body and soul, not idly but in a very necessary way, that we may learn whether our life is more wretched owing to Fortune or through our own fault. For disease is engendered in the body by nature, but vice and depravity in the soul is first its own doing, then its settled condition. And it is no slight aid to tranquillity of mind if what is bad be capable of cure, and lighter and less violent.

§ II. The fox in Æsop[313] disputing with the leopard as to their respective claims to variety, the latter showed its body and appearance all bright and spotted, while the tawny skin of the former was dirty and not pleasant to look at. Then the fox said, "Look inside me, sir judge, and you will see that I am more full of variety than my opponent," referring to his trickiness and versatility in shifts. Let us similarly say to ourselves, Many diseases and disorders, good sir, thy body naturally produces of itself, many also it receives from without; but if thou lookest at thyself within thou wilt find, to borrow the language of Democritus, a varied and susceptible storehouse and treasury of what is bad, not flowing in from without, but having as it were innate and native springs, which vice, being exceedingly rich and abundant in passion, produces. And if diseases are detected in the body by the pulse and by pallors and flushes,[314] and are indicated by heats and sudden pains, while the diseases of the mind, bad as they are, escape the notice of most people, the latter are worse because they deprive the sufferer of the perception of them. For reason if it be sound perceives the diseases of the body, but he that is diseased in his mind cannot judge of his sufferings, for he suffers in the very seat of judgement. We ought to account therefore the first and greatest of the diseases of the mind that ignorance,[315] whereby vice is incurable for most people, dwelling with them and living and dying with them. For the beginning of getting rid of disease is the perception of it, which leads the sufferer to the necessary relief, but he who through not believing he is ill knows not what he requires refuses the remedy even when it is close at hand. For amongst the diseases of the body those are the worst which are accompanied by stupor, as lethargies, headaches, epilepsies, apoplexies, and those fevers which raise inflammation to the pitch of madness, and disturb the brain as in the case of a musical instrument,

"And move the mind's strings hitherto untouched."[316]

§ III. And so doctors wish a man not to be ill, or if he is ill to be ignorant of it, as is the case with all diseases of the soul. For neither those who are out of their minds, nor the licentious, nor the unjust think themselves faulty--some even think themselves perfect. For no one ever yet called a fever health, or consumption a good condition of body, or gout swift-footedness, or paleness a good colour; but many call anger manliness, and love friendship, and envy competition, and cowardice prudence. Then again those that are ill in body send for doctors, for they are conscious of what they need to counteract their ailments; but those who are ill in mind avoid philosophers, for they think themselves excellent in the very matters in which they come short. And it is on this account that we maintain that ophthalmia is a lesser evil than madness, and gout than frenzy. For the person ill in body is aware of it and calls loudly for the doctor, and when he comes allows him to anoint his eye, to open a vein, or to plaster up his head; but you hear mad Agave in her frenzy not knowing her dearest ones, but crying out, "We bring from the mountain to the halls a young stag recently torn limb from limb, a fortunate capture."[317] Again he who is ill in body straightway gives up and goes to bed and remains there quietly till he is well, and if he toss and tumble about a little when the fit is on him, any of the people who are by saying to him,

"Gently, Stay in the bed, poor wretch, and take your ease,"[318]

restrain him and check him. But those who suffer from a diseased brain are then most active and least at rest, for impulses bring about action, and the passions are vehement impulses. And so they do not let the mind rest, but when the man most requires quiet and silence and retirement, then is he dragged into the open air, and becomes the victim of anger, contentiousness, lust, and grief, and is compelled to do and say many lawless things unsuitable to the occasion.

§ IV. As therefore the storm which prevents one's putting into harbour is more dangerous than the storm which will not let one sail, so those storms of the soul are more formidable which do not allow a man to take in sail, or to calm his reason when it is disturbed, but without a pilot and without ballast, in perplexity and uncertainty through contrary and confusing courses, he rushes headlong and falls into woeful shipwreck, and shatters his life. So that from these points of view it is worse to be diseased in mind than body, for the latter only suffer, but the former do ill as well as suffer ill. But why need I speak of our various passions? The very times bring them to our mind. Do you see yon great and promiscuous crowd jostling against one another and surging round the rostrum and forum? They have not assembled here to sacrifice to their country's gods, nor to share in one another's rites; they are not bringing to Ascræan Zeus the firstfruits of Lydian produce,[319] nor are they celebrating in honour of Dionysus the Bacchic orgies on festival nights with common revellings; but a mighty plague stirring up Asia in annual cycles drives them here for litigation and suits at law at stated times: and the mass of business, like the confluence of mighty rivers, has inundated one forum, and festers and teems with ruiners and ruined. What fevers, what agues, do not these things cause? What obstructions, what irruptions of blood into the air-vessels, what distemperature of heat, what overflow of humours, do not result? If you examine every suit at law, as if it were a person, as to where it originated, where it came from, you will find that one was produced by obstinate temper, another by frantic love of strife, a third by some sordid desire.[320]

[312] Homer, "Iliad," xvii. 446, 447.

[313] See the Fable [Greek: Alôpêx kai Pardalis]. No. 42, Ed. Halme.

[314] Reading with Wyttenbach, [Greek: ôchriasesi kai erythêmasi].

[315] Forte [Greek: agnoian]."--*Wyttenbach*. The ordinary reading is [Greek: anoian]. "E coelo descendit [Greek: gnôthi seauton]," says Juvenal truly, xi. 27.

[316] Compare the image in Shakspere, "Hamlet," A. iii. Sc. I. 165, 166.

"Now see that noble and most sovereign reason, Like sweet bells jangled, out of tune and harsh."

[317] Euripides, "Bacchæ," 1170-1172. Agave's treatment of her son Pentheus was a stock philosophical comparison. See for example Horace, ii. "Sat." iii. 303, 304, and context.

[318] Euripides, "Orestes," 258.

[319] "*Aurum* puta. Pactolus enim aurum fert. Videtur dictio e Pindaro desumta esse."--*Reiske*.

[320] "Libellus hic fine carere videtur. Quare autem opusculum hoc Plutarcho indignum atque suppositum visum Xylandro fuerit, non intelligo."--*Reiske*.

ON ABUNDANCE OF FRIENDS.

§ I. Menon the Thessalian, who thought he was a perfect adept in discourse, and, to borrow the language of Empedocles, "had attained the heights of wisdom," was asked by Socrates, what virtue was, and upon his answering quickly and glibly, that virtue was a different thing in boy and old man, and in man and woman, and in magistrate and private person, and in master and servant, "Capital," said Socrates, "you were asked about one virtue, but you have raised up a whole swarm of them,"[321] conjecturing not amiss that the man named many because he knew not one. Might not someone jeer at us in the same way, as being afraid, when we have not yet one firm friendship, that we shall without knowing it fall upon an abundance of friends? It is very much the same as if a man maimed and blind should be afraid of becoming hundred-handed like Briareus or all eyes like Argus. And yet we wonderfully praise the young man in Menander, who said that he thought anyone wonderfully good, if he had even the shadow of a friend.[322]

§ II. But among many other things what stands chiefly in the way of getting a friend is the desire for many friends, like a licentious woman who, through giving her favours indiscriminately, cannot retain her old lovers, who are neglected and drop off;[323] or rather like the foster-child of Hypsipyle, "sitting in the meadow and plucking flower after flower, snatching at each prize with gladsome heart, insatiable in its childish delight,"[324] so in the case of each of us, owing to our love of novelty and fickleness, the recent flower ever attracts, and makes us inconstant, frequently laying the foundations of many friendships and intimacies that come to nothing, neglecting in love of what we eagerly pursue what we have already possession of. To begin therefore with the domestic hearth,[325] as the saying is, with the traditions of life that time has handed down to us about constant friends, let us take the witness and counsel of antiquity, according to which friendships go in pairs, as in the cases of Theseus and Pirithous, Achilles and Patroclus,

Orestes and Pylades, Phintias and Damon, Epaminondas and Pelopidas. For friendship is a creature that goes in pairs, and is not gregarious, or crow-like,[326] and to think a friend a second self, and to call him companion as it were second one,[327] shows that friendship is a dual relation. For we can get neither many slaves nor many friends at small expense. What then is the purchase-money of friendship? Benevolence and complaisance conjoined with virtue, and yet nature has nothing more rare than these. And so to love or be loved very much cannot find place with many persons; for as rivers that have many channels and cuttings have a weak and thin stream, so excessive love in the soul if divided out among many is weakened. Thus love for their young is most strongly implanted in those that bear only one, as Homer calls a beloved son "the only one, the child of old age,"[328] that is, when the parents neither have nor are likely to have another child.

§ III. Not that we insist on only one friend, but among the rest there should be one eminently so, like a child of old age, who according to that well-known proverb has eaten a bushel of salt with one,[329] not as nowadays many so-called friends contract friendship from drinking together once, or playing at ball together, or playing together with dice, or passing the night together at some inn, or meeting at the wrestling-school or in the market. And in the houses of rich and leading men people congratulate them on their many friends, when they see the large and bustling crowd of visitors and handshakers and retainers: and yet they see more flies in their kitchens, and as the flies only come for the dainties, so they only dance attendance for what they can get. And since true friendship has three main requirements, virtue, as a thing good; and familiarity, as a thing pleasant; and use, as a thing serviceable; for we ought to choose a friend with judgement, and rejoice in his company, and make use of him in need; and all these things are prejudicial to abundance of friends, especially judgement, which is the most important point; we must first consider, if it is impossible in a short time to test dancers who are to form a chorus, or rowers who are to pull together, or slaves who are to act as stewards of estates, or as tutors of one's sons, far more difficult is it to meet with many friends who will take off their coats to aid you in every fortune, each of whom "offers his services to you in prosperity, and does not object to share your adversity." For neither does a ship encounter so many storms at sea, nor do they fortify places with walls, or harbours with defences and earthworks, in the expectation of so many and great dangers, as friendship tested well and soundly promises defence and refuge from. But if friends slip in without being tested, like money proved to be bad,

"Those who shall lose such friends may well be glad, And those who have such pray that they may lose them."[330]

Yet is it difficult and by no means easy to avoid and bring to a close an unpleasant friendship: as in the case of food which is injurious and harmful, we cannot retain it on the stomach without damage and hurt, nor can we expel it as it was taken into the mouth, but only in a putrid mixed up and changed form, so a bad friend is troublesome both to others and himself if retained, and if he be got rid of forcibly it is with hostility and hatred, and like the voiding of bile.

§ IV. We ought not, therefore, lightly to welcome or strike up an intimate friendship with any chance comers, or love those who attach themselves to us, but attach ourselves to those who are worthy of our friendship. For what is easily got is not always desirable: and we pass over and trample upon heather and brambles that stick to us[331] on our road to the olive and vine: so also is it good not always to make a friend of the person who is expert in twining himself around us, but after testing them to attach ourselves to those who are worthy of our affection and likely to be serviceable to us.

§ V. As therefore Zeuxis, when some people accused him of painting slowly, replied, "I admit that I do, but then I paint to last," so ought we to test for a long time the friendship and intimacy that we take up and mean to keep. Is it not easy then to put to the test many friends, and to associate with many friends at the same time, or is this impossible? For intimacy is the full enjoyment of friendship, and most pleasant is companying with and spending the day with a friend. "Never again shall we alive, apart from dear friends, sit and take counsel alone together."[332] And Menelaus said about Odysseus, "Nor did anything ever divide or separate us, who loved and delighted in one another, till death's black cloud overshadowed us."[333] The contrary effect seems to be produced by abundance of friends. For the friendship of a pair of friends draws them together and puts them together and holds them together, and is heightened by intercourse and kindliness, "as when the juice of the fig curdles and binds the white milk,"[334] as Empedocles says, such unity and complete union will such a friendship produce. Whereas having many friends puts people apart and severs and disunites them, by transferring and shifting the tie of friendship too frequently, and does not admit of a mixture and welding of goodwill by the diffusing and compacting of intimacy. And this causes at once an inequality and difficulty in respect of acts of kindness, for the uses of friendship become inoperative by being dispersed over too wide an area. "One man is acted upon by his character, another by his reflection."[335] For neither do our natures and impulses always incline in the same directions, nor are our fortunes in life identical, for opportunities of action are, like the winds, favourable to some, unfavourable to others.

§ VI. Moreover, if all our friends want to do the same things at the same time, it will be difficult to satisfy them all, whether they desire to deliberate, or to act in state affairs, or wish for office, or are going to entertain guests. If again at the same time they chance to be engaged in different occupations and interests and ask you all together, one who is going on a voyage that you will sail with him, another who is going to law that you will be his advocate, another who is going to try a case that you will try it with him, another who is selling or buying that you will go into partnership with him, another who is going to marry that you will join him in the sacrifice, another who is going to bury a relation that you will be one of the mourners,

"The town is full of incense, and at once Resounds with triumph-songs and bitter wailing,"[336]

that is the fruit of many friends; to oblige all is impossible, to oblige none is absurd, and to help one and offend many is grievous.

"No lover ever yet fancied neglect."[337]

And yet people bear patiently and without anger the carelessness and neglect of friends, if they get from them such excuses as "I forgot," "I did it unwittingly." But he who says, "I did not assist you in your lawsuit, for I was assisting another friend," or "I did not visit you when you had your fever, for I was helping so-and-so who was entertaining his friends," excusing himself for his inattention to one by his attention to another, so far from making the offence less, even adds jealousy to his neglect. But most people in friendship regard only, it seems, what can be got out of it, overlooking what will be asked in return, and not remembering that he, who has had many of his own requests granted, must oblige others in turn by granting their requests. And as Briareus with his hundred hands had to feed fifty stomachs, and was therefore no better provided than we are, who with two hands have to supply the necessities of only one belly, so in having many friends[338] one has to do many services for them, one has to share in their anxiety, and to toil and moil with them. For we must not listen to Euripides when he says, "mortals ought to join in moderate friendships for one another, and not love with all their heart, that the spell may be soon broken, and the friendship may either be ended or become closer at will,"[339] that so it may be adjusted to our requirements, like the sail of a ship that we can either slacken or haul tight. But let us transfer, Euripides, these lines of yours to enmities, and bid people make their animosities moderate, and not hate with all their heart, that their hatred, and wrath, and querulousness, and suspicions, may be easily broken. Recommend rather for our consideration that saying of Pythagoras, "Do not give many your right hand,"[340] that is, do not make many friends, do not go in for a common and vulgar friendship, which is sure to cause anyone much trouble; for its sharing in others' anxieties and griefs and labours and dangers is quite intolerable to free and noble natures. And that was a true saying of the wise Chilo[341] to one who told him he had no enemy. "Neither," said he, "do you seem to me to have a friend." For enmities inevitably accompany and are involved in friendships.

§ VII. It is impossible I say not to share with a friend in his injuries and disgraces and enmities, for enemies at once suspect and hate the friend of their enemies, and even friends are often envious and jealous and carp at him. As then the oracle given to Timesias about his colony foretold him, "that his swarm of bees would soon be followed by a swarm of wasps," so those that seek a swarm of friends have sometimes lighted unawares on a wasp's-nest of enemies. And the remembrance of wrongs done by an enemy and the kindness of a friend do not weigh in the same balance. See how Alexander treated the friends and intimates of Philotas and Parmenio, how Dionysius treated those of Dion, Nero those of Plautus, Tiberius those of Sejanus, torturing and putting them to death. For as neither the gold nor rich robes of Creon's daughter[342] availed her or her sire, but the flame that burst out suddenly involved him in the same fate as herself, as he ran up to embrace her and rescue her, so some friends, though they have had no enjoyment out of their friends' prosperity, are involved in their misfortunes. And this is especially the case with philosophers and kind people, as Theseus, when his friend Pirithous was punished and imprisoned, "was also bound in fetters not of brass."[343] And Thucydides tells us that during the plague at Athens those that most displayed their virtue perished with their friends that were ill, for they neglected their own lives in going to visit them.[344]

§ VIII. We ought not therefore to be too lavish with our virtue, binding it together and implicating it in various people's fortunes, but we ought to preserve our friendship for those who are worthy of it, and are capable of reciprocating it. For this is indeed the greatest argument against many friends that friendship is originated by similarity. For seeing that even the brutes can hardly be forced to mix with those that are unlike themselves, but crouch down, and show their dislike, and run away, while they mix freely with those that are akin to them and have a similar nature, and gently and gladly make friends with one another then, how is it possible that there should be friendship between people differing in characters and temperaments and ideas of life? For harmony on the harp or lyre is attained by notes in unison and not in unison, sharp and flat somehow or other producing concord, but in the harmony of friendship there must be no unlike, or uneven, or unequal element, but from all alike must come agreement in opinions and wishes and feeling, as if one soul were put into several bodies.

§ IX. What man then is so industrious, so changeable, and so versatile, as to be able to make himself like and adapt himself to many different persons, and not to laugh at the advice of Theognis, "Imitate the ingenuity of the polypus, that takes the colour of whatever stone it sticks to."[345] And yet the changes in the polypus do not go deep but are only on the surface, which, from its thickness or thinness takes the impression of everything that approaches it, whereas friends endeavour to be like one another in character, and feeling, and language, and pursuits, and disposition. It requires a not very fortunate or very good Proteus,[346] able by jugglery to assume various forms, to be frequently at the same time a student with the learned, and ready to try a fall with wrestlers, or to go a hunting with people fond of the chase, or to get drunk with tipplers, or to go a canvassing with politicians, having no fixed character of his own.[347] And as the natural philosophers say of unformed and colourless matter when subjected to external change, that it is now fire, now water, now air, now solid earth, so the soul suitable for many friendships must be impressionable, and versatile, and pliant, and changeable. But friendship requires a steady constant and unchangeable character, a person that is uniform in his intimacy. And so a constant friend is a thing rare and hard to find.

[321] Plato, "Men." p. 71 E.

[322] Quoted more fully by our author, "De Fraterno Amore," § iii.

[323] "Eadem comparatione utitur Lucianus in Toxari T. ii. p. 351: [Greek: hostis an polyphilos hê homoios hêmin dokei tais koinais tautais kai moicheuomenais gynaixi; kai oiometh' ouketh' homoiôs ischyran tên philian autou einai pros pollas eunoias diairetheisan]."--*Wyttenbach.*

[324] From the "Hypsipyle" of Euripides.

[325] A well-known proverb for beginning at the beginning. Aristophanes, "Vespæ." 846; Plato, "Euthryphro," 3 A; Strabo, 9.

[326] An allusion to the well-known proverb, [Greek: koloios poti koloion]. See Erasmus, "Adagia," p. 1644.

[327] The paronomasia is on [Greek: hetairos, heteros].

[328] "Iliad," ix. 482; "Odyssey," xvi. 19.

[329] Cf. Cicero, "De Amicitia," xix.

[330] Sophocles, Fragm. 741. Quoted again by our author, "On Love," § xxiii.

[331] For the image compare Lucio's speech, Shakspere, "Measure for Measure," A. iv. Sc. iii. 189, 190: "Nay, friar, I am a kind of burr; I shall stick."

[332] "Iliad," xxiii. 77, 78.

[333] "Odyssey," iv. 178-180.

[334] "Iliad," v. 902, altered somewhat.

[335] Bergk. p. 1344^3.

[336] Sophocles, "Oedipus Tyrannus," 4, 5. Quoted again "On Moral Virtue," § vi.

[337] A line from Menander. Quoted again "De Fraterno Amore," § xx.

[338] Reading with Halm and Hercher [Greek: en tôi pollois philois chrêsthai.]

[339] Euripides, "Hippolytus," 253-257, where Dindorf and Hercher agree in the reading.

[340] Compare "On Education," § xvii.

[341] Chilo was one of the Seven Wise Men. See Pausanias, iii. 16; X. 24.

[342] For the circumstances see Euripides, "Medea," 1136 sq.

[343] For the friendship of Theseus and Pirithous, see Pausanias, i. 17; x. 29. The line is from Euripides, "Pirithous," Fragm. 591. Cf. "On Shyness," § x.

[344] Thucydides, ii. 51.

[345] Bergk. p. 500^3.

[346] On Proteus, see Verg. "Georg." iv. 387 sq.; Ovid, "Art." i. 761; "Met." ii. 9; "Fasti," i. 367 sq., and especially Horace, "Epistles," i. i. 90: "Quo teneam vultus mutantem Protea nodo?"

[347] Literally, "having no hearth of character," the hearth being an emblem of stability. Compare "How One may Discern a Flatterer from a Friend," § vii., where the same image is employed.

HOW ONE MAY DISCERN A FLATTERER FROM A FRIEND.

§ I. Plato says,[348] Antiochus Philopappus, that all men pardon the man who acknowledges that he is excessively fond of himself, but that there is among many other defects this very grave one in self-love, that by it a man becomes incapable of being a just and impartial judge about himself, for love is blind in regard to the loved object, unless a person has learnt and accustomed himself to honour and pursue what is noble rather than his own selfish interests. This gives a great field for the flatterer in friendship, who finds a wonderful base of operations in our self-love, which makes each person his own first and greatest flatterer, and easily admits a flatterer from without, who will be, so he thinks and hopes, both a witness and confirmer of his good opinion of himself. For he that lies open to the reproach of being fond of flatterers is very fond of himself, and owing to his goodwill to himself wishes to possess all good qualities, and thinks he actually does; the wish is not ridiculous, but the thought is misleading and requires a good deal of caution. And if truth is a divine thing, and, according to Plato,[349] the beginning of all good things both to the gods and men, the flatterer is likely to be an enemy to the gods, and especially to Apollo, for he always sets himself against that famous saying, "Know thyself,"[350] implanting in everybody's mind self-deceit and ignorance of his own good or bad qualities, thus making his good points defective and imperfect, and his bad points altogether incorrigible.

§ II. If however, as is the case with most other bad things, the flatterer attacked only or chiefly ignoble or worthless persons, the evil would not be so mischievous or so difficult to guard against. But since, as wood-worms breed most in soft and sweet wood, those whose characters are honourable and good and equitable encourage and support the flatterer most,--and moreover, as Simonides says, "rearing of horses does not go with the oil-flask,[351] but with fruitful fields," so we see that flattery does not join itself to the poor, the obscure, or those without means, but is the snare and bane of great houses and estates, and often overturns kingdoms and principalities,--it is a matter of no small importance, needing much foresight, to examine the question, that so flattery may be easily detected, and neither injure nor discredit friendship. For just as lice leave dying persons, and abandon bodies when the blood on which they feed is drying up, so one never yet saw flatterers dancing attendance on dry and cold poverty, but they fasten on wealth and position and there get fat, but speedily decamp if reverses come. But we ought not to wait to experience that, which would be unprofitable, or rather injurious and dangerous. For not to find friends at a time when you want them is hard, as also not to be able to exchange an inconstant and bad friend for a constant and good one. For a friend should be like money tried before being required, not found faulty in our need. For we ought not to have our wits about us only when the mischief is done, but we ought to try and prevent the flatterer doing any harm to us: for otherwise we shall be in the same plight as people who test deadly poisons by first tasting them, and kill or nearly kill themselves in the experiment. We do not praise such, nor again all those who, looking at their friend simply from the point of view of decorum and utility, think that they can detect all agreeable and pleasant companions as flatterers in the very act. For a friend ought not to be disagreeable or unpleasant, nor ought friendship to be a thing high and mighty with sourness and austerity, but even its decorous deportment ought to be attractive and winning,[352] for by it

"The Graces and Desire have pitched their tents,"[353]

and not only to a person in misfortune "is it sweet to look into the eyes of a friendly person," as Euripides[354] says, but no less does it bring pleasure and charm in good fortune, than when it relieves the sorrows and difficulties of adversity. And as Evenus said "fire was the best sauce,"[355] so the deity, mixing up friendship with life, has made everything bright and sweet and acceptable by its presence and the enjoyment it brings. How else indeed could the flatterer insinuate himself by the pleasure he gives, unless he knew that friendship admitted the pleasurable element? It would be impossible to say. But just as spurious and mock gold only imitates the brightness and glitter of real gold, so the flatterer seems to imitate the pleasantness and agreeableness of the real friend, and to exhibit himself ever merry and bright, contradicting and opposing nothing. We must not however on that account suspect all who praise as simple flatterers. For friendship requires praise as much as censure on the proper occasion. Indeed peevishness and querulousness are altogether alien to friendship and social life: but when goodwill bestows praise ungrudgingly and readily upon good actions, people endure also easily and without pain admonition and plainspeaking, believing and continuing to love the person who took such pleasure in praising, as if now he only blamed out of necessity.

§ III. It is difficult then, someone may say, to distinguish between the flatterer and the friend, if they differ neither in the pleasure they give nor in the praise they bestow; for as to services and attentions you may often see friendship outstripped by flattery. Certainly it is so, I should reply, if we are trying to find the genuine flatterer who handles his craft with cleverness and art, but not if, like most people, we consider those persons flatterers who are called their own oil-flask-carriers and table-men, men who begin to talk, as one said, the moment their hands have been washed for dinner,[356] whose servility, ribaldry, and want of all decency, is apparent at the first dish and glass. It did not of course require very much discrimination to detect Melanthius the parasite of Alexander of Pheræ of flattery, who, to those who asked how Alexander was murdered, answered, "Through his side into my belly": or those who formed a circle round a wealthy table, "whom neither fire, nor sword, nor steel, would keep from running to a feast":[357] or those female flatterers in Cyprus, who after they crossed over into Syria were nicknamed "step-ladders,"[358] because they lay down and let the kings' wives use their bodies as steps to mount their carriages.

§ IV. What kind of flatterer then must we be on our guard against? The one who neither seems to be nor acknowledges himself to be one: whom you will not always find in the vicinity of your kitchen, who is not to be caught watching the dial to see how near it is to dinner-time,[359] nor gets so drunk as to throw himself down anyhow, but one who is generally sober, and a busybody, and thinks he ought to have a hand in your affairs, and wishes to share in your secrets, and as to friendship plays rather a tragic than a satyric or comic part. For as Plato says, "it is the height of injustice to appear to be just when you are not really so,"[360] so we must deem the most dangerous kind of flattery not the open but the secret, not the playful but the serious. For it throws suspicion even upon a genuine friendship, which we may often confound with it, if we are not careful. When Gobryas pursued one of the Magi into a dark room, and was on the ground wrestling with him, and Darius came up and was doubtful how he could kill one without killing both, Gobryas bade him thrust his sword boldly through both of them;[361] but we, since we give no assent to that saying, "Let friend perish so the enemy perish with him,"[362] in our endeavour to distinguish the flatterer from the friend, seeing that their resemblances are so many, ought to take great care that we do not reject the good with the bad, nor in sparing what is beneficial fall in with what is injurious. For as wild grains mixed up with wheat, if very similar in size and appearance, are not easily kept apart, for if the sieve have small holes they don't pass through, and if large holes they pass with the corn, so flattery is not easily distinguished from friendship, being mixed up with it in feeling and emotion, habit and custom.

§ V. Because however friendship is the most pleasant of all things, and nothing more glads the heart of man, therefore the flatterer attracts by the pleasure he gives, pleasure being in fact his field. And because favours and good services accompany friendship, as the proverb says "a friend is more necessary than fire or water,"[363] therefore the flatterer volunteers all sorts of services, and strives to show himself on all occasions zealous and obliging and ready. And since friendship is mainly produced by a similarity of tastes and habits, and to have the same likes and dislikes first brings people together and unites them through sympathy,[364] the flatterer observing this moulds himself like material and demeans himself accordingly, seeking completely to imitate and resemble those whom he desires to ingratiate himself with, being supple in change, and plausible in his imitations, so that one would say,

"Achilles' son, O no, it is himself."[365]

But his cleverest trick is that, observing that freedom of speech, is both spoken of and reckoned as the peculiar and natural voice of friendship, while not speaking freely is considered unfriendly and disingenuous, he has not failed to imitate this trait of friendship also. But just as clever cooks infuse bitter sauces and sharp seasoning to prevent sweet things from cloying, so these flatterers do not use a genuine or serviceable freedom of speech, but merely a winking and tickling innuendo. He is therefore difficult to detect, like those creatures which naturally change their colour and take that of the material or place near them.[366] But since he deceives and conceals his true character by his imitations, it is our duty to unmask him and detect him by the differences between him and the true friend, and to show that he is, as Plato says, "tricked out in other people's colours and forms, from lack of any of his own."[367]

§ VI. Let us examine the matter then from the beginning. I said that friendship originated in most cases from a similar disposition and nature, generally inclined to the same habits and morals, and rejoicing in the same pursuits, studies, and amusements, as the following lines testify: "To old man the voice of old man is sweetest, to boy that of boy, to woman is most acceptable that of woman, to the sick person that of sick person, while he that is overtaken by misfortune is a comforter to one in trouble." The flatterer knowing then that it is innate in us to delight in, and enjoy the company of, and to love, those who are like ourselves, attempts first to approach and get near a person in this direction, (as one tries to catch an animal in the pastures,) by the same pursuits and amusements and studies and modes of life quietly throwing out his bait, and disguising himself in false colours, till his victim give him an opportunity to catch him, and become tame and tractable at his touch. Then too he censures the things and modes of life and persons that he knows his victim dislikes, while he praises those he fancies immoderately, overdoing it indeed[368] with his show of surprise and excessive admiration, making him more and more convinced that his likes and dislikes are the fruits of judgement and not of caprice.

§ VII. How then is the flatterer convicted, and by what differences is he detected, of being only a counterfeit, and not really like his victim? We must first then look at the even tenor and consistency of his principles, if he always delights in the same things, and always praises the same things, and directs and governs his life after one pattern, as becomes the noble lover of consistent friendship and familiarity. Such a person is a friend. But the flatterer having no fixed character of his own,[369] and not seeking to lead the life suitable for him, but shaping and modelling himself after another's pattern, is neither simple nor uniform, but complex and unstable, assuming different appearances, like water poured from vessel to vessel, ever in a state of flux and accommodating himself entirely to the fashion of those who entertain him. The ape indeed, as it seems, attempting to imitate man, is caught imitating his movements and dancing like him, but the flatterer himself attracts and decoys other men, imitating not all alike, for with one he sings and dances, with another he wrestles and gets covered with the dust of the palæstra, while he follows a third fond of hunting and the chase all but shouting out the words of Phædra,

"How I desire to halloo on the dogs, Chasing the dappled deer,"[370]

and yet he has really no interest in the chase, it is the hunter himself he sets the toils and snares for. And if the object of his pursuit is some young scholar and lover of learning, he is all for books then, his beard flows down to his feet,[371] he's quite a sight with his threadbare cloak, has all the indifference of the Stoic, and speaks of nothing but the rectangles and triangles of Plato. But if any rich and careless fellow fond of drink come in his way,

"Then wise Odysseus stript him of his rags,"[372]

his threadbare cloak is thrown aside, his beard is shorn off like a fruitless crop, he goes in for wine-coolers and tankards, and laughs loudly in the streets, and jeers at philosophers. As they say happened at Syracuse, when Plato went there, and Dionysius was seized with a furious passion for philosophy, and so great was the concourse of geometricians that they raised up quite a cloud of dust in the palace, but when Plato fell out of favour, and Dionysius gave up philosophy, and went back again headlong to wine and women and trifles and debauchery, then all the court was metamorphosed, as if they all had drunk of Circe's cup, for ignorance and oblivion and silliness reigned rampant. I am borne out in what I say by the behaviour of great flatterers and demagogues,[373] the greatest of whom Alcibiades, a jeerer and horse-rearer at Athens, and living a gay and merry life, wore his hair closely shaven at Lacedæmon, and washed in cold water, and attired himself in a threadbare cloak; while in Thrace he fought[374] and drank; and at Tissaphernes' court lived delicately and luxuriously and in a pretentious style; and thus curried favour and was popular with everybody by imitating their habits and ways. Such was not the way however in which Epaminondas or Agesilaus acted, for though they associated with very many men and states and different modes of life, they maintained everywhere their usual demeanour, both in dress and diet and language and behaviour. So Plato[375] at Syracuse was exactly the same man as in the Academy, the same with Dionysius as with Dion.

§ VIII. As to the changes of the flatterer, which resemble those of the polypus,[376] a man may most easily detect them by himself pretending to change about frequently, and by censuring the kind of life he used formerly to praise, and anon approving of the words actions and modes of life that he used to be displeased with. He will then see that the flatterer is never consistent or himself, never loving hating rejoicing grieving at his own initiative, but like a mirror, merely reflecting the image of other people's emotions and manners and feelings. Such a one will say, if you censure one of your friends to him, "You are slow in finding the fellow out, he never pleased me from the first." But if on the other hand you change your language and praise him, he will swear by Zeus that he rejoices at it, and is himself under obligations to the man, and believes in him. And if you talk of the necessity of changing your mode of life, of retiring from public life to a life of privacy and ease, he says, "We ought long ago to have got rid of uproar[377] and envy." But if you think of returning again to public life, he chimes in, "Your sentiments do you honour: retirement from business is pleasant, but inglorious and mean." One ought to say at once to such a one, "Stranger, quite different now you look to what you did before.'[378] I do not need a friend to change his opinions with me and to assent to me in everything, my shadow will do that better, but I need one that will speak the truth and help me with his judgement." This is one way of detecting the flatterer.

§ IX. We must also observe another difference in the resemblance between the friend and flatterer. The true friend does not imitate you in everything, nor is he too keen to praise, but praises only what is excellent, for as Sophocles says,

"He is not born to share in hate but love,"[379]

yes, by Zeus, and he is born to share in doing what is right and in loving what is noble, and not to share in wrong-doing or misbehaviour, unless it be that, as a running of the eyes is catching, so through companionship and intimacy he may against his will contract by infection some vice or ill habit, as they say Plato's intimates imitated his stoop, Aristotle's his lisp, and king Alexander's his holding his head a little on one side, and rapidity of utterance in conversation,[380] for people mostly pick up unawares such traits of character. But the flatterer is exactly like the chameleon,[381] which takes every colour but white, and so he, though unable to imitate what is worth his while, leaves nothing that is bad unimitated. And just as poor painters unable to make a fine portrait from inefficiency in their craft, bring out the likeness by painting all the wrinkles, moles and scars, so the flatterer imitates his friend's intemperance, superstition, hot temper, sourness to domestics, suspicion of his friends and relations. For he is by nature inclined to what is worst, and thinks that imitation of what is bad is as far as possible removed from censure. For those are suspected who have noble aims in life, and seem to be vexed and disgusted at their friends' faults, for that injured and even ruined Dion with Dionysius, Samius with Philip, and Cleomenes with Ptolemy. But he that wishes to be and appear at the same time both agreeable and trustworthy pretends to rejoice more in what is bad, as being through excessive love for his friend not even offended at his vices, but as one with him in feeling and nature in all matters. And so they claim to share in involuntary and chance ailments, and pretend to have the same complaints, in flattery to those who suffer from any, as that their eyesight and sense of hearing are deficient, if their friends are somewhat blind or deaf, as the flatterers of Dionysius, who was rather short-sighted, jostled one another at a dinner party, and knocked the dishes off the table, *as if from defect of vision*.[382] And some to make their cases more similar wind themselves in closer, and dive even into family secrets for parallels. For seeing that their friends are unfortunate in marriage, or suspicious about the behaviour of their sons or relations, they do not spare themselves, but make quite a Jeremiad about their own sons, or wife, or kinsfolk, or relations, proclaiming loudly their own family secrets. For similarity in situation makes people more sympathetic, and their friends having received as it were hostages by their confessions, entrust them in return with their secrets, and having once made confidants of them, dare not take back their confidence.[383] I actually know of a man who turned his wife out of doors because his friend had put away his; but as he secretly visited her and sent messages to her, he was detected by his friend's wife noticing his conduct. So little did he know the nature of a flatterer that thought the following lines more applicable to a crab than a flatterer, "His whole body is belly, his eye is on everything, he is a creature creeping on his teeth," for such is a true picture of the parasite, "friends of the frying-pan, hunting for a dinner," to borrow the language of Eupolis.

§ X. However let us put off all this to its proper place in the discourse. But let us not fail to notice the wiliness of the flatterer's imitation, in that, even if he imitates any good points in the person he flatters, he always takes care to give him the palm. Whereas among real friends there is no rivalry or jealousy of one another, but they are satisfied and contented alike whether they are equal or one of them is superior. But the flatterer, ever remembering that he is to play second fiddle,[384] makes his copy always fall a little short of the original, for he admits that he is everywhere outstripped and left behind, except in vice. For in that alone he claims pre-eminence, for if his friend is peevish, he says he is atrabilious; if his friend is superstitious, he says he is a fanatic; if his friend is in love, he says he is madly in love; if his friend laughs, he will say, "You laughed a little unseasonably, but I almost died of laughter." But in regard to any good points his action is quite the opposite. He says he can run quickly, but his friend flies; he says he can ride pretty well, but his friend is a Centaur on horseback. He says "I am not a bad poet, and don't write very bad lines",

"'But your sonorous verse is like Jove's thunder.'"

Thus he shows at once that his friend's aims in life are good, and that his friend has reached a height he cannot soar to. Such then are the differences in the resemblances between the flatterer and the friend.

§ XI. But since, as has been said before, to give pleasure is common to both, for the good man delights in his friends as much as the bad man in his flatterers, let us consider the difference between them here too. The difference lies in the different aim of each in giving pleasure. Look at it this way. There is no doubt a sweet smell in perfume. So there is also in medicine. But the difference is that while in perfume pleasure and nothing else is designed, in medicine either purging, or warming, or adding flesh to the system, is the primary object, and the sweet smell is only a secondary consideration. Again painters mix gay colours and dyes: there are also some drugs which are gay in appearance and not unpleasing in colour. What then is the difference between these? Manifestly we distinguish by the end each aims at. So too the social life of friends employs mirth to add a charm to some good and useful end,[385] and sometimes makes joking and a good table and wine, aye, and even chaff and banter, the seasoning to noble and serious matters, as in the line,

"Much they enjoyed talking to one another,"[386]

and again,

"Never did ought else Disturb our love or joy in one another."[387]

But the flatterer's whole aim and end is to cook up and season his joke or word or action, so as to produce pleasure. And to speak concisely, the flatterer's object is to please in everything he does, whereas the true friend always does what is right, and so often gives pleasure, often pain, not wishing the latter, but not shunning it either, if he deems it best. For as the physician, if it be expedient, infuses saffron or spikenard, aye, or uses some soothing fomentation or feeds his patient up liberally, and sometimes orders castor,

"Or poley,[388] that so strong and foully smells,"

or pounds hellebore and compels him to drink it,--neither in the one case making unpleasantness, nor in the other pleasantness, his end and aim, but in both studying only the interest of his patient,--so the friend sometimes by praise and kindness, extolling him and gladdening his heart, leads him to what is noble, as Agamemnon,

"Teucer, dear head, thou son of Telamon, Go on thus shooting, captain of thy men;"[389]

or Diomede,

"How could I e'er forget divine Odysseus?"[390]

But where on the other hand there is need of correction, then he rebukes with biting words and with the freedom worthy of a friend,

"Zeus-cherished Menelaus, art thou mad, And in thy folly tak'st no heed of safety?"[391]

Sometimes also he joins action to word, as Menedemus sobered the profligate and disorderly son of his friend Asclepiades, by shutting him out of his house, and not speaking to him. And Arcesilaus forbade Bato his school, when he wrote a line in one of his plays against Cleanthes, and only got reconciled with him after he repented and made his peace with Cleanthes. For we ought to give our friend pain if it will benefit him, but not to the extent of breaking off our friendship; but just as we make use of some biting medicine, that will save and preserve the life of the patient. And so the friend, like a musician, in bringing about an improvement to what is good and expedient, sometimes slackens the chords, sometimes tightens them, and is often pleasant, but always useful. But the flatterer, always harping on one note, and accustomed to play his accompaniment only with a view to please and to ingratiate himself, knows not how either to oppose in deed, or give pain in word, but complies only with every wish, ever chiming in with and echoing the sentiments of his patron. As then Xenophon says Agesilaus took pleasure in being praised by those who would also censure him,[392] so ought we to think that to please and gratify us is friendly in the person who can also give us pain and oppose us, but to feel suspicion at an intercourse which is merely for pleasure and gratification, and never pungent, aye and by Zeus to have ready that saying of the Lacedæmonian, who, on hearing king Charillus praised, said, "How can he be a good man, who is not severe even to the bad?"

§ XII. They say the gadfly attacks bulls, and the tick dogs, in the ear: so the flatterer besieges with praise the ears of those who are fond of praise, and sticks there and is hard to dislodge. We ought therefore here to make a wide-awake and careful discrimination, whether the praise is bestowed on the action or the man. It is bestowed on the action, if people praise the absent rather than the present, if also those that have the same aims and aspirations praise not only us but all that are similarly disposed, and do not evidently say and do one thing at one time, and the direct contrary at another; and the greatest test is if we are conscious, in the matters for which we get the praise, that we have not regretted them, and are not ashamed at them, and would not rather have said and done differently. For our own inward judgement, testifying the contrary and not admitting the praise, is above passion, and impregnable and proof against the flatterer. But I know not how it is that most people in misfortune cannot bear exhortation, but are captivated more by condolence and sympathy, and when they have done something wrong and acted amiss, he that by censure and blame implants in them the stings of repentance is looked upon by them as hostile and an accuser, while they welcome and regard as friendly and well-disposed to them the person who bestows praise and panegyric on what they have done. Those then that readily praise and join in applauding some word or action on the part of someone whether in jest or earnest, only do temporary harm for the moment, but those who injure the character by their praise, aye, and by their flattery undermine the morals, act like those slaves who do not steal from the bin, but from the seed corn.[393] For they pervert the disposition, which is the seed of actions, and the character, which is the principle and fountain of life, by attaching to vice names that belong properly only to virtue. For as Thucydides says,[394] in times of faction and war "people change the accustomed meaning of words as applied to acts at their will and pleasure, for reckless daring is then considered bravery to one's comrades, and prudent delay specious cowardice, and sober-mindedness the cloak of the coward, and taking everything into account before action a real desire to do nothing." So too in the case of flattery we must observe and be on our guard against wastefulness being called liberality, and cowardliness prudence, and madness quick-wittedness, and meanness frugality, and the amorous man called social and affectionate, and the term manly applied to the passionate and vain man, and the term civil applied to the paltry and mean man. As I remember Plato[395] says the lover is a flatterer of the beloved one, and calls the snub nose graceful, and the aquiline nose royal, and swarthy people manly, and fair people the children of the gods, and the olive complexion is merely the lover's phrase to gloss over and palliate excessive pallor. And yet the ugly man persuaded he is handsome, or the short man persuaded he is tall, cannot long remain in the error, and receives only slight injury from it, and not irreparable mischief: but praise applied to vices as if they were virtues, so that one is not vexed but delighted with a vicious life, removes all shame from wrong-doing, and was the ruin of the Sicilians, by calling the savage cruelty of Dionysius and Phalaris detestation of wickedness and uprightness. It was the ruin of Egypt, by styling Ptolemy's effeminacy, and superstition, and howlings, and beating of drums, religion and service to the gods.[396] It was nearly the overthrow and destruction of the ancient manners of the Romans, palliating the luxury and intemperance and display of Antony as exhibitions of jollity and kindliness, when his power and fortune were at their zenith. What else invested Ptolemy[397] with his pipe and fiddle? What else brought Nero[398] on the tragic stage, and invested him with the mask and buskins? Was it not the praise of flatterers? And are not many kings called Apollos if they can just sing a song,[399] and Dionysuses if they get drunk, and Herculeses if they can wrestle, and do they not joy in such titles, and are they not dragged into every kind of disgrace by flattery?

§ XIII. Wherefore we must be especially on our guard against the flatterer in regard to praise; as indeed he is very well aware himself, and clever to avoid suspicion. If he light upon some dandy, or rustic in a thick leather garment, he treats him with nothing but jeers and mocks,[400] as Struthias insulted Bias, ironically praising him for his stupidity, saying, "You have drunk more than king Alexander,"[401] and, "that he was ready to die of laughing at his tale about the Cyprian."[402] But when he sees people more refined very much on their guard, and observing both time and place, he does not praise them directly, but draws off a little and wheels round and approaches them noiselessly, as one tries to catch a wild animal. For sometimes he reports to a man the panegyric of other persons upon him, (as orators do, introducing some third person,) saying that he had a very pleasant conversation in the market with some strangers and men of worth, who mentioned how they admired his many good points. On another occasion he concocts and fabricates some false and trifling charges against him, pretending he has heard them from other people, and runs up with a serious face and inquires, where he said or did such and such a thing. And upon his denying he ever did, he pounces on him at once[403] and compliments his man with, "I thought it strange that you should have spoken ill of your friends, seeing that you don't even treat your enemies so: and that you should have tried to rob other people, seeing that you are so lavish with your own money."

§ XIV. Other flatterers again, just as painters heighten the effect of their pictures by the combination of light and shade, so by censure abuse detraction and ridicule of the opposite virtues secretly praise and foment the actual vices of those they flatter. Thus they censure modesty as merely rustic behaviour in the company of profligates, and greedy people, and villains, and such as have got rich by evil and dishonourable courses; and contentment and uprightness they call having no spirit or energy in action; and when they associate with lazy and idle persons who avoid all public duties, they are not ashamed to call the life of a citizen wearisome meddling in other people's affairs, and the desire to hold office fruitless vain-glory. And some ere now to flatter an orator have depreciated a philosopher, and others won favour with wanton women by traducing those wives who are faithful to their husbands as constitutionally cold and countrybred. And by an acme of villainy flatterers do not always spare even themselves. For as wrestlers stoop that they may the easier give their adversaries a fall, so by censuring themselves they glide into praising others. "I am a cowardly slave," says such a one, "at sea, I shirk labour, I am madly in rage if a word is said against me; but this man fears nothing, has no vices, is a rare good fellow, patient and easy in all circumstances." But if a person has an excellent idea of his own good sense, and desires to be austere and self-opinionated, and in his moral rectitude is ever spouting that line of Homer,

"Tydides, neither praise nor blame me much,"[404]

the artistic flatterer does not attack him as he attacked others, but employs against such a one a new device. For he comes to him about his own private affairs, as if desirous to have the advice of one wiser than himself; he has, he says, more intimate friends, but he is obliged to trouble him; "for whither shall we that are deficient in judgement go? whom shall we trust?" And having listened to his utterance he departs, saying he has received an oracle not an opinion. And if he notices that somebody lays claim to experience in oratory, he gives him some of his writings, and begs him to read and correct them. So, when king Mithridates took a fancy to play the surgeon, several of his friends offered themselves for operating upon, as for cutting or cauterizing, flattering in deed and not in word, for his being credited by them would seem to prove his skill.[405]

"For Providence has many different aspects."[406]

But we can test this kind of negative praise, that needs more wary caution, by purposely giving strange advice and suggestions, and by adopting absurd corrections. For if he raises no objection but nods assent to everything, and approves of everything, and is always crying out, "Good! How admirable!" he is evidently

"Asking advice, but seeking something else,"

wishing by praise to puff you up.

§ XV. Moreover, as some have defined painting to be silent poetry,[407] so is there praise in silent flattery. For as hunters are more likely to catch the objects of their chase unawares, if they do not openly appear to be so engaged, but seem to be walking, or tending their sheep, or looking after the farm, so flatterers obtain most success in their praise, when they do not seem to be praising but to be doing something else. For he who gives up his place or seat to the great man when he comes in, and while making a speech to the people or senate breaks off even in the middle, if he observes any rich man wants to speak, and gives up to him alike speech and platform, shows by his silence even more than he would by any amount of vociferation that he thinks the other the better man, and superior to him in judgement. And consequently you may always see them occupying the best places at theatres and public assembly rooms, not that they think themselves worthy of them, but that they may flatter the rich by giving up their places to them; and at public meetings they begin speaking first, and then make way as for better men, and most readily take back their own view, if any influential or rich or famous person espouse the contrary view. And so one can see plainly that all such servility and drawing back on their part is a lowering their sails, not to experience or virtue or age, but to wealth and fame. Not so Apelles the famous painter, who, when Megabyzus sat with him, and wished to talk about lines and shades, said to him, "Do you see my lads yonder grinding colours, they admired just now your purple and gold, but now they are laughing at you for beginning to talk about what you don't understand."[408] And Solon, when Croesus asked him about happiness, replied that Tellus, an obscure Athenian, and Bito and Cleobis were happier than he was.[409] But flatterers proclaim kings and rich men and rulers not only happy and fortunate, but also pre-eminent for wisdom, and art, and every virtue.

§ XVI. Now some cannot bear to hear the assertion of the Stoics[410] that the wise man is at once rich, and handsome, and noble, and a king; but flatterers declare that the rich man is at once orator and poet, and (if he likes) painter, and flute-player, and swift-footed, and strong, falling down if he wrestles with them, and if contending with him in running letting him win the race, as Crisso of Himera purposely allowed Alexander to outrun him, which vexed the king very much when he heard of it.[411] And Carneades said that the sons of rich men and kings learnt nothing really well and properly except how to ride, for their master praised and flattered them in their studies, and the person who taught them wrestling always let them throw him, whereas the horse, not knowing or caring whether his rider were a private person or ruler, rich or poor, soon threw him over his head if he could not ride well. Simple therefore and fatuous was that remark of Bion, "If you could by encomiums make your field to yield well and be fruitful, you could not be thought wrong in tilling it so rather than digging it and labouring in it: nor would it be strange in you to praise human beings if by so doing you could be useful and serviceable to them." For a field does not become worse by being praised, but those who praise a man falsely and against his deserts puff him up and ruin him.

§ XVII. Enough has been said on this matter: let us now examine outspokenness. For just as Patroclus put on the armour of Achilles, and drove his horses to the battle, only durst not touch his spear from Mount Pelion, but let that alone, so ought the flatterer, tricked out and modelled in the distinctive marks and tokens of the friend, to leave untouched and uncopied only his outspokenness, as the special burden of friendship, "heavy, huge, strong."[412] But since flatterers, to avoid the blame they incur by their buffoonery, and drinking, and gibes, and jokes, sometimes work their ends by frowns and gravity, and intermix censure and reproof, let us not pass this over either without examination. And I think, as in Menander's Play the sham Hercules comes on the stage not with a club stout and strong, but with a light and hollow cane, so the outspokenness of the flatterer is to those who experience it mild and soft, and the very reverse of vigorous, and like those cushions for women's heads, which seem able to stand their ground, but in reality yield and give way under their pressure; so this sham outspokenness is puffed up and inflated with an empty and spurious and hollow bombast, that when it contracts and collapses draws in the person who relies on it. For true and friendly outspokenness attacks wrong-doers, bringing pain that is salutary and likely to make them more careful, like honey biting but cleansing ulcerated parts of the body,[413] but in other respects serviceable and sweet. But we will speak of this anon.[414] But the flatterer first exhibits himself as disagreeable and passionate and unforgiving in his dealings with others. For he is harsh to his servants, and a terrible fellow to attack and ferret out the faults of his kinsmen and friends, and to look up to and respect nobody who is a stranger, but to look down upon them, and is relentless and mischief-making in making people provoked with others, hunting after the reputation of hating vice, as one not likely knowingly to mince matters with the vicious, or ingratiate himself with them either in word or deed. Next he pretends to know nothing of real and great crimes, but he is a terrible fellow to inveigh against trifling and external shortcomings, and to fasten on them with intensity and vehemence, as if he sees any pot or pipkin out of its place, or anyone badly housed, or neglecting his beard or attire, or not adequately attending to a horse or dog. But contempt of parents, and neglect of children, and bad treatment of wife, and haughtiness to friends, and throwing away money, all this he cares nothing about, but is silent and does not dare to make any allusion to it: just as if the trainer in a gymnasium were to allow the athlete to get drunk and live in debauchery,[415] and yet be vexed at the condition of his oil-flask or strigil if out of order; or as if the schoolmaster scolded a boy about his tablet and pen, but paid no attention to a solecism or barbarism. The flatterer is like a man who should make no comment on the speech of a silly and ridiculous orator, but should find fault with his voice, and chide him for injuring his throat by drinking cold water; or like a person bidden to read some wretched composition, who should merely find fault with the thickness of the paper, and call the copyist a dirty and careless fellow. So too when Ptolemy seemed to desire to become learned, his flatterers used to spin out the time till midnight, disputing about some word or line or history, but not one of them all objected to his cruelty and outrages, his torturing and beating people to death.[416] Just as if, when a man has tumours and fistulas, one were to cut his hair and nails with a surgeon's knife, so flatterers use outspokenness only in cases where it gives no pain or distress.

§ XVIII. Moreover some of them are cleverer still and make their outspokenness and censure a means of imparting pleasure. As Agis the Argive,[417] when Alexander bestowed great gifts on a buffoon, cried out in envy and displeasure, "What a piece of absurdity!" and on the king turning angrily to him and saying, "What are you talking about?" he replied, "I admit that I am vexed and put out, when I see that all you descendants of Zeus alike take delight in flatterers and jesters, for Hercules had his Cercopes, and Dionysus his Sileni, and with you too I see that such are held in good repute." And on one occasion, when the Emperor Tiberius entered the senate, one of his flatterers got up and said, that being free men they ought to be outspoken, and not suppress or conceal anything that might be important, and having by this exordium engaged everybody's attention, a dead silence prevailing, and even Tiberius being all attention, he said, "Listen, Cæsar, to what we all charge you with, although no one ventures to tell you openly of it; you neglect yourself, and are careless about your health, and wear yourself out with anxiety and labour on our behalf, taking no rest either by night or day." And on his stringing much more together in the same strain, they say the orator Cassius Severus said, "This outspokenness will ruin the man."

§ XIX. These are indeed trifling matters: but the following are more important and do mischief to foolish people, when flatterers accuse them of the very contrary vices and passions to those to which they are really addicted; as Himerius the flatterer twitted a very rich, very mean, and very covetous Athenian with being a careless spendthrift, and likely one day to want bread as well as his children; or on the other hand if they rail at extravagant spendthrifts for meanness and sordidness, as Titus Petronius railed at Nero; or exhort rulers who make savage and cruel attacks on their subjects to lay aside their excessive clemency, and unseasonable and inexpedient mercy. Similar to these is the person who pretends to be on his guard against and afraid of a silly stupid fellow as if he were clever and cunning; and the one who, if any person fond of detraction, rejoicing in defamation and censure, should be induced on any occasion to praise some man of note, fastens on him and alleges against him that he has an itch for praising people. "You are always extolling people of no merit: for who is this fellow, or what has he said or done out of the common?" But it is in regard to the objects of their love that they mostly attack those they flatter, and additionally inflame them. For if they see people at variance with their brothers, or despising their parents, or treating their wives contemptuously, they neither take them to task nor scold them, but fan the flame of their anger still more. "You don't sufficiently appreciate yourself," they say, "you are yourself the cause of your being put upon in this way, through your constant submissiveness and humility." And if there is any tiff or fit of jealousy in regard to some courtesan or adulteress, the flatterer is at hand with remarkable outspokenness, adding fuel to flame,[418] and taking the lady's part, and accusing her lover of acting in a very unkind harsh and shameful manner to her,

"O ingrate, after all those frequent kisses!"[419]

Thus Antony's friends, when he was passionately in love with the Egyptian woman,[420] persuaded him that he was loved by her, and twitted him with being cold and haughty to her. "She," they said, "has left her mighty kingdom and happy mode of life, and is wasting her beauty, taking the field with you like some camp-follower,

"The while your heart is proof 'gainst all her charms,"[421]

as you neglect her love-lorn as she is." But he that is pleased at being reproached with his wrong-doing, and delights in those that censure him, as he never did in those that praised him, is unconscious that he is really perverted also by what seems to be rebuke. For such outspokenness is like the bites of wanton women,[422] that while seeming to hurt really tickle and excite pleasure. And just as if people mix pure wine, which is by itself an antidote against hemlock, with it and so offer it, they make the poison quite deadly, being rapidly carried to the heart by the warmth,[423] so ill-disposed men, knowing that outspokenness is a great antidote to flattery, make it a means of flattering. And so it was rather a bad answer Bias[424] made, to the person who inquired what was the most formidable animal, "Of wild animals the tyrant, and of tame the flatterer." For it would have been truer to observe that tame flatterers are those that are found round the baths and table, but the one that intrudes into the interior of the house and into the women's apartments with his curiosity and calumny and malignity, like the legs and arms of the polypus, is wild and savage and unmanageable.

§ XX. Now one kind of caution against his snares is to know and ever remember that, whereas the soul contains true and noble and reasoning elements, as also unreasoning and false and emotional ones, the friend is always a counsellor and adviser to the better instincts of the soul, as the physician improves and maintains health, whereas the flatterer works upon the emotional and unreasoning ones, and tickles and titillates them and seduces them from reason, employing sensuality as his bait. As then there are some kinds of food which neither benefit the blood or spirit, nor brace up the nerves and marrow, but stir the passions, excite the lower nature, and make the flesh unsound and rotten, so the language of the flatterer adds nothing to soberness and reason, but encourages some love passion, or stirs up foolish rage, or incites to envy, or produces the empty and burdensome vanity of pride, or joins in bewailing woes, or ever by his calumnies and hints makes malignity and illiberality and suspicion sharp and timid and jealous, and cannot fail to be detected by those that closely observe him. For he is ever anchoring himself upon some passion, and fattening it, and, like a bubo, fastens himself on some unsound and inflamed parts of the soul. Are you angry? Have your revenge, says he. Do you desire anything? Get it. Are you afraid? Let us flee. Do you suspect? Entertain no doubts about it. But if he is difficult to detect in thus playing upon our passions, since they often overthrow reason by their intensity and strength, he will give a handle to find him out in smaller matters, being consistent in them too. For if anyone feels a little uneasy after a surfeit or excess in drink, and so is a little particular about his food and doubts the advisability of taking a bath, a friend will try and check him from excess, and bid him be careful and not indulge, whereas the flatterer will drag him to the bath, bid him serve up some fresh food, and not starve himself and so injure his constitution. And if he see him reluctant about a journey or voyage or some business or other, he will say that there is no hurry, that it's all one whether the business be put off, or somebody else despatched to look after it. And if you have promised to lend or give some money to a friend, but have repented of your offer, and yet feel ashamed not to keep your promise, the flatterer will throw his influence into the worse scale, he will confirm your desire to save your purse, he will destroy your reluctance, and will bid you be careful as having many expenses, and others to think about besides that person. And so, unless we are entirely ignorant of our desires, our shamelessness, and our timidity, the flatterer cannot easily escape our detection. For he is ever the advocate of those passions, and outspoken when we desire to repress them.[425] But so much for this matter.

§ XXI. Now let us pass on to useful and kind services, for in them too the flatterer makes it very difficult and confusing to detect him from the friend, seeming to be zealous and ready on all occasions and never crying off. For, as Euripides says,[426] a friend's behaviour is, "like the utterance of truth, simple," and plain and inartificial, while that of the flatterer "is in itself unsound, and needs wise remedies," aye, by Zeus, and many such, and not ordinary ones. As for example in chance meetings the friend often neither speaks nor is spoken to, but merely looks and smiles, and then passes on, showing his inner affection and goodwill only by his countenance, which his friend also reciprocates, but the flatterer runs up, follows, holds out his hand at a distance, and if he is seen and addressed first, frequently protests with oaths, and calls witnesses to prove, that he did not see you. So in business friends neglect many unimportant points, are not too punctilious and officious, and do not thrust themselves upon every service, but the flatterer is persevering and unceasing and indefatigable in it, giving nobody else either room or place to help, but putting himself wholly at your disposal, and if you will not find him something to do for you, he is troubled, nay rather altogether dejected and lamenting loudly.[427]

§ XXII. To all sensible people all this is an indication, not of true or sober friendship, but of a meretricious one, that embraces you more warmly than there is any occasion for. Nevertheless let us first look at the difference between the friend and flatterer in their promises. For it has been well said by those who have handled this subject before us, that the friend's promise is,

"If I can do it, and 'tis to be done,"

but the flatterer's is,

"Speak out your mind, whate'er it is, to me."[428]

And the comic dramatists put such fellows on the stage,

"Nicomachus, pit me against that soldier, See if I beat him not into a jelly, And make his face e'en softer than a sponge."[429]

In the next place no friend participates in any matter, unless he has first been asked his advice, and put the matter to the test, and set it on a suitable and expedient basis. But the flatterer, if anyone allows him to examine a matter and give his opinion on it, not only wishes to gratify him by compliance, but also fearing to be looked upon with suspicion as unwilling and reluctant to engage in the business, gives in to and even urges on his friend's desire. For there is hardly any king or rich man who would say,

"O that a beggar I could find, or worse Than beggar, if, with good intent to me, He would lay bare his heart boldly and honestly;"[430]

but, like the tragedians, they require a chorus of sympathizing friends, or the applause of a theatre. And so Merope gives the following advice in the tragedy,

"Choose you for friends those who will speak their mind, For those bad men that only speak to please See that you bolt and bar out of your house."[431]

But they act just the contrary, for they turn away with horror from those who speak their mind, and hold different views as to what is expedient, while they welcome those bad and illiberal impostors (that only speak to please them) not only within their houses, but also to their affections and secrets. Now the simpler of these do not think right or claim to advise you in important matters, but only to assist in the carrying out of them: but the more cunning one stands by during the discussion, and knits his brows, and nods assent with his head, but says nothing, but if his friend express an opinion, he then says, "Hercules, you only just anticipated me, I was about to make that very remark." For as the mathematicians tell us that surfaces and lines neither bend nor extend nor move of themselves, being without body and only perceived by the mind, but only bend and extend and change their position with the bodies whose extremities they are: so you will catch the flatterer ever assenting with, and agreeing with, aye, and feeling with, and being angry with, another, so easy of detection in all these points of view is the difference between the friend and the flatterer. Moreover as regards the kind of good service. For the favour done by a friend, as the principal strength of an animal is within, is not for display or ostentation, but frequently as a doctor cures his patient imperceptibly, so a friend benefits by his intervention, or by paying off creditors, or by managing his friend's affairs, even though the person who receives the benefit may not be aware of it. Such was the behaviour of Arcesilaus on various occasions, and when Apelles[432] of Chios was ill, knowing his poverty, he took with him twenty drachmæ when he visited him, and sitting down beside him he said, "There is nothing here but those elements of Empedocles, 'fire and water and earth and balmy expanse of air,' but you don't lie very comfortably," and with that he moved his pillow, and privately put the money under it. And when his old housekeeper found it, and wonderingly told Apelles of it, he laughed and said, "This is some trick of Arcesilaus." And the saying is also true in philosophy that "children are like their parents."[433] For when Cephisocrates had to stand his trial on a bill of indictment, Lacydes (who was an intimate friend of Arcesilaus) stood by him with several other friends, and when the prosecutor asked for his ring, which was the principal evidence against him, Cephisocrates quietly dropped it on the ground, and Lacydes noticing this put his foot on it and so hid it. And after sentence was pronounced in his favour, Cephisocrates going up to thank the jury, one of them who had seen the artifice told him to thank Lacydes, and related to him all the matter, though Lacydes had not said a word about it to anybody. So also I think the gods do often perform benefits secretly, taking a natural delight in bestowing their favours and bounties.[434] But the good service of the flatterer has no justice, or genuineness, or simplicity, or liberality about it; but is accompanied with sweat, and running about, and noise, and knitting of the brow, creating an impression and appearance of toilsome and bustling service, like a painting over-curiously wrought in bold colours, and with bent folds wrinkles and angles, to make the closer resemblance to life. Moreover he tires one by relating what journeys and anxieties he has had over the matter, how many enemies he has made over it, the thousand bothers and annoyances he has gone through, so that you say, "The affair was not worth all this trouble." For being reminded of any favour done to one is always unpleasant and disagreeable and insufferable:[435] but the flatterer not only reminds us of his services afterwards, but even during the very moment of doing them upbraids us with them and is importunate. But the friend, if he is obliged to mention the matter, relates it modestly, and says not a word about himself. And so, when the Lacedæmonians sent corn to the people of Smyrna that needed it, and the people of Smyrna wondered at their kindness, the Lacedæmonians said, "It was no great matter, we only voted that we and our beasts of burden should go without our dinner one day, and sent what was so saved to you."[436] Not only is it handsome to do a favour in that way, but it is more pleasant to the receivers of it, because they think those who have done them the service have done it at no great loss to themselves.

§ XXIII. But it is not so much by the importunity of the flatterer in regard to services, nor by his facility in making promises, that one can recognize his nature, as by the honourable or dishonourable kind of service, and by the regard to please or to be of real use. For the friend is not as Gorgias defined him, one who will ask his friend to help him in what is right, while he will himself do many services for his friend that are not right.

"For friend should share in good not in bad action."[437]

He will therefore rather try and turn him away from what is not becoming, and if he cannot persuade him, good is that answer of Phocion to Antipater, "You cannot have me both as friend and flatterer,"[438] that is, as friend and no friend. For one must indeed assist one's friend but not do anything wrong for him, one must advise with him but not plot with him, one must bear witness for him but not join him in fraud, one must certainly share adversity with him but not crime. For since we should not wish even to know of our friends' dishonourable acts, much less should we desire to share their dishonour by acting with them. As then the Lacedæmonians, when conquered in battle by Antipater, on settling the terms of peace, begged that he would lay upon them what burdens he pleased, provided he enjoined nothing dishonourable, so the friend, if any necessity arise involving expense or danger or trouble, is the first to desire to be applied to and share in it with alacrity and without crying off, but if there be anything disgraceful in connection with it he begs to have nothing to do with it. The flatterer on the contrary cries off from toilsome and dangerous employments, and if you put him to the test by ringing him,[439] he returns a hollow and spurious sound, and finds some excuse; whereas use him in disgraceful and low and disreputable service, and trample upon him, he will think no treatment too bad or ignominious. Have you observed the ape? He cannot guard the house like the dog, nor bear burdens like the horse, nor plough like the ox, so he has to bear insult and ribaldry, and put up with being made sport of, exhibiting himself as an instrument to produce laughter. So too the flatterer, who can neither advocate your cause, nor give you useful counsel, nor share in your contention with anybody, but shirks all labour and toil, never makes any excuses in underhand transactions, is sure to lend a helping hand in any love affair, is energetic in setting free some harlot, and not careless in clearing off the account of a drinking score, nor remiss in making preparations for banquets, and obsequious to concubines, but if ordered to be uncivil to your relations, or to help in turning your wife out of doors, he is relentless and not to be put out of countenance. So that he is not hard to detect here too. For if ordered to do anything you please disreputable or dishonourable, he is ready to take any pains to oblige you.

§ XXIV. One might detect again how greatly the flatterer differs from the friend by his behaviour to other friends. For the friend is best pleased with loving and being beloved by many, and also always tries to contrive for his friend that he too may be much loved and honoured, for he believes in the proverb "the goods of friends are common property,"[440] and thinks it ought to apply to nothing more than to friends; but the false and spurious and counterfeit friend, knowing how much he debases friendship, like debased and spurious coin, is not only by nature envious, but shows his envy even of those who are like himself, striving to outdo them in scurrility and gossip, while he quakes and trembles at any of his betters, not by Zeus "merely walking on foot by their Lydian chariot," but, to use the language of Simonides, "not even, having pure lead by comparison with their refined gold."[441] Whenever then, being light and counterfeit and false, he is put to the test at close quarters with a true and solid and cast-iron friendship, he cannot stand the test but is detected at once, and imitates the conduct of the painter that painted some wretched cocks, for he ordered his lad to scare away all live cocks as far from his picture as possible. So he too scares away real friends and will not let them come near if he can help it, but if he cannot prevent that, he openly fawns upon them, and courts them, and admires them as his betters, but privately runs them down and spreads calumnies about them. And when secret detraction has produced a sore feeling,[442] if he has not effected his end completely, he remembers and observes the teaching of Medius, who was the chief of Alexander's flatterers, and a leading sophist in conspiracy against the best men. He bade people confidently sow their calumny broadcast and bite with it, teaching them that even if the person injured should heal his sore, the scar of the calumny would remain. Consumed by these scars, or rather gangrenes and cancers, Alexander put to death Callisthenes, and Parmenio, and Philotas; while he himself submitted to be completely outwitted by such as Agnon, and Bagoas, and Agesias, and Demetrius, who worshipped him and tricked him up and feigned him to be a barbaric god. So great is the power of flattery, and nowhere greater, as it seems, than among the greatest people. For their thinking and wishing the best about themselves makes them credit the flatterer, and gives him courage.[443] For lofty heights are difficult of approach and hard to reach for those who endeavour to scale them, but the highmindedness and conceit of a person thrown off his balance by good fortune or good natural parts is easily reached by mean and petty people.

§ XXV. And so we advised at the beginning of this discourse, and now advise again, to cut off self-love and too high an opinion of ourselves; for that flatters us first, and makes us more impressionable and prepared for external flatterers. But if we hearken to the god, and recognize the immense importance to everyone of that saying, "Know thyself,"[444] and at the same time carefully observe our nature and education and training, with its thousand shortcomings in respect to good, and the large proportion of vice and vanity mixed up with our words and deeds and feelings, we shall not make ourselves so easy a mark for flatterers. Alexander said that he disbelieved those who called him a god chiefly in regard to sleep and the sexual delight, for in both those things he was more ignoble and emotional than in other respects.[445] So we, if we observe the blots, blemishes, shortcomings, and imperfections of our private selves, shall perceive clearly that we do not need a friend who shall bestow upon us praise and panegyric, but one that will reprove us, and speak plainly to us, aye, by Zeus, and censure us if we have done amiss. For it is only a few out of many that venture to speak plainly to their friends rather than gratify them, and even among those few you will not easily find any who know how to do so properly, for they think they are outspoken when they abuse and scold. And yet, just as in the case of any other medicine, to employ freedom of speech unseasonably is only to give needless pain and trouble, and in a manner to do so as to produce vexation the very thing the flatterer does so as to produce pleasure. For it does people harm not only to praise them unseasonably but also to blame them unseasonably, and especially exposes them to the successful attack of flatterers, for, like water, they abandon the rugged hills for the soft grassy valleys. And so outspokenness ought to be tempered with kindness, and reason ought to be called in to correct its excessive tartness, (as we tone down the too powerful glare of a lamp), that people may not, by being troubled and grieved at continual blame and rebuke, fly for refuge to the shade of the flatterer, and turn aside to him to free themselves from annoyance. For we ought, Philopappus, to banish all vice by virtue, not by the opposite vice, as some hold,[446] by exchanging modesty for impudence, and countrified ways for town ribaldry, and by removing their character as far as possible from cowardice and effeminacy, even if that should make people get very near to audacity and foolhardiness. And some even make superstition a plea for atheism, and stupidity a plea for knavery, perverting their nature, like a stick bent double, from inability to set it straight. But the basest disowning of flattery is to be disagreeable without any purpose in view, and it shows an altogether inelegant and clumsy unfitness for social intercourse to shun by unpleasing moroseness the suspicion of being mean and servile in friendship; like the freedman in the comedy who thought railing only enjoying freedom of speech. Seeing then, that it is equally disgraceful to become a flatterer through trying only to please, as in avoiding flattery to destroy all friendship and intimacy by excessive freedom of speech, we must avoid both these extremes, and, as in any other case, make our freedom of speech agreeable by its moderation. So the subject itself seems next to demand that I should conclude it by discussing that point.

§ XXVI. As then we see that much trouble arises from excessive freedom of speech, let us first of all detach from it any element of self-love, being carefully on our guard that we may not appear to upbraid on account of any private hurt or injury. For people do not regard a speech on the speaker's own behalf as arising from goodwill, but from anger, and reproach rather than admonition. For freedom in speech is friendly and has weight, but reproach is selfish and little. And so people respect and admire those that speak their mind freely, but accuse back and despise those that reproach them: as Agamemnon would not stand the moderate freedom of speech of Achilles, but submitted to and endured the bitter attack and speech of Odysseus,

"Pernicious chief, would that thou didst command Some sorry host, and not such men as these!"[447]

for he was restrained by the carefulness and sobriety of his speech, and also Odysseus had no private motive of anger but only spoke out on behalf of Greece,[448] whereas Achilles seemed rather vexed on his own account. And Achilles himself, though not sweet-tempered or mild of mood, but "a terrible man, and one that would perchance blame an innocent person,"[449] yet silently listened to Patroclus bringing against him many such charges as the following,

"Pitiless one, thy sire never was Knight Peleus, nor thy mother gentle Thetis, But the blue sea and steep and rocky crags Thy parents were, so flinty is thy heart."[450]

For as Hyperides the orator bade the Athenians consider not only whether he spoke bitterly, but whether he spoke so from interested motives,[451] so the rebuke of a friend void of all private feeling is solemn and grave and what one dare not lightly face. And if anyone shows plainly in his freedom of speech, that he altogether passes over and dismisses any offences his friend has done to himself, and only blames him for other shortcomings, and does not spare him but gives him pain for the interests of others, the tone of his outspokenness is invincible, and the sweetness of his manner even intensifies the bitterness and austerity of his rebuke. And so it has well been said, that in anger and differences with our friends we ought more especially to act with a view to their interest or honour. And no less friendly is it, when it appears that we have been passed over and neglected, to boldly put in a word for others that are neglected too, and to remind people of them, as Plato, when he was out of favour with Dionysius, begged for an audience, and Dionysius granted it, thinking that Plato had some personal grievance and was going to enter into it, but Plato opened the conversation as follows, "If, Dionysius, you knew that some enemy had sailed to Sicily with a view to do you some harm, but found no opportunity, would you allow him to sail back again, and go off scot-free?" "Certainly not, Plato," replied Dionysius, "for we must not only hate and punish the deeds of our enemies, but also their intentions." "If then," said Plato, "anyone has come here for your benefit, and wishes to do you good, and you do not find him an opportunity, is it right to let him go away with neglect and without thanks?" And on Dionysius asking, who he meant, he replied, "I mean Æschines, a man of as good a character as any of Socrates' pupils whatever, and able to improve by his conversation any with whom he might associate: and he is neglected, though he has made a long voyage here to discuss philosophy with you." This speech so affected Dionysius, that he at once threw his arms round Plato and embraced him, admiring his benevolence and loftiness of mind, and treated Æschines well and handsomely.

§ XXVII. In the next place, let us clear away as it were and remove all insolence, and jeering, and mocking, and ribaldry, which are the evil seasonings of freedom of speech. For as, when the surgeon performs an operation, a certain neatness and delicacy of touch ought to accompany his use of the knife, but all pantomimic and venturesome and fashionable suppleness and over-finicalness ought to be far away from his hand, so freedom of speech admits of dexterity and politeness, provided that a pleasant way of putting it does not destroy the power of the rebuke, for impudence and coarseness and insolence, if added to freedom of speech, entirely mar and ruin the effect. And so the harper plausibly and elegantly silenced Philip, who ventured to dispute with him about proper playing on the harp, by answering him, "God forbid that you should be so unfortunate, O king, as to understand harping better than me." But that was not a right answer of Epicharmus, when Hiero a few days after putting to death some of his friends invited him to supper, "You did not invite me," he said, "the other day, when you sacrificed your friends." Bad also was that answer of Antiphon, who, when Dionysius asked him "which was the best kind of bronze," answered, "That of which the Athenians made statues of Harmodius and Aristogiton." For this unpleasant and bitter kind of language profits not those that use it, nor does scurrility and puerile jesting please, but such kind of speeches are indications of an incontinent tongue inspired by hate, and full of malignity and insolence, and those who use such language do but ruin themselves, recklessly dancing on the verge of a well.[452] For Antiphon was put to death by Dionysius, and Timagenes lost the friendship of Augustus, not by using on any occasion too free a tongue, but at supper-parties and walks always declining to talk seriously, "only saying what he knew would make the Argives laugh,"[453] and thus virtually charging friendship with being only a cloak for abuse. For even the comic poets have introduced on the stage many grave sentiments well adapted to public life, but joking and ribaldry being mixed with them, like insipid sauces with food, destroy their effect and make them lose their nourishing power, so that the comic poets only get a reputation for malignity and coarseness, and the audience get no benefit from what is said. We may on other occasions jest and laugh with our friends, but let our outspokenness be coupled with seriousness and gravity, and if it be on important matters, let our speech be trustworthy and moving from its pathos, and animation, and tone of voice. And on all occasions to let an opportunity slip by is very injurious, but especially does it destroy the usefulness of freedom of speech. It is plain therefore that we must abstain from freedom of speech when men are in their cups. For he disturbs the harmony of a social gathering[454] who, in the midst of mirth and jollity, introduces a topic that shall knit the brows and contract the face, and shall act as a damper to the Lysian[455] god, who, as Pindar says, "looses the rope of all our cares and anxieties." There is also great danger in such ill-timed freedom of speech. For wine makes people easily slip into rage, and oftentimes freedom of speech in liquor makes enemies. And generally speaking it is not noble or brave but cowardly to conceal your ideas when people are sober and to give free vent to them at table, snarling like cowardly dogs. We need say no more therefore on this head.

§ XXVIII. But since many people do not think fit or even dare to find fault with their friends when in prosperity, but think that condition altogether out of the reach and range of rebuke, but inveigh against them if they have made a slip or stumble, and trample upon them if they are in dejection and in their power, and, like a stream swollen above its banks, pour upon them then the torrent of all their eloquence,[456] and enjoy and are glad at their reverse of fortune, owing to their former contempt of them when they were poor themselves, it is not amiss to discuss this somewhat, and to answer those words of Euripides,

"What need of friends, when things go well with us?"[457]

for those in prosperity stand in especial need of friends who shall be outspoken to them, and abate their excessive pride. For there are few who are sensible in prosperity, most need to borrow wisdom from others, and such considerations as shall keep them lowly when puffed up and giving themselves airs owing to their good fortune. But when the deity has abased them and stripped them of their conceit, there is something in their very circumstances to reprove them and bring about a change of mind. And so there is no need then of a friendly outspokenness, nor of weighty or caustic words, but truly in such reverses "it is sweet to look into the eyes of a friendly person,"[458] consoling and cheering one up: as Xenophon[459] tells us that the sight of Clearchus in battle and dangers, and his calm benevolent face, inspired courage in his men when in peril. But he who uses to a man in adversity too great freedom and severity of speech, like a man applying too pungent a remedy to an inflamed and angry eye, neither cures him nor abates his pain, but adds anger to his grief, and exasperates his mental distress. For example anyone well is not at all angry or fierce with a friend, who blames him for his excesses with women and wine, his laziness and taking no exercise, his frequent baths, and his unseasonable surfeiting: but to a person ill all this is unsufferable, and even worse than his illness to hear, "All this has happened to you through your intemperance, and luxury, your dainty food, and love for women." The patient answers, "How unseasonable is all this, good sir! I am making my will, the doctors are preparing me a dose of castor and scammony, and you are scolding me and plying me with philosophy." And thus the affairs of the unfortunate do not admit of outspokenness and a string of Polonius-like saws, but they require kindness and help. For when children fall down their nurses do not run up to them and scold, but pick them up, and clean them, and tidy their dress, and afterwards find fault and correct them. The story is told of Demetrius of Phalerum, when an exile from his native country, and living a humble and obscure life at Thebes, that he was not pleased to see Crates approaching, for he expected to receive from him cynical outspokenness and harsh language. But as Crates talked kindly to him, and discussed his exile, and pointed out that there was no evil in it, or anything that ought to put him about, for he had only got rid of the uncertainties and dangers of public life, and at the same time bade him trust in himself and his condition of mind, Demetrius cheered up and became happier, and said to his friends, "Out upon all my former business and employments, that left me no leisure to know such a man as this!"

"For friendly speech is good to one in grief, While bitter language only suits the fool."[460]

This is the way with generous friends. But the ignoble and low flatterers of those in prosperity, as Demosthenes says fractures and sprains always give us pain again when the body is not well,[461] adhere to them in reverses, as if they were pleased at and enjoyed them. But indeed if there be any need of reminding a man of the blunders he committed through unadvisedly following his own counsel, it is enough to say, "This was not to my mind, indeed I often tried to dissuade you from it."[462]

§ XXIX. In what cases then ought a friend to be vehement, and when ought he to use emphatic freedom of language? When circumstances call upon him to check some headlong pleasure or rage or insolence, or to curtail avarice, or to correct some foolish negligence. Thus Solon spoke out to Croesus, who was corrupted and enervated by insecure good fortune, bidding him look to the end.[463] Thus Socrates restrained Alcibiades, and wrung from him genuine tears by his reproof, and changed his heart.[464] Such also was the plain dealing of Cyrus with Cyaxares, and of Plato with Dion, for when Dion was most famous and attracted to himself the notice of all men, by the splendour and greatness of his exploits, Plato warned him to fear and be on his guard against "pleasing only himself, for so he would lose all his friends."[465] Speusippus also wrote to him not to plume himself on being a great person only with lads and women, but to see to it that by adorning Sicily with piety and justice and good laws he might make the Academy glorious. On the other hand Euctus and Eulæus, companions of Perseus, in the days of his prosperity ingratiated themselves with him, and assented to him in all things, and danced attendance upon him, like all the other courtiers, but when he fled after his defeat by the Romans at Pydna, they attacked him and censured him bitterly, reminding him and upbraiding him in regard to everything he had done amiss or neglected to do, till he was so greatly exasperated both from grief and rage that he whipped out his sword and killed both of them.

§ XXX. Let so much suffice for general occasions of freedom of speech. There are also particular occasions, which our friends themselves furnish, that one who really cares for his friends will not neglect, but make use of. In some cases a question, or narrative, or the censure or praise of similar things in other people, gives as it were the cue for freedom of speech. Thus it is related that Demaratus came to Macedonia from Corinth at the time when Philip was at variance with his wife and son, and when the king asked if the Greeks were at harmony with one another, Demaratus, being his well-wisher and friend, answered, "It is certainly very rich of you, Philip, inquiring as to concord between the Athenians and Peloponnesians, when you don't observe that your own house is full of strife and variance."[466] Good also was the answer of Diogenes, who, when Philip was marching to fight against the Greeks, stole into his camp, and was arrested and brought before him, and the king not recognizing him asked if he was a spy, "Certainly," replied he, "Philip, I have come to spy out your inconsiderate folly, which makes you, under no compulsion, come here and hazard your kingdom and life on a moment's[467] cast of the die." This was perhaps rather too strong a remark.

§ XXXI. Another suitable time for reproof is when people have been abused by others for their faults, and have consequently become humble, and abated their pride. The man of tact will ingeniously seize the occasion, checking and baffling those that used the abuse, but privately speaking seriously to his friend, and reminding him, that he ought to be more careful if for no other reason than to take off the edge of his enemies' satire. He will say, "How can they open their mouths against you, or what can they urge, if you give up and abandon what you get this bad name about?" Thus pain comes only from abuse, but profit from reproof. And some correct their friends more daintily by blaming others; censuring others for what they know are their friends' faults. Thus my master Ammonius in afternoon school, noticing that some of his pupils had not dined sufficiently simply, bade one of his freedmen scourge his own son, charging him with being unable to get through his dinner without vinegar,[468] but in acting thus he had an eye to us, so that this indirect rebuke touched the guilty persons.

§ XXXII. We must also beware of speaking too freely to a friend in the company of many people, remembering the well-known remark of Plato. For when Socrates reproved one of his friends too vehemently in a discussion at table, Plato said, "Would it not have been better to have said this privately?" Whereupon Socrates replied, "And you too, sir, would it not have become you to make this remark also privately?" And Pythagoras having rebuked one of his pupils somewhat harshly before many people, they say the young fellow went off and hung himself, and from that moment Pythagoras never again rebuked anyone in another's presence. For, as in the case of some foul disease, so also in the case of wrong-doing we ought to make the detection and exposure private, and not ostentatiously public by bringing witnesses and spectators. For it is not the part of a friend but a sophist to seek glory by the ill-fame of another, and to show off in company, like the doctors that perform wonderful cures in the theatres as an advertisement.[469] And independently of the insult, which ought not to be an element in any cure, we must remember that vice is contentious and obstinate. For it is not merely "love," as Euripides says, that "if checked becomes more vehement," but an unsparing rebuke before many people makes every infirmity and vice more impudent. As then Plato[470] urges old men who want to teach the young reverence to act reverently to them first themselves, so among friends a gentle rebuke is gently taken, and a cautious and careful approach and mild censure of the wrong-doer undermines and destroys vice, and makes its own modesty catching. So that line is most excellent, "holding his head near, that the others might not hear."[471] And most especially indecorous is it to expose a husband in the hearing of his wife, or a father before his children, or a lover in the presence of the loved one, or a master before his scholars. For people are beside themselves with pain and rage if reproached before those with whom they desire to be held in good repute. And I think it was not so much wine that exasperated Alexander with Clitus, as his seeming to put him down in the presence of many people. And Aristomenes, the tutor of Ptolemy,[472] because he went up to the king and woke him as he was asleep in an audience of some ambassadors, gave a handle to the king's flatterers who professed to be indignant on his behalf, and said, "If after your immense state-labours and many vigils you have been overpowered by sleep, he ought to have rebuked you privately, and not put his hands upon you before so many people." And Ptolemy sent for a cup of poison and ordered the poor man to drink it up. And Aristophanes said Cleon blamed him for "railing against the state when strangers were present,"[473] and so irritating the Athenians. We ought therefore to be very much on our guard in relation to this point too as well as others, if we wish not to make a display and catch the public ear, but to use our freedom of speech for beneficial purposes and to cure vice. Moreover, what Thucydides has represented the Corinthians saying of themselves, that "they had a right to blame their neighbours,"[474] is not a bad precept for those to remember who intend to use freedom of speech. Lysander, it seems, on one occasion said to a Megarian, who was speaking somewhat boldly on behalf of Greece among the allies, "Your words require a state to back them":[475] similarly every man's freedom of speech requires character behind it, and especially true is this in regard to those who censure and correct others. Thus Plato said that his life was a tacit rebuke to Speusippus: and doubtless Xenocrates by his mere presence in the schools, and by his earnest look at Polemo, made a changed man of him. Whereas a man of levity and bad character, if he ventures to rebuke anybody, is likely to hear the line,

"He doctors others, all diseased himself."[476]

§ XXXIII. Yet since circumstances frequently call on people who are bad themselves in association with other such to reprove them, the most convenient mode of reproof will be that which contrives to include the reprover in the same indictment as the reproved, as in the case of the line,

"Tydides, how on earth have we forgot Our old impetuous courage?"[477]

and,

"Now are we all not worth one single Hector."[478]

In this mild way did Socrates rebuke young men, as not himself without ignorance, but one that needed in common with them to prosecute virtue, and seek truth. For they gain goodwill and influence, who seem to have the same faults as their friends, and desire to correct themselves as well as them. But he who is high and mighty in setting down another, as if he were himself perfect and without any imperfections, unless he be of a very advanced age, or has an acknowledged reputation for virtue and worth, does no good, but is only regarded as a tiresome bore. And so it was wisely done of Phoenix to relate his own mishaps, how he had meant killing his father, but quickly repented at the thought "that he would be called by the Achæans parricide,"[479] that he might not seem to be rebuking Achilles, as one that had himself never suffered from excess of rage. For kindness of this sort has great influence, and people yield more to those who seem to be sympathetic and not supercilious. And since we ought not to expose an inflamed eye to a strong light, and a soul a prey to the passions cannot bear unmixed reproof and rebuke, one of the most useful remedies will be found to be a slight mixture of praise, as in the following lines,

"Ye will not sure give up your valiant courage, The best men in the host! I should not care If any coward left the fight, not I; But you to do so cuts me to the heart."[480]

And,

"Where is thy bow, where thy wing'd arrows, Pandarus, Where thy great fame, which no one here can match?"[481]

Such language again plainly cheers very much those that are down as,

"Where now is Oedipus, and his famous riddles?"[482]

and,

"Does much-enduring Hercules say this?"[483]

For not only does it soften the harsh imperiousness of censure, but also, by reminding a man of former noble deeds, implants a desire to emulate his former self in the person who is ashamed of what is low, and makes himself his own exemplar for better things. But if we make a comparison between him and other men, as his contemporaries, his fellow-citizens, or his relations, then the contentious spirit inherent in vice is vexed and exasperated, and is often apt to chime in angrily, "Why don't you go off to my betters then, and leave off bothering me?" We must therefore be on our guard against praising others, when we are rebuking a man, unless indeed it be their parents, as Agamemnon says in Homer,

"Little like Tydeus is his father's son!"[484]

or as Odysseus in the play called "The Scyrians,"[485]

"Dost thou card wool, and thus the lustre smirch Of thy illustrious sire, thy noble race?"

§ XXXIV. But it is by no means fitting when rebuked to rebuke back, and when spoken to plainly to answer back, for that soon kindles a flame and causes dissension; and generally speaking such altercation will not look so much like a retort as an inability to bear freedom of speech. It is better therefore to listen patiently to a friend's rebuke, for if he should afterwards do wrong himself and so need rebuke, he has set you the example of freedom of speech. For being reminded without any malice, that he himself has not been accustomed to spare his friends when they have done wrong, but to convince them and show them their fault, he will be the more inclined to yield and give himself up to correction, as it will seem a return of goodwill and kindness rather than scolding or rage.

§ XXXV. Moreover, as Thucydides says "he is well advised who [only] incurs envy in the most important matters,"[486] so the friend ought only to take upon himself the unpleasant duty of reproof in grave and momentous cases. For if he is always in a fret and a fume, and rates his acquaintances more like a tutor than a friend, his rebuke will be blunt and ineffective in cases of the highest importance, and he will resemble a doctor who dispenses some sharp and bitter, but important and costly, drug in trifling cases of common occurrence, where it was not at all needed, and so will lose all the advantages that might come from a judicious use of freedom of speech. He will therefore be very much on his guard against continual fault-finding, and if his friend is always pettifogging about minute matters, and is needlessly querulous, it will give him a handle against him in more important shortcomings. Philotimus the doctor, when a patient who had abscesses on his liver showed him his sore finger, said to him, "My friend, it is not the whitlow that matters."[487] So an opportunity sometimes offers itself to a friend to say to a man, who is always finding fault on small and trivial points, "Why are we always discussing mere child's play, tippling,[488] and trifles? Let such a one, my dear sir, send away his mistress, or give up playing at dice, he will then be in my opinion in all respects an excellent fellow." For he who receives pardon on small matters is content that his friend should rebuke him on matters of more moment: but the man who is ever on the scold, everywhere sour and glum, knowing and prying into everything, is scarcely tolerable to his children or brothers, and insufferable to his slaves.

§ XXXVI. But since "neither," to use the words of Euripides, "do all troubles proceed only from old age,"[489] nor from the stupidity of our friends, we ought to observe not only the shortcomings but also the good points of our friends, aye, by Zeus, and to be ready to praise them first, and only censure them afterwards. For as iron receives its consistency and temper by first being submitted to fire and so made soft and then dipped into cold water, so when friends have been first warmed and melted with praises we can afterwards use gentle remonstrance, which has a similar effect to that of dipping in the case of the metal. For an opportunity will offer itself to say, "Are those actions worthy to be compared with these? Do you see what fruits virtue yields? These are the things we your friends ask of you, these become you, for these you are designed by nature; but all that other kind of conduct we must reject with abhorrence, 'cast it away on a mountain, or throw it into the roaring sea.'"[490] For as a clever doctor would prefer to cure the illness of his patient by sleep and diet rather than by castor or scammony, so a kind friend and good father or teacher delight to use praise rather than blame to correct the character. For nothing makes rebuke less painful or more beneficial than to refrain from anger, and to inveigh against wrong-doing mildly and kindly. And so we ought not sharply to drive home the guilt of those who deny it, or prevent their making their defence, but even contrive to furnish them with specious excuses, and if they seem reluctant to give a bad motive for their action we ought ourselves to find for them a better, as Hector did for his brother Paris,

"Unhappy man, thy anger was not good,"[491]

suggesting that his absconding from the battle was not running away or cowardice, but only anger. And Nestor says to Agamemnon,

"You only yielded to your lofty passion."[492]

For it has, I think, a better moral tendency to say "You forgot," or "You did it inadvertently," than to say "You acted unfairly," or "You behaved shamefully:" as also "Don't contend with your brother," than "Don't envy your brother;" and "Avoid the woman who is your ruin," than "Stop ruining the woman." Such is the language employed in rebuke that desires to reform and not to wound; that rebuke which looks merely at the effect to be produced acts on another principle. For when it is necessary to stop people on the verge of wrong-doing, or to check some violent and irregular impulse, or if we wish to rouse and infuse vigour in those who prosecute virtue only feebly and languidly, we may then assign strange and unbecoming motives for their behaviour. As Odysseus in Sophocles' play,[493] striving to rouse Achilles, says he is not angry about his supper,[494] but "that he is afraid now that he looks upon the walls of Troy," and when Achilles was vexed at this, and talked of sailing home again, he said,

"I know what 'tis you shun: 'tis not ill fame: But Hector's near, it is not safe to beard him."

Thus by frightening the high-spirited and courageous man by the imputation of cowardice, and the sober and orderly man by that of licentiousness, and the liberal and munificent man by that of meanness and avarice, people urge them on to what is good, and deter them from what is bad, showing moderation in cases past remedy, and exhibiting in their freedom of speech more sorrow and sympathy than fault-finding; but in the prevention of wrong-doing and in earnest fighting against the passions they are vehement and inexorable and assiduous: for that is the time for downright plainness and truth. Besides we see that enemies censure one another for what they have done amiss, as Diogenes said,[495] he who wished to lead a good life ought to have good friends or red-hot enemies, for the former told you what was right, and the latter blamed you if you did what was wrong. But it is better to be on our guard against wrong actions, through listening to the persuasion of those that advise us well, than to repent, after we have done wrong, in consequence of the reproaches of our enemies. And so we ought to employ tact in our freedom of speech, as it is the greatest and most powerful remedy in friendship, and always needs a well-chosen occasion, and moderation in applying it.

§ XXXVII. Since then, as I have said before, freedom of speech is often painful to the person who is to receive benefit from it, we must imitate the surgeons, who, when they have performed an operation, do not leave the suffering part to pain and smart, but bathe and foment it; so those who do their rebuking daintily run[496] off after paining and smarting, and by different dealing and kind words soothe and mollify them, as statuaries smooth and polish images which have been broken or chipped. But he that is broken and wounded by rebuke, if he is left sullen and swelling with rage and off his equilibrium, is henceforth hard to win back or talk over. And so people who reprove ought to be especially careful on this point, and not to leave them too soon, nor break off their conversation and intercourse with their acquaintances at the exasperating and painful stage.

[348] Plato, "Laws," v. p. 731 D, E.

[349] "Laws," v. p. 730 C.

[350] Inscribed in the vestibule of the temple of Apollo at Delphi. See Pausanias, x. 24.

[351] Used here apparently proverbially for poverty or low position in life.

[352] Wyttenbach well compares Cicero, "De Amicitia," xviii.: "Accedat huc suavitas quædam oportet sermonum atque morum, haudquaquam mediocre condimentum amicitiæ. Tristitia autem et in omni re severitas, habet illa quidem gravitatem: sed amicitia remissior esse debet, et liberior, et dulcior, et ad omnem comitatem facilitatemque proclivior."

[353] Hesiod, "Theogony," 64.

[354] Euripides, "Ion," 732.

[355] Our author assigns this saying to Prodicus, "De Sanitate Præcepta," § viii. But to Evenus, "Quæst. Conviv." Lib. vii. Prooemium, and "Platonicæ Quæstiones," x. § iii.

[356] As was usual. See Homer, "Odyssey," i. 146. Cf. Plautus, "Persa," v. iii. 16: "Hoc age, accumbe: hunc diem suavem meum natalem agitemus amoenum: date aquam manibus: apponite mensam."

[357] From a play of Eupolis called "The Flatterers." Cf. Terence, "Eunuchus," 489-491.

[358] See Athenæus, 256 D. Compare also Valerius Maximus, ix. 1.

[359] "Videatur Casaubonus ad Athenæum, vi. p. 243 A."--*Wyttenbach.*

[360] "Republic," p. 361 A.

[361] See Herodotus, iii. 78.

[362] See Erasmus, "Adagia," p. 1883.

[363] "Proverbium etiam a Cicerone laudatum 'De Amicitia,' cap. vi.: Itaque non aqua, non igne, ut aiunt, pluribus locis utimur, quam amicitia. Notavit etiam Erasmus 'Adag.' p. 112."--*Wyttenbach.*

[364] Compare Sallust, "De Catilinæ Conjuratione," cap. xx.: "Nam idem velle atque idem nolle, ea demum firma amicitia est."

[365] "Proverbiale, quo utitur Plutarchus in Alcibiade, p. 203 D. Iambus Tragici esse videtur, ad Neoptolemum dictus."--*Wyttenbach.*

[366] As the polypus, or chameleon.

[367] Plato, "Phædrus," p. 239 D.

[368] Wyttenbach compares Juvenal, iii. 100-108.

[369] See my note "On Abundance of Friends," § ix. Wyttenbach well points out the felicity of the expression here, "siquidem parasitus est [Greek: aoikos kai anestios]."

[370] Euripides, "Hippolytus," 219, 218. Cf. Ovid, "Heroides," iv. 41, 42.

[371] Compare "How one may be aware of one's progress in virtue," § x. Cf. also Horace, "Satires," ii. iii. 35; Quintilian, xi. 1.

[372] "Odyssey," xxii. 1.

[373] The demagogue is a kind of flatterer. See Aristotle, "Pol." iv. 4.

[374] Cf. Aristophanes, "Acharnians," 153, [Greek: hoper machimôtaton thrakôn ethnos].

[375] Plato was somewhat of a traveller, he three times visited Syracuse, and also travelled in Egypt.

[376] As to the polypus, see "On Abundance of Friends," § ix.

[377] As "Fumum et opes *strepitumque* Romæ."--Horace, "Odes," iii. 29. 12.

[378] Homer, "Odyssey," xvi. 181.

[379] Sophocles, "Antigone," 523.

[380] As to these traits in Plato and Aristotle, compare "De Audiendis Poetis," § viii. And as to Alexander, Plutarch tells us in his Life that he used to hold his head a little to the left, "Life," p. 666 B. See also "De Alexandri Fortuna aut Virtute," § ii.

[381] "De Chamæleonte Aristoteles 'Hist. Animal.' i. 11; 'Part. Animal.' iv. 11; Theophrastus Eclog. ap. Photium edit. Aristot. Sylburg. T. viii. p. 329: [Greek: metaballei de ho chamaileôn eis panta ta chrômata; plên ten eis to leukon kai to eruthron ou dechetai metabolên.] Similiter Plinius 'Hist. Nat.' viii. 51."--*Wyttenbach.*

[382] See Athenæus, 249 F; 435 E.

[383] Cf. Juv. iii. 113; "Scire volunt secreta domus, atque inde timeri."

[384] Cf. Menander apud Stob. p. 437: [Greek: Ta deuter aiei tên gynaika dei legein, Tên d' êgemonian tôn olôn ton andr' echein].

[385] As Lord Stowell used to say that "dinners lubricated business."

[386] Homer, "Iliad," xi. 643.

[387] Homer, "Odyssey," iv. 178, 179.

[388] Perhaps the poley-germander. See Pliny, "Nat. Hist," xxi. 84. The line is from Nicander Theriac. 64.

[389] "Iliad," viii. 281, 282.

[390] "Iliad," x. 243.

[391] "Iliad," vii. 109, 110.

[392] Xenophon, "Agesilaus," xi. 5. p. 673 C.

[393] To filch the grain from the bin or granary would not of course be so important a theft as to steal the seed-stock preserved for sowing. So probably Cato, "De Re Rustica," v. § iv.: "Segetem ne defrudet," sc. villicus.

[394] Thucydides, iii. 82.

[395] Plato, "Republic," v. p. 474 E. Compare also Lucretius, iv. 1160-1170; Horace, "Satires," i. 3. 38 sq.

[396] This Ptolemy was a votary of Cybele, and a spiritual ancestor of General Booth. The worship of Cybele is well described by Lucretius, ii. 598-643.

[397] This was Ptolemy Auletes, as the former was Ptolemy Philopator.

[398] See Suetonius, "Nero," ch. 21.

[399] "Plerumque *minuta voce cantillare*."--*Wyttenbach*. What Milton would have called "a lean and flashy song."

[400] Naso suspendit adunco, as Horace, "Sat." i. 6. 5.

[401] See Athenæus, p. 434 C.

[402] As Gnatho in Terence, "Eunuch." 496-498.

[403] Reading [Greek: Helôn], as Courier, Hercher.

[404] "Iliad," x. 249. They are words of Odysseus.

[405] This was carrying flattery rather far. "Mithridatis medicinæ scientia multis memorata veterum."--*Wyttenbach*.

[406] Euripides, "Alcestis," 1159.

[407] Our author gives this definition to Simonides, "De Gloria Atheniensium," § iii.

[408] So our author again, "On Contentedness of Mind," § xii.

[409] See Herodotus, i. 30, 33; Juvenal, x. 274, 275; and Pausanias, ii. 20.

[410] "Nobile Stoæ Paradoxum. Cicero Fin. iii. 22, ex persona Catonis. Horatius ridet Epistol. i. 1. 106-108. Ad summam sapiens uno minor est Jove: dives, Liber, honoratus, pulcher, rex denique regum; Præcipue sanus, nisi quum pituita molesta est."--*Wyttenbach*.

[411] See also "On Contentedness of Mind," § xii.

[412] Homer, "Iliad," xvi. 141. See the context also from 130 sq.

[413] Our author has used this illustration again in "Phocion," p. 742 B.

[414] Namely in § xxvii. where [Greek: parrhêsia] is discussed.

[415] Contrary to the severe training he ought to undergo, well expressed by Horace, "De Arte Poetica," 412-414.

[416] Reading with Hercher [Greek: apotympanizontos kai streblountos]. This was Ptolemy Physcon.

[417] "Unus ex Alexandri adulatoribus: memoratus Curtio viii. 5, 6."--*Wyttenbach.*

[418] A common proverb among the ancients. See "Conjugal Precepts," § xl.; Erasmus, "Adagia," pp. 1222, 1838.

[419] A line out of Æschylus' "Myrmidons." Quoted again by our author, "Of Love," § V.

[420] Cleopatra.

[421] Homer, "Odyssey," x. 329. They are the words of Circe to Odysseus. But the line was suspected even by old grammarians, and is put in brackets in modern editions of the "Odyssey."

[422] See Lucretius, iv. 1079-1085.

[423] So Pliny, "Hist. Nat." xxv. 95: "Remedio est (cicutæ), priusquam perveniat ad vitalia, vini natura excalfactoria: sed in vino pota irremediabilis existimatur."

[424] Assigned to Pittacus by our author, "Septem Sapientum Convivium," § ii.

[425] So Wyttenbach, who reads [Greek: enstaseis], and translates, "et libertate loquendi in nobis reprehendendis utitur, quando nos cupiditatibus morbisque animi nostri non indulgere, sed resistere, volumus."

[426] "Phoenissæ," 469-472.

[427] Like Juvenal's "Græculus esuriens in cælum, jusseris, ibit."--Juvenal, iii, 78.

[428] These are two successive lines found three times in Homer, "Iliad," xiv. 195, 196; xviii. 426, 427; "Odyssey," v. 89, 90. The two lines are in each case spoken by one person.

[429] Probably lines from "The Flatterer" of Menander.

[430] From the "Ino" of Euripides.

[431] From the "Erechtheus" of Euripides.

[432] We know from Athenæus, p. 420 D, that Apelles and Arcesilaus were friends.

[433] An allusion to Hesiod, "Works and Days," 235. Cf. Horace, "Odes," iv. 5. 23.

[434] See the beautiful story of Baucis and Philemon, Ovid, "Metamorphoses," viii. 626-724: "Cura pii dis

sunt, et qui coluere coluntur."

[435] Compare Terence, "Andria," 43, 44. So too Seneca, "De Beneficiis," ii. 10: "Hæc enim beneficii inter duos lex est: alter statim oblivisci debet dati, alter accepti nunquam. Lacerat animum et premit frequens meritorum commemoratio."

[436] A similar story about the Samians and Lacedæmonians is told by Aristotle, "Oeconom." ii. 9.

[437] A line from Euripides, "Iphigenia in Aulis," 407.

[438] Also in "Conjugal Precepts," § xxix.

[439] See Persius, iii. 21, 22, with Jahn's Note.

[440] See "On Love," § xxi.

[441] "Auri plumbique oppositio fere proverbialis est. Petronius, 'Satyricon,' 43. Plane fortunæ filius: in manu illius plumbum aureum fiebat."--*Wyttenbach.* The passage about the Lydian chariot is said to be by Pindar in our author, "Nicias," p. 523 D.

[442] Wyttenbach compares Seneca, "Epist." cxxiii. p. 495: "Horum sermo multum nocet: nam etiamsi non statim officit, semina in animo relinquit, sequiturque nos etiam cum ab illis discesserimus, resurrecturum postea malum."

[443] Compare Cicero, "De Amicitia," xxvi.: "Assentatio, quamvis perniciosa sit, nocere tamen nemini potest, nisi ei, qui eam recipit atque ea delectatur. Ita fit, ut is assentatoribus patefaciat aures suas maxime, qui ipse sibi assentetur et se maxime ipse delectet."

[444] Compare § i.

[445] Compare our Author, "Quaestiones Convivalium," viii. p. 717 F.

[446] So Horace, "Satires," i. 2, 24: "Dum vitant stulti vitia in contraria currunt."

[447] Homer, "Iliad," xiv. 84, 85.

[448] Compare Cicero, "De Officiis," i. 25: "Omnis autem animadversio et castigatio contumelia vacare debet: neque ad ejus, qui punitur aliquem aut verbis fatigat, sed ad reipublicæ utilitatem referri."

[449] "Iliad," xi. 654.

[450] "Iliad," xvi. 33-35.

[451] Cf. Plutarch, "Phocion," p. 746 D.

[452] A proverb of persons on the brink of destruction. Wells among the ancients were uncovered.

[453] "Iliad," ii. 215, of Thersites. As to Theagenes, see Seneca, "De Ira," ii. 23.

[454] Literally, "brings a cloud over fair weather."

[455] The MSS. have Lydian. Lysian Dionysus is also found in Pausanias, ix. 16. Lyæus is suggested by

Wyttenbach, and read by Hercher. Lysius or Lyæus will both be connected with [Greek: luô], and so refer to Dionysus as the god that looses or frees us from care. See Horace, "Epodes," ix. 37, 38.

[456] Compare Juvenal, iii. 73, 74: "Sermo Promptus et Isæo torrentior."

[457] "Orestes," 667.

[458] Euripides, "Ion," 732.

[459] "Anabasis," ii. 6, 11.

[460] Perhaps by Euripides.

[461] "Olynth." ii. p. 8 C; "Pro Corona," 341 C.

[462] Homer, "Iliad," ix. 108, 109. They are the words of Nestor to Agamemnon.

[463] See Herodotus, i. 30-32.

[464] See Plato's "Symposium," p. 215 E.

[465] See Plato, "Epist." iv. p. 321 B.

[466] See our author, "Apophthegmata," p. 179 C.

[467] Compare Horace, "Satires," i. 1. 7, 8: "Quid enim, concurritur: horæ Momento cita mors venit aut victoria læta."

[468] And so being dainty. See Athenæus, ii. ch. 76.

[469] We see from this and other places that the mountebanks and quacks of the Middle Ages and later times existed also among the ancients. Human nature in its great leading features is ever the same. "Omne ignotum pro magnifico est."

[470] "Laws," p. 729 C.

[471] Homer, "Odyssey," i. 157; iv. 70; xvii. 592.

[472] Ptolemy V., Epiphanes. The circumstances are related by Polybius, xv. 29; xvii. 35.

[473] See "Acharnians," 501, 502.

[474] Thucydides, i. 70: [Greek: kai hama, eiper tines kai alloi, nomizomen axioi einai tois pelas psogon epenenkein].

[475] See our Author, "Apophthegmata," p. 190 E.

[476] A line of Euripides, quoted again in "How a Man may be benefited by his Enemies," § iv.

[477] Homer, "Iliad," xi. 313.

[478] Do. viii. 234, 235.

[479] Do. ix. 461.

[480] "Iliad," xiii. 116-119.

[481] Do. v. 171, 172.

[482] Euripides, "Phoenissæ," 1688.

[483] Euripides, "Hercules Furens," 1250.

[484] "Iliad," v. 800. Athene is the speaker.

[485] A play by Sophocles, now only in fragments, relating the life of Achilles in the island of Scyros, the scene of his amour with Deidamia, the daughter of Lycomedes, by whom he became the father of Pyrrhus.

[486] Thucydides, ii. 64. Quoted again in "On Shyness," § xviii.

[487] See also "De Audiendo," § x.

[488] [Greek: potous] comes in rather curiously here. Can any other word lurk under it?

[489] "Phoenissæ," 528, 529.

[490] Homer, "Iliad," vi. 347.

[491] Do. vi. 326.

[492] Homer, "Iliad," ix. 109, 110.

[493] In Dindorf's "Poetæ Scenici Græci," Fragment 152.

[494] As it is not quite clear why Achilles should have been angry about his supper, [Greek: dia to deipnon], apropos of the context, Wyttenbach ingeniously suggests, as this lost play of Sophocles was called [Greek: Syn deipnon], that Plutarch may have written [Greek: en tô Deipnô].

[495] Compare "How One may be aware of one's Progress in Virtue," § xi.

[496] "Ductum e proverbiali dictione [Greek: balonta ekpheugein], emisso telo aufugere."--*Wyttenbach.*

HOW A MAN MAY BE BENEFITED BY HIS ENEMIES.

§ I. I am well aware, Cornelius Pulcher, that you prefer the mildest manners in public life, by which you can be at once most useful to the community, and most agreeable in private life to those who have any dealings with you. But since it is difficult to find any region without wild beasts, though it is related of Crete;[497] and hitherto there has been no state that has not suffered from envy, rivalry, and strife, the most fruitful seeds of hostility; (for, even if nothing else does, our friendships involve us in enmities, as Chilo[498] the wise man perceived, who asked the man who told him he had no enemy, whether he had a friend either), it seems to me that a public man ought not only to examine the whole question of enemies in its various ramifications, but also to listen to the serious remark of Xenophon,[499] that a sensible man will receive profit even from his enemies. The ideas therefore that lately occurred to me to deliver, I have now put together nearly in the identical words and send them to you, with the exception of some matter also in "Political Precepts,"[500] a treatise which I have often noticed in your hands.

§ II. People in old times were well satisfied if they were not injured by strange and wild beasts, and that was the only motive of their fights with them, but those of later days have by now learnt to make use of them, for they feed on their flesh, and clothe themselves with their wool, and make medical use of their gall and beestings, and turn their hides into shields, so that we might reasonably fear, if beasts failed man, that his life would become brutish, and wild, and void of resources. Similarly since all others are satisfied with not being injured by their enemies, but the sensible will also (as Xenophon says) get profit out of them, we must not be incredulous, but seek a method and plan how to obtain this advantage, seeing that life without an enemy is impossible. The husbandman cannot cultivate every tree, nor can the hunter tame every kind of animal, so both seek means to derive profit according to their several necessities, the one from his barren trees, the other from his wild animals. Sea-water also is undrinkable and brackish, but it feeds fish, and is a sort of vehicle to convey and transport travellers anywhere. The Satyr, when he saw fire for the first time, wished to kiss it and embrace it, but Prometheus warned him,

"Goat, thou wilt surely mourn thy loss of beard."[501]

For fire burns whoever touches it, but it also gives light and warmth, and is an instrument of art to all those who know how to use it.[502] Consider also in the case of the enemy, if he is in other respects injurious and intractable, he somehow or other gives us a handle to make use of him by, and so is serviceable. And many things are unpleasant and detestable and antagonistic to those to whom they happen, but you must have noticed that some use even illnesses as a period of rest for the body, and others by excessive toil have strengthened and trained their bodily vigour, and some have made exile and the loss of money a passage to leisure and philosophy, as did Diogenes and Crates. And Zeno, when he heard of the wreck of the ship which contained all his property, said, "Thou hast done well, Fortune, to confine me to my threadbare cloak."[503]

For as those animals that have the strongest and healthiest stomachs eat and digest serpents and scorpions, and some even feed on stones and shells, which they convert into nourishment by the strength and heat of their stomachs, while fastidious people out of health almost vomit if offered bread and wine, so foolish people spoil even their friendships, while the wise know how to turn to account even their enmities.

§ III. In the first place then it seems to me that what is most injurious in enmity may become most useful to those that pay attention to it? To what do I refer? Why, to the way in which your enemy ever wide awake pries into all your affairs, and analyzes your whole life, trying to get a handle against you somewhere, able not only to look through a tree, like Lynceus,[504] or through stones and shells, but through your friend and domestic and every intimate acquaintance, as far as possible detecting your doings, and digging and ferreting into your designs. For our friends are ill and often die without our knowing anything about it through our delay and carelessness, but we almost pry into even the dreams of our enemies; and our enemy knows even more than we do ourselves of our diseases and debts and differences with our wives.[505] But they pay most attention to our faults and hunt them out: and as vultures follow the scent of putrid carcases, and cannot perceive sound and wholesome ones, so the diseases and vices and crimes of life attract the enemy, and on these those that hate us pounce, these they attack and tear to pieces. Is not this an advantage to us? Certainly it is. For it teaches us to live warily and be on our guard, and neither to do or say anything carelessly or without circumspection, but ever to be vigilant by careful mode of living that we give no handle to an enemy. For the cautiousness that thus represses the passions and follows reason implants a care and determination to live well and without reproach. For as those states that have been sobered by wars with their neighbours and continual campaigns love the blessings of order and peace, so those people who are compelled to lead a sober life owing to their enemies, and to be on their guard against carelessness and negligence, and to do everything with an eye to utility, imperceptibly glide into a faultless mode of life, and tone down their character, even without requiring much assistance from precepts. For those who always remember the line,

"Ah! how would Priam and his sons rejoice,"[506]

are by it diverted from and learn to shun all such things as their enemies would rejoice and laugh at. Again we see actors[507] and singers on the stage oftentimes slack and remiss, and not taking sufficient pains about their performances in the theatres when they have it all to themselves; but when there is a competition and contest with others, they not only wake up but tune their instruments, and adjust their chords, and play on the flute with more care. Similarly whoever knows that his enemy is antagonistic to his life and character, pays more attention to himself, and watches his behaviour more carefully, and regulates his life. For it is peculiar to vice to be more afraid of enemies than friends in regard to our faults. And so Nasica, when some expressed their opinion that the Roman Republic was now secure, since Carthage was rased to the ground and Achaia reduced to slavery, said, "Nay rather we are now in a critical position, since we have none left to fear or respect."

§ IV. Consider also that very philosophical and witty answer of Diogenes to the man who asked, "How shall I avenge myself on my enemy?" "By becoming a good and honest man."[508] Some people are terribly put about if they see their enemies' horses in a good condition, or hear their dogs praised; if they see their farm well-tilled, their garden well-kept, they groan aloud. What a state think you then they would be in, if you were to exhibit yourself as a just man, sensible and good, in words excellent, in deeds pure, in manner of life decorous, "reaping fruit from the deep soil of the soul, where good counsels grow."[509] Pindar says[510] "those that are conquered are reduced to complete silence:" but not absolutely, not all men, only those that see they are outdone by their enemies in industry, in goodness, in magnanimity, in humanity, in kindnesses; these, as Demosthenes says, "stop the tongue, block up the mouth, choke people, and make them silent."[511]

"Be better than the bad: 'tis in your power."[512]

If you wish to vex the man who hates you, do not abuse him by calling him a pathick, or effeminate, or intemperate, or a low fellow, or illiberal; but be yourself a man, and temperate, and truthful, and kind and just in all your dealings with those you come across. But if you are tempted to use abuse, mind that you yourself are very far from what you abuse him for, dive down into your own soul, look for any rottenness in yourself, lest someone suggest to you the line of the tragedian,

"You doctor others, all diseased yourself."[513]

If you say your enemy is uneducated, increase your own love of learning and industry; if you call him coward, stir up the more your own spirit and manliness; and if you say he is wanton and licentious, erase from your own soul any secret trace of the love of pleasure. For nothing is more disgraceful or more unpleasant than slander that recoils on the person who sets it in motion; for as the reflection of light seems most to injure weak eyes, so does censure when it recoils on the censurer, and is borne out by the facts. For as the north-east wind attracts clouds, so does a bad life draw upon itself rebukes.

§ V. Whenever Plato was in company with people who behaved in an unseemly manner, he used to say to himself, "Am I such a person as this?"[514] So he that censures another man's life, if he straightway examines and mends his own, directing and turning it into the contrary direction, will get some advantage from his censure, which will be otherwise idle and unprofitable. Most people laugh if a bald-pate or hump-back jeer and mock at others who are so too: it is quite as ridiculous to jeer and mock if one lies open to retort oneself, as Leo of Byzantium showed in his answer to the hump-back who jeered at him for weakness of eyes, "You twit me with an infirmity natural to man, while you yourself carry your Nemesis on your back."[515] And so do not abuse another as an adulterer, if you yourself are mad after boys: nor as a spendthrift, if you yourself are niggardly. Alcmæon said to Adrastus, "You are near kinsman to a woman that slew her husband." What was his reply? He retaliated on him with the appropriate retort, "But you killed with your own hand the mother that bore you."[516] And Domitius said to Crassus, "Did you not weep for the lamprey that was bred in your fishpond, and died?" To which Crassus replied, "Did you weep, when you buried your three wives?" He therefore that intends to abuse others must not be witty and noisy and impudent, but a man that does not lie open to counter-abuse and retort, for the god seems to have enjoined upon no one the precept "Know thyself" so much as on the person who is censorious, to prevent people saying just what they please, and hearing what don't please them. For such a one is wont, as Sophocles[517] says, "idly letting his tongue flow, to hear against his will, what he willingly says ill of others."

§ VI. This use and advantage then there is in abusing one's enemy, and no less arises from being abused and ill-spoken of oneself by one's enemies. And so Antisthenes[518] said well that those who wish to lead a good life ought to have genuine friends or red-hot enemies; for the former deterred you from what was wrong by reproof, the latter by abuse. But since friendship has nowadays become very mealy-mouthed in freedom of speech, voluble in flattery and silent in rebuke, we can only hear the truth from our enemies. For as Telephus[519] having no surgeon of his own, submitted his wound to be cured by his enemy's spear, so those who cannot procure friendly rebuke must content themselves with the censure of an enemy that hates them, reprehending and castigating their vices, and regard not the animus of the person, but only his matter. For as he who intended to kill the Thessalian Prometheus[520] only stabbed a tumour, and so lanced it that the man's life was saved, and he was rid of the tumour by its bursting, so oftentimes abuse, suddenly thrust on a man in anger or hatred, has cured some disease in his soul which he was ignorant of or neglected. But most people when they are abused do not consider whether the abuse really belongs to them properly, but look round to see what abuse they can heap on the abuser, and, as wrestlers get smothered with the dust of the arena, do not wipe off the abuse hurled at themselves, but bespatter others, and at last get on both sides grimy and discoloured. But if anyone gets a bad name from an enemy, he ought to clear himself of the imputation even more than he would remove any stain on his clothes that was pointed out to him; and if it be wholly untrue, yet he ought to investigate what originated the charge, and to be on his guard and be afraid lest he had unawares done something very near akin to what was imputed to him. As Lacydes, the king of the Argives, by the way he wore his hair and by his mincing walk got charged with effeminacy: and Pompey's scratching his head with one finger was construed in the same way, though both these men were very far from effeminacy or wantonness. And Crassus was accused of an intrigue with one of the Vestal Virgins, because he wished to purchase from her a pleasant estate, and therefore frequently visited her and waited upon her. And Postumia, from her readiness to laugh and talk somewhat freely with men, got accused and even had to stand her trial for incest,[521] but was, however, acquitted of that charge: but Spurius Minucius the Pontifex Maximus, when he pronounced her innocent, urged her not to be freer in her words than she was in her life. And though Themistocles[522] was guiltless of treason, his intimacy with Pausanias, and the letters and messages that frequently passed between them, laid him under suspicion.

§ VII. Whenever therefore any false charge is made against us, we ought not merely to despise and neglect it as false, but to see what word or action, either in jest or earnest, has made the charge seem probable, and this we must for the future be earnestly on our guard against and shun. For if others falling into unforeseen trouble and difficulties teach us what is expedient, as Merope says,

"Fortune has made me wise, though she has ta'en My dearest ones as wages,"[523]

why should we not take an enemy, and pay him no wages, to teach us, and give us profit and instruction, in matters which had escaped our notice? For an enemy has keener perception than a friend, for, as Plato[524] says, "the lover is blind as respects the loved one," and hatred is both curious and talkative. Hiero was twitted by one of his enemies for his foul breath, so he went home and said to his wife, "How is this? You never told me of it." But she being chaste and innocent replied, "I thought all men's breath was like that."[525] Thus perceptible and material things, and things that are plain to everybody, are sooner learnt from enemies than from friends and intimates.

§ VIII. Moreover to keep the tongue well under control, no small factor in moral excellence, and to make it always obedient and submissive to reason, is not possible, unless by practice and attention and painstaking a man has subdued his worst passions, as for example anger. For such expressions as "a word uttered involuntarily," and "escaping the barrier of the teeth,"[526] and "words darting forth spontaneously," well illustrate what happens in the case of ill-disciplined souls, ever wavering and in an unsettled condition through infirmity of temper, through unbridled fancy, or through faulty education. But, according to divine Plato,[527] though a word seems a very trivial matter, the heaviest penalty follows upon it both from gods and men. But silence can never be called to account, is not only not thirsty, to borrow the language of Hippocrates, but when abused is dignified and Socratic, or rather Herculean, if indeed it was Hercules who said,

"Sharp words he heeded not so much as flies."[528]

Not more dignified and noble than this is it to keep silent when an enemy reviles you, "as one swims by a smooth and mocking cliff," but in practice it is better. If you accustom yourself to bear silently the abuse of an enemy, you will very easily bear the attack of a scolding wife, and will remain undisturbed when you hear the sharp language of a friend or brother, and will be calm and placid when you are beaten or have something thrown at your head by your father or mother. For Socrates put up with Xanthippe, a passionate and forward woman, which made him a more easy companion with others, as being accustomed to submit to her caprices; and it is far better to train and accustom the temper to bear quietly the insults and rages and jeers and taunts of enemies and estranged persons, and not to be distressed at it.

§ IX. Thus then must we exhibit in our enmities meekness and forbearance, and in our friendships still more simplicity and magnanimity and kindness. For it is not so graceful to do a friend a service, as disgraceful to refuse to do so at his request; and not to revenge oneself on an enemy when opportunity offers is generous. But the man who sympathizes with his enemy in affliction, and assists him in distress, and readily holds out a helping hand to his children and family and their fortunes when in a low condition, whoever does not admire such a man for his humanity, and praise his benevolence,

"He has a black heart made of adamant Or iron or bronze."[529]

When Cæsar ordered the statues of Pompey that had been thrown down to be put up again,[530] Cicero said, "You have set up again Pompey's statues, and in so doing have erected statues to yourself." We ought not therefore to be niggardly in our praise and honour of an enemy that deserves a good name. For he who praises another receives on that account greater praise himself, and is the more credited on another occasion when he finds fault, as not having any personal ill-feeling against the man, but only disapproving of his act; and what is most noble and advantageous, the man who is accustomed to praise his enemies, and not to be vexed or malignant at their prosperity, is as far as possible from envying the good fortune of his friends, and the success of his intimates. And yet what practice will be more beneficial to our minds, or bring about a happier disposition, than that which banishes from us all jealousy and envy? For as in war many necessary things, otherwise bad, are customary and have as it were the sanction of law, so that they cannot be abolished in spite of the injury they do, so enmity drags along in its train hatred, and envy, and jealousy, and malignity, and revenge, and stamps them on the character. Moreover knavery, and deceit, and villainy, that seem neither bad nor unfair if employed against an enemy, if they once get planted in the mind are difficult to dislodge; and eventually from force of habit get used also against friends, unless they are forewarned and forearmed through their previous acquaintance with the tricks of enemies. If then Pythagoras,[531] accustoming his disciples to abstain from all cruelty and inhumanity to the brute creation, did right to discountenance bird-fowling, and to buy up draughts of fishes and bid them be thrown into the water again, and to forbid killing any but wild animals, much more noble is it, in dissensions and differences with human beings, to be a generous, just and true enemy, and to check and tame all bad and low and knavish propensities, that in all intercourse with friends a man may keep the peace and abstain from doing an injury. Scaurus was an enemy and accuser of Domitius, but when one of Domitius' slaves came to him to reveal some important matters which were unknown to Scaurus, he would not hear him, but seized him and sent him back to his master. And when Cato was prosecuting Murena for canvassing, and was getting together his evidence, he was accompanied as was usual by people who watched what he was doing,[532] and would often ask him if he intended that day to get together his witnesses and open the case, and if he said "No," they believed him and went their way. All this is the greatest proof of the credit which was reposed in Cato, but it is better and more important, that we should accustom ourselves to deal justly even with our enemies, and then there will be no fear that we should ever act unjustly and treacherously to our friends and intimates.

§ X. But since, as Simonides says, "all larks must have their crests,"[533] and every man's nature contains in it pugnacity and jealousy and envy, which last is, as Pindar says, "the companion of empty-headed men," one might get considerable advantage by purging oneself of those passions against enemies, and by diverting them, like sewers, as far as possible from companions and friends.[534] And this it seems the statesmanlike Onomademus had remarked, for being on the victorious side in a disturbance at Chios, he urged his party not to expel all of the different faction, but to leave some, "in order," he said, "that we may not begin to quarrel with our friends, when we have got entirely rid of our enemies." So too our expending these passions entirely on our enemies will give less trouble to our friends. For it ought not to be, as Hesiod[535] says, that "potter envies potter, and singer envies singer, and neighbour neighbour," and cousin cousin, and brother brother, "if hastening to get rich" and enjoying prosperity. But if there is no other way to get rid of strife and envy and quarrels, accustom yourself to be vexed at your enemies' good fortune, and sharpen and accentuate on them your acerbity. For as judicious gardeners think they produce finer roses and violets by planting alongside of them garlic and onions, that any bitter or strong elements may be transferred to them, so your enemy's getting and attracting your envy and malignity will render you kinder and more agreeable to your prosperous friends. And so let us be rivals of our enemies for glory or office or righteous gain, not only being vexed if they get ahead of us, but also carefully observing all the steps by which they get ahead, and trying to outdo them in industry, and hard work, and soberness, and prudence; as Themistocles said Miltiades' victory at Marathon would not let him sleep.[536] For he who thinks his enemy gets before him in offices, or advocacies, or state affairs, or in favour with his friends or great men, if from action and emulation he sinks into envy and despondency, makes his life become idle and inoperative. But he who is not blinded by hate,[537] but a discerning spectator of life and character and words and deeds, will perceive that most of what he envies comes to those who have them from diligence and prudence and good actions, and exerting himself in the same direction he will increase his love of what is honourable and noble, and will eradicate his vanity and sloth.

§ XI. But if our enemies seem to us to have got either by flattery, or fraud, or bribery, or venal services, ill-got and discreditable power at court or in state, it ought not to trouble us but rather inspire pleasure in us, when we compare our own liberty and purity and independence of life. For, as Plato[538] says, "all the gold above or below the earth is not of equal value with virtue." And we ought ever to remember the precept of Solon, "We will not exchange our virtue for others' wealth."[539] Nor will we give up our virtue for the applause of banqueting theatres, nor for honours and chief seats among eunuchs and harlots, nor to be monarchs' satraps; for nothing is to be desired or noble that comes from what is bad. But since, as Plato[540] says, "the lover is blind as respects the loved one," and we notice more what our enemies do amiss, we ought not to let either our joy at their faults or our grief at their success be idle, but in either case we ought to reflect, how we may become better than them by avoiding their errors, and by imitating their virtues not come short of them.

[497] So Pliny, viii. 83: "In Creta Insula non vulpes ursive, atque omnino millum maleficum animal præter phalangium."

[498] See the same remark of Chilo, "On Abundance of Friends," § vi.

[499] "Oeconom." i. 15.

[500] A treatise of Plutarch still extant.

[501] A line from a lost Satyric Play of Æschylus, called "Prometheus Purphoros."

[502] So fire is called [Greek: pantechnon] in Æschylus, "Prometheus Desmotes," 7.

[503] Compare Seneca, "De Animi Tranquillitate," cap. xiii.: "Zeno noster cum omnia sua audiret submersa, Jubet, inquit, me fortuna expeditius philosophari."

[504] See Horace, "Epistles," i. l. 28; Pausanias, iv. 2.

[505] See Plautus, "Trinummus," 205-211.

[506] Homer, "Iliad," i. 255.

[507] Literally "the artists of Dionysus." We know what they were from our author's "Quæstiones Romanæ," § 107: [Greek: dia ti tous peri ton Dionuson technitas histriônas Rhômaioi kalousin];

[508] Compare "De Audiendis Poetis," § iv.

[509] Æschylus, "Septem contra Thebas," 593, 594.

[510] Pindar, "Fragm." 253.

[511] Demosthenes, "De Falsa Legatione," p. 406.

[512] Euripides, "Orestes," 251.

[513] A line from Euripides. Quoted also "De Adulatore et Amico," § xxxii.

[514] Compare "De Audiendo," §vi. See also Horace, "Satires," i, 4. 136, 137.

[515] The story is somewhat differently told, "Quæst. Conviv.," Lib. ii. § ix.

[516] From a lost play of Euripides.

[517] In some lost play. Compare Hesiod, "Works and Days," 719-721; Terence, "Andria," 920.

[518] The sentiment is assigned to Diogenes twice elsewhere by our author, namely, "How One may be aware of one's Progress in Virtue," § xi., and "How One may discern a Flatterer from a Friend," § xxxvi.

[519] See Propertius, ii. 1. 63, 64; Ovid, "Metamorphoses," xii. 112; xiii. 171; "Tristia," v. 2. 15, 16; "Remedia Amoris," 47, 48; Erasmus, "Adagia," p. 221.

[520] "Jason Pheræus cognomine Prometheus dictus est. Vide Ciceronem, 'Nat. Deor.' iii. 29; Plinium, vii. 51; Valerium Maximum, i. 8, Extem. 6."--*Wytttenbach.*

[521] She was a Vestal Virgin. See Livy, iv. 44.

[522] See Thucydides, i. 135, 136.

[523] From a lost play of Euripides. Compare the proverb, [Greek: pathêmata mathêmata].

[524] "Laws," v. p. 731 E.

[525] Told again "Reg. et Imperator. Apophthegm.," p. 175 B.

[526] A favourite image of Homer, employed "Iliad," iv. 350; xiv. 83; "Odyssey," i. 64; xxiii. 70.

[527] "Laws," xi. p. 935 A. Quoted again "On Talkativeness," § vii.

[528] See Pausanias, v. 14.

[529] From a Fragment of Pindar.

[530] See Suetonius, "Divus Julius," 75: "Sed et statuas L. Sullæ atque Pompeii a plebe disjectas reposuit."

[531] Compare our author, "Quaestiones Convivalium," viii. p. 729 E.

[532] No doubt in the interest of the defendant. See our author, "Cato Minor," p. 769 B.

[533] A Greek proverb, see Erasmus, "Adagia," p. 921.

[534] So Cicero, "Nat. Deor." ii. 56: "In ædibus architecti avertunt ab oculis naribusque dominorum ea quæ profluentia necessario tætri essent aliquid habitura."

[535] "Works and Days," 23-26. Our "Two of a trade seldom agree."

[536] Compare "How One may be aware of one's Progress in Virtue," § xiv.

[537] For as the English proverb says, "Hatred is blind as well as love."

[538] "Laws," v. p. 728 A.

[539] Quoted more fully "How One may be aware of one's Progress in Virtue," § vi.

[540] "Laws," v. p. 731 E. See also above, § vii.

ON TALKATIVENESS.[541]

§ 1. Philosophy finds talkativeness a disease very difficult and hard to cure. For its remedy, conversation, requires hearers: but talkative people hear nobody, for they are ever prating. And the first evil this inability to keep silence produces is an inability to listen. It is a self-chosen deafness of people who, I take it, blame nature for giving us one tongue and two ears. If then the following advice of Euripides to a foolish hearer was good,

"I cannot fill one that can nought retain, Pumping up wise words for an unwise man;"

one might more justly say to a talkative man, or rather about a talkative man,

"I cannot fill one that will nothing take, Pumping up wise words for an unwise man;"

or rather deluging with words one that talks to those who don't listen, and listens not to those who talk. Even if he does listen for a short time, talkativeness hurries off what is said like the retiring sea, and anon brings it up again multiplied with the approaching tide. The portico at Olympia that returns many echoes to one utterance is called seven-voiced,[542] and if the slightest utterance catches the ear of talkativeness, it at once echoes it all round,

"Moving the mind's chords all unmoved before."[543]

For their ears can certainly have no passages leading to the brain but only to the tongue. And so while other people retain what they hear, talkative people lose it altogether, and, being empty-headed, they resemble empty vessels, and go about making much noise.[544]

§ II. If however it seems that no attempt at cure has been left untried, let us say to the talkative person,

"Be silent, boy; silence has great advantages;"

two of the first and foremost of which are hearing and being heard, neither of which can happen to talkative people, for however they desire either so unhappy are they that they must desist from it. For in all other diseases of the soul, as love of money, love of glory, or love of pleasure, people at any rate attain the desired object: but it is the cruel fate of talkative people to desire hearers but not to get them, for everyone flees from them with headlong speed; and if people are sitting or walking about in any public place,[545] and see one coming they quickly pass the word to one another to shift quarters. And as when there is dead silence in any assembly they say Hermes has joined the company, so when any prater joins some drinking party or social gathering of friends, all are silent, not wishing to give him a chance to break in, and if he uninvited begin to open his mouth, they all, "like before a storm at sea, when Boreas is blowing a gale round some headland," foreseeing tossing about and nausea, disperse. And so it is their destiny to find neither willing table-companions, nor messmates when they are travelling by land or by sea, but only such as cannot help themselves; for such a fellow is always at you, plucking hold of your clothes or chin, or giving you a dig in the ribs with his elbow. "Most valuable are the feet in such a conjuncture," according to Archilochus, nay according to the wise Aristotle himself. For he being bothered with a talkative fellow, and wearied out with his absurd tales, and his frequent question, "Is not this wonderful, Aristotle?" "Not at all," said he, "but it is wonderful that anyone with a pair of legs stops here to listen to you." And to another such fellow, who said after a long rigmarole, "Did I weary you, philosopher, by my chatter?" "Not you, by Zeus," said he, "for I paid no attention to you." For even if talkative people force you to listen,[546] the mind can give them only its outward ears to deluge, while it unfolds and pursues some other thoughts within; so they find neither hearers to attend to them, nor credit them. They say those that are prone to Venus are commonly barren: so the prating of talkative people is ineffectual and fruitless.

§ III. And yet nature has fenced and barricaded in us nothing so much as the tongue, having put the teeth before it as a barrier, so that if, when reason holds tight her "glossy reins,"[547] it hearken not, nor keep within bounds, we may check its intemperance, biting it till the blood comes. For Euripides tells us that, not from unbolted houses or store-rooms, but "from unbridled mouths the end is misfortune."[548] But those persons who think that houses without doors and open purses are no good to their possessors, and yet keep their mouths open and unshut, and allow their speech to flow continually like the waves of the Euxine,[549] seem to regard speech as of less value than anything. And so they never get believed, though credit is the aim of every speech; for to inspire belief in one's hearers is the proper end of speech, but praters are disbelieved even when they tell the truth. For as corn stowed away in a granary is found to be larger in quantity but inferior in quality, so the speech of a talkative man is increased by a large addition of falsehood, which destroys his credit.

§ IV. Then again every man of modesty and propriety would avoid drunkenness, for anger is next door neighbour to madness as some think,[550] but drunkenness lives in the same house: or rather drunkenness is madness, more short-lived indeed, but more potent also through volition, for it is self-chosen. Nor is drunkenness censured for anything so much as its intemperate and endless talk.

"Wine makes a prudent man begin to sing, And gently laugh, and even makes him dance."[551]

And yet there is no harm in all this, in singing and laughing and dancing. But the poet adds--

"And it compels to say what's best unsaid."[552]

This is indeed dreadful and dangerous. And perhaps the poet in this passage has solved that problem of the philosophers, and stated the difference between being under the influence of wine and being drunk, mirth being the condition of the former, foolish talk of the latter. For as the proverb tells us, "What is in the heart of the sober is on the tongue of the drunken."[553] And so Bias, being silent at a drinking bout, and jeered at by some young man in the company as stupid, replied, "What fool could hold his tongue in liquor?" And at Athens a certain person gave an entertainment to the king's ambassadors, and at their desire contrived to get the philosophers there too, and as they were all talking together and comparing ideas, and Zeno alone was silent, the strangers greeted him and pledged him, and said, "What are we to tell the king about you, Zeno?" And he replied, "Nothing, but that there is an old man at Athens that can hold his tongue at a drinking bout." So profound and mysterious and sober is silence, while drunkenness is talkative: for it is void of sense and understanding, and so is loquacious. And so the philosophers define drunkenness to be silly talk in wine. Drinking therefore is not censured, if silence go with it, but foolish prating turns being under the influence of wine into drunkenness. And the drunken man prates only in his cups; but the talkative man prates everywhere, in the market-place, in the theatre, out walking, by night and by day. If he is your doctor, he is more trouble to you than your disease: if he is on board ship with you, he disgusts you more than sea-sickness; if he praises you, he is more fulsome than blame. It is more pleasure associating with bad men who have tact than with good men who prate. Nestor indeed in Sophocles' Play, trying by his words to soothe exasperated Ajax, said to him mildly,

"I blame you not, for though your words are bad, Your acts are good:"

but we cannot feel so to the talkative man, for his want of tact in words destroys and undoes all the grace of his actions.

§ V. Lysias wrote a defence for some accused person, and gave it him, and he read it several times, and came to Lysias in great dejection and said, "When I first perused this defence, it seemed to me wonderful, but when I read it a second and third time, it seemed altogether dull and ineffective. Then Lysias laughed, and said, "What then? Are you going to read it more than once to the jury?" And yet do but consider the persuasiveness and grace of Lysias' style;[554] for he "I say was a great favourite with the dark-haired Muses."[555] And of the things which have been said of Homer the truest is that he alone of all poets has survived the fastidiousness of mankind, as being ever new and still at his acme as regards giving pleasure, and yet saying and proclaiming about himself, "I hate to spin out a plain tale over and over again,"[556] he avoids and fears that satiety which lies in ambush for every narrative, and takes the hearer from one subject to another, and relieves by novelty the possibility of being surfeited. But the talkative worry one's ears to death with their tautologies, as people scribble the same things over and over again on palimpsests.[557]

§ VI. Let us remind them then first of this, that just as in the case of wine, which was intended for pleasure and mirth, those who compel people to drink it neat and in large quantities bring some into a disgusting condition of drunkenness, so with speech, which is the pleasantest social tie amongst mankind, those who make a bad and ill-advised use of it render it unpleasing and unfit for company, paining those whom they think to gratify, and become a laughing-stock to those who they think admire them, and objectionable to those who they think love them. As then he cannot be a favourite of the goddess who with Aphrodite's charmed girdle[558] repels and drives away those who associate with him, so he who with his speech bores and disgusts one is without either taste or refinement.

§ VII. Of all other passions and disorders some are dangerous, some hateful, some ridiculous, but in talkativeness all these elements are combined. For praters are jeered at for their commonplaces, and hated when they bring bad news, and run into danger when they reveal secrets. And so Anacharsis, when he was feasted by Solon and lay down to sleep, and was observed with his left hand on his private parts, and his right hand on his mouth, for he thought his tongue needed the stronger restraint, was right in his opinion. For it would be difficult to find as many men who have been ruined by venereal excesses as cities and leading states that have been undone by the utterance of a secret. When Sulla was besieging Athens, and had no time to waste there, "for he had other fish to fry,"[559] as Mithridates was ravaging Asia, and the party of Marius was again in power at Rome, some old men in a barber's shop happened to observe to one another that the Heptachalcon was not well guarded, and that their city ran a great risk of being captured at that point, and some spies who overheard this conversation reported it to Sulla. And he at once marched up his forces, and about midnight entered the city with his army, and all but rased it to the ground, and filled it with slaughter and dead bodies, insomuch that the Ceramicus ran with blood: and he was thus savage against the Athenians for their words rather than their deeds, for they had spoken ill of him and his wife Metella, jumping on to the walls and calling out in a jeering way,

"Sulla is a mulberry bestrewn with barley meal,"

and much similar banter. Thus they drew down upon themselves for words, which, as Plato[560] says, are a very small matter, a very heavy punishment.[561] The prating of one man also prevented Rome from becoming free by the removal of Nero. For it was only the night before the tyrant was to be murdered, and all preparations had been made, when he that was to do the deed going to the theatre, and seeing someone in chains near the doors who was about to be taken before Nero, and was bewailing his sad fortune, went up close to him and whispered, "Pray only, good sir, that to-day may pass by, to-morrow you will owe me many thanks." He guessing the meaning of the riddle, and thinking, I take it, "he is a fool who gives up what is in his hand for a remote contingency,"[562] preferred certain to honourable safety. For he informed Nero of what the man had said, and he was immediately arrested, and torture, and fire, and scourging were applied to him, who denied now in his necessity what before he had divulged without necessity.

§ VIII. Zeno the philosopher,[563] that he might not against his will divulge any secrets when put to the torture, bit off his tongue, and spit it at the tyrant. Famous also was the reward which Leæna had for her taciturnity.[564] She was the mistress of Harmodius and Aristogiton, and, although a woman, participated in their hopes of success in the conspiracy against the tyrants: for she had revelled in the glorious cup of love, and had been initiated in their secrets through the god. When then they had failed in their attempt and been put to death, and she was examined and bidden to reveal the names of the other conspirators, she refused to do so, and held out to the end, showing that those famous men in loving such a one as her had done nothing unworthy of them. And the Athenians erected to her memory a bronze lioness without a tongue, and placed it near the entrance to the Acropolis, signifying her dauntless courage by the nobleness of that animal, and by its being without a tongue her silence and fidelity. For no spoken word has done as much good as many unspoken ones. For at some future day we can give utterance if we like to what has been not said, but a word once spoken cannot be recalled, but flies about and runs all round the world. And this is the reason, I take it, why men teach us to speak, but the gods teach us to be silent, silence being enjoined on us in the mysteries and in all religious rites. Thus Homer has described the most eloquent Odysseus, and Telemachus, and Penelope, and the nurse, as all remarkable for their taciturnity. You remember the nurse saying,

"I'll keep it close as heart of oak or steel."[565]

And Odysseus sitting by Penelope,

"Though in his heart he pitied her sad grief, His eyes like horn or steel impassive stood Within their lids, and craft his tears repressed."[566]

So great control had he over all his body, and so much were all his members under the sway and rule of reason, that he commanded his eyes not to weep, his tongue not to speak, and his heart not to tremble or quake.[567]

"So calm and passive did his heart remain,"[568]

reason penetrating even to the irrational instincts, and making spirit and blood obedient and docile to it. Such also were most of his companions, for though they were dashed to the ground and dragged along by the Cyclops, they said not a word about Odysseus, nor did they show the stake of wood that had been put into the fire and prepared to put out Polyphemus' eye, but they would rather have been eaten alive than divulge secrets, such wonderful self-control and fidelity had they.[569] And so it was not amiss of Pittacus, when the king of Egypt sent him a victim, and bade him take from it the best and worst piece of it, to pull out the tongue and send that to the king, as being the instrument of the greatest blessings and withal the greatest mischiefs.

§ IX. So Ino in Euripides, speaking plainly about herself, says she knows "how to be silent when she should, and to speak when speech is safe."[570] For those who have enjoyed a truly noble and royal education learn first to be silent and then to speak. So the famous king Antigonus, when his son asked him, "When are we going to shift our quarters?" answered, "Are you afraid that you only will not hear the trumpet?" Was he afraid then to entrust a secret to him, to whom he intended one day to leave his kingdom? Nay rather, it was to teach him to be close and guarded on such matters. Metellus[571] also, the well-known veteran, when questioned somewhat similarly about an expedition, said, "If I thought my coat knew the secret, I would strip it off and throw it into the fire." And Eumenes, when he heard that Craterus was marching against him, told none of his friends, but pretended that it was Neoptolemus; for his soldiers despised Neoptolemus, but they admired the glory and loved the virtue of Craterus; and no one but Eumenes knew the truth, and they engaged and were victorious, and unwittingly killed Craterus, and only recognized his dead body. So great a part did silence play in the battle, concealing the name of the enemy's general: so that Eumenes' friends marvelled more than found fault at his not having told them the truth. And if anyone should receive blame in such a case, it is better to be censured when one has done well by keeping one's counsel, rather than to have to accuse others through having come to grief by trusting them.

§ X. But, generally speaking, who has the right to blame the person who has not kept his secret? For if it was not to be known, it was not well to tell another person of it at all, and if you divulged your secret yourself and expected another person to keep it, you had more faith in another than in yourself. And so should he be such another as yourself you are deservedly undone, and should he be a better man than yourself, your safety is more than you could have reckoned on, as it involved finding a man more to be trusted than yourself. But you will say, He is my friend. Yes, but he has another friend, whom he reposes confidence in as much as you do in your friend, and that other friend has one of his own, and so on, so that the secret spreads in many quarters from inability to keep it close in one. For as the unit never deviates from its orbit, but (as its name signifies) always remains one, but the number two contains within it the seeds of infinity, for when it departs from itself it becomes plurality at once by doubling, so speech confined in one person's breast is truly secret, but if it be communicated to another it soon gets noised abroad. And so Homer calls words "winged," for as he that lets a bird go from his hands cannot easily get it back again, so he that lets a word go from his mouth cannot catch or stop it, but it is borne along "whirling on swift wings," and dispersed from one person to another. When a ship scuds before the gale the mariners can stop it, or at least check its course with cables and anchors, but when the spoken word once sails out of harbour, so to speak, there is no roadstead or anchorage for it, but borne along with much noise and echo it dashes its utterer on the rocks, and brings him into imminent danger of shipwreck,

"As one might set on fire Ida's woods With a small torch, so what one tells one person Is soon the property of all the citizens."[572]

§ XI. The Roman Senate had been discussing for several days a secret matter, and there was much doubt and suspicion about it. And one of the senator's wives, discreet in other matters but a very woman in curiosity, pressed her husband close, and entreated him to tell her what the secret was; she vowed and swore she would not divulge it, and did not refrain from shedding tears at her not being trusted. And he, nothing loth to convince her of her folly, said, "Your importunity, wife, has prevailed, listen to a dreadful and portentous matter. It has been told us by the priests that a lark has been seen flying in the air with a golden helmet and spear: it is this portent that we are considering and discussing with the augurs, as to whether it be a good or bad omen. But say nothing about it." Having said these words he went into the Forum. But his wife seized on the very first of her maids that entered the room, and smote her breast, and tore her hair, and said, "Alas! for my husband and country! What will become of us?" wishing and teaching her maid to say, "Whatever's up?"

So when she inquired she told her all about it, adding that refrain common to all praters, "Tell no one a word about it." The maid however had scarce left her mistress when she told one of her fellow-servants who was doing little or nothing, and she told her lover who happened to call at that moment. So the news spread to the Forum so quickly that it got the start of its original author, and one of his friends meeting him said, "Have you only just left your house?" "Only just," he replied. "Didn't you hear the news?" said his friend. "What news?" said he. "Why, that a lark has been seen flying in the air with a golden helmet and spear, and the Senate are met to discuss the portent." And he smiled and said to himself, "You are quick, wife, for the tale to get before me to the Forum!" Then meeting some of the Senators he disabused them of their panic. But to punish his wife, he said when he got home, "You have undone me, wife: for the secret has got abroad from my house, so that I must be an exile from my country for your inability to keep a secret." And on her trying to deny it, and saying, "Were there not three hundred Senators that heard of it as well as you? Might not one of them have divulged it?" he replied, "Stuff o' your three hundred! It was at your importunity that I invented the story, to put you to the test!" This fellow tested his wife warily and cunningly, as one pours water, and not wine or oil, into a leaky vessel. And Fabius,[573] the friend of Augustus, hearing the Emperor in his old age mourning over the extinction of his family, how two of his daughter Julia's sons were dead, and how Posthumus Agrippa, the only remaining one, was in exile through false accusation,[574] and how he was compelled to put his wife's son[575] into the succession to the Empire, though he pitied Agrippa and had half a mind to recall him from banishment, repeated the Emperor's words to his wife, and she to Livia.[576] And Livia bitterly upbraided Augustus, if he meant recalling his grandson, for not having done so long ago, instead of bringing her into hatred and hostility with the heir to the Empire. When Fabius came in the morning as usual into the Emperor's presence, and said, "Hail, Cæsar!" the Emperor replied, "Farewell,[577] Fabius." And he understanding the meaning of this straightway went home, and sent for his wife, and said, "The Emperor knows that I have not kept his secret, so I shall kill myself." And his wife replied, "You have deserved your fate, since having been married to me so long you did not remember and guard against my incontinence of speech, but suffer me to kill myself first." So saying she took his sword, and slew herself first.

§ XII. That was a good answer therefore that the comic poet Philippides made to king Lysimachus, who greeted him kindly, and said to him,[578] "What shall I give you of all my possessions?" "Whatever you like, O king, except your secrets." And talkativeness has another plague attached to it, even curiosity: for praters wish to hear much that they may have much to say, and most of all do they gad about to investigate and pry into secrets and hidden things, providing as it were an antiquated stock of rubbish[579] for their twaddle, in fine like children who cannot[580] hold ice in their hands, and yet are unwilling to let it go,[581] or rather taking secrets to their bosoms and embracing them as if they were so many serpents, that they cannot control, but are sure to be gnawed to death by. They say that garfish and vipers burst in giving life to their young, so secrets by coming out ruin and destroy those who cannot keep them. Seleucus Callinicus having lost his army and all his forces in a battle against the Galati, threw off his diadem, and fled on a swift horse with an escort of three or four of his men a long day's journey by bypaths and out-of-the-way tracks, till faint and famishing for want of food he drew rein at a small farmhouse, where by chance he found the master at home, and asked for some bread and water. And he supplied him liberally and courteously not only with what he asked for but with whatever else was on the farm, and recognized the king, and being very joyful at this opportunity of ministering to the king's necessities, he could not contain himself, nor dissemble like the king who wished to be incognito, but he accompanied him to the road, and on parting from him, said, "Farewell, king Seleucus." And he stretching out his right hand, and drawing the man to him as if he was going to kiss him, gave a sign to one of his escort to draw his sword and cut the man's head off;

"And at his word the head roll'd in the dust."[582]

Whereas if he had been silent then, and kept his counsel for a time, as the king afterwards became prosperous and great, he would have received, I take it, greater favour for his silence than for his hospitality. And yet he had I admit some excuse for his want of reticence, namely hope and joy.

§ XIII. But most talkative people have no excuse for ruining themselves. As for example in a barber's shop one day there was some conversation about the tyranny of Dionysius, that it was as hard as adamant and invincible, and the barber laughed and said, "Fancy your saying this to me, who have my razor at his throat most days!" And Dionysius hearing this had him crucified. Barbers indeed are generally a talkative race, for people fond of prating flock to them and sit in their shops, so that they pick up the habit from their customers. It was a witty answer therefore of king Archelaus,[583] when a talkative barber put the towel round his neck, and asked him, "How shall I shave you, O king?" "Silently," said the monarch. It was a barber that first spread the news of the great reverse of the Athenians in Sicily, having heard of it at the Piræus from a slave that had escaped from the island. He at once left his shop, and ran into the city at full speed, "that no one else should reap the fame, and he come in the second,"[584] of carrying the news into the town. And an uproar arising, as was only to be expected, the people assembled in the ecclesia, and began to investigate the origin of the rumour. So the barber was dragged up and questioned, but knew not the person's name who had told him, so was obliged to refer its origin to an anonymous and unknown person. Then anger filled the theatre, and the multitude cried out, "Torture the cursed fellow, put him to the rack: he has fabricated and concocted this news: who else heard it? who credits it?" The wheel was brought, the poor fellow stretched on it. Meantime those came up who had brought the news, who had escaped from the carnage in Sicily. Then all the multitude dispersed to weep over their private sorrows, and abandoned the poor barber, who remained fastened to the wheel. And when released late in the evening he actually asked the executioner, if they had heard how Nicias the General was slain. So invincible and incorrigible a vice does habit make talkativeness to be.

§ XIV. And yet, as those that drink bitter and strong-smelling physic are disgusted even with the cups they drink it out of, so those that bring evil tidings are disliked and hated by their hearers. Wittily therefore has Sophocles described the conversation between Creon and the guard.

"*G.* Is't in your ears or in your mind you're grieved? *C.* Why do you thus define the seat of grief? *G.* The doer pains your mind, but I your ears."[585]

However those that tell the tale grieve us as well as those that did the deed: and yet there is no means of checking or controlling the running tongue. At Lacedæmon the temple of Athene Chalcioecus[586] was broken into, and an empty flagon was observed lying on the ground inside, and a great concourse of people came up and discussed the matter. And one of the company said, "If you will allow me, I will tell you what I think about this flagon. I cannot help being of opinion that these sacrilegious wretches drank hemlock, and brought wine with them, before commencing their nefarious and dangerous work: that so, if they should fail to be detected, they might depart in safety, drinking the wine neat as an antidote to the hemlock: whereas should they be caught in the act, before they were put to the torture they would die of the poison easily and painlessly." When he had uttered these words, the idea seemed so ingenious and farfetched that it looked as if it could not emanate from fancy, but only from knowledge of the real facts. So the crowd surrounded this man, and asked him one after the other, "Who are you? Who knows you? How come you to know all this?" And at last he was convicted in this way, and confessed that he was one of those that had committed the sacrilege. And were not the murderers of Ibycus similarly captured? They were sitting in the theatre, and some cranes flew over their heads, and they laughed and whispered to one another, "Behold the avengers of Ibycus." And this being overheard by some who sat near, as Ibycus had now been some time missing and inquired after, they laid hold of this remark, and reported it to the magistrates. And so they were convicted and dragged off to punishment, being brought to justice not by the cranes but by their own inability to hold their tongues, being compelled by some Fury or Vengeance as it were to divulge the murder.[587] For as in the body there is an attraction to sore and suffering parts from neighbouring parts, so the tongue of talkative persons, ever suffering from inflammation and a throbbing pulse, attracts and draws to it secret and hidden things. And so the tongue ought to be fenced in, and have reason ever before it, as a bulwark, to prevent its tripping: that we may not seem to be more silly than geese, of whom it is said that, when they fly from Cilicia over Mt. Taurus which swarms with eagles, they carry in their mouths a large stone, which they employ as a gag or bridle for their scream, and so they cross over by night unobserved.

§ XV. Now if anyone were to ask who is the worst and most abandoned man, no one would pass over the traitor, or mention anyone else. It was as the reward of treason that Euthycrates roofed his house with Macedonian wood, as Demosthenes tells us; and that Philocrates got a large sum of money, and spent it on women and fish; and it was for betraying Eretria that Euphorbus and Philagrus got an estate from king Philip. But the talkative man is an unhired and officious traitor, not of horses[588] or walls, but of secrets which he divulges in the law courts, in factions, in party-strife, no one thanking him for his pains; but should anyone listen to him he thinks he is the obliged party. So that what was said to a man who rashly and indiscriminately squandered away all his means and bestowed them on others,

"It is not kindness in you but disease, This itch for giving,"[589]

is appropriate also to the prater, "You don't communicate to us all this out of friendship or goodwill, but it is a disease in you, this itch for talking and prating."

§ XVI. But all this must not be looked upon merely as an indictment against talkativeness, but an attempt to cure it: for we overcome the passions by judgement and practice, but judgement is the first step. For no one is wont to shun, and eradicate from his soul, what he does not dislike. And we dislike the passions only when we discern by reason the harm and shame that results to us by indulging them. As we see every day in the case of talkative people: if they wish to be loved, they are hated; if they desire to please, they bore; when they think they are admired, they are really laughed at; they spend, and get no gain from so doing; they injure their friends, benefit their enemies, and ruin themselves. So that the first cure and remedy of this disorder will be to reckon up the shame and trouble that results from it.

§ XVII. In the next place we must consider the opposite virtue to talkativeness, always listening to and having on our lips the encomiums passed upon reserve, and remembering the decorum sanctity and mysterious power of silence, and ever bearing in mind that terse and brief speakers, who put the maximum of matter into the minimum of words, are more admired and esteemed and thought wiser[590] than unbridled windbags. And so Plato[591] praises, and compares to clever javelin-men, such as speak tersely, compressedly, and concisely. And Lycurgus by using his citizens from boyhood to silence taught them to perfection their brevity and terseness. For as the Celtiberians make steel of iron only after digging down deep in the soil, and carefully separating the iron ore, so Laconian oratory has no rind,[592] but by the removal of all superfluous matter goes home straight to the point like steel. For its sententiousness,[593] and pointed suppleness in repartee, comes from the habit of silence. And we ought to quote such pointed sayings especially to talkative people, such neatness and vigour have they, as, for example, what the Lacedæmonians said to Philip, "[Remember] Dionysius at Corinth."[594] And again, when Philip wrote to them, "If I invade Laconia, I will drive you all out of house and home," they only wrote back, "If." And when king Demetrius was indignant and cried out, "The Lacedæmonians have only sent me one ambassador," the ambassador was not frightened but said, "Yes, one to one man." Certainly among the ancients men of few words were admired. So the Amphictyones did not write extracts from the Iliad or Odyssey, or the Pæans of Pindar, in the temple of Pythian Apollo at Delphi, but "Know thyself," "Not too much of anything,"[595] and "Be a surety, trouble is near;"[596] so much did they admire compactness and simplicity of speech, combining brevity with shrewdness of mind. And is not the god himself short and concise in his oracles? Is he not called Loxias,[597] because he prefers ambiguity to longwindedness? And are not those who express their meaning by signs without words wonderfully praised and admired? As Heraclitus, when some of the citizens asked him to give them his opinion about concord, got on the platform, and took a cup of cold water, and put some barley-meal in it, and stirred it up with penny-royal, thus showing them that it is being content with anything, and not needing costly dainties, that keeps cities in peace and concord. Scilurus, the king of the Scythians, left eighty sons, and on his death-bed asked for a bundle of sticks, and bade his sons break it when it was tied together, and when they could not, he took the sticks one by one and easily broke them all up: thus showing them that their harmony and concord would make them strong and hard to overthrow, while dissension would make them feeble and insecure.

§ XVIII. If then anyone were continually to recollect and repeat these or similar terse sayings, he would probably cease to be pleased with idle talk. As for myself, when I consider of what importance it is to attend to reason, and to keep to one's purpose, I confess I am quite put out of countenance by the example of the slave of Pupius Piso the orator. He, not wishing to be annoyed by their prating, ordered his slaves merely to answer his questions, and not say a word more. On one occasion wishing to pay honour to Clodius who was then in power, he ordered him to be invited to his house, and provided for him no doubt a sumptuous entertainment. At the time fixed all the guests were present except Clodius, for whom they waited, and the host frequently sent the slave who used to invite guests to see if he was coming, but when evening came, and he was now quite despaired of, he said to his slave, "Did you not invite him?" "Certainly," said the slave. "Why then has he not come?" said the master. "Because he declined," said the slave. "Why then did you not tell me of it at once?" said the master. "Because you never asked me," said the slave. This was a Roman slave. But an Athenian slave "while digging will tell his master on what terms peace was made." So great is the force of habit in all matters. And of it we will now speak.

§ XIX. For it is not by applying bit or bridle that we can restrain the talkative person, we must master the disease by habit. In the first place then, when you are in company and questions are going round, accustom yourself not to speak till all the rest have declined giving an answer. For as Sophocles says, "counsel is not like a race;" no more are question and answer. For in a race the victory belongs to him who gets in first, but in company, if anyone has given a satisfactory answer, it is sufficient by assenting and agreeing to his view to get the reputation of being a pleasant fellow; and if no satisfactory answer is given, then to enlighten ignorance and supply the necessary information is well-timed and does not excite envy. But let us be especially on our guard that, if anyone else is asked a question, we do not ourselves anticipate and intercept him in giving an answer. It is indeed perhaps nowhere good form, if another is asked a favour, to push him aside and undertake to grant it ourselves; for we shall seem so to upbraid two people at once, the one who was asked as not able to grant the favour, and the other as not knowing how to ask in the right quarter. But especially insulting is such forwardness and impetuosity in answering questions. For he that anticipates by his own answer the person that was asked the question seems to say, "What is the good of asking him? What does he know about it? In my presence nobody else ought to be asked about these matters." And yet we often put questions to people, not so much because we want an answer, as to elicit from them conversation and friendly feeling, and from a wish to fit them for company, as Socrates drew out Theætetus and Charmides. For it is all one to run up and kiss one who wishes to be kissed by another, or to divert to oneself the attention that he was bestowing on another, as to intercept another person's answers, and to transfer people's ears, and force their attention, and fix them on oneself; when, even if he that was asked declines to give an answer, it will be well to hold oneself in reserve, and only to meet the question modestly when one's turn comes, so framing one's answer as to seem to oblige the person who asked the question, and as if one had been appealed to for an answer by the other. For if people are asked questions and cannot give a satisfactory answer they are with justice excused; but he who without being asked undertakes to answer a question, and anticipates another, is disagreeable even if he succeeds, while, if his answer is unsatisfactory, he is ridiculed by all the company, and his failure is a source of the liveliest satisfaction to them.

§ XX. The next thing to practise oneself to in answering the questions put to one,--a point to which the talkative person ought to pay the greatest attention,--is not through inadvertence to give serious answers to people who only challenge you to talk in fun and sport. For some people concoct questions not for real information, but simply for amusement and to pass the time away, and propound them to talkative people, just to have them on. Against this we must be on our guard, and not rush into conversation too hastily, or as if we were obliged for the chance, but we must consider the character of the inquirer and his purpose. When it seems that he really desires information, we should accustom ourselves to pause, and interpose some interval between the question and answer; during which time the questioner can add anything if he chooses, and the other can reflect on his answer, and not be in too great a hurry about it, nor bury it in obscurity, nor, as is frequently the case in too great haste, answer some other question than that which was asked. The Pythian Priestess indeed was accustomed to utter some of her oracles at the very moment before the question was put: for the god whom she serves "understands the dumb, and hears the mute."[598] But he that wishes to give an appropriate answer must carefully consider both the question and the mind of the questioner, lest it be as the proverb expresses it,

"I asked for shovels, they denied me pails."[599]

Besides we ought to check this greediness and hunger for words, that it may not seem as if we had a flood on our tongue which was dammed up, but which we were only too glad to discharge[600] on a question being put. Socrates indeed so repressed his thirst, that he would not allow himself to drink after exercise in the gymnasium, till he had first drawn from the well one bucket of water and poured it on to the ground, that he might accustom his irrational part to wait upon reason.

§ XXI. There are moreover three kinds of answers to questions, the necessary, the polite, and the superfluous. For instance, if anyone asked, "Is Socrates at home?" one, as if backward and disinclined to answer, might say, "Not at home;" or, if he wished to speak with Laconic brevity, might cut off "at home," and simply say "No;" as, when Philip wrote to the Lacedæmonians to ask if they would receive him in their city, they sent him back merely a large "No." But another would answer more politely, "He is not at home, but with the bankers," and if he wished to add a little more, "he expects to see some strangers there." But the superfluous prater, if he has read Antimachus of Colophon,[601] says, "He is not at home, but with the bankers, waiting for some Ionian strangers, about whom he has had a letter from Alcibiades who is in the neighbourhood of Miletus, staying with Tissaphernes the satrap of the great king, who used long ago to favour the Lacedæmonian party, but now attaches himself to the Athenians for Alcibiades' sake, for Alcibiades desires to return to his country, and so has succeeded in changing the views of Tissaphernes." And then he will go over the whole of the Eighth Book of Thucydides, and deluge the man, till before he is aware Miletus is captured, and Alcibiades is in exile the second time. In such a case most of all ought we to curtail talkativeness, by following the track of a question closely, and tracing out our answer according to the need of the questioner with the same accuracy as we describe a circle. When Carneades was disputing in the gymnasium before the days of his great fame, the superintendent of the gymnasium sent to him a message to bid him modulate his voice (for it was of the loudest), and when he asked him to fix a standard, the superintendent replied not amiss, "The standard of the person talking with you." So the meaning of the questioner ought to be the standard for the answer.

§ XXII. Moreover as Socrates urged his disciples to abstain from such food as tempted them to eat when they were not hungry, and from such drinks as tempted them to drink when they were not thirsty, so the talkative person ought to be afraid most of such subjects of conversation as he most delights in and repeats *ad nauseam*, and to try and resist their influence. For example, soldiers are fond of descriptions about war, and thus Homer introduces Nestor frequently narrating his prowess and glorious deeds. And generally speaking those who have been successful in the law courts, or beyond their hopes been favourites of kings and princes, are possessed, as it were by some disease, with the itch for frequently recalling and narrating, how they got on and were advanced, what struggles they underwent, how they argued on some famous occasion, how they won the day either as plaintiffs or defendants, what panegyrics were showered upon them. For joy is much more inclined to prate than the well-known sleeplessness represented in comedies, frequently rousing itself, and finding something fresh to relate. And so at any excuse they slip into such narratives. For not only,

"Where anyone does itch, there goes his hand,"[602]

but also delight has a voice of its own, and leads about the tongue in its train, ever wishing to fortify it with memory. Thus lovers spend most of their time in conversations that revive the memory of their loves; and if they cannot talk to human beings about them, they talk about them to inanimate objects, as, "O dearest bed," and,

"O happy lamp, Bacchis deems you a god, And if she thinks so, then you are indeed The greatest of the gods."

The talkative person therefore is merely as regards words a white line,[603] but he that is especially inclined to certain subjects should be especially on his guard against talking about them, and should avoid such topics, since from the pleasure they give him they may entice him to be very prolix and tedious. The same is the case with people in regard to such subjects as they think they are more experienced in and acquainted with than others. For such a one, being self-appreciative and fond of fame, "spends most of the day in that particular branch of study in which he chances to be proficient."[604] Thus he that is fond of reading will give his time to research; the grammarian his to syntax; and the traveller, who has wandered over many countries, his to geography. We must therefore be on our guard against our favourite topics, for they are an enticement to talkativeness, as its wonted haunts are to an animal. Admirable therefore was the behaviour of Cyrus in challenging his companions, not to those contests in which he was superior to them, but to those in which he was inferior, partly that he might not give them pain through his superiority, partly for his own benefit by learning from them. But the talkative person acts just contrary, for if any subject is introduced from which he might learn something he did not know, this he rejects and refuses, not being able to earn a good deal by a short silence,[605] but he rambles round the subject and babbles out stale and commonplace rhapsodies. As one amongst us, who by chance had read two or three of the books of Ephorus,[606] bored everybody, and dispersed every social party, by always narrating the particulars of the battle of Leuctra and its consequences, so that he got nicknamed Epaminondas.

§ XXIII. Nevertheless this is one of the least of the evils of talkativeness, and we ought even to try and divert it into such channels as these, for prating is less of a nuisance when it is on some literary subject. We ought also to try and get some persons to write on some topic, and so discuss it by themselves. For Antipater the Stoic philosopher,[607] not being able or willing it seems to dispute with Carneades, who inveighed vehemently against the Stoic philosophy, writing and filling many books of controversy against him, got the nickname of *Noisy-with-the-pen*; and perhaps the exercise and excitement of writing, keeping him very much apart from the community, might make the talkative man by degrees better company to those he associated with; as dogs, bestowing their rage on sticks and stones, are less savage to men. It will also be very advantageous for such to mix with people better and older than themselves, for they will accustom themselves to be silent by standing in awe of their reputation. And withal it will be well, when we are going to say something, and the words are on our lips, to reflect and consider, "What is this word that is so eager for utterance? To what is this tongue marching? What good will come of speaking now, or what harm of silence?" For we ought not to drop words as we should a burden that pressed upon us, for the word remains still after it has been spoken just the same; but men speak either on their own behalf if they want something, or to benefit those that hear them, or, to gratify one another, they season everyday life with speech, as one seasons food with salt. But if words are neither useful to the speaker, nor necessary for the hearer, nor contain any pleasure or charm, why are they spoken? For words may be idle and useless as well as deeds. And besides all this we must ever remember as most important the dictum of Simonides, that he had often repented he had spoken, but never that he had been silent: while as to the power and strength of practice consider how men by much toil and painstaking will get rid even of a cough or hiccough. And silence is not only never thirsty, as Hippocrates says, but also never brings pain or sorrow.

[541] Or *Garrulity, Chattering, Prating*. It is Talkativeness in a bad sense.

[542] Or *Heptaphonos*. See Pausanias, v. 21.

[543] Some unknown poet's words. I suppose they mean driving one mad, making one "Like sweet bells jangled, out of tune and harsh."

[544] So our English proverb, "Empty vessels make the greatest sound."

[545] Literally in a semi-circular place. It is not quite clear whether the front seats of the theatre are meant, or, as I have taken it, more generally, of some public place for entertainment or meeting, some promenade or piazza.

[546] Reading [Greek: akouein], which seems far the best reading.

[547] Homer, "Iliad," v. 226; "Odyssey," vi. 81.

[548] "Bacchæ," 385-387.

[549] See Ovid, "Tristia," iv. 4, 55-58.

[550] For example, Horace, "Epistles," i. 2, 62: "Ira furor brevis est" I read [Greek: homotoichos] with Mez.

[551] Homer, "Odyssey," xiv. 463-465.

[552] Ibid. 466.

[553] Compare the German proverb, "Thought when sober, said when drunk"--"Nuchtern gedacht, voll gesagt."

[554] Cf. Quintilian, x. 1, 78: "His ætate Lysias major, subtilis atque elegans et quo nihil, si oratori satis est docere, quæras perfectius. Nihil enim est inane, nihil arcessitum; puro tamen fonti quam magno flumini propior." Cf. ix. 4, 17.

[555] Somewhat like Pindar, "Pyth." i. 1. 1, 2.

[556] "Odyssey," xii. 452, 453.

[557] See Cicero, "Ad Fam." vii. 18; Catullus, xxii. 5, 6.

[558] See "Iliad," xiv. 214-217.

[559] "Allusio ad Homericum [Greek: epei ponos allos epeigei.]"--*Xylander*.

[560] "Laws," xi. p. 935 A.

[561] So true are the words of Æschylus, [Greek: glôssê mataia zêmia prostribetai].--"Prom." 329.

[562] Our "A bird in the hand is worth two in the bush."

[563] "Non Citticus, sed Eleates. v. Cic. Tuscul. ii. 22, et Nat. Deor. 3, 33."--*Reiske*.

[564] See Pausanias, i. 23. Leæna means "lioness." On the conspiracy see Thucydides, vi. 54-59.

[565] Homer, "Odyssey," xix. 494. Plutarch quotes from memory. The nurse's name was Euryclea.

[566] Odyssey," xix. 210-212. Quoted again "On Moral Virtue," § iv.

[567] Literally *bark*. See "Odyssey," xx. 13, 16.

[568] "Odyssey," xx. 23.

[569] See "Odyssey," ix. [Greek: Kyklôpeia].

[570] Euripides, "Ino." Fragment, 416.

[571] "Significat Q. Cæcilium Metellum, de quo Liv. xl. 45, 46."--*Reiske*.

[572] Euripides, "Ino." Fragm. 415. Compare St. James, iii. 5, 6.

[573] Fabius Maximus. So Tacitus, "Annals," i. 5, who relates this story somewhat differently.

[574] See Tacitus, "Annals," i. 3. As to his fate, see "Annals," i. 6.

[575] Tiberius Nero, who actually did succeed Augustus.

[576] The Emperor's wife.

[577] So it is in § xii. But perhaps here it means, "I wish you had more sense, Fabius!"

[578] Adopting the reading of Reiske.

[579] Reading [Greek: phorutou] or [Greek: phorytôn], as Wyttenbach.

[580] Reading [Greek: katechein dynantai] with Reiske.

[581] See Sophocles, Fragm. 162.

[582] Homer, "Iliad," x. 457.

[583] Compare "Moralia," p. 177 A; Horace, "Satires," i. 7. 3: "Omnibus et lippis notum et tonsoribus."

[584] Homer, "Iliad," xxii. 207.

[585] Sophocles, "Antigone," 317-319.

[586] See Pausanias, iii. 17; iv. 15; x. 5.

[587] Compare the idea of the people of Melita, Acts xxviii. 4.

[588] An Allusion to Dolon in Homer, "Iliad," x., 374, sq. according to Xylander.

[589] Quoted again by our author in his "Publicola," p. 105 B., and assigned to Epicharmus.

[590] So Shakspere has taught us, "Brevity is the soul of wit."--*Hamlet*, Act ii Sc. 2.

[591] "In Protagora."--*Xylander*.

[592] That is, is all kernel. See passim our author's "Apophthegmata Laconica."

[593] Or, *apophthegmatic nature*.

[594] Dionysius the younger, tyrant of Syracuse, was expelled, and afterwards kept a school at Corinth. That is the allusion. It would be like saying "Remember Napoleon at St. Helena."

[595] See Pausanias, x. 24.

[596] See Plato, "Charmides," 165 A.

[597] A title applied to Apollo first by Herodotus, i. 91, from his ambiguous ([Greek: loxa]) oracles.

[598] Part of the words of an oracle of the Pythian Priestess, slightly changed. The whole oracle may be seen in Herodotus, i. 47.

[599] Proverb of cross purposes.

[600] Reading [Greek: exerasthai] with Dübner.

[601] Catullus calls him "tumidus," *i.e.* long-winded, 95, 10. See also Propertius, iii. 34-32. He was a Greek poet, a contemporary of Socrates and Plato, and author of a Thebaid. Pausanias mentions him, viii. 25; ix. 35.

[602] The mediæval proverb, *Ubi dolor ibi digitus*.

[603] A proverbial expression for having no judgment. See Sophocles, Fragm. 307; Plato, "Charmides," 154 B; Erasmus, "Adagia." So we say a person's mind is a blank sheet on a subject he knows nothing about.

[604] Euripides, Fragm. 202. Quoted also by Plato, "Gorgias," 484 E.

[605] Reading with Reiske, [Greek: misthon autô dounai tô mikron siôpêsai mê dynamenos].

[606] A celebrated Greek historian, and pupil of Isocrates. See Cicero, "De Oratore," ii. 13.

[607] Of Tarsus. See Cicero, "De Officiis," iii. 12.

ON CURIOSITY.[608]

§ I. If a house is dark, or has little air, is in an exposed position, or unhealthy, the best thing will probably be to leave it; but if one is attached to it from long residence in it, one can improve it and make it more light and airy and healthy by altering the position of the windows and stairs, and by throwing open new doors and shutting up old ones. So some towns have been altered for the better, as my native place,[609] which did lie to the west and received the rays of the setting sun from Parnassus, was they say turned to the east by Chæron. And Empedocles the naturalist is supposed to have driven away the pestilence from that district, by having closed up a mountain gorge that was prejudicial to health by admitting the south wind to the plains. Similarly, as there are certain diseases of the soul that are injurious and harmful and bring storm and darkness to it, the best thing will be to eject them and lay them low by giving them open sky, pure air and light, or, if that cannot be, to change and improve them some way or other. One such mental disease, that immediately suggests itself to one, is curiosity, the desire to know other people's troubles, a disease that seems neither free from envy nor malignity.

"Malignant wretch, why art so keen to mark Thy neighbour's fault, and seest not thine own?"[610]

Shift your view, and turn your curiosity so as to look inwards: if you delight to study the history of evils, you have copious material at home, "as much as there is water in the Alizon, or leaves on the oak," such a quantity of faults will you find in your own life, and passions in your soul, and shortcomings in your duty. For as Xenophon says[611] good managers have one place for the vessels they use in sacrificing, and another for those they use at meals, one place for their farm instruments, and another for their weapons of war, so your faults arise from different causes, some from envy, some from jealousy, some from cowardice, some from meanness. Review these, consider these; bar up the curiosity that pries into your neighbours' windows and passages, and open it on the men's apartments, and women's apartments, and servant's attics, in your own house. There this inquisitiveness and curiosity will find full vent, in inquiries that will not be useless or malicious, but advantageous and serviceable, each one saying to himself,

"What have I done amiss? What have I done? What that I ought to have done left undone?"

§ II. And now, as they say of Lamia that she is blind when she sleeps at home, for she puts her eyes on her dressing-table, but when she goes out she puts her eyes on again, and has good sight, so each of us turns, like an eye, our malicious curiosity out of doors and on others, while we are frequently blind and ignorant about our own faults and vices, not applying to them our eyes and light. So that the curious man is more use to his enemies than to himself, for he finds fault with and exposes their shortcomings, and shows them what they ought to avoid and correct, while he neglects most of his affairs at home, owing to his excitement about things abroad. Odysseus indeed would not converse with his mother till he had learnt from the seer Tiresias what he went to Hades to learn; and after receiving that information, then he turned to her, and asked questions about the other women, who Tyro was, and who the fair Chloris, and why Epicaste[612] had died, "having fastened a noose with a long drop to the lofty beam."[613] But we, while very remiss and ignorant and careless about ourselves, know all about the pedigrees of other people, that our neighbour's grandfather was a Syrian, and his grandmother a Thracian woman, and that such a one owes three talents, and has not paid the interest. We even inquire into such trifling matters as where somebody's wife has been, and what those two are talking in the corner about. But Socrates used to busy himself in examining the secret of Pythagoras' persuasive oratory, and Aristippus, meeting Ischomachus at the Olympian games, asked him how Socrates conversed so as to have so much influence over the young men, and having received from him a few scraps and samples of his style, was so enthusiastic about it that he wasted away, and became quite pale and lean, thirsty and parched, till he sailed to Athens and drew from the fountain-head, and knew the wonderful man himself and his speeches and philosophy, the object of which was that men should recognize their faults and so get rid of them.

§ III. But some men cannot bear to look upon their own life, so unlovely a spectacle is it, nor to throw and flash on themselves, like a lantern, the reflection of reason; but their soul being burdened with all manner of vices, and dreading and shuddering at its own interior, sallies forth and wanders abroad, feeding and fattening its malignity there. For as a hen, when its food stands near its coop,[614] will frequently slip off into a corner and scratch up,

"Where I ween some poor little grain appears on the dunghill,"

so curious people neglecting conversation or inquiry about common matters, such as no one would try and prevent or be indignant at their prying into, pick out the secret and hidden troubles of every family. And yet that was a witty answer of the Egyptian, to the person who asked him, "What he was carrying wrapped up;" "It was wrapped up on purpose that you should not know." And you too, Sir, I would say to a curious person, why do you pry into what is hidden? If it were not something bad it would not be hidden. Indeed it is not usual to go into a strange house without knocking at the door, and nowadays there are porters, but in old times there were knockers on doors to let the people inside know when anyone called, that a stranger might not find the mistress or daughter of the house *en déshabille*, or one of the slaves being corrected, or the maids bawling out. But the curious person intrudes on all such occasions as these, although he would be unwilling to be a spectator, even if invited, of a well-ordered family: but the things for which bars and bolts and doors are required, these he reveals and divulges openly to others. Those are the most troublesome winds, as Aristo says, that blow up our clothes: but the curious person not only strips off the garments and clothes of his neighbours, but breaks through their walls, opens their doors, and like the wanton wind, that insinuates itself into maidenly reserve, he pries into and calumniates dances and routs and revels.

§ IV. And as Cleon is satirized in the play[615] as having "his hands among the Ætolians, but his soul in Peculation-town," so the soul of the curious man is at once in the mansions of the rich, and the cottages of the poor, and the courts of kings, and the bridal chambers of the newly married; he pries into everything, the affairs of foreigners, the affairs of princes, and sometimes not without danger. For just as if one were to taste aconite to investigate its properties, and kill oneself before one had discovered them, so those that pry into the troubles of great people ruin themselves before they get the knowledge they desire; even as those become blind who, neglecting the wide and general diffusion all over the earth of the sun's rays, impudently attempt to gaze at its orb and penetrate to its light. And so that was a wise answer of Philippides the Comic Poet, when King Lysimachus asked him on one occasion, "What would you like to have of mine?" "Anything, O king, but your secrets." For the pleasantest and finest things to be got from kings are public, as banquets, and riches, and festivities, and favours: but come not near any secret of theirs, pry not into it. There is no concealment of the joy of a prosperous monarch, or of his laugh when he is in a playful mood, or of any tokens of his goodwill and favour; but dreadful is what he conceals, his gloominess, his sternness, his reserve, his store of latent wrath, his meditation on stern revenge, his jealousy of his wife, or suspicion of his son, or doubt about the fidelity of a friend. Flee from this cloud that is so black and threatening, for when its hidden fury bursts forth, you will not fail to hear its thunder and see its lightning.

§ V. How shall you flee from it? Why, by dissipating and distracting your curiosity, by turning your soul to better and pleasanter objects: examine the phenomena of sky, and earth, and air, and sea. Are you by nature fond of gazing at little or great things? If at great, turn your attention to the sun, consider its rising and setting: view the changes of the moon, like the changes of our mortal life, see how it waxes and wanes,

"How at the first it peers out small and dim Till it unfolds its full and glorious Orb, And when its zenith it has once attained, Again it wanes, grows small, and disappears."[616]

These are indeed Nature's secrets, but they bring no trouble on those that study them. But if you decline the study of great things, inspect with curiosity smaller matters, see how some plants flourish, are green and gay, and exhibit their beauty, all the year round, while others are sometimes gay like them, at other times, like some unthrift, run through their resources entirely, and are left bare and naked. Consider again their various shapes, how some produce oblong fruits, others angular, others smooth and round. But perhaps you will not care to pry into all this, since you will find nothing bad. If you must then ever bestow your time and attention on what is bad, as the serpent lives but in deadly matter, go to history, and turn your eye on the sum total of human misery. For there you will find "the falls of men, and murders of their lives,"[617] rapes of women, attacks of slaves, treachery of friends, mixing of poisons, envyings, jealousies, "shipwrecks of families," and dethroning of princes. Sate and cloy yourself on these, you will by so doing vex and enrage none of your associates.

§ VI. But it seems curiosity does not rejoice in stale evils, but only in fresh and recent ones, gladly viewing the spectacle of tragedies of yesterday, but backward in taking part in comic and festive scenes. And so the curious person is a languid and listless hearer to the narrator of a marriage, or sacrifice, or solemn procession, he says he has heard most of all that before, bids the narrator cut it short and come to the point; but if his visitor tell him of the violation of some girl, or the adultery of some married woman, or the disputes and intended litigation of brothers, he doesn't go to sleep then, nor pretend want of leisure,

"But he pricks up his ears, and asks for more."

And indeed those lines,

"Alas! how quicker far to mortals' ears Do ill news travel than the news of good!"

are truly said of curious people. For as cupping-glasses take away the worst blood, so the ears of curious people attract only the worst reports; or rather, as cities have certain ominous and gloomy gates, through which they conduct only condemned criminals, or convey filth and night soil, for nothing pure or holy has either ingress into or egress from them, so into the ears of curious people goes nothing good or elegant, but tales of murders travel and lodge there, wafting a whiff of unholy and obscene narrations.

"And ever in my house is heard alone The sound of wailing;"

this is to the curious their one Muse and Siren, this the sweetest note they can hear. For curiosity desires to know what is hidden and secret; but no one conceals his good fortune, nay sometimes people even pretend to have such advantages as they do not really possess. So the curious man, eager to hear a history of what is bad, is possessed by the passion of malignity, which is brother to envy and jealousy. For envy is pain at another's blessings, and malignity is joy at another's misfortunes: and both proceed from the same savage and brutish vice, ill-nature.

§ VII. But so unpleasant is it to everybody to have his private ills brought to light, that many have died rather than acquaint the doctors with their secret ailments. For suppose Herophilus, or Erasistratus, or even Æsculapius himself during his sojourn on earth, had gone with their drugs and surgical instruments from house to house, to inquire what man had a fistula in ano, or what woman had a cancer in her womb;--and yet their curiosity would have been professional[618]--who would not have driven them away from their house, for not waiting till they were sent for, and for coming without being asked to spy out their neighbours' ailments? But curious people pry into these and even worse matters, not from a desire to heal them, but only to expose them to others, which makes them deservedly hated. For we are not vexed and mortified with custom-house officers when they levy toll on goods *bona fide* imported, but only when they seek for contraband articles, and rip up bags and packages: and yet the law allows them to do even this, and sometimes it is injurious to them not to do so. But curious people abandon and neglect their own affairs, and are busy about their neighbours' concerns. Seldom do they go into the country, for they do not care for its quiet and stillness and solitude, but if once in a way they do go there, they look more at their neighbours' vines than their own, and inquire how many cows of their neighbour have died, or how much of his wine has turned sour, and when they are satisfied on these points they soon return to town again. But the genuine countryman does not willingly listen to any rumour that chances to come from the town, for he quotes the following lines,

"Even with spade in hand he'll tell the terms On which peace was concluded: all these things The cursèd fellow walks about and pries into."

§ VIII. But curious people shun the country as stale and dull and too quiet, and push into warehouses and markets and harbours, asking, "Any news? Were you not in the market in the forenoon?" and sometimes receiving for answer, "What then? Do you think things in the town change every three hours?" Notwithstanding if anyone brings any news, he'll get off his horse, and embrace him, and kiss him, and stand to listen. If however the person who meets him says he has no news, he will say somewhat peevishly, "No news, Sir? Have you not been in the market? Did you not pass by the officers' quarters? Did you exchange no words with those that have just arrived from Italy?" To stop such people the Locrian authorities had an excellent rule; they fined everyone coming from abroad who asked what the news was. For as cooks pray for plenty of meat, and fishmongers for shoals of fish, so curious people pray for shoals of trouble, and plenty of business, and innovations and changes, that they may have something to hunt after and tittle-tattle about. Well also was it in *Charondas*, the legislator of the people of Thurii,[619] to forbid any of the citizens but adulterers and curious persons to be ridiculed on the stage. Adultery itself indeed seems to be only the fruit of curiosity about another man's pleasures, and an inquiring and prying into things kept close and hidden from the world; while curiosity is a tampering with and seduction of and revealing the nakedness of secrets.[620]

§ IX. As it is likely that much learning will produce wordiness, and so Pythagoras enjoined five years' silence on his scholars, calling it a truce from words,[621] so defamation of character is sure to go with curiosity. For what people are glad to hear they are glad to talk about, and what they eagerly pick up from others they joyfully retail to others. And so, amongst the other mischiefs of curiosity, the disease runs counter to their desires; for all people fight shy of them, and conceal their affairs from them, and neither care to do or say anything in their presence, but defer consultations, and put off investigations, till such people are out of the way; and if, when some secret is just about to be uttered, or some important business is just about to be arranged, some curious man happen to pop in, they are mum at once and reserved, as one puts away fish if the cat is about; and so frequently things seen and talked about by all the rest of the world are unknown only to them. For the same reason the curious person never gets the confidence of anybody. For we would rather entrust our letters and papers and seals to slaves and strangers than to curious friends and intimates. The famous Bellerophon,[622] though he carried letters against his life, opened them not, but abstained from reading the letter to the king, as he had refused to sell his honour to Proetus' wife, so great was his continence.[623] For curiosity and adultery both come from incontinence, and to the latter is added monstrous folly and insanity. For to pass by so many common and public women, and to intrude oneself on some married woman,[624] who is sure to be more costly, and possibly less pretty to boot, is the acme of madness. Yet such is the conduct of curious people. They neglect many gay sights, fail to hear much that would be well worth hearing, lose much fine sport and pastime, to break open private letters, to put their ears to their neighbour's walls, and to whisper to their slaves and women-servants, practices always low, and frequently dangerous.

§ X. It will be exceedingly useful, therefore, to deter the curious from these propensities, for them to remember their past experience. Simonides used to say that he occasionally opened two chests for rewards and thanks that he had by him, and found the one full for rewards, but the one for thanks always empty.[625] So if anyone were to open occasionally the stores that curiosity had amassed, and observe what a cargo there was of useless and idle and unlovely things, perhaps the sight of all this poor stuff would inspire him with disgust. Suppose someone, in studying the writings of the ancients, were to pick out only their worst passages, and compile them into a volume, as Homer's imperfect lines, and the solecisms of the tragedians, and Archilochus' indecent and bitter railings against women, by which he so exposed himself, would he not be worthy of the curse of the tragedian,

"Perish, compiler of thy neighbours' ills?"

And independently of such a curse, the piling up of other people's misdoings is indecent and useless, and like the town which Philip founded and filled with the vilest and most dissolute wretches, and called *Rogue Town*. Curious persons, indeed, making a collection of the faults and errors and solecisms, not of lines or poems but of people's lives, render their memory a most inelegant and unlovely register of dark deeds. Just as there are in Rome some people who care nothing for pictures and statues, or even handsome boys or women exposed for sale, but haunt the monster-market, and make eager inquiries about people who have no calves, or three eyes, or arms like weasels, or heads like ostriches, and look about for some

"Unnatural monster like the Minotaur,"[626]

and for a time are greatly captivated with them, but if anyone continually gazes at such sights, they will soon give him satiety and disgust; so let those who curiously inquire into the errors and faults of life, and disgraces of families, and disorders in other people's houses, first remember what little favour or advantage such prying has brought them on previous occasions.

§ XI. Habit will be of the utmost importance in stopping this propensity, if we begin early to practise self-control in respect to it, for as the disease increases by habit and degrees, so will its cure, as we shall see when we discuss the necessary discipline. In the first place, let us begin with the most trifling and unimportant matters. What hardship will it be when we walk abroad not to read the epitaphs on graves, or what detriment shall we suffer by not glancing at the inscriptions on walls in the public walks? Let us reflect that there is nothing useful or pleasant for us in these notices, which only record that so-and-so remembered so-and-so out of gratitude, and, "Here lies the best of friends," and much poor stuff of that kind;[627] which indeed do not seem to do much harm, except indirectly, to those that read them, by engendering the practice of curiosity about things immaterial. And as huntsmen do not allow the hounds to follow any scent and run where they please, but check and restrain them in leashes, keeping their sense of smell pure and fresh for the object of their chase, that they may the keener dart on their tracks, "following up the traces of the unfortunate beasts by their scent," so we must check and repress the sallies and excursions of the curious man to every object of interest, whether of sight or hearing, and confine him to what is useful. For as eagles and lions on the prowl keep their claws sheathed that they may not lose their edge and sharpness, so, when we remember that curiosity for learning has also its edge and keenness, let us not entirely expend or blunt it on inferior objects.

§ XII. Next let us accustom ourselves when we pass a strange house not to look inside at the door, or curiously inspect the interior, as if we were going to pilfer something, remembering always that saying of Xenocrates, that it is all one whether one puts one's feet or eyes in another person's house. For such prying is neither honourable, nor comely, nor even agreeable.

"Stranger, thou'lt see within untoward sights."

For such is generally the condition inside houses, utensils kicking about, maids lolling about, no work going on, nothing to please the eye; and moreover such side glances, and stray shots as it were, distort the soul, and are unhandsome, and the practice is a pernicious one. When Diogenes saw Dioxippus, a victor at Olympia, driving up in his chariot and unable to take his eyes off a handsome woman who was watching the procession, but still turning round and casting sheep's eyes at her, he said, "See you yon athlete straining his neck to look at a girl?" And similarly you may see curious people twisting and straining their necks at every spectacle alike, from the habit and practice of turning their eyes in all directions. And I think the senses ought not to rove about, like an ill-trained maid, when sent on an errand by the soul, but to do their business, and then return quickly with the answer, and afterwards to keep within the bounds of reason, and obey her behests. But it is like those lines of Sophocles,

"Then did the Ænianian's horses bolt, Unmanageable quite;"[628]

for so the senses not having, as we said, right training and practice, often run away, and drag reason along with them, and plunge her into unlawful excesses. And so, though that story about Democritus is false, that he purposely destroyed his eyesight by the reflection from burning-glasses (as people sometimes shut up windows that look into the street), that they might not disturb him by frequently calling off his attention to external things, but allow him to confine himself to purely intellectual matters, yet it is very true in every case that those who use the mind most are least acted upon by the senses. And so the philosophers erected their places for study as far as possible from towns, and called Night the time propitious to thought,[629] thinking quiet and withdrawal from worldly distractions a great help towards meditating upon and solving the problems of life.

§ XIII. Moreover, when men are abusing and reviling one another in the market-place, it is not very difficult or tiresome not to go near them; or if a tumultuous concourse of people crowd together, to remain seated; or to get up and go away, if you are not master of yourself. For you will gain no advantage by mixing yourself up with curious people: but you will derive the greatest benefit from putting a force upon your inclinations, and bridling your curiosity, and accustoming it to obey reason. Afterwards it will be well to extend the practice still further, and not to go to the theatre when some fine piece is performing, and if your friends invite you to see some dancer or actor to decline, and, if there is some shouting in the stadium and hippodrome, not even to turn your head to look what is up. For as Socrates advised people to abstain from food that made them eat when they were not hungry, and from drinks that made them drink when they were not thirsty, so ought we also to shun and flee from those objects of interest, whether to eye or ear, that master us and attract us when we stand in no need of them. Thus Cyrus would not look at Panthea, but when Araspes told him that her beauty was well worth inspection, he replied, "For that very reason must I the more abstain from seeing her, for if at your persuasion I were to pay her a visit, perhaps she would persuade me to visit her again when I could ill spare the time, so that I might neglect important business to sit with her and gaze on her charms."[630] Similarly Alexander would not see the wife of Darius, who was reputed to be very beautiful, but visited her mother who was old, and would not venture to look upon the young and handsome queen. We on the contrary peep into women's litters, and hang about their windows, and think we do no harm, though we thus make our curiosity a loop-hole[631] for all manner of vice.

§ XIV. Moreover, as it is of great help to fair dealing sometimes not to seize some honest gain, that you may accustom yourself as far as possible to flee from unjust gains, and as it makes greatly for virtue to abstain sometimes from your own wife, that you may not ever be tempted by another woman, so, applying the habit to curiosity, try not to see and hear at times all that goes on in your own house even, and if anyone wishes to tell you anything about it give him the go-by, and decline to hear him. For it was nothing but his curiosity that involved Oedipus in his extreme calamities: for it was to try and find out his extraction that he left Corinth and met Laius, and killed him, and got his kingdom, and married his own mother, and when he then seemed at the acme of felicity, he must needs make further inquiries about himself; and though his wife tried to prevent him, he none the less compelled the old man that had been an eye-witness of the deed to tell him all the circumstances of it, and though he long suspected how the story would end, yet when the old man cried out,

"Alas! the dreadful tale I must then tell,"

so inflamed was he with curiosity and trembling with impatience, that he replied,

"I too must hear, for hear it now I will."[632]

So bitter-sweet and uncontrollable is the itch of curiosity, like a sore, shedding its blood when lanced. But he that is free from this disease, and calm by nature, being ignorant of many unpleasant things, may say,

"Holy oblivion of all human ills, What wisdom dost thou bring!"[633]

§ XV. We ought therefore also to accustom ourselves, when we receive a letter, not to be in a tremendous hurry about breaking the seal, as most people are, even tearing it open with their teeth if their hands are slow; nor to rise from our seat and run up to meet him, if a messenger comes; and if a friend says, "I have some news to tell you," we ought to say, "I had rather you had something useful or advantageous to tell me." When I was on one occasion lecturing at Rome, one of my audience was the well-known Rusticus, whom the Emperor Domitian afterwards had put to death through envy of his glory, and a soldier came in in the middle and brought him a letter from the Emperor, and silence ensuing, and I stopping that he might have time to read his letter, he would not, and did not open it till I had finished my lecture, and the audience had dispersed; so that everybody marvelled at his self-control. But whenever anyone who has power feeds his curiosity till it is strong and vehement, he can no longer easily control it, when it hurries him on to illicit acts, from force of habit; and such people open their friends' letters, thrust themselves in at private meetings, become spectators of rites they ought not to witness, enter holy grounds they ought not to, and pry into the lives and conversations of kings.

§ XVI. Indeed tyrants themselves, who must know all things, are made unpopular by no class more than by their spies[634] and talebearers. Darius in his youth, when he mistrusted his own powers, and suspected and feared everybody, was the first who employed spies; and the Dionysiuses introduced them at Syracuse: but in a revolution they were the first that the Syracusans took and tortured to death. Indeed informers are of the same tribe and family as curious people. However informers only investigate wicked acts or plots, but curious people pry into and publish abroad the involuntary misfortunes of their neighbours. And it is said that impious people first got their name from curiosity, for it seems there was a mighty famine at Athens, and those people that had wheat not producing it, but grinding it stealthily by night in their houses, some of their neighbours went about and noticed the noise of the mills grinding, and so they got their name.[635] This also is the origin of the well-known Greek word for informer, (Sycophant, *quasi* Fig-informer), for when the people were forbidden to export figs, those who informed against those who did were called Fig-informers. It is well worth the while of curious people to give their attention to this, that they may be ashamed of having any similarity or connection in habit with a class of people so universally hated and disliked as informers.

[608] Jeremy Taylor has largely borrowed from this Treatise in his "Holy Living," chap. ii. § v. Of Modesty.

[609] Chæronea in Boeotia.

[610]   Lines   from   some   comic   poet,   no   doubt.

[611] "Oeconomicus," cap. viii.

[612] The mother of Oedipus, better known as "Jocasta."

[613] Homer, "Odyssey," xi. 278. Epicaste hung herself.

[614] "[Greek: oikiskô] corrigit Valekenarius ad Herodot. p. 557."--*Wyttenbach.*

[615] Aristophanes, "Equites," 79.

[616] Sophocles, Fragm. 713. The lines are quoted more fully by our author in his "Lives," p. 911. There are there four preceding lines that compare human life to the moon's changes.

[617] Æschylus, "Supplices," 937. [618]

All three being eminent doctors. [619]

"Intelligo Charondam."--*Xylander.*

[620] Plutarch wants to show that curiosity and adultery are really the same vice in principle. Hence his imagery here. Jeremy Taylor has very beautifully dealt with this passage, "Holy Living," chap. ii. § v. I cannot pretend to his felicity of language. Thus Plutarch makes adultery mere curiosity, and curiosity a sort of adultery in regard to secrets. A profoundly ethical and moral view. Compare § ix.

[621] Compare Lucian's [Greek: echeglôttia], after [Greek: echecheiria] (*armistice*), *Lexiph.* 9.

[622] See the story in Homer, "Iliad," vi. 155 sq.

[623] Or self-control.

[624] Literally, some woman *shut up*, or *enclosed.*

[625] See also our author's "On those who are punished by the Deity late," § xi.

[626] See Euripides, Fragm., 389. Also Plutarch's "Theseus," cap. xv.

[627] Plutarch rather reminds one, in his evident contempt for *Epitaphs*, of the cynic who asked, "Where are all the bad people buried?" Where indeed?

[628] Sophocles, "Electra," 724, 725.

[629] *euphronê*, a stock phrase for night, is here defined.

[630] "Historia exstat initio libri quinti Cyropædiæ."--*Reiske.*

[631] Literally, "slippery and prone to." For the metaphor of "slippery" compare Horace, "Odes," i. 19-8, "Et vultus nimium lubricus adspici."

[632] This and the line above are in Sophocles, "Oedipus Tyrannus," 1169, 1170.

[633] Euripides, "Orestes," 213.

[634] Literally, *ears*.

[635] The paronomasia is as follows. The word for impious people is supposed to mean *listeners to mills grinding*.

ON SHYNESS.[636]

§ I. Some of the things that grow on the earth are in their nature wild and barren and injurious to the growth of seeds and plants, yet those who till the ground consider them indications not of a bad soil but of a rich and fat one;[637] so also there are passions of the soul that are not good, yet are as it were offshoots of a good disposition, and one likely to improve with good advice. Among these I class shyness, no bad sign in itself, though it affords occasion to vice. For the modest oftentimes plunge into the same excesses as the shameless, but then they are pained and grieved at them, and not pleased like the others. For the shameless person is quite apathetic at what is disgraceful, while the modest person is easily affected even at the very appearance of it. Shyness is in fact an excess of modesty. And thus it is called shamefacedness, because the face exhibits the changes of the mind. For as dejection is defined to be the grief that makes people look on the ground, so shamefacedness is that shyness that cannot look people in the face. And so the orator said the shameless person had not pupils[638] in his eyes but harlots. The bashful person on the other hand shows his delicacy and effeminacy of soul in his countenance, and palliates his weakness, which exposes him to defeat at the hands of the impudent, by the name of modesty. Cato used to say he was better pleased with those lads that blushed than with those that turned pale, rightly teaching us to fear censure more than labour,[639] and suspicion than danger. However we must avoid too much timidity and fear of censure, since many have played the coward, and abandoned noble ventures, more from fear of a bad name than of the dangers to be undergone, not being able to bear a bad reputation.

§ II. As we must not disregard their weakness, so neither again must we praise that rigid and stubborn insensibility, "that recklessness and frantic energy to rush anywhere, that seemed like a dog's courage in Anaxarchus."[640] But we must contrive a harmonious blending of the two, that shall remove the shamelessness of pertinacity, and the weakness of excessive modesty; seeing its cure is difficult, and the correction of such excesses not without danger. For as the husbandman, in rooting up some wild and useless weed, at once plunges his spade vigorously into the ground, and digs it up by the root, or burns it with fire, but if he has to do with a vine that needs pruning, or some apple-tree, or olive, he puts his hand to it very carefully, being afraid of injuring any sound part; so the philosopher, eradicating from the soul of the young man that ignoble and untractable weed, envy, or unseasonable avarice, or amputating the excessive love of pleasure, may bandage and draw blood, make deep incision, and leave scars: but if he has to apply reason as a corrective to a tender and delicate part of the soul, such as shyness and bashfulness, he is careful that he may not inadvertently root up modesty as well. For nurses who are often rubbing the dirt off their infants sometimes tear their flesh and put them to torture. We ought not therefore, by rubbing off the shyness of youths too much, to make them too careless and contemptuous; but as those that pull down houses close to temples prop up the adjacent parts, so in trying to get rid of shyness we must not eradicate with it the virtues akin to it, as modesty and meekness and mildness, by which it insinuates itself and becomes part of a man's character, flattering the bashful man that he has a nature courteous and civil and affable, and not hard as flint or self-willed. And so the Stoics from the outset verbally distinguished shame and shyness from modesty, that they might not by identity of name give the vice opportunity to inflict harm. But let it be granted to us to use the words indiscriminately, following indeed the example of Homer. For he said,

"Modesty does both harm and good to men;"[641]

and he did well to mention the harm it does first. For it becomes advantageous only through reason's curtailing its excess, and reducing it to moderate proportions.

§ III. In the first place, then, the person who is afflicted with shyness ought to be persuaded that he suffers from an injurious disease, and that nothing injurious can be good: nor must he be wheedled and tickled with the praise of being called a nice and jolly fellow rather than being styled lofty and dignified and just; nor, like Pegasus in Euripides, "who stooped and crouched lower than he wished"[642] to take up his rider Bellerophon, must he humble himself and grant whatever favours are asked him, fearing to be called hard and ungentle. They say that the Egyptian Bocchoris, who was by nature very severe, had an asp sent him by Isis, which coiled round his head, and shaded him from above, that he might judge righteously. Bashfulness on the contrary, like a dead weight on languid and effeminate persons, not daring to refuse or contradict anybody, makes jurors deliver unjust verdicts, and shuts the mouth of counsellors, and makes people say and do many things against their wish; and so the most headstrong person is always master and lord of such, through his own impudence prevailing against their modesty. So bashfulness, like soft and sloping ground, being unable to repel or avert any attack, lies open to the most shameful acts and passions. It is a bad guardian of youth, as Brutus said he didn't think that person had spent his youth well who had not learnt how to say No. It is a bad duenna of the bridal bed and of women's apartments, as the penitent adultress in Sophocles said to her seducer,

"You did persuade, and coax me into sin."[643]

Thus shyness, being first seduced by vice,[644] leaves its citadel unbarred, unfortified, and open to attack. By gifts people ensnare the worse natures, but by persuasion and playing upon their bashfulness people often seduce even good women. I pass over the injury done to worldly affairs by bashfulness causing people to lend to those whose credit is doubtful, and to go security against their wish, for though they commend that saying, "Be a surety, trouble is at hand,"[645] they cannot apply it when business is on hand.

§ IV. It would not be easy to enumerate how many this vice has ruined. When Creon said to Medea,

"Lady, 'tis better now to earn your hate, Than through my softness afterwards to groan,"[646]

he uttered a pregnant maxim for others; for he himself was overcome by his bashfulness, and granted her one day more, and so was the undoing of his family. And some, when they suspected murder or poison, have failed through it to take precautions for their safety. Thus perished Dion, not ignorant that Callippus was plotting against him, but ashamed to be on his guard against a friend and host. So Antipater, the son of Cassander, having invited Demetrius to supper, and being invited back by him for the next day, was ashamed to doubt another as he had been trusted himself, and went, and got his throat cut after supper. And Polysperchon promised Cassander for a hundred talents to murder Hercules, the son of Alexander by Barsine, and invited him to supper, and, as the stripling suspected and feared the invitation, and pleaded as an excuse that he was not very well, Polysperchon called on him, and addressed him as follows, "Imitate, my lad, your father's good-nature and kindness to his friends, unless indeed you fear us as plotting against you." The young man was ashamed to refuse any longer, so he went with him, and some of those at the supper-party strangled him. And so that line of Hesiod,[647]

"Invite your friend to supper, not your enemy,"

is not ridiculous, as some say, or stupid advice, but wise. Show no bashfulness in regard to an enemy, and do not suppose him trustworthy, though he may seem so.[648] For if you invite you will be invited back, and if you entertain others you will be entertained back to your hurt, if you let the temper as it were of your caution be weakened by shame.

§ V. As then this disease is the cause of much mischief, we must try and exterminate it by assiduous effort, beginning first, as people are wont to do in other matters, with small and easy things. For example, if anyone pledge you to drink with him at a dinner when you have had enough, do not be bashful, or do violence to nature, but put the cup down without drinking. Again, if somebody else challenge you to play at dice with him in your cups, be not bashful or afraid of ridicule, but imitate Xenophanes, who, when Lasus of Hermione called him coward because he would not play at dice with him, admitted that he was a great coward and had no courage for what was ignoble. Again, if you meet with some prating fellow who attacks you and sticks to you, do not be bashful, but get rid of him, and hasten on and pursue your undertaking. For such flights and repulses, keeping you in practice in trying to overcome your bashfulness in small matters, will prepare you for greater occasions. And here it is well to record a remark of Demosthenes. When the Athenians were going to help Harpalus, and to war against Alexander, all of a sudden Philoxenus, who was Alexander's admiral, was sighted in the offing. And the populace being greatly alarmed, and speechless for fear, Demosthenes said, "What will they do when they see the sun, if they cannot lift their eyes to face a lamp?" And what will you do in important matters, if the king desires anything, or the people importune you, if you cannot decline to drink when your friend asks you, or evade the onset of some prating fellow, but allow the trifler to waste all your time, from not having nerve to say, "I will see you some other time, I have no leisure now."[649]

§ VI. Moreover, the use and practice of restraining one's bashfulness in small and unimportant matters is advantageous also in regard to praise. For example, if a friend's harper sings badly at a drinking party, or an actor hired at great cost murders[650] Menander, and most of the party clap and applaud, I find it by no means hard, or bad manners, to listen silently, and not to be so illiberal as to praise contrary to one's convictions. For if in such matters you are not master of yourself, what will you do if your friend reads a poor poem, or parades a speech stupidly and ridiculously written?[651] You will praise it of course, and join the flatterers in loud applause. But how then will you find fault with your friend if he makes mistakes in business? How will you be able to correct him, if he acts improperly in reference to some office, or marriage, or the state? For I cannot indeed assent to the remark of Pericles to his friend, who asked him to bear false witness in his favour even to the extent of perjury, "I am your friend as far as the altar." He went too far. But he that has long accustomed himself never to go against his convictions in praising a speaker, or clapping a singer, or laughing at a dull buffoon, will never go to this length, nor say to some impudent fellow in such matters, "Swear on my behalf, bear false witness, pronounce an unjust verdict."

§ VII. So also we ought to refuse people that want to borrow money of us, from being accustomed to say No in small and easily refused matters. Thus Archelaus, king of the Macedonians, being asked at supper for a gold cup by a man who thought *Receive* the finest word in the language, bade a boy give it to Euripides,[652] and gazing intently on the man said to him, "You are fit to ask, and not to receive, and he is fit to receive without asking." Thus did he make judgement and not bashfulness the arbiter of his gifts and favours. Yet we oftentimes pass over our friends who are both deserving and in need, and give to others who continually and impudently importune us, not from the wish to give but from the inability to say No. So the older Antigonus, being frequently annoyed by Bion, said, "Give a talent to Bion and necessity." Yet he was of all the kings most clever and ingenious at getting rid of such importunity. For on one occasion, when a Cynic asked him for a drachma, he replied, "That would be too little for a king to give;"[653] and when the Cynic rejoined, "Give me then a talent," he met him with, "That would be too much for a Cynic to receive."[654] Diogenes indeed used to go round begging to the statues in the Ceramicus, and when people expressed their astonishment said he was practising how to bear refusals. And we must practise ourselves in small matters, and exercise ourselves in little things, with a view to refusing people who importune us, or would receive from us when inconvenient, that we may be able to avoid great miscarriages. For no one, as Demosthenes says,[655] if he expends his resources on unnecessary things, will have means for necessary ones. And our disgrace is greatly increased, if we are deficient in what is noble, and abound in what is trivial.

§ VIII. But bashfulness is not only a bad and inconsiderate manager of money, but also in more important matters makes us reject expediency and reason. For when we are ill we do not call in the experienced doctor, because we stand in awe of the family one; and instead of the best teachers for our boys we select those that importune us;[656] and in our suits at law we frequently refuse the aid of some skilled advocate, to oblige the son of some friend or relative, and give him a chance to make a forensic display; and lastly, you will find many so-called philosophers Epicureans or Stoics, not from deliberate choice or conviction, but simply from bashfulness, to have the same views as their friends and acquaintances. Since this is the case, let us accustom ourselves betimes in small and everyday matters to employ no barber or fuller merely from bashfulness, nor to put up at a sorry inn, when a better is at hand, merely because the innkeeper has on several occasions been extra civil to us, but for the benefit of the habit to select the best even in a small matter; as the Pythagoreans were careful never to put their left leg across the right, nor to take an even number instead of an odd, all other matters being indifferent. We must accustom ourselves also, at a sacrifice or marriage or any entertainment of that kind, not to invite the person who greets us and runs up to meet us, but the friend who is serviceable to us. For he that has thus practised and trained himself will be difficult to catch tripping, nay even unassailable, in greater matters.

§ IX. Let so much suffice for practice. And of useful considerations the first is that which teaches and reminds us, that all passions and maladies of the soul are accompanied by the very things which we think we avoid through them. Thus infamy comes through too great love of fame, and pain comes from love of pleasure, and plenty of work to the idle, and to the contentious defeats and losses of lawsuits. And so too it is the fate of bashfulness, in fleeing from the smoke of ill-repute, to throw itself into the fire of it.[657] For the bashful, not venturing to say No to those that press them hard, afterwards feel shame at just rebuke, and, through standing in awe of slight blame, frequently in the end incur open disgrace. For if a friend asks some money of them, and through bashfulness they cannot refuse, a little time after they are disgraced by the facts becoming known;[658] or if they have promised to help friends in a lawsuit, they turn round and hide their diminished heads, and run away from fear of the other side. Many also, who have accepted on behalf of a daughter or sister an unprofitable offer of marriage at the bidding of bashfulness, have afterwards been compelled to break their word, and break off the match.

§ X. He that said all the dwellers in Asia were slaves to one man because they could not say the one syllable No, spoke in jest and not in earnest; but bashful persons, even if they say nothing, can by raising or dropping their eyebrows decline many disagreeable and unpleasant acts of compliance. For Euripides says, "Silence is an answer to wise men,"[659] but we stand more in need of it to inconsiderate persons, for we can talk over the sensible. And indeed it is well to have at hand and frequently on our lips the sayings[660] of good and famous men to quote to those who importune us, as that of Phocion to Antipater, "You cannot have me both as a friend and flatterer;" or his remark to the Athenians, when they applauded him and bade him contribute to the expenses of a festival, "I am ashamed to contribute anything to you, till I have paid yonder person my debts to him," pointing out his creditor Callicles. For, as Thucydides says, "It is not disgraceful to admit one's poverty, but it is very much so not to try to mend it."[661] But he who through stupidity or softness is too bashful to say to anyone that importunes him,

"Stranger, no silver white is in my caves,"

but goes bail for him as it were through his promises,

"Is bound by fetters not of brass but shame."[662]

But Persæus,[663] when he lent a sum of money to one of his friends, had the fact duly attested by a banker in the market-place, remembering belike that line in Hesiod,[664]

"E'en to a brother, smiling, bring you witness."

And he wondering and saying, "Why all these legal forms, Persæus?" he replied, "Ay, verily, that my money may be paid back in a friendly way, and that I may not have to use legal forms to get it back." For many, at first too bashful to see to security, have afterwards had to go to law, and lost their friend.[665]

§ XI. Plato again, giving Helicon of Cyzicus a letter for Dionysius, praised the bearer as a man of goodness and moderation, but added at the end of the letter, "I write you this about a man, an animal by nature apt to change." But Xenocrates, though a man of austere character, was prevailed upon through his bashfulness to recommend to Polysperchon by letter, one who was no good man as the event showed; for when the Macedonian welcomed him, and inquired if he wanted any money, he asked for a talent, and Polysperchon gave it him, but wrote to Xenocrates advising him for the future to be more careful in the choice of people he recommended. But Xenocrates knew not the fellow's true character; we on the other hand very often when we know that such and such men are bad, yet give them testimonials and money, doing ourselves injury, and not getting any pleasure for it, as people do get in the company of whores and flatterers, but being vexed and disgusted at the importunity that has upset and forced our reason. For the line

"I know that what I'm going to do is bad,"[666]

is especially applicable to people that importune us, when one is going to perjure oneself, or deliver an unjust verdict, or vote for a measure that is inexpedient, or borrow money for someone who will never pay it back.

§ XII. And so repentance follows more closely upon bashfulness than upon any emotion, and that not afterwards, but in the very act. For we are vexed with ourselves when we give, and ashamed when we perjure ourselves, and get ill-fame from our advocacies, and are put to the blush, when we cannot fulfil our promises. For frequently, from inability to say No, we promise impossibilities to persevering applicants, as introductions at court, and audiences with princes, from reluctance or want of nerve to say, "The king does not know us, others have his regard far more." But Lysander, when he was out of favour with Agesilaus, though he was thought to have very great influence with him owing to his great reputation, was not ashamed to dismiss suitors, and bid them go and pay their court to others who had more influence with the king. For not to be able to do everything carries no disgrace with it, but to undertake and try and force your way to what you are unable to do, or unqualified by nature for, is in addition to the disgrace incurred a task full of trouble.

§ XIII. To take another element into consideration, all seemly and modest requests we ought readily to comply with, not bashfully but heartily, whereas in injurious or unreasonable requests we ought ever to remember the conduct of Zeno, who, meeting a young man he knew walking very quietly near a wall, and learning from him that he was trying to get out of the way of a friend who wanted him to perjure himself on his behalf, said to him, "O stupid fellow, what do you tell me? Is he not afraid or ashamed to press you to what is not right? And dare not you stand up boldly against him for what is right?" For he that said "villainy is no bad weapon against villainy"[667] taught people the bad practice of standing on one's defence against vice by imitating it; but to get rid of those who shamelessly and unblushingly importune us by their own effrontery, and not to gratify the immodest in their disgraceful desires through false modesty, is the right and proper conduct of sensible people.

§ XIV. Moreover it is no great task to resist disreputable and low and worthless fellows who importune you, but some send such off with a laugh or a jest, as Theocritus did, who, when two fellows in the public baths, one a stranger, the other a well-known thief, wanted to borrow his scraper,[668] put them both off with a playful answer, "You, sir, I don't know, and you I know too well." And Lysimache,[669] the priestess of Athene Polias at Athens, when some muleteers that bore the sacred vessels asked her to give them a drink, answered, "I hesitate to do so from fear that you would make a practice of it." And when a certain young man, the son of a distinguished officer, but himself effeminate and far from bold, asked Antigonus for promotion, he replied, "With me, young man, honours are given for personal prowess, not for the prowess of ancestors."

§ XV. But if the person that importunes us be famous or a man of power, for such persons are very hard to move by entreaty or to get rid of when they come to sue for your vote and interest, it will not perhaps be easy or even necessary to behave as Cato, when quite a young man, did to Catulus. Catulus was in the highest repute at Rome, and at that time held the office of censor, and went to Cato, who then held the office of quæstor, and tried to beg off someone whom he had fined, and was urgent and even violent in his petitions, till Cato at last lost all patience, and said, "To have you, the censor, removed by my officers against your will, Catulus, would not be a seemly thing for you." So Catulus felt ashamed, and went off in a rage. But see whether the answers of Agesilaus and Themistocles are not more modest and in better form. Agesilaus, when he was asked by his father to pronounce sentence contrary to the law, said, "Father, I was taught by you even from my earliest years to obey the laws, so now I shall obey you and do nothing contrary to law." And Themistocles, when Simonides asked him to do something unjust, replied, "Neither would you be a good poet if your lines violated the laws of metre, nor should I be a good magistrate if I gave decisions contrary to law."

§ XVI. And yet it is not on account of want of metrical harmony in respect to the lyre, to borrow the words of Plato, that cities quarrel with cities and friends with friends, and do and suffer the worst woes, but on account of deviations[670] from law and justice. And yet some, who themselves pay great attention to melody and letters and measures, do not think it wrong for others to neglect what is right in magistracies and judicial sentences and business generally. One must therefore deal with them in the following manner. Does an orator ask a favour of you when you are acting as juryman, or a demagogue when you are sitting in council? Say you will grant his request if he first utter a solecism, or introduce a barbarism into his speech; he will refuse because of the shame that would attach itself to him; at any rate we see some that will not in a speech let two vowels come together. If again some illustrious and distinguished person importune you to something bad, bid him come into the market-place dancing or making wry faces, and if he refuse you will have an opportunity to speak, and ask him which is more disgraceful, to utter a solecism and make wry faces, or to violate the law and one's oath, and contrary to justice to do more for a bad than for a good man. Nicostratus the Argive, when Archidamus offered him a large sum of money and any Lacedæmonian bride he chose if he would deliver up Cromnum, said Archidamus could not be a descendant of Hercules, for he travelled about and killed evil-doers, whereas Archidamus tried to make evil-doers of the good. In like manner, if a man of good repute tries to force and importune us to something bad, let us tell him that he is acting in an ignoble way, and not as his birth and virtue would warrant.

§ XVII. But in the case of people of no repute you must see whether you can persuade the miser by your importunity to lend you money without a bond, or the proud man to yield you the better place, or the ambitious man to surrender some office to you when he might take it himself. For truly it would seem monstrous that, while such remain firm and inflexible and unmoveable in their vicious propensities, we who wish to be, and profess to be, men of honour and justice should be so little masters of ourselves as to abandon and betray virtue. For indeed, if those who importune us do it for glory and power, it is absurd that we should adorn and aggrandize others only to get infamy and a bad name ourselves; like unfair umpires in the public games, or like people voting only to ingratiate themselves, and so bestowing improperly offices and prizes[671] and glory on others, while they rob themselves of respect and fair fame. And if we see that the person who importunes us only does so for money, does it not occur to one that it is monstrous to be prodigal of one's own fame and reputation merely to make somebody else's purse heavier? Why the idea must occur to most people, they sin with their eyes open; like people who are urged hard to toss off big bumpers, and grunt and groan and make wry faces, but at last do as they are told.

§ XVIII. Such weakness of mind is like a temperament of body equally susceptible to heat and cold; for if such people are praised by those that importune them they are overcome and yield at once, whereas they are mortally afraid of the blame and suspicions of those whose desires they do not comply with. But we ought to be stout and resolute in either case, neither yielding to bullying nor cajolery. Thucydides indeed tells us, since envy necessarily follows ability, that "he is well advised who incurs envy in matters of the highest importance."[672] But we, thinking it difficult to escape envy, and seeing that it is altogether impossible not to incur blame or give offence to those we live with, shall be well advised if we prefer the hatred of the perverse to that of those who might justly find fault with us for having iniquitously served their turn. And indeed we ought to be on our guard against praise from those who importune us, which is sure to be altogether insincere, and not to resemble swine, readily allowing anyone that presses to make use of us from our pleasure at itching and tickling, and submitting ourselves to their will. For those that give their ears to flatterers differ not a whit from such as let themselves be tripped up at wrestling, only their overthrow and fall is more disgraceful; some forbearing hostility and reproof in the case of bad men, that they may be called merciful and humane and compassionate; and others on the contrary persuaded to take up unnecessary and dangerous animosities and charges by those who praise them as the only men, the only people that never flatter, and go so far as to entitle them their mouthpieces and voices. Accordingly Bio[673] compared such people to jars, that you could easily take by the ears and turn about at your will. Thus it is recorded that the sophist Alexinus in one of his lectures said a good many bad things about Stilpo the Megarian, but when one of those that were present said, "Why, he was speaking in your praise only the other day," he replied, "I don't doubt it; for he is the best and noblest of men." Menedemus on the contrary, having heard that Alexinus[674] frequently praised him, replied, "But I always censure him, for that man is bad who either praises a bad man or is blamed by a good." So inflexible and proof was he against such flattery, and master of that advice which Hercules in Antisthenes[675] gave, when he ordered his sons to be grateful to no one that praised them; which meant nothing else than that they should not be dumbfoundered at it, nor flatter again those who praised them. Very apt, I take it, was the remark of Pindar to one who told him that he praised him everywhere and to all persons, "I am greatly obliged to you, and will make your account true by my actions."

§ XIX. A useful precept in reference to all passions is especially valuable in the case of the bashful. When they have been overcome by this infirmity, and against their judgement have erred and been confounded, let them fix it in their memories, and, remembering the pain and grief it gave them, let them recall it to their mind and be on their guard for a very long time. For as travellers that have stumbled against a stone, or pilots that have been wrecked off a headland, if they remember these occurrences, not only dread and are on their guard continually on those spots, but also on all similar ones; so those that frequently remember the disgrace and injury that bashfulness brought them, and its sorrow and anguish, will in similar cases be on their guard against their weakness, and will not readily allow themselves to be subjugated by it again.

[636] Or *bashfulness*, *shamefacedness*, what the French call *mauvaise honte*.

[637] Shakespeare puts all this into one line: "Most subject is the fattest soil to weeds."--*2 Henry IV.*, A. iv. Sc. iv.

[638] Or *girls*. [Greek: korê] means both a girl, and the pupil of the eye.

[639] So Wyttenbach.

[640] These lines are quoted again "On Moral Virtue," § vi.

[641] "Iliad," xxiv. 44, 45.

[642] Euripides, "Bellerophon," Fragm., 313.

[643] Soph., Fragm., 736.

[644] Surely it is necessary to read [Greek: prodiaphthareisa tô akolastô].

[645] See Plato, "Charmides," 165 A.

[646] Euripides, "Medea," 290, 291.

[647] "Works and Days," 342.

[648] Reading with Wyttenbach, [Greek: mêd hypolabe pisteuein, dokounta].

[649] See Horace's very amusing "Satire," i. ix., on such tiresome fellows.

[650] [Greek: epitribô] is used in the same sense by Demosthenes, p. 288.

[651] On such social pests see Juvenal, i. 1-14.

[652] See Pausanias, i. 2. Euripides left Athens about 409 B.C., and took up his abode for good in Macedonia at the court of Archelaus, where he died 406 B.C.

[653] For a drachma was only worth 6 obols, or 9¾d. of our money, nearly = Roman denarius.

[654] A talent was 6,000 drachmæ, or 36,000 obols, about £243 15s. of our money.

[655] "Olynth." iii. p. 33, § 19.

[656] Compare "On Education," § vii.

[657] Our "Out of the frying-pan into the fire." Cf. "Incidit in Scyllam cupiens vitare Charybdim."

[658] By their having to borrow themselves.

[659] Fragm. 947.

[660] Or apophthegms, of which Plutarch and Lord Verulam have both left us collections.

[661] Thucydides, ii. 40. Pericles is the speaker.

[662] A slightly-changed line from Euripides' "Pirithous," Fragm. 591. Quoted correctly "On Abundance of Friends," § vii.

[663] "Zenonis discipulus."--*Reiske*.

[664] "Works and Days," 371.

[665] Cf. Shakspere, "Hamlet," i. iii. 76.

[666] Euripides, "Medea," 1078.

[667] Our "Set a thief to catch a thief."

[668] Or strigil. See Otto Jahn's note on Persius, v. 126.

[669] "Forsitan illa quam nominat Pausanias, i. 27."--*Reiske*.

[670] Literally "want of tune in." We cannot well keep up the metaphor. Compare with this passage, "That virtue may be taught," § ii.

[671] Literally "crowns."

[672] Thucydides, ii. 64. Pericles is the speaker. Quoted again in "How one may discern a flatterer from a friend," § XXXV.

[673] "Est Bio Borysthenita, de quo vide Diog. Laërt."--*Reiske*.

[674] "De Alexino Eleo vide Diog. Laërt., ii. 109. Nostri p. 1063, 3."--*Reiske*.

[675] Antisthenes wrote a book called "Hercules." See Diogenes Laertius, vi. 16.

ON RESTRAINING ANGER.

A DIALOGUE BETWEEN SYLLA AND FUNDANUS.

§ I. *Sylla.* Those painters, Fundanus, seem to me to do well who, before giving the finishing touches to their paintings, lay them by for a time and then revise them; because by taking their eyes off them for a time they gain by frequent inspection a new insight, and are more apt to detect minute differences, that continuous familiarity would have hidden. Now since a human being cannot so separate himself from himself for a time, and make a break in his continuity, and then approach himself again--and that is perhaps the chief reason why a man is a worse judge of himself than of others--the next best thing will be for a man to inspect his friends after an interval, and likewise offer himself to their scrutiny, not to see whether he has aged quickly, or whether his bodily condition is better or worse, but to examine his moral character, and see whether time has added any good quality, or removed any bad one. On my return then to Rome after an absence of two years, and having been with you now five months, I am not at all surprised that there has been a great increase and growth in those good points which you formerly had owing to your admirable nature; but when I see how gentle and obedient to reason your former excessive impetuosity and hot temper has become, it cannot but occur to me to quote the line,

"Ye gods, how much more mild is he become!"[676]

And this mildness has not wrought in you sloth or weakness, but like cultivation of the soil it has produced a smoothness and depth fit for action, instead of the former impetuosity and vehemence. And so it is clear that your propensity to anger has not been effaced by any declining vigour or through some chance, but has been cured by good precepts. And indeed, for I will tell you the truth, when our friend Eros[677] reported this change in you to me, I suspected that owing to goodwill he bare witness not of the actual state of the case, but of what was becoming to all good and virtuous men, although, as you know, he can never be persuaded to depart from his real opinion to ingratiate himself with anyone. But now he is acquitted of false witness, and do you, as your journey gives you leisure, narrate to me the mode of cure you employed to make your temper so under control, so natural, gentle and obedient to reason.

Fundanus. Most friendly Sylla, take care that you do not in your goodwill and affection to me rest under any misconception of my real condition. For it is possible that Eros, not being able always himself to keep his temper in its place in the obedience that Homer speaks of,[678] but sometimes carried away by his hatred of what is bad, may think me grown milder than I really am, as in changes of the scale in music the lowest notes become the highest.

Sylla. Neither of these is the case, Fundanus, but oblige me by doing as I ask.

§ II. *Fundanus.* One of the excellent precepts then of Musonius that I remember, Sylla, is this, that those who wish to be well should diet themselves all their life long. For I do not think we must employ reason as a cure, as we do hellebore, by purging it out with the disease, but we must retain it in the soul, to restrain and govern the judgement. For the power of reason is not like physic, but wholesome food, which co-operates with good health in producing a good habit of body in those by whom it is taken. But admonition and reproof, when passion is at its height and swelling, does little or no good, but resembles very closely those strong-smelling substances, that are able to set on their legs again those that have fallen in epileptic fits, but cannot rid them of their disease. For although all other passions, even at the moment of their acme, do in some sort listen to reason and admit it into the soul, yet anger does not, for, as Melanthius says,

"Fell things it does when it the mind unsettles,"

for it absolutely turns reason out of doors, and bolts it out, and, like those persons who burn themselves and houses together, it makes all the interior full of confusion and smoke and noise, so that what would be advantageous can neither be seen nor heard. And so an empty ship in a storm at open sea would sooner admit on board a pilot from without, than a man in a tempest of rage and anger would listen to another's advice, unless his own reason was first prepared to hearken. But as those who expect a siege get together and store up supplies, when they despair of relief from without, so ought we by all means to scour the country far and wide to derive aids against anger from philosophy, and store them up in the soul: for, when the time of need comes, we shall find it no easy task to import them. For either the soul doesn't hear what is said without because of the uproar, if it have not within its own reason (like a boatswain as it were) to receive at once and understand every exhortation; or if it does hear, it despises what is uttered mildly and gently, while it is exasperated by harsh censure. For anger being haughty and self-willed and hard to be worked upon by another, like a fortified tyranny, must have someone born and bred within it[679] to overthrow it.

§ III. Now long-continued anger, and frequent giving way to it, produces an evil disposition of soul, which people call irascibility, and which ends in passionateness, bitterness, and peevishness, whenever the mind becomes sore and vexed at trifles and querulous at everyday occurrences, like iron thin and beaten out too fine. But when the judgement checks and suppresses at once the rising anger, it not only cures the soul for the moment, but restores its tone and balance for the future. It has happened to myself indeed twice or thrice, when I strongly fought against anger, that I was in the same plight as the Thebans, who after they had once defeated the Lacedæmonians, whom they had hitherto thought invincible, never lost a battle against them again. I then felt confident that reason can win the victory. I saw also that anger is not only appeased by the sprinkling of cold water, as Aristotle attested, but is also extinguished by the action of fear; aye, and, as Homer tells us, anger has been cured and has melted away in the case of many by some sudden joy. So that I came to the conclusion that this passion is not incurable for those who wish to be cured. For it does not arise from great and important causes, but banter and joking, a laugh or a nod, and similar trifles make many angry, as Helen by addressing her niece,

"Electra, maiden now for no short time,"[680]

provoked her to reply,

"Your wisdom blossoms late, since formerly You left your house in shame;"[681]

and Callisthenes incensed Alexander, by saying, when a huge cup was brought to him, "I will not drink to Alexander till I shall require the help of Æsculapius."

§ IV. As then it is easy to put out a flame kindled in the hair of hares and in wicks and rubbish, but if it once gets hold of things solid and thick, it quickly destroys and consumes them, "raging amidst the lofty work of the carpenters," as Æschylus[682] says; so he that observes anger in its rise, and sees it gradually smoking and bursting forth into fire from some chatter or rubbishy scurrility, need have no great trouble with it, but can frequently smother it merely by silence and contempt. For as a person puts out a fire by bringing no fuel to it, so with respect to anger, he that does not in the beginning fan it, and stir up its rage in himself, keeps it off and destroys it. And so, though Hieronymus has given us many useful sayings and precepts, I am not pleased with his remark that there is no perception of anger in its birth, but only in its actual developement, so quick is it. For none of the passions when stirred up and set in motion has so palpable a birth and growth as anger. As indeed Homer skilfully shows us, where he represents Achilles as seized at once with grief, when word was brought him *of Patroclus' death*, in the line,

"Thus spake he, and grief's dark cloud covered him;"[683]

whereas he represents him as waxing angry with Agamemnon slowly, and as inflamed by his many words, which if either of them[684] had abstained from, their quarrel would not have attained such growth and magnitude. And so Socrates, as often as he perceived any anger rising in him against any of his friends, "setting himself like some ocean promontory to break the violence of the waves," would lower his voice, and put on a smiling countenance, and give his eye a gentler expression, by inclining in the other direction and running counter to his passion, thus keeping himself from fall and defeat.

§ V. For the first way, my friend, to overcome anger, like the putting down of some tyrant, is not to obey or listen to it when it bids you speak loud, and look fierce, and beat yourself, but to remain quiet, and not to make the passion more intense, as one would a disease, by tossing about and crying out. In love affairs indeed, such things as revellings, and serenadings, and crowning the loved one's door with garlands, may indeed bring, some pleasant and elegant relief.

"I went, but asked not who or whose she was, I merely kissed her door-post. If that be A crime, I do plead guilty to the same."[685]

In the case of mourners also giving up to weeping and wailing takes away with the tears much of the grief. But anger on the contrary is much more fanned by what angry persons do and say. It is best therefore to be calm, or to flee and hide ourselves and go to a haven of quiet, when we feel the fit of temper coming upon us as an epileptic fit, that we fall not, or rather fall not on others, for it is our friends that we fall upon most and most frequently. For we do not love all, nor envy all, nor fear all men; but nothing is untouched or unassailed by anger; for we are angry with friends and enemies, parents and children, aye, and with the gods, and beasts, and even things inanimate, as was Thamyris,

"Breaking his gold-bound horn, breaking the music Of well-compacted lyre;"[686]

and Pandarus, who called down a curse upon himself, if he did not burn his bow "after breaking it with his hands."[687] And Xerxes inflicted stripes and blows on the sea, and sent letters to Mount Athos, "Divine Athos, whose top reaches heaven, put not in the way of my works stones large and difficult to deal with, or else I will hew thee down, and throw thee into the sea." For anger has many formidable aspects, and many ridiculous ones, so that of all the passions it is the most hated and despised. It will be well to consider both aspects.

§ VI. To begin then, whether my process was wrong or right I know not, but I began my cure of anger by noticing its effects in others, as the Lacedæmonians study the nature of drunkenness in the Helots. And in the first place, as Hippocrates tells us that disease is most dangerous in which the face of the patient is most unlike himself, so observing that people beside themselves with anger change their face, colour, walk, and voice, I formed an impression as it were of that aspect of passion, and was very disgusted with myself if ever I should appear so frightful and like one out of his mind to my friends and wife and daughters, not only wild and unlike oneself in appearance, but also with a voice savage and harsh, as I had noticed in some[688] of my acquaintance, who could neither preserve for anger their ordinary behaviour, or demeanour, or grace of language, or persuasiveness and gentleness in conversation. Caius Gracchus, indeed, the orator, whose character was harsh and style of oratory impassioned, had a pitch-pipe made for him, such as musicians use to heighten or lower their voices by degrees, and this, when he was making a speech, a slave stood behind him and held, and used to give him a mild and gentle note on it, whereby he lowered his key, and removed from his voice the harsh and passionate element, charming and laying the heat of the orator,

"As shepherds' wax-joined reed sounds musically With sleep provoking strain."[689]

For myself if I had some elegant and sprightly companion, I should not be vexed at his showing me a looking-glass in my fits of anger, as they offer one to some after a bath to little useful end. For to behold oneself unnaturally distorted in countenance will condemn anger in no small degree. The poets playfully tell us that Athene when playing on the pipe was rebuked thus by a Satyr,

"That look no way becomes you, take your armour, Lay down your pipes, and do compose your cheeks,"

and though she paid no attention to him, yet afterwards when she saw her face in a river, she felt vexed and threw her pipes away, although art had made melody a compensation for her unsightliness. And Marsyas, it seems, by a sort of mouthpiece forcibly repressed the violence of his breath, and tricked up and hid the contortion of his face,

"Around his shaggy temples put bright gold, And o'er his open mouth thongs tied behind."

Now anger, that puffs up and distends the face so as to look ugly, utters a voice still more harsh and unpleasant,

"Moving the mind's chords undisturbed before."

They say that the sea is cleansed when agitated by the winds it throws up tangle and seaweed; but the intemperate and bitter and vain words, which the mind throws up when the soul is agitated, defile the speakers of them first of all and fill them with infamy, as always having those thoughts within their bosom and being defiled with them, but only giving vent to them in anger. And so for a word which is, as Plato styles it, "a very small matter," they incur a most heavy punishment, for they get reputed to be enemies, and evil speakers, and malignant in disposition.

§ VII. Seeing and observing all this, it occurs to me to take it as a matter of fact, and record it for my own general use, that if it is good to keep the tongue soft and smooth in a fever, it is better to keep it so in anger. For if the tongue of people in a fever be unnatural, it is a bad sign, but not the cause of their malady; but the tongue of angry people, being rough and foul, and breaking out into unseemly speeches, produces insults that work irremediable mischief, and argue deep-rooted malevolence within. For wine drunk neat does not exhibit the soul in so ungovernable and hateful a condition as temper does: for the outbreaks of the one smack of laughter and fun, while those of the other are compounded with gall: and at a drinking-bout he that is silent is burdensome to the company and tiresome, whereas in anger nothing is more highly thought of than silence, as Sappho advises,

"When anger's busy in the brain Thy idly-barking tongue restrain."

§ VIII. And not only does the consideration of all this naturally arise from observing ourselves in the moments of anger, but we cannot help seeing also the other properties of rage, how ignoble it is, how unmanly, how devoid of dignity and greatness of mind! And yet to most people its noise seems vigour, its threatening confidence, and its obstinacy force of character; some even not wisely entitle its savageness magnanimity, and its implacability firmness, and its morosity hatred of what is bad. For their actions and motions and whole demeanour argue great littleness and meanness, not only when they are fierce with little boys, and peevish with women, and think it right to treat dogs and horses and mules with harshness, as Otesiphon the pancratiast thought fit to kick back a mule that had kicked him, but even in the butcheries that tyrants commit their littleness of soul is apparent in their savageness, and their suffering in their action, so that they are like the bites of serpents, that, when they are burnt and smart with pain, violently thrust their venom on those that have hurt them. For as a swelling is produced in the flesh by a heavy blow, so in softest souls the inclination to hurt others gets its greater strength from greater weakness. Thus women are more prone to anger than men, and people ill than people well, and old men than men in their prime, and the unfortunate than the prosperous; the miser is most prone to anger with his steward, the glutton with his cook, the jealous man with his wife, the vain man when he is spoken ill of; and worst of all are those "men who are too eager in states for office, or to head a faction, a manifest sorrow," to borrow Pindar's words. So from the very great pain and suffering of the soul there arises mainly from weakness anger, which is not like the nerves of the soul, as some one defined it, but like its strainings and convulsions when it is excessively vehement in its thirst for revenge.

§ IX. Such bad examples as these were not pleasant to look at but necessary, but I shall now proceed to describe people who have been mild and easy in dealing with anger, conduct gratifying either to see or hear about, being utterly disgusted[690] with people who use such language as,

"You have a man wronged: shall a man stand this?"

and,

"Put your heel upon his neck, and dash his head against the ground,"

and other provoking expressions such as these, by which some not well have transferred anger from the woman's side of the house to the man's. For manliness in all other respects seems to resemble justice, and to differ from it only in respect to gentleness, with which it has more affinities. For it sometimes happens to worse men to govern better ones, but to erect a trophy in the soul against anger (which Heraclitus says it is difficult to contend against, for whatever it wishes is bought at the price of the soul), is a proof of power so great and victorious as to be able to apply the judgement as if it were nerves and sinews to the passions. So I always try to collect and peruse the remarks on this subject not only of the philosophers, who foolish[691] people say had no gall in their composition, but still more of kings and tyrants. Such was the remark of Antigonus to his soldiers, when they were abusing him near his tent as if he were not listening, so he put his staff out, and said, "What's to do? can you not go rather farther off to run me down?" And when Arcadio the Achæan, who was always railing against Philip, and advising people to flee

"Unto a country where they knew not Philip,"

visited Macedonia afterwards on some chance or other, the king's friends thought he ought to be punished and the matter not looked over; but Philip treated him kindly, and sent him presents and gifts, and afterwards bade inquiry to be made as to what sort of account of him Arcadio now gave to the Greeks; and when all testified that the fellow had become a wonderful praiser of the king, Philip said, "You see I knew how to cure him better than all of you." And at the Olympian games when there was defamation of Philip, and some of his suite said to him, that the Greeks ought to smart for it, because they railed against him when they were treated well by him, he replied, "What will they do then if they are treated badly by me?" Excellent also was the behaviour of Pisistratus to Thrasybulus, and of Porsena to Mucius, and of Magas to Philemon. As to Magas, after he had been publicly jeered at by Philemon in one of his comedies at the theatre in the following words,

"Magas, the king hath written thee a letter, Unhappy Magas, since thou can'st not read,"

after having taken Philemon, who had been cast on shore by a storm at Parætonium, he commanded one of his soldiers only to touch his neck with the naked sword and then to go away quietly, and dismissed him, after sending him a ball and some dice as if he were a silly boy. And Ptolemy on one occasion, flouting a grammarian for his ignorance, asked him who was the father of Peleus, and he answered, "I will tell you, if you tell me first who was the father of Lagus." This was a jeer at the obscure birth of the king, and all his courtiers were indignant at it as an unpardonable liberty; but Ptolemy said, "If it is not kingly to take a flout, neither is it kingly to give one." And Alexander was more savage than usual in his behaviour to Callisthenes and Clitus. So Porus, when he was taken captive, begged Alexander to use him as a king. And on his inquiring, "What, nothing more?" he replied "No. For everything is included in being used as a king." So they call the king of the gods Milichius,[692] while they call Ares Maimactes;[693] and punishment and torture they assign to the Erinnyes and to demons, not to the gods or Olympus.

§ X. As then a certain person passed the following remark on Philip when he had razed Olynthus to the ground, "He certainly could not build such another city," so we may say to anger, "You can root up, and destroy, and throw down, but to raise up and save and spare and tolerate is the work of mildness and moderation, the work of a Camillus, a Metellus, an Aristides, a Socrates; but to sting and bite is to resemble the ant and horse-fly. For, indeed, when I consider revenge, I find its angry method to be for the most part ineffectual, since it spends itself in biting the lips and gnashing the teeth, and in vain attacks, and in railings coupled with foolish threats, and eventually resembles children running races, who from feebleness ridiculously tumble down before they reach the goal they are hastening to. So that speech of the Rhodian to a lictor of the Roman prætor who was shouting and talking insolently was not inapt, "It is no matter to me what you say, but what your master thinks."[694] And Sophocles, when he had introduced Neoptolemus and Eurypylus as armed for the battle, gives them this high commendation,[695]

"They rushed into the midst of armed warriors,"

Some barbarians indeed poison their steel, but bravery has no need of gall, being dipped in reason, but rage and fury are not invincible but rotten. And so the Lacedæmonians by their pipes turn away the anger of their warriors, and sacrifice to the Muses before commencing battle, that reason may abide with them, and when they have routed a foe do not follow up the victory,[696] but relax their rage, which like small daggers they can easily take back. But anger kills myriads before it is glutted with revenge, as happened in the case of Cyrus and Pelopidas the Theban. But Agathocles bore mildly the revilings of those he was besieging, and when one of them cried out, "Potter, how are you going to get money to pay your mercenaries?" he replied laughingly, "Out of your town if I take it." And when some of those on the wall threw his ugliness into the teeth of Antigonus, he said to them, "I thought I was rather a handsome fellow." But after he had taken the town, he sold for slaves those that had flouted him, protesting that, if they insulted him again, he would bring the matter before their masters. I have noticed also that hunters and orators are very unsuccessful when they give way to anger.[697] And Aristotle tells us that the friends of Satyrus stopped up his ears with wax when he was to plead a cause, that he might not make any confusion in the case through rage at the abuse of his enemies. And does it not frequently happen with ourselves that a slave who has offended escapes punishment, because they abscond in fear of our threats and harsh words? What nurses then say to children, "Give up crying, and you shall have it," may usefully be applied to anger, thus, "Do not be in a hurry, or bawl out, or be vehement, and you will sooner and better get what you want." For a father, seeing his boy trying to cut or cleave something with a knife, takes the knife from him and does it himself: and similarly a person, taking revenge out of the hand of passion, does himself safely and usefully and without harm punish the person who deserves punishment, and not himself instead, as anger often does.

§ XI. Now though all the passions need such discipline as by exercise shall tame and subdue their unreasoning and disobedient elements, yet there is none which we ought to keep under by such discipline so much as the exhibition of anger to our servants. For neither envy, nor fear, nor rivalry come into play between them and us; but our frequent displays of anger to them, creating many offences and faults, make us to slip as if on slippery ground owing to our autocracy with our servants, which no one resists or prevents. For it is impossible to check irresponsible power so as never to break out under the influence of passion, unless one wields power with much meekness, and refuses to listen to the frequent complaints of one's wife and friends charging one with being too easy and lax with one's servants. And by nothing have I been more exasperated against them, as if they were being ruined for want of correction. At last, though late, I got to see that in the first place it is better to make them worse by forbearance, than by bitterness and anger to distort oneself for the correction of others. In the next place I observed that many for the very reason that they were not corrected were frequently ashamed to be bad, and made pardon rather than punishment the commencement of their reformation, aye, and made better slaves to some merely at their nod silently and cheerfully than to others with all their beatings and brandings, and so I came to the conclusion that reason gets better obeyed than temper, for it is not as the poet said,

"Where there is fear, there too is self-respect,"

but it is just the other way about, for self-respect begets that kind of fear that corrects the behaviour. But perpetual and pitiless beating produces not so much repentance for wrong-doing as contrivances to continue in it without detection. In the third place, ever remembering and reflecting within myself that, just as he that teaches us the use of the bow does not forbid us to shoot but only to miss the mark, so it will not prevent punishment altogether to teach people to do it in season, and with moderation, utility, and decorum, I strive to remove anger most especially by not forbidding those who are to be corrected to speak in their defence, but by listening to them. For the interval of time gives a pause to passion, and a delay that mitigates it, and so judgement finds out both the fit manner and adequate amount of punishment. Moreover he that is punished has nothing to allege against his correction, if he is punished not in anger but only after his guilt is brought home to him. And the greatest disgrace will not be incurred, which is when the servant seems to speak more justly than the master. As then Phocion, after the death of Alexander, to stop the Athenians from revolting and believing the news too soon, said to them, "Men of Athens, if he is dead to-day, he will certainly also be dead to-morrow and the next day," so I think the man who is in a hurry to punish anyone in his rage ought to consider with himself, "If this person has wronged you to-day, he will also have wronged you to-morrow and the next day; and there will be no harm done if he shall be punished somewhat late; whereas if he shall be punished at once, he will always seem to you to have been innocent, as has often happened before now." For which of us is so savage as to chastise and scourge a slave because five or ten days before he over-roasted the meat, or upset the table, or was somewhat tardy on some errand? And yet these are the very things for which we put ourselves out and are harsh and implacable, immediately after they have happened and are recent. For as bodies seem greater in a mist, so do little matters in a rage. We ought therefore to consider such arguments as these at once, and if, when there is no trace of passion left, the matter appear bad to calm and clear reason, then it ought to be taken in hand, and the punishment ought not to be neglected or abandoned, as we leave food when we have lost our appetites. For nothing causes people to punish so much when their anger is fierce, as that when it is appeased they do not punish at all, but forget the matter entirely, and resemble lazy rowers, who lie in harbour when the sea is calm, and then sail out to their peril when the wind gets up. So we, condemning reason for slackness and mildness in punishing, are in a hurry to punish, borne along by passion as by a dangerous gale. He that is hungry takes his food as nature dictates, but he that punishes should have no hunger or thirst for it, nor require anger as a sauce to stimulate him to it, but should punish when he is as far as possible from having any desire for it, and has to compel his reason to it. For we ought not, as Aristotle tells us slaves in his time were scourged in Etruria to the music of the flute, to go headlong into punishing with a desire and zest for it, and to delight in punishing, and then afterwards to be sorry at it--for the first is savage, and the last womanish--but we should without either sorrow or pleasure chastise at the dictates of reason, giving anger no opportunity to interfere.

§ XII. But this perhaps will not appear a cure of anger so much as a putting away and avoiding such faults as men commit in anger. And yet, though the swelling of the spleen is only a symptom of fever, the fever is assuaged by its abating, as Hieronymus tells us. Now when I contemplated the origin of anger itself, I observed that, though different persons fell into it for different reasons, yet in nearly all of them was the idea of their being despised and neglected to be found. So we ought to help those who try to get rid of anger, by removing as far as possible from them any action savouring of contempt or contumely, and by looking upon their anger as folly or necessity, or emotion, or mischance, as Sophocles says,

"In those that are unfortunate, O king, No mind stays firm, but all their balance lose."[698]

And so Agamemnon, ascribing to Ate his carrying off Briseis, yet says to Achilles,

"I wish to please you in return, and give Completest satisfaction."[699]

For suing is not the action of one who shews his contempt, and when he that has done an injury is humble he removes all idea of slighting one. But the angry person must not expect this, but rather take to himself the answer of Diogenes, who, when it was said to him, "These people laugh at you," replied, "But I am not one to be laughed at," and not think himself despised, but rather despise the person who gave the offence, as acting from weakness, or error, or rashness, or heedlessness, or illiberality, or old age, or youth. Nor must we entertain such notions with regard to our servants and friends. For they do not despise us as void of ability or energy, but owing to our evenness and good-nature, some because we are mild, and others presuming on our affection for them. But as it is we not only fly into rages with wife and slaves and friends, as if we were slighted by them, but we also frequently, from forming the same idea of being slighted, fall foul of innkeepers and sailors and muleteers, and are vexed at dogs that bark and asses that are in our way: like the man who was going to beat an ass-driver, but when he cried out he was an Athenian, he said to the ass, "You are not an Athenian anyway," and beat it with many stripes.

§ XIII. Moreover those continuous and frequent fits of anger that gather together in the soul by degrees, like a swarm of bees or wasps, are generated within us by selfishness and peevishness, luxury and softness. And so nothing causes us to be mild to our servants and wife and friends so much as easiness and simplicity, and the learning to be content with what we have, and not to require a quantity of superfluities.

"He who likes not his meat if over-roast Or over-boiled, or under-roast or under-boiled, And never praises it however dressed,"

but will not drink unless he have snow to cool his drink, nor eat bread purchased in the market, nor touch food served on cheap or earthenware plates, nor sleep upon any but a feather bed that rises and falls like the sea stirred up from its depths, and with rods and blows hastens his servants at table, so that they run about and cry out and sweat as if they were bringing poultices to sores, he is slave to a weak querulous and discontented mode of life, and, like one who has a continual cough or various ailments, whether he is aware of it or not, he is in an ulcerous and catarrh-like condition as regards his proneness to anger. We must therefore train the body to contentment by plain living, that it may be easily satisfied: for they that require little do not miss much; and it is no great hardship to begin with our food, and take it silently whatever it is, and not by being choleric and peevish to thrust upon ourselves and friends the worst sauce to meat, anger.

"No more unpleasant supper could there be"[700]

than that wherein the servants are beaten, and the wife scolded, because something is burnt or smoked or not salt enough, or because the bread is too cold. Arcesilaus was once entertaining some friends and strangers, and when dinner was served, there was no bread, through the servants having neglected to buy any. In such a case as this which of us would not have broken the walls with vociferation? But he only smiled and said, "How unfit a sage is to give an entertainment!" And when Socrates once took Euthydemus home with him from the wrestling-school, Xanthippe was in a towering rage, and scolded, and at last upset the table, and Euthydemus rose and went away full of sorrow. But Socrates said to him, "Did not a hen at your house the other day fly in and act in the very same way? And we did not put ourselves out about it." We ought to receive our friends with gaiety and smiles and welcome, not knitting our brows, or inspiring fear and trembling in the attendants. We ought also to accustom ourselves to the use of any kind of ware at table, and not to stint ourselves to one kind rather than another, as some pick out a particular tankard or horn, as they say Marius did, out of many, and will not drink out of anything else; and some act in the same way with regard to oil-flasks and scrapers,[701] being content with only one out of all, and so, if such an article is broken or lost, they are very much put out about it, and punish with severity. He then that is prone to anger should not use rare and dainty things, such as choice cups and seals and precious stones: for if they are lost they put a man beside himself much more than the loss of ordinary and easily got things would do. And so when Nero had got an eight-cornered tent constructed, a wonderful object both for its beauty and costliness, Seneca said to him, "You have now shown yourself to be poor, for if you should lose this, you will not be able to procure such another." And indeed it did so happen that the tent was lost by shipwreck, but Nero bore its loss patiently, remembering what Seneca had said. Now this easiness about things generally makes a man also easy and gentle to his servants, and if to them, then it is clear he will be so to his friends also, and to all that serve under him in any capacity. So we observe that newly-purchased slaves do not inquire about the master who has bought them, whether he is superstitious or envious, but only whether he is a bad-tempered man: and generally speaking we see that neither can men put up with chaste wives, nor wives with loving husbands, nor friends with one another, if they be ill-tempered to boot. So neither marriage nor friendship is bearable with anger, though without anger even drunkenness is a small matter. For the wand of Dionysus punishes sufficiently the drunken man, but if anger be added it turns wine from being the dispeller of care and inspirer of the dance into a savage and fury. And simple madness can be cured by Anticyra,[702] but madness mixed with anger is the producer of tragedies and dreadful narratives.

§ XIV. So we ought to give anger no vent, either in jest, for that draws hatred to friendliness; or in discussion, for that turns love of learning into strife; or on the judgement-seat, for that adds insolence to power; or in teaching, for that produces dejection and hatred of learning: or in prosperity, for that increases envy; or in adversity, for that deprives people of compassion, when they are peevish and run counter to those who condole with them, like Priam,

"A murrain on you, worthless wretches all, Have you no griefs at home, that here you come To sympathize with me?"[703]

Good temper on the other hand is useful in some circumstances, adorns and sweetens others, and gets the better of all peevishness and anger by its gentleness. Thus Euclides,[704] when his brother said to him in a dispute between them, "May I perish, if I don't have my revenge on you!" replied, "May I perish, if I don't persuade you!" and so at once turned and changed him. And Polemo, when a man reviled him who was fond of precious stones and quite crazy for costly seal-rings, made no answer, but bestowed all his attention on one of his seal-rings, and eyed it closely; and he being delighted said, "Do not look at it so, Polemo, but in the light of the sun, and it will appear to you more beautiful." And Aristippus, when there was anger between him and Æschines, and somebody said, "O Aristippus, where is now your friendship?" replied, "It is asleep, but I will wake it up," and went to Æschines, and said to him, "Do I seem to you so utterly unfortunate and incurable as to be unworthy of any consideration?" And Æschines replied, "It is not at all wonderful that you, being naturally superior to me in all things, should have been first to detect in this matter too what was needful."

"For not a woman only, but young child Tickling the bristly boar with tender hand, Will lay him prostrate sooner than an athlete."

But we that tame wild beasts and make them gentle, and carry in our arms young wolves and lions' whelps, inconsistently repel our children and friends and acquaintances in our rage, and let loose our temper like some wild beast on our servants and fellow-citizens, speciously trying to disguise it not rightly under the name of hatred of evil, but it is, I suppose, as with the other passions and diseases of the soul, we cannot get rid of any of them by calling one prudence, and another liberality, and another piety.

§ XV. And yet, as Zeno said the seed was a mixture and compound drawn from all the faculties of the soul, so anger seems a universal seed from all the passions. For it is drawn from pain and pleasure and haughtiness, and from envy it gets its property of malignity--and it is even worse than envy,[705] for it does not mind its own suffering if it can only implicate another in misery--and the most unlovely kind of desire is innate in it, namely the appetite for injuring another. So when we go to the houses of spendthrifts we hear a flute-playing girl early in the morning, and see "the dregs of wine," as one said, and fragments of garlands, and the servants at the doors reeking of yesterday's debauch; but for tokens of savage and peevish masters these you will see by the faces, and marks, and manacles of their servants: for in the house of an angry man

"The only music ever heard is wailing,"

stewards being beaten within, and maids tortured, so that the spectators even in their jollity and pleasure pity these victims of passion.

§ XVI. Moreover those to whom it happens through their genuine hatred of what is bad to be frequently overtaken by anger, can abate its excess and acerbity by giving up their excessive confidence in their intimates. For nothing swells the anger more, than when a good man is detected of villainy, or one who we thought loved us falls out and jangles with us. As for my own disposition, you know of course how mightily it inclines to goodwill and belief in mankind. As then people walking on empty space,[706] the more confidently I believe in anybody's affection, the more sorrow and distress do I feel if my estimate is a mistaken one. And indeed I could never divest myself of my ardour and zeal in affection, but as to trusting people I could perhaps use Plato's caution as a curb. For he said he so praised Helicon the mathematician, because he was by nature a changeable animal, but that he was afraid of those that were well educated in the city, lest, being human beings and the seed of human beings, they should reveal by some trait or other the weakness of human nature. But Sophocles' line,

"Trace out most human acts, you'll find them base,"

seems to trample on human nature and lower its merits too much. Still such a peevish and condemnatory verdict as this has a tendency to make people milder in their rage, for it is the sudden and unexpected that makes people go distracted. And we ought, as Panætius somewhere said, to imitate Anaxagoras, and as he said at the death of his son, "I knew that I had begotten a mortal," so ought every one of us to use the following kind of language in those contretemps that stir up our anger, "I knew that the slave I bought was not a philosopher," "I knew that the friend I had was not perfect," "I knew that my wife was but a woman." And if anyone would also constantly put to himself that question of Plato, "Am I myself all I should be?" and look at home instead of abroad, and curb his propensity to censoriousness, he would not be so keen to detect evil in others, for he would see that he stood in need of much allowance himself. But now each of us, when angry and punishing, quote the words of Aristides and Cato, "Do not steal, Do not tell lies," and "Why are you lazy?" And, what is most disgraceful of all, we blame angry people when we are angry ourselves, and chastise in temper faults that were committed in temper, unlike the doctors who

"With bitter physic purge the bitter bile,"

for we rather increase and aggravate the disease. Whenever then I busy myself with such considerations as these, I try also to curtail my curiosity. For to scrutinize and pry into everything too minutely, and to overhaul every business of a servant, or action of a friend, or pastime of a son, or whisper of a wife, produces frequent, indeed daily, fits of anger, caused entirely by peevishness and harshness of character. Euripides says that the Deity

"In great things intervenes, but small things leaves To fortune;"[707]

but I am of opinion that a prudent man should commit nothing to fortune, nor neglect anything, but should put some things in his wife's hands to manage, others in the hands of his servants, others in the hands of his friends, (as a governor has his stewards, and financiers, and controllers), while he himself superintends the most important and weighty matters. For as small writing strains the eyes, so small matters even more strain and bother people, and stir up their anger, which carries this evil habit to greater matters. Above all I thought that saying of Empedocles, "Fast from evil,"[708] a great and divine one, and I approved of those promises and vows as not ungraceful or unphilosophical, to abstain for a year from wine and Venus, honouring the deity by continence, or for a stated time to give up lying, taking great heed to ourselves to be truthful always whether in play or earnest. With these I compared my own vow, as no less pleasing to the gods and holy, first to abstain from anger for a few days, like spending days without drunkenness or even without wine at all, offering as it were wineless offerings of honey.[709] Then I tried for a month or two, and so in time made some progress in forbearance by earnest resolve, and by keeping myself courteous and without anger and using fair language, purifying myself from evil words and absurd actions, and from passion which for a little unlovely pleasure pays us with great mental disturbance and the bitterest repentance. In consequence of all this my experience, and the assistance of the deity, has made me form the view, that courtesy and gentleness and kindliness are not so agreeable, and pleasant, and delightful, to any of those we live with as to ourselves, that have those qualities.[710]

[676] Homer, "Iliad," xxii. 373.

[677] Alluded to again "On the tranquillity of the mind," § i.

[678] The allusion is to Homer's "Odyssey," xx. 23.

[679] Reading [Greek: ex heautou] with Reiske.

[680] Euripides, "Orestes," 72.

[681] Euripides, "Orestes," 99.

[682] Fragment 361.

[683] Homer, "Iliad," xvii. 591.

[684] The reading of the MSS. is [Greek: autôn].

[685] Lines of Callimachus. [Greek: phliên] is the admirable emendation of Salmasius.

[686] Sophocles, "Thamyras," Fragm. 232.

[687] "Iliad," v. 214-216.

[688] Reading [Greek: eniois], as Wyttenbach suggests.

[689] Aeschylus, "Prometheus," 574, 575.

[690] It will be seen I adopt the reading and punctuation of Xylander.

[691] This is the reading of Reiske and Dübner.

[692] That is *mild*. Zeus is so called, Pausanias, i. 37; ii. 9, 20.

[693] That is, *fierce, furious*. It will be seen I adopt the suggestion of Reiske.

[694] Literally "is silent about." It is like the saying about Von Moltke that he can be silent in six or seven languages.

[695] Adopting Reiske's reading.

[696] Compare Pausanias, iv. 8.

[697] Dübner puts this sentence in brackets.

[698] Sophocles, "Antigone," 563, 564.

[699] Homer, "Iliad," xix. 138.

[700] Homer, "Odyssey," xx. 392.

[701] Or strigils.

[702] Anticyra was famous for its hellebore, which was prescribed in cases of madness. See Horace, "Satires," ii. 3. 82, 83.

[703] Homer, "Iliad," xxiv. 239, 240.

[704] A philosopher of Megara, and disciple of Socrates. Compare our author, "De Fraterno Amore," § xviii.

[705] So Reiske. Dübner reads [Greek: phobou]. The MSS. have [Greek: phonou], which Wyttenbach retains, but is evidently not quite satisfied with the text. Can [Greek: phthonou]--[Greek: heteron] be an account of [Greek: epichairekakia]?

[706] Up in the clouds. Cf. [Greek: aerobateô].

[707] Horace, remembering these lines no doubt, says "De Arte Poetica," 191, 192,

"Nec deus intersit nisi dignus vindice nodus Inciderit."

[708] It is quite likely that the delicious poet Robert Herrick borrowed hence his "To starve thy sin not bin, That is to keep thy Lent." For we know he was a student of the "Moralia" when at the University of Cambridge.

[709] See Æschylus, "Eumenides," 107. Sophocles, "Oedipus Colonæus," 481. See also our author's "De Sanitate Præcepta," § xix.

[710] Jeremy Taylor has closely imitated parts of this Dialogue in his "Holy Living," chapter iv. sect. viii., "Twelve remedies against anger, by way of exercise," "Thirteen remedies against anger, by way of consideration." Such a storehouse did he make of the "Moralia."

ON CONTENTEDNESS OF MIND.[711]

PLUTARCH SENDS GREETING TO PACCIUS.

§ I. It was late when I received your letter, asking me to write to you something on contentedness of mind, and on those things in the Timæus that require an accurate explanation. And it so fell out that at that very time our friend Eros was obliged to set sail at once for Rome, having received a letter from the excellent Fundanus, urging haste according to his wont. And not having as much time as I could have wished to meet your request, and yet not thinking for one moment of letting my messenger go to you entirely empty-handed, I copied out the notes that I had chanced to make on contentedness of mind. For I thought that you did not desire this discourse merely to be treated to a subject handled in fine style, but for the real business of life. And I congratulate you that, though you have friendships with princes, and have as much forensic reputation as anybody, yet you are not in the same plight as the tragic Merops, nor have you like him by the felicitations of the multitude been induced to forget the sufferings of humanity; but you remember, what you have often heard, that a patrician's slipper[712] is no cure for the gout, nor a costly ring for a whitlow, nor a diadem for the headache. For how can riches, or fame, or power at court help us to ease of mind or a calm life, unless we enjoy them when present, but are not for ever pining after them when absent? And what else causes this but the long exercise and practice of reason, which, when the unreasoning and emotional part of the soul breaks out of bounds, curbs it quickly, and does not allow it to be carried away headlong from its actual position? And as Xenophon[713] advised that we should remember and honour the gods most especially in prosperity, that so, when we should be in any strait, we might confidently call upon them as already our well-wishers and friends; so sensible men would do well before trouble comes to meditate on remedies how to bear it, that they may be the more efficacious from being ready for use long before. For as savage dogs are excited at every sound, and are only soothed by a familiar voice, so also it is not easy to quiet the wild passions of the soul, unless familiar and well-known arguments be at hand to check its excitement.

§ II. He then that said, that the man that wished to have an easy mind ought to have little to do either public or private, first of all makes ease of mind a very costly article for us, if it is to be bought at the price of doing nothing, as if he should advise every sick person,

"Lie still, poor wretch, in bed."[714]

And indeed stupor is a bad remedy for the body against despair,[715] nor is he any better physician of the soul who removes its trouble and anxiety by recommending a lazy and soft life and a leaving our friends and relations and country in the lurch. In the next place, it is false that those that have little to do are easy in mind. For then women would be easier in mind than men, since they mostly stay at home in inactivity, and even now-a-days it is as Hesiod says,[716]

"The North Wind comes not near a soft-skinned maiden;"

yet griefs and troubles and unrest, proceeding from jealousy or superstition or ambition or vanity, inundate the women's part of the house with unceasing flow. And Laertes, though he lived for twenty years a solitary life in the country,

"With an old woman to attend on him, Who duly set on board his meat and drink,"[717]

and fled from his country and house and kingdom, yet had sorrow and dejection[718] as a perpetual companion with leisure. And some have been often thrown into sad unrest merely from inaction, as the following,

"But fleet Achilles, Zeus-sprung, son of Peleus, Sat by the swiftly-sailing ships and fumed, Nor ever did frequent th' ennobling council, Nor ever join the war, but pined in heart, Though in his tent abiding, for the fray."[719]

And full of emotion and distress at this state of things he himself says,

"A useless burden to the earth I sit Beside the ships."[720]

So even Epicurus thinks that those who are desirous of honour and glory should not rust in inglorious ease, but use their natural talents in public life for the benefit of the community at large, seeing that they are by nature so constituted that they would be more likely to be troubled and afflicted at inaction, if they did not get what they desired. But he is absurd in that he does not urge men of ability to take part in public life, but only the restless. But we ought not to estimate ease or unrest of mind by our many or few actions, but by their fairness or foulness. For the omission of fair actions troubles and distresses us, as I have said before, quite as much as the actual doing of foul actions.

§ III. As for those who think that one kind of life is especially free from trouble, as some think that of farmers, others that of bachelors, others that of kings, Menander sufficiently exposes their error in the following lines:

"Phania, I thought those rich who need not borrow, Nor groan at nights, nor cry out 'Woe is me,' Kicked up and down in this untoward world, But sweet and gentle sleep they may enjoy."

He then goes on to remark that he saw the rich suffering the same as the poor,

"Trouble and life are truly near akin. With the luxurious or the glorious life Trouble consorts, and in the life of poverty Lasts with it to the end."

But just as people on the sea, timid and prone to sea-sickness, think they will suffer from it less on board a merchantman than on a boat, and for the same reason shift their quarters to a trireme, but do not attain anything by these changes, for they take with them their timidity and qualmishness, so changes of life do not remove the sorrows and troubles of the soul; which proceed from want of experience and reflection, and from inability or ignorance rightly to enjoy the present. These afflict the rich as well as the poor; these trouble the married as well as the unmarried; these make people shun the forum, but find no happiness in retirement; these make people eagerly desire introductions at court, though when got they straightway care no more about them.

"The sick are peevish in their straits and needs."[721]

For the wife bothers them, and they grumble at the doctor, and they find the bed uneasy, and, as Ion says,

"The friend that visits them tires their patience, And yet they do not like him to depart."

But afterwards, when the illness is over, and a sounder condition supervenes, health returns and makes all things pleasant and acceptable. He that yesterday loathed eggs and cakes of finest meal and purest bread will to-day eat eagerly and with appetite coarsest bread with a few olives and cress.

§ IV. Such contentedness and change of view in regard to every kind of life does the infusion of reason bring about. When Alexander heard from Anaxarchus of the infinite number of worlds, he wept, and when his friends asked him what was the matter, he replied, "Is it not a matter for tears that, when the number of worlds is infinite, I have not conquered one?" But Crates, who had only a wallet and threadbare cloak, passed all his life jesting and laughing as if at a festival. Agamemnon was troubled with his rule over so many subjects,

"You look on Agamemnon, Atreus' son, Whom Zeus has plunged for ever in a mass Of never-ending cares."[722]

But Diogenes when he was being sold sat down and kept jeering at the auctioneer, and would not stand up when he bade him, but said joking and laughing, "Would you tell a fish you were selling to stand up?" And Socrates in prison played the philosopher and discoursed with his friends. But Phäethon,[723] when he got up to heaven, wept because nobody gave to him his father's horses and chariot. As therefore the shoe is shaped by the foot, and not the foot by the shoe, so does the disposition make the life similar to itself. For it is not, as one said, custom that makes the best life seem sweet to those that choose it, but it is sense that makes that very life at once the best and sweetest. Let us cleanse therefore the fountain of contentedness, which is within us, that so external things may turn out for our good, through our putting the best face on them.

"Events will take their course, it is no good Our being angry at them, he is happiest Who wisely turns them to the best account."[724]

§ V. Plato compared human life to a game at dice, wherein we ought to throw according to our requirements, and, having thrown, to make the best use of whatever turns up. It is not in our power indeed to determine what the throw will be, but it is our part, if we are wise, to accept in a right spirit whatever fortune sends, and so to contrive matters that what we wish should do us most good, and what we do not wish should do us least harm. For those who live at random and without judgement, like those sickly people who can stand neither heat nor cold, are unduly elated by prosperity, and cast down by adversity; and in either case suffer from unrest, but 'tis their own fault, and perhaps they suffer most in what are called good circumstances. Theodorus, who was surnamed the Atheist, used to say that he held out arguments with his right hand, but his hearers received them with their left; so awkward people frequently take in a clumsy manner the favours of fortune; but men of sense, as bees extract honey from thyme which is the strongest and driest of herbs,[725] so from the least auspicious circumstances frequently derive advantage and profit.

§ VI. We ought then to cultivate such a habit as this, like the man who threw a stone at his dog, and missed it, but hit his step-mother, and cried out, "Not so bad." Thus we may often turn the edge of fortune when things turn not out as we wish. Diogenes was driven into exile; "not so bad;" for his exile made him turn philosopher. And Zeno of Cittium,[726] when he heard that the only merchantman he had was wrecked, cargo and all, said, "Fortune, you treat me handsomely, since you reduce me to my threadbare cloak and piazza."[727] What prevents our imitating such men as these? Have you failed to get some office? You will be able to live in the country henceforth, and manage your own affairs. Did you court the friendship of some great man, and meet with a rebuff? You will live free from danger and cares. Have you again had matters to deal with that required labour and thought? "Warm water will not so much make the limbs soft by soaking," to quote Pindar,[728] as glory and honour and power make "labour sweet, and toil to be no toil."[729] Or has any bad luck or contumely fallen on you in consequence of some calumny or from envy? The breeze is favourable that will waft you to the Muses and the Academy, as it did Plato when his friendship with Dionysius came to an end. It does indeed greatly conduce to contentedness of mind to see how famous men have borne the same troubles with an unruffled mind. For example, does childlessness trouble you? Consider those kings of the Romans, none of whom left his kingdom to a son. Are you distressed at the pinch of poverty? Who of the Boeotians would you rather prefer to be than Epaminondas, or of the Romans than Fabricius? Has your wife been seduced? Have you never read that inscription at Delphi,

"Agis the king of land and sea erected me;"

and have you not heard that his wife Timæa was seduced by Alcibiades, and in her whispers to her handmaidens called the child that was born Alcibiades? Yet this did not prevent Agis from being the most famous and greatest of the Greeks. Neither again did the licentiousness of his daughter prevent Stilpo from leading the merriest life of all the philosophers that were his contemporaries. And when Metrocles reproached him with her life, he said, "Is it my fault or hers?" And when Metrocles answered, "Her fault, but your misfortune," he rejoined, "How say you? Are not faults also slips?" "Certainly," said he. "And are not slips mischances in those matters wherein we slip?" Metrocles assented. "And are not mischances misfortunes in those matters wherein we mischance?" By this gentle and philosophical argument he demonstrated the Cynic's reproach to be an idle bark.

§ VII. But most people are troubled and exasperated not only at the bad in their friends and intimates, but also in their enemies. For railing and anger and envy and malignity and jealousy and ill-will are the bane of those that suffer from those infirmities, and trouble and exasperate the foolish: as for example the quarrels of neighbours, and peevishness of acquaintances, and the want of ability in those that manage state affairs. By these things you yourself seem to me to be put out not a little, as the doctors in Sophocles, who

"With bitter physic purge the bitter bile,"[730]

so vexed and bitter are you at people's weaknesses and infirmities, which is not reasonable in you. Even your own private affairs are not always managed by simple and good and suitable instruments, so to speak, but very frequently by sharp and crooked ones. Do not think it then either your business, or an easy matter either, to set all these things to rights. But if you take people as they are, as the surgeon uses his bandages and instruments for drawing teeth, and with cheerfulness and serenity welcome all that happens, as you would look upon barking dogs as only following their nature, you will be happier in the disposition you will then have than you will be distressed at other people's disagreeableness and shortcomings. For you will forget to make a collection of disagreeable things,[731] which now inundate, as some hollow and low-lying ground, your littleness of mind and weakness, which fills itself with other people's bad points. For seeing that some of the philosophers censure compassion to the unfortunate (on the ground that it is good to help our neighbours, and not to give way to sentimental sympathy in connection with them), and, what is of more importance, do not allow those that are conscious of their errors and bad moral disposition to be dejected and grieved at them, but bid them cure their defects without grief at once, is it not altogether unreasonable, look you, to allow ourselves to be peevish and vexed, because all those who have dealings with us and come near us are not good and clever? Let us see to it, dear Paccius, that we do not, whether we are aware of it or not, play a part, really looking[732] not at the universal defects of those that approach us, but at our own interests through our selfishness, and not through our hatred of evil. For excessive excitement about things, and an undue appetite and desire for them, or on the other hand aversion and dislike to them, engender suspiciousness and peevishness against persons, who were, we think, the cause of our being deprived of some things, and of being troubled with others. But he that is accustomed to adapt himself to things easily and calmly is most cheerful and gentle in his dealings with people.

§ VIII. Wherefore let us resume our argument. As in a fever everything seems bitter and unpleasant to the taste, but when we see others not loathing but fancying the very same eatables and drinkables, we no longer find the fault to be in them but in ourselves and our disease, so we shall cease to blame and be discontented with the state of affairs, if we see others cheerfully and without grief enduring the same. It also makes for contentedness, when things happen against our wish, not to overlook our many advantages and comforts, but by looking at both good and bad to feel that the good preponderate. When our eyes are dazzled with things too bright we turn them away, and ease them by looking at flowers or grass, while we keep the eyes of our mind strained on disagreeable things, and force them to dwell on bitter ideas, well-nigh tearing them away by force from the consideration of pleasanter things. And yet one might apply here, not unaptly, what was said to the man of curiosity,[733]

"Malignant wretch, why art so keen to mark Thy neighbour's fault, and seest not thine own?"

Why on earth, my good sir, do you confine your view to your troubles, making them so vivid and acute, while you do not let your mind dwell at all on your present comforts? But as cupping-glasses draw the worst blood from the flesh, so you force upon your attention the worst things in your lot: acting not a whit more wisely than that Chian, who, selling much choice wine to others, asked for some sour wine for his own supper; and one of his slaves being asked by another, what he had left his master doing, replied, "Asking for bad when good was by." For most people overlook the advantages and pleasures of their individual lives, and run to their difficulties and grievances. Aristippus, however, was not such a one, for he cleverly knew as in a scale to make the better preponderate over the worse. So having lost a good farm, he asked one of those who made a great show of condolence and sympathy, "Have you not only one little piece of ground, while I have three fields left?" And when he admitted that it was so, he went on to say, "Ought I not then to condole with you rather than you with me?" For it is the act of a madman to distress oneself over what is lost, and not to rejoice at what is left; but like little children, if one of their many playthings be taken away by anyone, throw the rest away and weep and cry out, so we, if we are assailed by fortune in some one point, wail and mourn and make all other things seem unprofitable in our eyes.

§ IX. Suppose someone should say, What blessings have we? I would reply, What have we not? One has reputation, another a house, another a wife, another a good friend. When Antipater of Tarsus was reckoning up on his death-bed his various pieces of good fortune, he did not even pass over his favourable voyage from Cilicia to Athens. So we should not overlook, but take account of everyday blessings, and rejoice that we live, and are well, and see the sun, and that no war or sedition plagues our country, but that the earth is open to cultivation, the sea secure to mariners, and that we can speak or be silent, lead a busy or an idle life, as we choose. We shall get more contentedness from the presence of all these blessings, if we fancy them as absent, and remember from time to time how people ill yearn for health, and people in war for peace, and strangers and unknown in a great city for reputation and friends, and how painful it is to be deprived of all these when one has once had them. For then each of these blessings will not appear to us only great and valuable when it is lost, and of no value while we have it. For not having it cannot add value to anything. Nor ought we to amass things we regard as valuable, and always be on the tremble and afraid of losing them as valuable things, and yet, when we have them, ignore them and think little of them; but we ought to use them for our pleasure and enjoyment, that we may bear their loss, if that should happen, with more equanimity. But most people, as Arcesilaus said, think it right to inspect minutely and in every detail, perusing them alike with the eyes of the body and mind, other people's poems and paintings and statues, while they neglect to study their own lives, which have often many not unpleasing subjects for contemplation, looking abroad and ever admiring other people's reputations and fortunes, as adulterers admire other men's wives, and think cheap of their own.

§ X. And yet it makes much for contentedness of mind to look for the most part at home and to our own condition, or if not, to look at the case of people worse off than ourselves, and not, as most people do, to compare ourselves with those who are better off. For example, those who are in chains think those happy who are freed from their chains, and they again freemen, and freemen citizens, and they again the rich, and the rich satraps, and satraps kings, and kings the gods, content with hardly anything short of hurling thunderbolts and lightning. And so they ever want something above them, and are never thankful for what they have.

"I care not for the wealth of golden Gyges,"

and,

"I never had or envy or desire To be a god, or love for mighty empire, Far distant from my eyes are all such things."

But this, you will say, was the language of a Thasian. But you will find others, Chians or Galatians or Bithynians, not content with the share of glory or power they have among their fellow-citizens, but weeping because they do not wear senators' shoes; or, if they have them, that they cannot be prætors at Rome; or, if they get that office, that they are not consuls; or, if they are consuls, that they are only proclaimed second and not first. What is all this but seeking out excuses for being unthankful to fortune, only to torment and punish oneself? But he that has a mind in sound condition, does not sit down in sorrow and dejection if he is less renowned or rich than some of the countless myriads of mankind that the sun looks upon, "who feed on the produce of the wide world,"[734] but goes on his way rejoicing at his fortune and life, as far fairer and happier than that of myriads of others. In the Olympian games it is not possible to be the victor by choosing one's competitors. But in the race of life circumstances allow us to plume ourselves on surpassing many, and to be objects of envy rather than to have to envy others, unless we pit ourselves against a Briareus or a Hercules. Whenever then you admire anyone carried by in his litter as a greater man than yourself, lower your eyes and look at those that bear the litter. And when you think the famous Xerxes happy for his passage over the Hellespont, as a native of those parts[735] did, look too at those who dug through Mount Athos under the lash, and at those whose ears and noses were cut off because the bridge was broken by the waves, consider their state of mind also, for they think your life and fortunes happy. Socrates, when he heard one of his friends saying, "How dear this city is! Chian wine costs one mina,[736] a purple robe three, and half a pint of honey five drachmæ," took him to the meal market, and showed him half a peck of meal for an obol, then took him to the olive market, and showed him a peck of olives for two coppers, and lastly showed him that a sleeveless vest[737] was only ten drachmæ. At each place Socrates' friend exclaimed, "How cheap this city is!" So also we, when we hear anyone saying that our affairs are bad and in a woful plight, because we are not consuls or governors, may reply, "Our affairs are in an admirable condition, and our life an enviable one, seeing that we do not beg, nor carry burdens, nor live by flattery."

§ XI. But since through our folly we are accustomed to live more with an eye to others than ourselves, and since nature is so jealous and envious that it rejoices not so much in its own blessings as it is pained by those of others, do not look only at the much-cried-up splendour of those whom you envy and admire, but open and draw, as it were, the gaudy curtain of their pomp and show, and peep within, you will see that they have much to trouble them, and many things to annoy them. The well-known Pittacus,[738] whose fame was so great for fortitude and wisdom and uprightness, was once entertaining some guests, and his wife came in in a rage and upset the table, and as the guests were dismayed he said, Every one of you has some trouble, and he who has mine only is not so bad off.

"Happy is he accounted at the forum, But when he opens the door of his own house Thrice miserable; for his wife rules all, Still lords it over him, and is ever quarrelling. Many griefs has he that I wot not of."

Many such cases are there, unknown to the public, for family pride casts a veil over them, to be found in wealth and glory and even in royalty.

"O happy son of Atreus, child of destiny, Blessed thy lot;"[739]

congratulation like this comes from an external view, from a halo of arms and horses and the pomp of war, but the inward voice of emotion testifies against all this vain glory;

"A heavy fate is laid on me by Zeus The son of Cronos."[740]

And,

"Old man, I think your lot one to be envied, As that of any man who free from danger Passes his life unknown and in obscurity."[741]

By such reflections as these one may wean oneself from that discontent with one's fortune, which makes one's own condition look low and mean from too much admiring one's neighbour's.

§ XII. Another thing, which is a great hindrance to peace of mind, is not to proportion our desires to our means, but to carry too much sail, as it were, in our hopes of great things and then, if unsuccessful, to blame destiny and fortune, and not our own folly. For he is not unfortunate who wishes to shoot with a plough, or hunt the hare with an ox; nor has he an evil genius opposed to him, who does not catch deer with fishing nets, but merely is the dupe of his own stupidity and folly in attempting impossibilities. Self-love is mainly to blame, making people fond of being first and aspiring in all matters, and insatiably desirous to engage in everything. For people not only wish at one and the same time to be rich, and learned, and strong, and boon-companions, and agreeable, and friends of kings, and governors of cities, but they are also discontented if they have not dogs and horses and quails and cocks of the first quality. Dionysius the elder was not content with being the most powerful monarch of his times, but because he could not beat Philoxenus the poet in singing, or surpass Plato in dialectics, was so angry and exasperated that he put the one to work in his stone quarries, and sent the other to Ægina and sold him there. Alexander was of a different spirit, for when Crisso the famous runner ran a race with him, and seemed to let the king outrun him on purpose, he was greatly displeased. Good also was the spirit of Achilles in Homer, who, when he said,

"None of the Achæan warriors is a match For me in war,"

added,

"Yet in the council hall Others there are who better are than me."[742]

And when Megabyzus the Persian visited the studio of Apelles, and began to chatter about art, Apelles stopped him and said, "While you kept silence you seemed to be somebody from your gold and purple, but now these lads that are grinding colours are laughing at your nonsense." But some who think the Stoics only talk idly, in styling their wise man not only prudent and just and brave but also orator and general and poet and rich man and king, yet claim for themselves all those titles, and are indignant if they do not get them. And yet even among the gods different functions are assigned to different personages; thus one is called the god of war, another the god of oracles, another the god of gain, and Aphrodite, as she has nothing to do with warlike affairs, is despatched by Zeus to marriages and bridals.

§ XIII. And indeed there are some pursuits which cannot exist together, but are by their very nature opposed. For example oratory and the study of the mathematics require ease and leisure; whereas political ability and the friendship of kings cannot be attained without mixing in affairs and in public life. Moreover wine and indulgence in meat make the body indeed strong and vigorous, but blunt the intellect; and though unremitting attention to making and saving money will heap up wealth, yet despising and contemning riches is a great help to philosophy. So that all things are not within any one's power, and we must obey that saying inscribed in the temple of Apollo at Delphi, *Know thyself*,[743] and adapt ourselves to our natural bent, and not drag and force nature to some other kind of life or pursuit. "The horse to the chariot, and the ox to the plough, and swiftly alongside the ship scuds the dolphin, while he that meditates destruction for the boar must find a staunch hound."[744] But he that chafes and is grieved that he is not at one and the same time "a lion reared on the mountains, exulting in his strength,"[745] and a little Maltese lap-dog[746] reared in the lap of a rich widow, is out of his senses. And not a whit wiser is he who wishes to be an Empedocles, or Plato, or Democritus, and write about the world and the real nature of things, and at the same time to be married like Euphorion to a rich wife, or to revel and drink with Alexander like Medius; and is grieved and vexed if he is not also admired for his wealth like Ismenias, and for his virtue like Epaminondas. But runners are not discontented because they do not carry off the crowns of wrestlers, but rejoice and delight in their own crowns. "You are a citizen of Sparta: see you make the most of her." So too said Solon:

"We will not change our virtue for their wealth, For virtue never dies, but wealth has wings, And flies about from one man to another."

And Strato the natural philosopher, when he heard that Menedemus had many more pupils than he had, said, "Is it wonderful at all that more wish to wash than to be anointed?" And Aristotle, writing to Antipater, said, "Not only has Alexander a right to plume himself on his rule over many subjects, but no less legitimate is satisfaction at entertaining right opinions about the gods." For those that think so highly of their own walk in life will not be so envious about their neighbours'. We do not expect a vine to bear figs, nor an olive grapes, yet now-a-days, with regard to ourselves, if we have not at one and the same time the privilege of being accounted rich and learned, generals and philosophers, flatterers and outspoken, stingy and extravagant, we slander ourselves and are dissatisfied, and despise ourselves as living a maimed and imperfect life. Furthermore, we see that nature teaches us the same lesson.[747] For as she provides different kinds of beasts with different kinds of food, and has not made all carnivorous, or seed-pickers, or root-diggers, so she has given to mankind various means of getting a livelihood, "one by keeping sheep, another by ploughing, another by fowling,"[748] and another by catching the fish of the sea. We ought each therefore to select the calling appropriate for ourselves and labour energetically in it, and leave other people to theirs, and not demonstrate Hesiod as coming short of the real state of things when he said,

"Potter is wroth with potter, smith with smith."[749]

For not only do people envy those of the same trade and manner of life, but the rich envy the learned, and the famous the rich, and advocates sophists, aye, and freemen and patricians admire and think happy comedians starring it at the theatres, and dancers, and the attendants at kings' courts, and by all this envy give themselves no small trouble and annoyance.

§XIV. But that every man has in himself the magazines of content or discontent, and that the jars containing blessings and evils are not on the threshold of Zeus,[750] but lie stored in the mind, is plain from the differences of men's passions. For the foolish overlook and neglect present blessings, through their thoughts being ever intent on the future; but the wise make the past clearly present to them through memory. For the present giving only a moment of time to the touch, and then evading our grasp, does not seem to the foolish to be ours or to belong to us at all. And like that person[751] painted as rope-making in Hades and permitting an ass feeding by to eat up the rope as fast as he makes it, so the stupid and thankless forgetfulness of most people comes upon them and takes possession of them, and obliterates from their mind every past action, whether success, or pleasant leisure, or society, or enjoyment, and breaks the unity of life which arises from the past being blended with the present; for detaching to-day from both yesterday and to-morrow, it soon makes every event as if it had never happened from lack of memory. For as those in the schools, who deny the growth of our bodies by reason of the continual flux of substance, make each of us in theory different from himself and another man, so those who do not keep or recall to their memory former things, but let them drift, actually empty themselves daily, and hang upon the morrow, as if what happened a year ago, or even yesterday and the day before yesterday, had nothing to do with them, and had hardly occurred at all.

§ XV. This is one great hindrance to contentedness of mind, and another still greater is whenever, like flies that slide down smooth places in mirrors, but stick fast in rough places or where there are cracks, men let pleasant and agreeable things glide from their memory, and pin themselves down to the remembrance of unpleasant things; or rather, as at Olynthus they say beetles, when they get into a certain place called Destruction-to-beetles, cannot get out, but fly round and round till they die, so men will glide into the remembrance of their woes, and will not give themselves a respite from sorrow. But, as we use our brightest colours in a picture, so in the mind we ought to look at the cheerful and bright side of things, and hide and keep down the gloomy, for we cannot altogether obliterate or get rid of it. For, as the strings of the bow and lyre are alternately tightened and relaxed, so is it with the order of the world; in human affairs there is nothing pure and without alloy. But as in music there are high and low notes, and in grammar vowels and mutes, but neither the musician nor grammarian decline to use either kinds, but know how to blend and employ them both for their purpose, so in human affairs which are balanced one against another,--for, as Euripides says,

"There is no good without ill in the world, But everything is mixed in due proportion,"--

we ought not to be disheartened or despondent; but as musicians drown their worst music with the best, so should we take good and bad together, and make our chequered life one of convenience and harmony. For it is not, as Menander says,

"Directly any man is born, a genius Befriends him, a good guide to him for life,"

but it is rather, as Empedocles states, two fates or genii take hold of each of us when we are born and govern us. "There were Chthonia and far-seeing Heliope, and cruel Deris, and grave Harmonia, and Callisto, and Æschra, and Thoosa, and Denæa, and charming Nemertes, and Asaphea with the black fruit."

§ XVI. And as[752] at our birth we received the mingled seeds of each of these passions, which is the cause of much irregularity, the sensible person hopes for better things, but expects worse, and makes the most of either, remembering that wise maxim, *Not too much of anything.* For not only will he who is least solicitous about to-morrow best enjoy it when it comes, as Epicurus says, but also wealth, and renown, and power and rule, gladden most of all the hearts of those who are least afraid of the contrary. For the immoderate desire for each, implanting a most immoderate fear of losing them, makes the enjoyment of them weak and wavering, like a flame under the influence of a wind. But he whom reason enables to say to fortune without fear or trembling,

"If you bring any good I gladly welcome it, But if you fail me little does it trouble me,"

he can enjoy the present with most zest through his confidence, and absence of fear of the loss of what he has, which would be unbearable. For we may not only admire but also imitate the behaviour of Anaxagoras, which made him cry out at the death of his son, "I knew I had begot a mortal," and apply it to every contingency. For example, "I know that wealth is ephemeral and insecure; I know that those who gave power can take it away again; I know that my wife is good, but still a woman; and that my friend, since a human being, is by nature a changeable animal, to use Plato's expression." For such a prepared frame of mind, if anything happens unwished for but not unexpected, not admitting of such phrases as "I shouldn't have dreamed of it," or "I expected quite a different lot," or "I didn't look for this," abates the violent[753] beatings and palpitations of the heart, and quickly causes wild unrest to subside. Carneades indeed reminds us that in great matters the unexpected makes the sum total of grief and dejection. Certainly the kingdom of Macedonia was many times smaller than the Roman Empire, but when Perseus lost Macedonia, he not only himself bewailed his wretched fate, but seemed to all men the most unfortunate and unlucky of mankind; yet Æmilius who conquered him, though he had to give up to another the command both by land and sea, yet was crowned, and offered sacrifice, and was justly esteemed happy. For he knew that he had taken a command which he would have to give up, but Perseus lost his kingdom without expecting it. Well also has the poet[754] shown the power of anything that happens unexpectedly. For Odysseus wept bitterly at the death of his dog, but was not so moved when he sat by his wife who wept, for in the latter case he had come fully determined to keep his emotion under the control of reason, whereas in the former it was against his expectation, and therefore fell upon him as a sudden blow.

§ XVII. And since generally speaking some things which happen against our will pain and trouble us by their very nature, while in the case of most we accustom ourselves and learn to be disgusted with them from fancy, it is not unprofitable to counteract this to have ever ready that line of Menander,

"You suffer no dread thing but in your fancy."

For what, if they touch you neither in soul nor body, are such things to you as the low birth of your father, or the adultery of your wife, or the loss of some prize or precedence, since even by their absence a man is not prevented from being in excellent condition both of body and soul. And with respect to the things that seem to pain us by their very nature, as sickness, and anxieties, and the deaths of friends and children, we should remember, that line of Euripides,

"Alas! and why alas? we only suffer What mortals must expect."

For no argument has so much weight with emotion when it is borne down with grief, as that which reminds it of the common and natural necessity to which man is exposed owing to the body, the only handle which he gives to fortune, for in his most important and influential part[755] he is secure against external things. When Demetrius captured Megara, he asked Stilpo if any of his things had been plundered, and Stilpo answered, "I saw nobody carrying off anything of mine."[756] And so when fortune has plundered us and stripped us of everything else, we have that within ourselves

"Which the Achæans ne'er could rob us of."[757]

So that we ought not altogether to abase and lower nature, as if she had no strength or stability against fortune; but on the contrary, knowing that the rotten and perishable part of man, wherein alone he lies open to fortune, is small, while we ourselves are masters of the better part, wherein are situated our greatest blessings, as good opinions and teaching and virtuous precepts, all which things cannot be abstracted from us or perish, we ought to look on the future with invincible courage, and say to fortune, as Socrates is supposed to have said to his accusers Anytus and Melitus before the jury, "Anytus and Melitus can kill me, but they cannot hurt me." For fortune can afflict us with disease, take away our money, calumniate us to the people or king, but cannot make a good and brave and high-souled man bad and cowardly and low and ignoble and envious, nor take away that disposition of mind, whose constant presence is of more use for the conduct of life than the presence of a pilot at sea. For the pilot cannot make calm the wild wave or wind, nor can he find a haven at his need wherever he wishes, nor can he await his fate with confidence and without trembling, but as long as he has not despaired, but uses his skill, he scuds before the gale, "lowering his big sail, till his lower mast is only just above the sea dark as Erebus," and sits at the helm trembling and quaking. But the disposition of a wise man gives calm even to the body, mostly cutting off the causes of diseases by temperance and plain living and moderate exercise; but if some beginning of trouble arise from without, as we avoid a sunken rock, so he passes by it with furled sail, as Asclepiades puts it; but if some unexpected and tremendous gale come upon him and prove too much for him, the harbour is at hand, and he can swim away from the body, as from a leaky boat.

§ XVIII. For it is the fear of death, and not the desire of life, that makes the foolish person to hang to the body, clinging to it, as Odysseus did to the fig-tree from fear of Charybdis that lay below,

"Where the wind neither let him stay, or sail,"

so that he was displeased at this, and afraid of that. But he who understands somehow or other the nature of the soul, and reflects that the change it will undergo at death will be either to something better or at least not worse, he has in his fearlessness of death no small help to ease of mind in life. For to one who can enjoy life when virtue and what is congenial to him have the upper hand, and that can fearlessly depart from life, when uncongenial and unnatural things are in the ascendant, with the words on his lips,

"The deity shall free me, when I will,"[758]

what can we imagine could befall such a man as this that would vex him and wear him and harass him? For he who said, "I have anticipated you, O fortune, and cut off all your loopholes to get at me," did not trust to bolts or keys or walls, but to determination and reason, which are within the power of all persons that choose. And we ought not to despair or disbelieve any of these sayings, but admiring them and emulating them and being enthusiastic about them, we ought to try and test ourselves in smaller matters with a view to greater, not avoiding or rejecting that self-examination, nor sheltering ourselves under the remark, "Perhaps nothing will be more difficult." For inertia[759] and softness are generated by that self-indulgence which ever occupies itself only with the easiest tasks, and flees from the disagreeable to what is most pleasant. But the soul that accustoms itself to face steadily sickness and grief and exile, and calls in reason to its help in each case, will find in what appears so sore and dreadful much that is false, empty, and rotten, as reason will show in each case.

§ XIX. And yet many shudder at that line of Menander,

"No one can say, I shall not suffer this or that,"

being ignorant how much it helps us to freedom from grief to practise to be able to look fortune in the face with our eyes open, and not to entertain fine and soft fancies, like one reared in the shade on many hopes that always yield and never resist. We can, however, answer Menander's line,

"No one can say, I shall not suffer this or that,"

for a man can say, "I will not do this or that, I will not lie, I will not play the rogue, I will not cheat, I will not scheme." For this is in our power, and is no small but great help to ease of mind. As on the contrary

"The consciousness of having done ill deeds,"[760]

like a sore in the flesh, leaves in the mind a regret which ever wounds it and pricks it. For reason banishes all other griefs, but itself creates regret when the soul is vexed with shame and self-tormented. For as those who shudder in ague-fits or burn in fevers feel more trouble and distress than those who externally suffer the same from cold or heat, so the grief is lighter which comes externally from chance, but that lament,

"None is to blame for this but I myself,"

coming from within on one's own misdeeds, intensifies one's bitterness by the shame felt. And so neither costly house, nor quantity of gold, nor pride of race, nor weighty office, nor grace of language, nor eloquence, impart so much calm and serenity to life, as a soul pure from evil acts and desires, having an imperturbable and undefiled character as the source of its life; whence good actions flow, producing an enthusiastic and cheerful energy accompanied by loftiness of thought, and a memory sweeter and more lasting than that hope which Pindar says is the support of old age. Censers do not, as Carneades said, after they are emptied, long retain their sweet smell; but in the mind of the wise man good actions always leave a fresh and fragrant memory, by which joy is watered and flourishes, and despises those who wail over life and abuse it as a region of ills, or as a place of exile for souls in this world.

§ XX. I am very taken with Diogenes' remark to a stranger at Lacedæmon, who was dressing with much display for a feast, "Does not a good man consider every day a feast?" And a very great feast too, if we live soberly. For the world is a most holy and divine temple, into which man is introduced at his birth, not to behold motionless images made by hands, but those things (to use the language of Plato) which the divine mind has exhibited as the visible representations of invisible things, having innate in them the principle of life and motion, as the sun moon and stars, and rivers ever flowing with fresh water, and the earth affording maintenance to plants and animals. Seeing then that life is the most complete initiation into all these things, it ought to be full of ease of mind and joy; not as most people wait for the festivals of Cronos[761] and Dionysus and the Panathenæa and other similar days, that they may joy and refresh themselves with bought laughter, paying actors and dancers for the same. On such occasions indeed we sit silently and decorously, for no one wails when he is initiated, or groans when he beholds the Pythian games, or when he is drinking at the festival of Cronos:[761] but men shame the festivals which the deity supplies us with and initiates us in, passing most of their time in lamentation and heaviness of heart and distressing anxiety. And though men delight in the pleasing notes of musical instruments, and in the songs of birds, and behold with joy the animals playing and frisking, and on the contrary are distressed when they roar and howl and look savage; yet in regard to their own life, when they see it without smiles and dejected, and ever oppressed and afflicted by the most wretched sorrows and toils and unending cares, they do not think of trying to procure alleviation and ease. How is this? Nay, they will not even listen to others' exhortation, which would enable them to acquiesce in the present without repining, and to remember the past with thankfulness, and to meet the future hopefully and cheerfully without fear or suspicion.

[711] Or cheerfulness, or tranquillity of mind. Jeremy Taylor has largely borrowed again from this treatise in his "Holy Living," ch. ii. § 6, "Of Contentedness in all Estates and Accidents."

[712] Reading with Salmasius [Greek: kaltios patrikios].

[713] "Locus Xenophontis est Cyropæd.," l. i. p. 52.--*Reiske*.

[714] Euripides, "Orestes," 258.

[715] So Wyttenbach, Dübner. Vulgo [Greek: anaisthêsias--aponia.]

[716] "Works and Days," 519.

[717] "Odyssey," i. 191, 192.

[718] I read [Greek: katêpheian].

[719] "Iliad," i. 488-492.

[720] "Iliad," xviii. 104.

[721] Euripides, "Orestes," 232.

[722] Homer, "Iliad," x. 88, 89.

[723] The story of Phäethon is a very well-known one, and is recorded very fully by Ovid in the "Metamorphoses," Book ii.

[724] Euripides, "Bellerophon." Fragm. 298.

[725] Supplying [Greek: phytôn] with Reiske.

[726] In Cyprus. Zeno was the founder of the Stoics.

[727] Zeno and his successors taught in the Piazza at Athens called the Painted Piazza. See Pausanias, i. 15.

[728] Pindar, Nem. iv. 6.

[729] Euripides, "Bacchæ," 66.

[730] Quoted again by our author "On Restraining Anger," § xvi.

[731] As will be seen, I follow Wyttenbach's guidance in this very corrupt passage, which is a true crux.

[732] Reading [Greek: dedorkotes].

[733] See "On Curiosity," § i.

[734] Simonides.

[735] See Herodotus, vii. 56.

[736] A mina was 100 drachmæ (*i.e.* £4. 1*s.* 3*d.*), and 600 obols.

[737] A slave's ordinary dress.

[738] One of the Seven Wise Men.

[739] Homer, "Iliad," iii. 182.

[740] Homer, "Iliad," ii. 111.

[741] Words of Agamemnon to the House Porter. Euripides, "Iphigenia in Aulis," 17-19.

[742] "Iliad," xviii. 105, 106.

[743] See Pausanias, x. 24.

[744] Pindar, Fragm., 258. Quoted "On Moral Virtue," § xii.

[745] Homer, "Iliad," xvii. 61; "Odyssey," vi. 130.

[746] A famous breed of dogs from the island Melita, near Dalmatia. See Pliny, "Hist. Nat.," iii. 26, extr. § 30; xxx. 5, extr. § 14.

[747] That *Non omnia possumus omnes.*

[748] Pindar, "Isthm.," i. 65-70.

[749] Hesiod, "Works and Days," 25. Our "two of a trade seldom agree."

[750] An allusion to "Iliad," xxiv. 527-533.

[751] Ocnus. See Pausanias, x. 29.

[752] So Wyttenbach, who reads [Greek: Hôs de toutôn].

[753] Reading [Greek: oia] with Reiske.

[754] Homer to wit.

[755] The soul.

[756] The reading here is rather doubtful. That I have adopted is Reiske's and Wyttenbach's.

[757] "Iliad," v. 484.

[758] Euripides, "Bacchæ," 498. Compare Horace, "Epistles," i. xvi. 78, 79.

[759] Reading with Dübner [Greek: argian]. Reiske has [Greek: atonian].

[760] Euripides, "Orestes," 396.

[761] The *Saturnalia* (as the Romans called this feast) was well known as a festival of merriment and license.

ON ENVY AND HATRED.

§ I. Outwardly there seems no difference between hatred and envy, but they seem identical. For generally speaking, as vice has many hooks, and is swayed hither and thither by the passions that hang on it, there are many points of contact and entanglement between them, for as in the case of illnesses there is a sympathy between the various passions. Thus the prosperous man is equally a source of pain to hate and envy. And so we think benevolence the opposite of both these passions, being as it is a wish for our neighbour's good, and we think hate and envy identical, for the desire of both is the very opposite of benevolence. But since their similarities are not so great as their dissimilarities, let us investigate and trace out these two passions from their origin.

§ II. Hatred then is generated by the fancy that the person hated is either bad generally or bad to oneself. For those who think they are wronged naturally hate those who they think wrong them, and dislike and are on their guard against those who are injurious or bad to others;[762] but people envy merely those they think prosperous. So envy seems illimitable, being, like ophthalmia, troubled at everything bright, whereas hatred is limited, since it settles only on what seems hostile.

§ III. In the second place people feel hatred even against the brutes; for some hate cats and beetles and toads and serpents. Thus Germanicus could not bear the crowing or sight of a cock, and the Persian magicians kill their mice, not only hating them themselves but thinking them hateful to their god, and the Arabians and Ethiopians abominate them as much. Whereas we envy only human beings.

§ IV. Indeed among the brutes it is not likely that there should be any envy, for they have no conception of prosperity or adversity, nor have they any idea of reputation or want of reputation, which are the things that mainly excite envy; but they hate one another, and are hostile to one another, and fight with one another to the death, as eagles and dragons, crows and owls, titmice and finches, insomuch that they say that even the blood of these creatures will not mix, and if you try to mix it it will immediately separate again. It is likely also that there is strong hatred between the cock and the lion, and the pig and the elephant, owing to fear. For what people fear they naturally hate. We see also from this that envy differs from hatred, for the animals are capable of the one, but not of the other.

§ V. Moreover envy against anyone is never just, for no one wrongs another by his prosperity, though that is what he is envied for; but many are hated with justice, for we even think others[763] worthy of hatred, if they do not flee from such, and are not disgusted and vexed at them. A great indication of this is that some people admit they hate many, but declare they envy nobody. Indeed hatred of evil is reckoned among praiseworthy things; and when some were praising Charillus, the nephew of Lycurgus and king of Sparta, for his mildness and gentleness, his colleague said, "How can Charillus be good, who is not even harsh to the bad?" And so the poet described the bodily defects of Thersites at much length, whereas he expressed his vile moral character most shortly and by one remark, "He was most hateful both to Achilles and Odysseus."[764] For to be hated by the most excellent is the height of worthlessness. But people deny that they are envious, and, if they are charged with being so, they put forward ten thousand pleas, saying they are angry with the man or fear him or hate him, suggesting any other passion than envy, and concealing it as the only disorder of the soul which is abominable.

§ VI. Of necessity then these two passions cannot, like plants, be fed and nourished and grow on the same roots; for they are by nature different.[765] For we hate people more as they grow worse, but they are envied only the more the more they advance in virtue. And so Themistocles, when quite a lad, said he had done nothing remarkable, for he was not yet envied. For as insects attack most ripe corn and roses in their bloom, so envy fastens most on the good and on those who are growing in virtue and good repute for moral character. Again extreme badness intensifies hatred. So hated indeed and loathed were the accusers of Socrates, as guilty of extreme vileness, by their fellow-citizens, that they would neither supply them with fire, nor answer their questions, nor touch the water they had bathed in, but ordered the servants to pour it away as polluted, till they could bear this hatred no longer and hung themselves. But splendid and exceptional success often extinguishes envy. For it is not likely that anyone envied Alexander or Cyrus, after their conquests made them lords of the world. But as the sun, when it is high over our heads and sends down its rays, makes next to no shadow, so at those successes that attain such a height as to be over its head envy is humbled, and retires completely dazzled. So Alexander had none to envy him, but many to hate him, by whom he was plotted against till he died. So too misfortunes stop envy, but they do not remove hatred. For people hate their enemies even when they lie prostrate at their feet, but no one envies the unfortunate. But the remark of one of the sophists of our day is true, that the envious are very prone to pity; so here too there is a great difference between these two passions, for hatred abandons neither the fortunate nor unfortunate, whereas envy is mitigated in the extreme of either fortune.

§ VII. Let as look at the same again from opposite points of view. Men put an end to their enmity and hatred, either if persuaded they have not been wronged, or if they come round to the view that those they hated are good men and not bad, or thirdly if they receive a kindness. For, as Thucydides says, the last favour conferred, even though a smaller one, if it be seasonable, outweighs a greater offence.[766] Yet the persuasion that they have not been wronged does not put an end to envy, for people envy although absolutely persuaded that they have not been wronged; and the two other cases actually increase envy; for people look with an evil eye even more on those they think good, as having virtue, which is the greatest blessing; and if they are treated kindly by the prosperous it grieves them, for they envy both their will and power to do kindnesses, the former proceeding from their goodness, the latter from their prosperity, but both being blessings. Thus envy is a passion altogether different from hatred, seeing that what abates the one pains and exasperates the other.

§ VIII. Let us now look at the intent of each of these passions. The intent of the person who hates is to do as much harm as he can, so they define hatred to be a disposition and intent on the watch for an opportunity to do harm. But this is altogether foreign to envy.[767] For those who envy their relations and friends would not wish them to come to ruin, or fall into calamity, but are only annoyed at their prosperity; and would hinder, if they could, their glory and renown, but they would not bring upon them irremediable misfortunes: they are content to remove, as in the case of a lofty house, what stands in their light.

[762] [Greek: allôs] MSS. Wyttenbach [Greek: allôn]. Malo [Greek: allois].

[763] So Wyttenbach.

[764] Homer, "Iliad," ii. 220.

[765] So Wyttenbach. The reading in this passage is very doubtful.

[766] Thucydides, i. 42.

[767] Reading [Greek: apestin holôs. Oi gar phthonountes]. What can be made of [Greek: pollous] here?

HOW ONE CAN PRAISE ONESELF WITHOUT EXCITING ENVY.

§ I. To speak to other people about one's own importance or ability, Herculanus, is universally declared to be tiresome and illiberal, but in fact not many even of those who censure it avoid its unpleasantness. Thus Euripides, though he says,

"If words had to be bought by human beings, No one would wish to trumpet his own praises. But since one can get words *sans* any payment From lofty ether, everyone delights In speaking truth or falsehood of himself, For he can do it with impunity;"

yet uses much tiresome boasting, intermixing with the passion and action of his plays irrelevant matter about himself. Similarly Pindar says, that "to boast unseasonably is to play an accompaniment to madness,"[768] yet he does not cease to talk big about his own merit, which indeed is well worthy of encomium, who would deny it? But those who are crowned in the games leave it to others to celebrate their victories, to avoid the unpleasantness of singing their own praises. So we are with justice disgusted at Timotheus[769] for trumpeting his own glory inelegantly and contrary to custom in the inscription for his victory over Phrynis, "A proud day for you, Timotheus, was it when the herald cried out, 'The Milesian Timotheus is victorious over the son of Carbo and his Ionic notes.'" As Xenophon says, "Praise from others is the pleasantest thing a man can hear,"[770] but to others a man's self-praise is most nauseous. For first we think those impudent who praise themselves, since modesty would be becoming even if they were praised by others; secondly, we think them unjust in giving themselves what they ought to receive from others; thirdly, if we are silent we seem to be vexed and to envy them, and if we are afraid of this imputation, we are obliged to heap praise upon them contrary to our real opinion, and to bear them out, undertaking a task more befitting gross flattery than honour.

§ II. And yet, in spite of all this, there are occasions when a statesman may venture to speak in his own praise, not to cry up his own glory and merit, but when the time and matter demand that he should speak the truth about himself, as he would about another; especially when it is mentioned that another has done good and excellent things,[771] there is no need for him to suppress the fact that he has done as well. For such self-praise bears excellent fruit, since much more and better praise springs from it as from seed. For the statesman does not ask for reputation as a reward or consolation, nor is he merely pleased at its attending upon his actions, but he values it because credit and character give him opportunities to do good on a larger scale. For it is both easy and pleasant to benefit those who believe in us and are friendly to us, but it is not easy to act virtuously against suspicion and calumny, and to force one's benefits on those that reject them. Let us now consider, if there are any other reasons warranting self-praise in a statesman, what they are, that, while we avoid vain glory and disgusting other people, we may not omit any useful kind of self-praise.

§ III. That is vain glory then when men seem to praise themselves that they may call forth the laudation of others; and it is especially despised because it seems to proceed from ambition and an unseasonable opinion of oneself. For as those who cannot obtain food are forced to feed on their own flesh against nature, and that is the end of famine, so those that hunger after praise, if they get no one else to praise them, disgrace themselves by their anxiety to feed their own vanity. But when, not merely content with praising themselves, they vie with the praise of others, and pit their own deeds and actions against theirs, with the intent of outshining them, they add envy and malignity to their vanity. The proverb teaches us that to put our foot into another's dance is meddlesome and ridiculous; we ought equally to be on our guard against intruding our own panegyric into others' praises out of envy and spite, nor should we allow others either to praise us then, but we should make way for those that are being honoured, if they are worthy of honour, and even if they seem to us undeserving of honour and worthless, we ought not to strip them of their praise by self-laudation, but by direct argument and proof that they are not worthy of all these encomiums. It is plain then that we ought to avoid all such conduct as this.

§ IV. But self-praise cannot be blamed, if it is an answer to some charge or calumny, as those words of Pericles, "And yet you are angry with such a man as me, a man I take it inferior to no one either in knowledge of what should be done, or in ability to point out the same, and a lover of my country to boot, and superior to bribes."[772] For not only did he avoid all swagger and vainglory and ambition in talking thus loftily about himself, but he also exhibited the spirit and greatness of his virtue, which could abase and crush envy because it could not be abased itself. For people will hardly condemn such men, for they are elevated and cheered and inspired by noble self-laudation such as this, if it have a true basis, as all history testifies. Thus the Thebans, when their generals were charged with not returning home, and laying down their office of Boeotarchs when their time had expired, but instead of that making inroads into Laconia, and helping Messene, hardly acquitted Pelopidas, who was submissive and suppliant, but for Epaminondas,[773] who gloried in what he had done, and at last said that he was ready to die, if they would confess that he had ravaged Laconia, and restored Messene, and made Arcadia one state, against the will of the Thebans, they would not pass sentence upon him, but admired his heroism, and with rejoicing and smiles set him free. So too we must not altogether find fault with Sthenelus in Homer saying,

"We boast ourselves far better than our fathers,"[774]

when we remember the words of Agamemnon,

"How now? thou son of brave horse-taming Tydeus, Why dost thou crouch for fear, and watch far off The lines of battle? How unlike thy father!"[775]

For it was not because he was defamed himself, but he stood up for his friend[776] that was abused, the occasion giving him a reasonable excuse for self-commendation. So too the Romans were far from pleased at Cicero's frequently passing encomiums upon himself in the affair of Catiline, yet when Scipio said they ought not to try him (Scipio), since he had given them the power to try anybody, they put on garlands, and accompanied him to the Capitol, and sacrificed with him. For Cicero was not compelled to praise himself, but only did so for glory, whereas the danger in which Scipio stood removed envy from him.

§ V. And not only on one's trial and in danger, but also in misfortune, is tall talk and boasting more suitable than in prosperity. For in prosperity people seem to clutch as it were at glory and enjoy it, and so gratify their ambition; but in adversity, being far from ambition owing to circumstances, such self-commendation seems to be a bearing up and fortifying the spirit against fortune, and an avoidance altogether of that desire for pity and condolence, and that humility, which we often find in adversity. As then we esteem those persons vain and without sense who in walking hold themselves very erect and with a stiff neck, yet in boxing or fighting we commend such as hold themselves up and alert, so the man struggling with adversity, who stands up straight against his fate, "in fighting posture like some boxer,"[777] and instead of being humble and abject becomes through his boasting lofty and dignified, seems to be not offensive and impudent, but great and invincible. This is why, I suppose, Homer has represented Patroclus modest and without reproach in prosperity, yet at the moment of death saying grandiloquently,

"Had twenty warriors fought me such as thou, All had succumbed to my victorious spear."[778]

And Phocion, though in other respects he was gentle, yet after his sentence exhibited his greatness of soul to many others, and notably to one of those that were to die with him, who was weeping and wailing, to whom he said, "What! are you not content to die with Phocion?"

§ VI. Not less, but still more, lawful is it for a public man who is wronged to speak on his own behalf to those who treat him with ingratitude. Thus Achilles generally conceded glory to the gods, and modestly used such language as,

"If ever Zeus Shall grant to me to sack Troy's well-built town;"[779]

but when insulted and outraged contrary to his deserts, he utters in his rage boastful words,

"Alighting from my ships twelve towns I sacked,"[780]

and,

"For they will never dare to face my helmet When it gleams near."[781]

For frank outspokenness, when it is part of one's defence, admits of boasting. It was in this spirit no doubt that Themistocles, who neither in word nor deed had given any offence, when he saw the Athenians were tired of him and treating him with neglect, did not abstain from saying, "My good sirs, why do you tire of receiving benefits so frequently at the same hands?" and[782] "When the storm is on you fly to me for shelter as to a tree, but when fine weather comes again, then you pass by and strip me of my leaves."

§ VII. They then that are wronged generally mention what they have done well to those who are ungrateful. And the person who is blamed for what he has done well is altogether to be pardoned, and not censured, if he passes encomiums on his own actions: for he is in the position of one not scolding but making his defence. This it was that made Demosthenes' freedom of speech splendid, and prevented people being wearied out by the praise which in all his speech *On the Crown* he lavished on himself, pluming himself on those embassies and decrees in connection with the war with which fault had been found.

§ VIII. Not very unlike this is the grace of antithesis, when a person shows that the opposite of what he is charged with is base and low. Thus Lycurgus when he was charged at Athens with having bribed an informer to silence, replied, "What kind of a citizen do you think me, who, having had so long time the fingering of your public money, am detected in giving rather than taking unjustly?" And Cicero, when Metellus told him that he had destroyed more as a witness than he had got acquitted as an advocate, answered, "Who denies that my honesty is greater than my eloquence?" Compare such sayings of Demosthenes as, "Who would not have been justified in killing me, had I tried in word only to impair the ancient glory of our city?"[783] And, "What think you these wretches would have said, if the states had departed, when I was curiously discussing these points?"[784] And indeed the whole of that speech *On the Crown* most ingeniously introduces his own praises in his antitheses, and answers to the charges brought against him.

§ IX. However it is worth while to notice in his speech that he most artistically inserts praise of his audience in the remarks about himself, and so makes his speech less egotistical and less likely to raise envy. Thus he shows how the Athenians behaved to the Euboeans and to the Thebans, and what benefits they conferred on the people of Byzantium and on the Chersonese, claiming for himself only a subordinate part in the matter. Thus he cunningly insinuates into the audience with his own praises what they will gladly hear, for they rejoice at the enumeration of their successes,[785] and their joy is succeeded by admiration and esteem for the person to whom the success was due. So also Epaminondas, when Meneclidas once jeered at him as thinking more of himself than Agamemnon ever did, replied, "It is your fault then, men of Thebes, by whose help alone I put down the power of the Lacedæmonians in one day."

§ X. But since most people very much dislike and object to a man's praising himself, but if he praises some one else are on the contrary often glad and readily bear him out, some are in the habit of praising in season those that have the same pursuits business and characters as themselves, and so conciliate and move the audience in their own favour; for the audience know at the moment such a one is speaking that, though he is speaking about another, yet his own similar virtue is worthy of their praise.[786] For as one who throws in another's teeth things of which he is guilty himself must know that he upbraids himself most, so the good in paying honour to the good remind those who know their character of themselves, so that their hearers cry out at once, "Are not you such a one yourself?" Thus Alexander honouring Hercules, and Androcottus again honouring Alexander, got themselves honoured on the same grounds. Dionysius on the contrary pulling Gelon to pieces, and calling him the Gelos[787] of Sicily, was not aware that through his envy he was weakening the importance and dignity of his own authority.

§ XI. These things then a public man must generally know and observe. But those that are compelled to praise themselves do so less offensively if they do not ascribe all the honour to themselves, but, being aware that their glory will be tiresome to others, set it down partly to fortune, partly to the deity. So Achilles said well,

"Since the gods granted us to kill this hero."[788]

Well also did Timoleon, who erected a temple at Syracuse to the goddess of Fortune after his success, and dedicated his house to the Good Genius. Excellently again did Pytho of Ænos, (when he came to Athens after killing Cotys, and when the demagogues vied with one another in praising him to the people, and he observed that some were jealous and displeased,) in coming forward and saying, "Men of Athens, this is the doing of one of the gods, I only put my hands to the work." Sulla also forestalled envy by ever praising fortune, and eventually he proclaimed himself as under the protection of Aphrodite.[789] For men would rather ascribe their defeat to fortune than the enemy's valour, for in the former case they consider it an accident, whereas in the latter case they would have to blame themselves and set it down to their own shortcomings. So they say the legislation of Zaleucus pleased the Locrians not least, because he said that Athene visited him from time to time, and suggested to him and taught him his laws, and that none of those he promulgated were his own idea and plan.

§ XII. Perhaps this kind of remedy by talking people over must be contrived for those who are altogether crabbed or envious; but for people of moderation it is not amiss to qualify excessive praise. Thus if anyone should praise you as learned, or rich, or influential, it would be well to bid him not talk about you in that strain, but say that you were good and harmless and useful. For the person that acts so does not introduce his own praise but transfers it, nor does he seem to rejoice in people passing encomiums upon him, but rather to be vexed at their praising him inappropriately and on wrong grounds, and he seems to hide bad traits by better ones, not wishing to be praised, but showing how he ought to be praised. Such seems the intent of such words as the following, "I have not fortified the city with stones or bricks, but if you wish to see how I have fortified it, you will find arms and horses and allies."[790] Still more in point are the last words of Pericles. For as he was dying, and his friends very naturally were weeping and wailing, and reminded him of his military services and his power, and the trophies and victories and towns he had won for Athens, and was leaving as a legacy, he raised himself up a little and blamed them as praising him for things common to many, and some of them the results of fortune rather than merit, while they had passed over the best and greatest of his deeds and one peculiarly his own, that he had never been the cause of any Athenian's wearing mourning. This gives the orator an example, if he be a good man, when praised for his eloquence, to transfer the praise to his life and character, and the general who is admired for his skill and good fortune in war to speak with confidence about his gentleness and uprightness. And again, if any very extravagant praise is uttered, such as many people use in flattery which provokes envy, one can reply,

"I am no god; why do you liken me To the immortals?"[791]

If you really know me, praise my integrity, or my sobriety, or my kindheartedness, or my philanthropy. For even envy is not reluctant to give moderate praise to one that deprecates excessive praise, and true panegyric is not lost by people refusing to accept idle and false praise. So those kings who would not be called gods or the sons of gods, but only fond of their brothers or mother, or benefactors,[792] or dear to the gods, did not excite the envy of those that honoured them by those titles, that were noble but still such as men might claim. Again, people dislike those writers or speakers who entitle themselves wise, but they welcome those who content themselves with saying that they are lovers of philosophy, and have made some progress, or use some such moderate language about themselves as that, which does not excite envy. But rhetorical sophists, who expect to hear "Divine, wonderful, grand," at their declamations, are not even welcomed with "Pretty fair, so so."

§ XIII. Moreover, as people anxious not to injure those who have weak eyes, draw a shade over too much light, so some people make their praise of themselves less glaring and absolute, by pointing out some of their small defects, or miscarriages, or errors, and so remove all risk of making people offended or envious. Thus Epeus, who boasts very much of his skill in boxing, and says very confidently,

"I can your body crush, and break your bones,"[793]

yet says,

"Is't not enough that I'm in fight deficient?"[794]

But Epeus is perhaps a ridiculous instance, excusing his bragging as an athlete by his confession of timidity and want of manliness. But agreeable and graceful is that man who mentions his own forgetfulness, or ignorance, or ambition, or eager desire for knowledge and conversation. Thus Odysseus of the Sirens,

"My heart to listen to them did incline, I bade my comrades by a nod to unloose me."[795]

And again of the Cyclops,

"I did not hearken (it had been far better), I wished to see the Cyclops, and to taste His hospitality."[796]

And generally speaking the admixture with praise of such faults as are not altogether base and ignoble stops envy. Thus many have blunted the point of envy by admitting and introducing, when they have been praised, their past poverty and straits, aye, and their low origin. So Agathocles pledging his young men in golden cups beautifully chased, ordered some earthenware pots to be brought in, and said, "See the fruits of perseverance, labour, and bravery! Once I produced pots like these, but now golden cups." For Agathocles it seems was so low-born and poor that he was brought up in a potter's shop, though afterwards he was king of almost all Sicily.

§ XIV. These are external remedies against self-praise. There are other internal ones as it were, such as Cato applied, when he said "he was envied, because he had to neglect his own affairs, and lie awake every night for the interests of his country." Compare also the following lines,

"How should I boast? who could with ease have been Enrolled among the many in the army, And had a fortune equal to the wisest;"[797]

and,

"I shrink from squandering past labours' grace, Nor do I now reject all present toil."[797]

For as it is with house and farm, so also is it with glory and reputation, people for the most part envy those who have got them easily or for nothing, not those who have bought them at the cost of much toil and danger.

§ XV. Since then we can praise ourselves not only without causing pain or envy but even usefully and advantageously, let us consider, that we may not seem to have only that end in view but some other also, if we might praise ourselves to excite in our hearers emulation and ambition. For Nestor, by reciting his battles and acts of prowess, stirred up Patroclus and nine others to single combat with Hector. For the exhortation that adds deed to word and example and proper emulation is animating and moving and stimulating, and with its impulse and resolution inspires hope that the things we aim at are attainable and not impossible. That is why in the choruses at Lacedæmon the old men sing,

"We once were young and vigorous and strong,"

and then the boys,

"We shall be stronger far than now we are,"

and then the youths,

"We now are strong, look at us if you like."

In this wise and statesmanlike manner did the legislator exhibit to the young men the nearest and dearest examples of what they should do in the persons of those who had done so.

§ XVI. Moreover it is not amiss sometimes, to awe and repress and take down and tame the impudent and bold, to boast and talk a little big about oneself. As Nestor did, to mention him again,

"For I have mixed ere now with better men Than both of you, and ne'er did they despise me."[798]

So also Aristotle told Alexander that not only had they that were rulers over many subjects a right to think highly of themselves, but also those that had right views about the gods. Useful too against our enemies and foes is the following line,

"Ill-starred are they whose sons encounter me."[799]

Compare also the remark of Agesilaus about the king of the Persians, who was called great, "How is he greater than me, if he is not also more upright?" And that also of Epaminondas to the Lacedæmonians who were inveighing against the Thebans, "Anyhow we have made you talk at greater length than usual." But these kind of remarks are fitting for enemies and foes; but our boasting is also good on occasion for friends and fellow-citizens, not only to abate their pride and make them more humble, but also when they are in fear and dejection to raise them up again and give them confidence. Thus Cyrus talked big in perils and on battle-fields, though at other times he was no boaster. And the second Antigonus, though he was on all other occasions modest and far from vanity, yet in the sea-fight off Cos, when one of his friends said to him, "See you not how many more ships the enemy have got than we have?" answered, "How many do you make me equal to then?" This Homer also seems to have noticed. For he has represented Odysseus, when his comrades were dreadfully afraid of the noise and whirlpool of Charybdis, reminding them of his former cleverness and valour;

"We are in no worse plight than when the Cyclops By force detained us in his hollow cave; But even then, thanks to my valour, judgement, And sense, we did escape."[800]

For such is not the self-praise of a demagogue or sophist, or of one that asks for clapping or applause, but of one who makes his valour and experience a pledge of confidence to his friends. For in critical conjunctures the reputation and credit of one who has experience and capacity in command plays a great part in insuring safety.

§ XVII. As I have said before, to pit oneself against another's praise and reputation is by no means fitting for a public man: however, in important matters, where mistaken praise is injurious and detrimental, it is not amiss to confute it, or rather to divert the hearer to what is better by showing him the difference between true and false merit. Anyone would be glad, I suppose, when vice was abused and censured, to see most people voluntarily keep aloof from it; but if vice should be well thought of, and honour and reputation come to the person who promoted its pleasures or desires, no nature is so well constituted or strong that it would not be mastered by it. So the public man must oppose the praise not of men but of bad actions, for such praise is corrupting, and causes people to imitate and emulate what is base as if it were noble. But it is best refuted by putting it side by side with the truth: as Theodorus the tragic actor is reported to have said once to Satyrus the comic actor, "It is not so wonderful to make an audience laugh as to make them weep and cry." But what if some philosopher had answered him, "To make an audience weep and cry is not so noble a thing as to make them forget their sorrows." This kind of self-laudation benefits the hearer, and changes his opinion. Compare the remark of Zeno in reference to the number of Theophrastus' scholars, "His is a larger body, but mine are better taught." And Phocion, when Leosthenes was still in prosperity, being asked by the orators what benefit he had conferred on the city, replied, "Only this, that during my period of office there has been no funeral oration, but all the dead have been buried in their fathers' sepulchres." Wittily also did Crates parody the lines,

"Eating and wantonness and love's delights Are all I value,"

with

"Learning and those grand things the Muses teach one Are all I value."

Such self-praise is good and useful and teaches people to admire and love what is valuable and expedient instead of what is vain and superfluous. Let so much suffice on the question proposed.

§ XVIII. It remains to me now to point out, what our subject next demands and calls for, how everyone may avoid unseasonable self-praise. For there is a wonderful incentive to talking about oneself in self-love, which is frequently strongly implanted in those who seem to have only moderate aspirations for fame. For as it is one of the rules to preserve good health to avoid altogether places where sickness is, or to exercise the greatest precaution if one must go there, so talking about oneself has its slippery times and places that draw it on on any pretext. For first, when others are praised, as I said before, ambition makes people talk about themselves, and a certain desire and impulse for fame which is hard to check bites and tickles that ambition, especially if the other person is praised for the same things or less important things than the hearer thinks he is a proficient in. For as hungry people have their appetite more inflamed and sharpened by seeing others eat, so the praise of one's neighbours makes those who eagerly desire fame to blaze out into jealousy.

§ XIX. In the second place the narration of things done successfully and to people's mind entices many unawares to boasting and bragging in their joy; for falling into conversation about their victories, or success in state affairs, or their words or deeds commended by great men, they cannot keep themselves within bounds. With this kind of self-laudation you may see that soldiers and sailors are most taken. To be in this state of mind also frequently happens to those who have returned from important posts and responsible duties, for in their mention of illustrious men and men of royal rank they insert the encomiums they have passed on themselves, and do not so much think they are praising themselves as merely repeating the praises of others about themselves. Others think their hearers do not detect them at all of self-praise, when they recount the greeting and welcome and kindness they have received from kings and emperors, but only imagine them to be enumerating the courtesy and kindliness of those great personages. So we must be very much on our guard in praising others to free ourselves from all suspicion of self-love and self-recommendation, and not to seem to be really praising ourselves "under pretext of Patroclus."[801]

§ XX. Moreover that kind of conversation that mainly consists of censuring and running down others is dangerous as giving opportunity for self-laudation to those who pine for fame. A fault into which old men especially fall, when they are led to scold others and censure their bad ways and faulty actions, and so extol themselves as being remarkably the opposite. In old men we must allow all this, especially if to age they add reputation and merit, for such fault-finding is not without use, and inspires those who are rebuked with both emulation and love of honour.[802] But all other persons must especially avoid and fear that roundabout kind of self-praise. For since generally speaking censuring one's neighbours is disagreeable and barely tolerable and requires great wariness, he that mixes up his own praise with blame of another, and hunts for fame by defaming another, is altogether tiresome and inspires disgust, for he seems to wish to get credit through trying to prove others unworthy of credit.

§ XXI. Furthermore, as those that are naturally prone and inclined to laughter must be especially on their guard against tickling and touching, such as excites that propensity by contact with the smoothest parts of the body, so those that have a great passion for reputation ought to be especially advised to abstain from praising themselves when they are praised by others. For a person ought to blush when praised, and not to be past blushing from impudence, and ought to check those who extol him too highly, and not to rebuke them for praising him too little; though very many people do so, themselves prompting and reminding their praisers of others of their own acts and virtues, till by their own praise they spoil the effect of the praise that others give them. For some tickle and puff themselves up by self-praise, while others, malignantly holding out the small bait of eulogy, provoke others to talk about themselves, while others again ask questions and put inquiries, as was done to the soldier in Menander, merely to poke fun at him;

"'How did you get this wound?' 'Sir, by a javelin.' 'How in the name of Heaven?' 'I was on A scaling ladder fastened to a wall.' I show my wound to them in serious earnest, But they for their part only mock at me."

§ XXII. As regards all these points then we must be on our guard as much as possible not to launch out into praise of ourselves, or yield to it in consequence of questions put to us to draw us. And the best caution and security against this is to pay attention to others who praise themselves, and to consider how disagreeable and objectionable the practice is to everybody, and that no other conversation is so offensive and tiring. For though we cannot say that we suffer any other evil at the hands of those who praise themselves, yet being naturally bored by the practice, and avoiding it, we are anxious to get rid of them and breathe again; insomuch that even the flatterer and parasite and needy person in his distress finds the rich man or satrap or king praising himself hard to bear and wellnigh intolerable; and they say that having to listen to all this is paying a very large shot to their entertainment, like the fellow in Menander;

"To hear their foolish[803] saws, and soldier talk, Such as this cursed braggart bellows forth, Kills me; I get lean even at their feasts."

For as we may use this language not only about soldiers or men who have newly become rich,[804] who spin us a long yarn of their great and grand doings, being puffed up with pride and talking big about themselves; if we remember that the censure of others always follows our self-praise, and that the end of this vain-glory is a bad repute, and that, as Demosthenes says,[805] the result will be that we shall only tire our hearers, and not be thought what we profess ourselves to be, we shall cease talking about ourselves, unless by so doing we can bestow great benefit on ourselves or our hearers.

[768] Pindar, "Olymp." ix. 57, 58.

[769] Mentioned by Pausanias, iii. 12; viii. 50.

[770] "Memorabilia," ii. l. 31.

[771] Reading as Wyttenbach suggests, [Greek: malista de hotan legêtai ta allô pepragmena] *sq.*

[772]   Thucydides,   ii.   60.

[773] See Pausanias, ix. 14, 15.

[774] Homer, "Iliad," iv. 405.

[775] Homer, "Iliad," iv. 370, 371.

[776] Diomede.

[777] Sophocles, "Trachiniæ," 442.

[778] Homer, "Iliad," xvi. 847, 848. Plutarch only quotes the first line. I have added the second for the English reader, as necessary for the sense.

[779] Homer, "Iliad," i. 128, 129.

[780] "Iliad," ix. 328.

[781] "Iliad," xvi. 70, 71. [782] So Wyttenbach.

[783] Demosthenes, "De Corona," p. 260.

[784] "De Corona," p. 307.

[785] After Wyttenbach.

[786] After Wyttenbach.

[787] That is, laughing-stock. A play on the word Gelon.

[788] Homer, "Iliad," xxii. 379. He speaks of Hector.

[789] Others take it "as fortune's favourite."

[790] Words of Demosthenes, "De Corona," p. 325. Plutarch condenses them.

[791] Homer, "Odyssey," xvi. 187.

[792] Titles of the Ptolemies, Philadelphus Philometor, Euergetes.

[793] Homer, "Iliad," xxiii. 673.

[794] Ibid. 670.

[795] Homer, "Odyssey," xii. 192-194.

[796] Ibid. ix. 228, 229.

[797] Fragments from the "Philoctetes" of Euripides.

[798] Homer, "Iliad," i. 260, 261.

[799] Homer, "Iliad," vi. 127.

[800] Homer, "Odyssey," xii. 209-212.

[801] An allusion to Homer, "Iliad," xix. 302.

[802] Adopting the reading of Dübner.

[803] Adopting the reading of Salmasius.

[804] *Nouveaux riches, novi homines.*

[805] Demosthenes, "De Corona," p. 270.

ON THOSE WHO ARE PUNISHED BY THE DEITY LATE.

A discussion between Patrocleas, Plutarch, Timon, and Olympicus.

§ I. When Epicurus had made these remarks, Quintus, and before any of us who were at the end of the porch[806] could reply, he went off abruptly. And we, marvelling somewhat at his rudeness, stood still silently but looked at one another, and then turned and pursued our walk as before. And Patrocleas was the first to speak. "Are we," said he, "to leave the question unanswered, or are we to reply to his argument in his absence as if he were present?" Then said Timon, "Because he went off the moment he had thrown his missile at us, it would not be good surely to leave it sticking in us; for we are told that Brasidas plucked the javelin that had been thrown at him out of his body, and with it killed the hurler of it; but there is of course no need for us to avenge ourselves so on those that have launched on us an absurd or false argument, it will be enough to dislodge the notion before it gets fixed in us." Then said I, "Which of his words has moved you most? For the fellow seemed to rampage about, in his anger and abusive language, with a long disconnected and rambling rhapsody drawn from all sources, and at the same time inveighed against Providence."

§ II. Then said Patrocleas, "The slowness and delay of the deity in punishing the wicked used to seem[807] to me a very dreadful thing, but now in consequence of his speech I come as it were new and fresh to the notion. Yet long ago I was vexed when I heard that line of Euripides,

"He does delay, such is the Deity In nature."[808]

For indeed it is not fitting that the deity should be slow in anything, and least of all in the punishment of the wicked, seeing that they are not slow or sluggish in doing evil, but are hurried by their passions into crime at headlong speed. Moreover, as Thucydides[809] says, when punishment follows as closely as possible upon wrong-doing, it blocks up the road at once for those who would follow up their villainy if it were successful. For no debt so much as that of justice paid behind time damps the hopes and dejects the mind of the wronged person, and aggravates the audacity and daring of the wrong-doer; whereas the punishment that follows crime immediately not only checks future outbreaks but is also the greatest possible comfort to the injured. And so I am often troubled when I consider that remark of Bias, who told, it seems, a bad man that he was not afraid that he would escape punishment, but that he would not live to see it. For how did the Messenians who were killed long before derive any benefit from the punishment of Aristocrates? For he had been guilty of treason at the battle of *The Great Trench*, but had reigned over the Arcadians for more than twenty years without being found out, but afterwards was detected and paid the penalty, but they were no longer alive.[810] Or what consolation was brought to the people of Orchomenus, who lost their sons and friends and relatives in consequence of the treason of Lyciscus, by the disease which settled upon him long afterwards and spread all over his body? For he used to go and dip and soak his feet in the river, and uttered imprecations and prayed that they might rot off if he was guilty of treason or crime. Nor was it permitted to the children's children of those that were slain to see at Athens the tearing out of their graves the bodies of those atrocious criminals that had killed them, and the carrying them beyond their borders. And so it seems strange in Euripides using the following argument to deter people from vice:

"Fear not, for vengeance will not strike at once Your heart, or that of any guilty wretch, But silently and with slow foot it moves,[811] And when their time's come will the wicked reach."

This is no doubt the very reason why the wicked incite and cheer themselves on to commit lawless acts, for crime shows them a fruit visible and ripe at once, but a punishment late, and long subsequent to the enjoyment."

§ III. When Patrocleas had said thus much, Olympicus interfered, "There is another consideration, Patrocleas, the great absurdity involved in these delays and long-suffering of the deity. For the slowness of punishment takes away belief in providence, and the wicked, observing that no evil follows each crime except long afterwards, attribute it when it comes to mischance, and look upon it in the light more of accident than punishment, and so receive no benefit from it, being grieved indeed when the misfortune comes, but feeling no remorse for what they have done amiss. For, as in the case of a horse, the whipping or spurring that immediately follows upon a stumble or some other fault is a corrective and brings him to his duty, but pulling and backing him with the bit and shouting at him long afterwards seems to come from some other motive than a desire to teach him, for he is put to pain without being shown his fault; so the vice which each time it stumbles or offends is at once punished and checked by correction is most likely[812] to come to itself and be humble and stand in awe of the deity, as one that beholds men's acts and passions and does not punish behind time; whereas that justice that, according to Euripides, "steals on silently and with slow foot," and falls upon the wicked some time or other, seems to resemble more chance than providence by reason of its uncertainty, delay, and irregularity. So that I do not see what benefit there is in those mills of the gods that are said to grind late,[813] since they obscure the punishment, and obliterate the fear, of evil-doing."

§ IV. When Olympicus had done speaking, and I was musing with myself on the matter, Timon said, "Am I to put the finishing touch of difficulty on our subject, or am I to let him first contend earnestly against these views?" Then said I, "Why should we bring up the third wave[814] and drown the argument, if he is not able to refute or evade the charges already brought? To begin then with the domestic hearth, as the saying is,[815] let us imitate that cautious manner of speaking about the deity in vogue among the Academic philosophers, and decline to speak about these things as if we thoroughly understood them. For it is worse in us mortals than for people ignorant of music to discuss music, or for people ignorant of military matters to discuss the art of war, to examine too closely into the nature of the gods and demons, like people with no knowledge of art trying to get at the intention of artists from opinion and fancy and probabilities. For if[816] it is no easy matter for anyone not a professional to conjecture why the surgeon performed an operation later rather than sooner, or why he ordered his patient to take a bath to-day rather than yesterday, how is it easy or safe for a mortal to say anything else about the deity than that he knows best the time to cure vice, and applies to each his punishment as the doctor administers a drug, and that a punishment not of the same magnitude, or applied at the same time, in all cases. For that the cure of the soul, which is called justice, is the greatest of all arts is testified by Pindar as well as by ten thousand others, for he calls God, the ruler and lord of all things, the greatest artificer as the creator of justice, whose function it is to determine when, and how, and how far, each bad man is to be punished. And Plato says that Minos, the son of Zeus, was his father's pupil in this art, not thinking it possible that any one could succeed in justice, or understand how to succeed in it, without he had learned or somehow got that science. For the laws which men make are not always merely reasonable, nor is their meaning always apparent, but some injunctions seem quite ridiculous, for example, the Ephors at Lacedæmon make proclamation, directly they take office, that no one is to let his moustache grow, but that all are to obey the laws, that they be not grievous to them. And the Romans lay a light rod on the bodies of those they make freemen, and when they make their wills, they nominate some as their heirs, while to others they sell the property, which, seems strange. But strangest of all is that ordinance of Solon, that the citizen who, when his city is in faction, will not side with either party is to lose his civic rights. And generally one might mention many absurdities in laws, if one did not know the mind of the legislator, or understand the reason for each particular piece of legislation. How is it wonderful then, if human affairs are so difficult to comprehend, that it is no easy task to say in connection with the gods, why they punish some offenders early, and others late?

§ V. This is not a pretext for evading the subject, but merely a request for lenient judgement, that our discourse, looking as it were for a haven and place of refuge, may rise to the difficulty with greater confidence basing itself on probability. Consider then first that, according to Plato, god, making himself openly a pattern of all things good, concedes human virtue, which is in some sort a resemblance to himself, to those who are able to follow him. For all nature, being in disorder, got the principle of change and became order[817] by a resemblance to and participation in the nature and virtue of the deity. The same Plato also tells us that nature put eyesight into us, in order that the soul by beholding and admiring the heavenly bodies might accustom itself to welcome and love harmony and order, and might hate disorderly and roving propensities, and avoid aimless reliance on chance, as the parent of all vice and error. For man can enjoy no greater blessing from god than to attain to virtue by the earnest imitation of the noblest qualities of the divine nature. And so he punishes the wicked leisurely and long after, not being afraid of error or after repentance through punishing too hastily, but to take away from us that eager and brutish thirst for revenge, and to teach us that we are not to retaliate on those that have offended us in anger, and when the soul is most inflamed and distorted with passion and almost beside itself for rage, like people satisfying fierce thirst or hunger, but to imitate the mildness and long-suffering of the deity, and to avenge ourselves in an orderly and decent manner, only when we have taken counsel with time long enough to give us the least possible likelihood of after repentance. For it is a smaller evil, as Socrates said, to drink dirty water when excessively thirsty, than, when one's mind is disturbed and full of rage and fury, before it is settled and becomes pure, to glut our revenge on the person of a relation and kinsman. For it is not the punishment that follows as closely as possible upon wrong-doing, as Thucydides said,[818] but that which is more remote, that observes decorum. For as Melanthius says of anger,

"Fell things it does when it the mind unsettles,"[819]

so also reason acts with justice and moderation, when it banishes rage and passion. So also people are made milder by the example of other men, as when they hear that Plato, when he held his stick over his slave to correct him, waited some time, as he himself has told us, to compose his anger; and that Archytas, having learned of some wrong or disorderly action on the part of some of his farm labourers, knowing that at the time he was in a very great rage and highly incensed at them, did nothing to them, but merely departed, saying, "You may thank your stars that I am in a rage with you." If then the remembrance of the words and recorded acts of men abates the fierceness and intensity of our rage, much more likely is it that we (observing that the deity, though without either fear or repentance in any case, yet puts off his punishments and defers them for some time) shall be reserved in our views about such matters, and shall think that mildness and long-suffering which the god exhibits a divine part of virtue, reforming a few by speedy punishment, but benefiting and correcting many by a tardy one.

§ VI. Let us consider in the second place that punishments inflicted by men for offences regard only retaliation, and, when the offender is punished, stop and go no further; so that they seem to follow offences yelping at them like a dog, and closely pursuing at their heels as it were. But it is likely that the deity would look at the state of any guilty soul that he intended to punish, if haply it might turn and repent, and would give[820] time for reformation to all whose vice was not absolute and incurable. For knowing how great a share of virtue souls come into the world with, deriving it from him, and how strong and lasting is their nobility of nature, and how it breaks out into vice against its natural disposition through the corruption of bad habits and companions, and afterwards in some cases reforms itself, and recovers its proper position, he does not inflict punishment on all persons alike; but the incorrigible he at once removes from life and cuts off, since it is altogether injurious to others, but most of all to a man's own self, to live in perpetual vice, whereas to those who seem to have fallen into wrong-doing, rather from ignorance of what was good than from deliberate choice of what was bad, he gives time to repent. But if they persist in vice he punishes them too, for he has no fear that they will escape him. Consider also how many changes take place in the life and character of men, so that the Greeks give the names [Greek: tropos] and [Greek: êthos] to the character, the first word meaning *change*, and the latter the immense force and power of *habit*. I think also that the ancients called Cecrops half man and half dragon[821] not because, as some say, he became from a good king wild and dragon-like, but contrariwise because he was originally perverse and terrible, and afterwards became a mild and humane king. And if this is uncertain, at any rate we know that Gelon and Hiero, both Sicilians, and Pisistratus the son of Hippocrates, though they got their supreme power by bad means, yet used it for virtuous ends, and though they mounted the throne in an irregular way, yet became good and useful princes. For by good legislation and by encouraging agriculture they made the citizens earnest and industrious instead of scoffers and chatterers. As for Gelon, after fighting valiantly and defeating the Carthaginians in a great battle, he would not conclude with them the peace they asked for until they inserted an article promising to cease sacrificing their sons to Cronos. And Lydiades was tyrant in Megalopolis, yet in the very height of his power changing his ideas and being disgusted with injustice, he restored their old constitution to the citizens,[822] and fell gloriously, fighting against the enemy in behalf of his country. And if any one had slain prematurely Miltiades the tyrant of the Chersonese, or had prosecuted and got a conviction against Cimon for incest with his sister, or had deprived Athens of Themistocles for his wantonness and revellings and outrages in the market, as in later days Athens lost Alcibiades, by an indictment, should we not have had to go without the glory of Marathon, and Eurymedon, and beautiful Artemisium, "where the Athenian youth laid the bright base of liberty?"[823] For great natures produce nothing little, nor can their energy and activity rust owing to their keen intellect, but they toss to and fro as at sea till they come to a settled and durable character. As then one inexperienced in farming, seeing a spot full of thick bushes and rank growth, full of wild beasts and streams and mud, would not think much of it, while to one who has learnt how to discriminate and discern between different kind of soils all these are various tokens of the richness and goodness of the land, so great natures break out into many strange excesses, which exasperate us at first beyond bearing, so that we think it right to cut off such offenders and stop their career at once, whereas a better judge, seeing the good and noble even in these, waits for age and the season which nature appoints for gathering fruit to bring sense and virtue.

§ VII. So much for this point. Do you not think also that some of the Greeks did well to adopt that Egyptian law which orders a pregnant woman condemned to death not to suffer the penalty till after she has given birth?" "Certainly," said all the company. I continued, "Put the case not of a woman pregnant, but of a man who can in process of time bring to light and reveal some secret act or plan, point out some unknown evil, or devise some scheme of safety, or invent something useful and necessary, would it not be better to defer his execution, and wait the result of his meditation? That is my opinion, at least." "So we all think," said Patrocleas. "Quite right," said I. "For do but consider, had Dionysius had vengeance taken on him at the beginning of his tyranny, none of the Greeks would have dwelt in Sicily, which was laid waste by the Carthaginians. Nor would the Greeks have dwelt in Apollonia, or Anactorium, or the peninsula of the Leucadians, had not Periander's chastisement been postponed for a long time. I think also that Cassander's punishment was deferred that Thebes might be repeopled. And of the mercenaries that plundered this very temple most crossed over into Sicily with Timoleon, and after they had conquered the Carthaginians and put down their authority, perished miserably, miserable wretches that they were. For no doubt the deity makes use of some wicked men, as executioners, to punish others, and so I think he crushes as it were most tyrants. For as the gall of the hyena and rennet of the seal, both nasty beasts in all other respects, are useful in certain diseases, so when some need sharp correction, the deity casts upon them the implacable fury of some tyrant, or the savage ferocity of some prince, and does not remove the bane and trouble till their fault be got rid of and purged. Such a potion was Phalaris to the Agrigentines, and Marius to the Romans. And to the people of Sicyon the god distinctly foretold that their city needed a scourge, when they took away from the Cleonæans (as if he was a Sicyonian) the lad Teletias, who was crowned in the Pythian games, and tore him to pieces. As for the Sicyonians, Orthagoras became their tyrant, and subsequently Myro and Clisthenes, and these three checked their wanton outbreaks; but the Cleonæans, not getting such a cure, went to ruin. You have of course heard Homer's lines,

"'From a bad father sprang a son far better, Excelling in all virtue;'[824]

"and yet that son of Copreus never performed any brilliant or notable action: but the descendants of Sisyphus and Autolycus and Phlegyas nourished in the glory and virtues of great kings. Pericles also sprang of a family under a curse,[825] and Pompey the Great at Rome was the son of Pompeius Strabo, whose dead body the Roman people cast out and trampled upon, so great was their hatred of him. How is it strange then, since the farmer does not cut down the thorn till he has taken his asparagus, nor do the Libyans burn the twigs till they have gathered the ledanum, that god does not exterminate the wicked and rugged root of an illustrious and royal race till it has produced its fit fruit? For it would have been better for the Phocians to have lost ten thousand of the oxen and horses of Iphitus, and for more gold and silver to have gone from Delphi, than that Odysseus and Æsculapius should not have been born, nor those others who from bad and wicked men became good and useful."

§ VIII. "And do you not all think that it is better that punishment should take place at the fitting time and in the fitting manner rather than quickly and on the spur of the moment? Consider the case of Callippus, who with the very dagger with which he slew Dion, pretending to be his friend, was afterwards slain by his own friends. And when Mitius the Argive was killed in a tumult, a brazen statue in the market-place fell on his murderer and killed him during the public games. And of course, Patrocleas, you know all about Bessus the Pæonian, and about Aristo the Oetæan leader of mercenaries." "Not I, by Zeus," said Patrocleas, "but I should like to hear." "Aristo," I continued, "at the permission of the tyrants removed the necklace of Eriphyle[826] which was hung up in this temple, and took it to his wife as a present; but his son being angry with his mother for some reason or other, set the house on fire, and burnt all that were in it. As for Bessus, it seems he had killed his father, though his crime was long undiscovered. But at last going to sup with some strangers, he knocked down a nest of swallows, pricking it with his lance, and killed all the young swallows. And when the company said, as it was likely they would, 'Whatever makes you act in such a strange manner?' 'Have they not,' he replied, 'been long bearing false witness against me, crying out that I had killed my father?' And the company, astonished at his answer, laid the matter before the king, and the affair was inquired into, and Bessus punished."

§ IX. "These cases," I continued, "we cite supposing, as has been laid down, that there is a deferring of punishment to the wicked; and, for the rest, I think we ought to listen to Hesiod, who tells us--not like Plato, who asserts that punishment is a condition that follows crime--that it is contemporaneous with it, and grows with it from the same source and root. For Hesiod says,

"Evil advice is worst to the adviser;"[827]

and,

"He who plots mischief 'gainst another brings It first on his own pate."[828]

The cantharis is said to have in itself the antidote to its own sting, but wickedness, creating its own pain and torment, pays the penalty of its misdeeds not afterwards but at the time of its ill-doing. And as every malefactor about to pay the penalty of his crime in his person bears his cross, so vice fabricates for itself each of its own torments, being the terrible author of its own misery in life, wherein in addition to shame it has frequent fears and fierce passions and endless remorse and anxiety. But some are just like children, who, seeing malefactors in the theatres in golden tunics and purple robes with crowns on and dancing, admire them and marvel at them, thinking them happy, till they see them goaded and lashed and issuing fire from their gaudy but cheap garments.[829] For most wicked people, though they have great households and conspicuous offices and great power, are yet being secretly punished before they are seen to be murdered or hurled down rocks, which is rather the climax and end of their punishment than the punishment itself. For as Plato tells us that Herodicus the Selymbrian having fallen into consumption, an incurable disease, was the first of mankind to mix exercise with the art of healing, and so prolonged his own life and that of others suffering from the same disease, so those wicked persons who seem to avoid immediate punishment, receive a longer and not slower punishment, not later but extending over a wider period; for they are not punished in their old age, but rather grow old in perpetual punishment. I speak of course of long time as a human being, for to the gods all the period of man's life is as nothing, and so to them 'now and not thirty years ago' means no more than with us torturing or hanging a malefactor in the evening instead of the morning would mean; especially as man is shut up in life as in a prison from which there is no egress or escape, and though doubtless during his life he has much feasting and business and gifts and favours and amusement, yet, just like people playing at dice or draughts in a prison, the rope is all the time hanging over his head."[830]

§ X. "And indeed what prevents our asserting that people in prison under sentence of death are not punished till their heads are cut off, or that the person who has taken hemlock, and walks about till he feels it is getting into his legs, suffers not at all till he is deprived of sensation by the freezing and curdling of his blood, if we consider the last moment of punishment all the punishment, and ignore all the intermediate sufferings and fears and anxiety and remorse, the destiny of every guilty wretch? That would be arguing that the fish that has swallowed the hook is not caught, till we see it boiled by the cook or sliced at table. For every wrong-doer is liable to punishment, and soon swallows the pleasantness of his wrong-doing like a bait, while his conscience still vexes and troubles him,

"As through the sea the impetuous tunny darts."

For the recklessness and audacity of vice is strong and rampant till the crime is committed, but afterwards, when the passion subsides like a storm, it becomes timid and dejected and a prey to fears and superstitions. So that Stesichorus in his account of Clytæmnestra's dream may have represented the facts and real state of the case, where he says, "A dragon seemed to appear to her with its lofty head smeared all over with blood, and out of it seemed to come king Orestes the grandson of Plisthenes." For visions in dreams, and apparitions during the day, and oracles, and lightning, and whatever is thought to come from the deity, bring tempests of apprehension to the guilty. So they say that one time Apollodorus in a dream saw himself flayed by the Scythians, and then boiled, and that his heart out of the caldron spoke to him in a low voice and said, "I am the cause of this;" and at another time he dreamed that he saw his daughters running round him in a circle all on fire and in flames. And Hipparchus the son of Pisistratus, a little before his death, dreamt that Aphrodite threw some blood on his face out of a certain phial. And the friends of Ptolemy Ceraunus dreamed that he was summoned for trial by Seleucus, and that the judges were vultures and wolves, who tore his flesh and distributed it wholesale among his enemies. And Pausanias at Byzantium, having sent for Cleonice a free-born maiden, intending to outrage her and pass the night with her, being seized with some alarm or suspicion killed her, and frequently saw her in his dreams saying to him, "Come near for judgement, lust is most assuredly a grievous bane to men," and as this apparition did not cease, he sailed, it seems, to Heraclea to the place where the souls of the dead could be summoned, and by propitiations and sacrifices called up the soul of the maiden, and she appeared to him and told him that this trouble would end when he got to Lacedæmon, and directly he got there he died."[831]

§ XI. "And so, if nothing happens to the soul after death, but that event is the end of all enjoyment or punishment, one would be rather inclined to say that the deity was lax and indulgent in quickly punishing the wicked and depriving them of life. For even if we were to say that the wicked had no other trouble in a long life, yet, when their wrong-doing was proved to bring them no profit or enjoyment, no good or adequate return for their many and great anxieties, the consciousness of that would be quite enough to throw[832] their mind off its balance. So they record of Lysimachus that he was so overcome by thirst that he surrendered himself and his forces to the Getæ for some drink, but after he had drunk and bethought him that he was now a captive, he said, "Alas! How guilty am I for so brief a gratification to lose so great a kingdom!" And yet it is very difficult to resist a necessity of nature. But when a man, either for the love of money, or for political place or power, or carried away by some amorous propensity, does some lawless and dreadful deed, and, after his eager desire is satisfied, sees in process of time that only the base and terrible elements of his crime remain, while nothing useful, or necessary, or advantageous has flowed from it, is it not likely that the idea would often present itself to him that, moved by vain-glory, or for some illiberal and unlovely pleasure, he had violated the greatest and noblest rights of mankind, and had filled his life with shame and trouble? For as Simonides used to say playfully that he always found his money-chest full but his gratitude-chest empty,[833] so the wicked contemplating their own vice soon find out that their gratification is joyless and hopeless,[834] and ever attended by fears and griefs and gloomy memories, and suspicions about the future, and distrust about the present. Thus we hear Ino, repenting for what she had done, saying on the stage,

"Dear women, would that I could now inhabit For the first time the house of Athamas, Guiltless of any of my awful deeds!"[835]

It is likely that the soul of every wicked person will meditate in this way, and consider how it can escape the memory of its ill-deeds, and lay its conscience to sleep, and become pure, and live another life over again from the beginning. For there is no confidence, or reality, or continuance, or security, in what wickedness proposes to itself, unless by Zeus we shall say that evil-doers are wise, but wherever the greedy love of wealth or pleasure or violent envy dwells with hatred and malignity, there will you also see and find stationed superstition, and remissness for labour, and cowardice in respect to death, and sudden caprice in the passions, and vain-glory and boasting. Those that censure them frighten them, and they even fear those that praise them as wronged by their deceit, and as most hostile to the bad because they readily praise those they think good. For as in the case of ill-tempered steel the hardness of vice is rotten, and its strength easily shattered. So that in course of time, understanding their real selves, they are vexed and disgusted with their past life and abhor it. For if a bad man who restores property entrusted to his care, or becomes surety for a friend, or contributes very generously and liberally to his country out of love of glory or honour, at once repents and is sorry for what he has done from the fickleness and changeableness of his mind; and if men applauded in the theatres directly afterwards groan, their love of glory subsiding into love of money; shall we suppose that those who sacrificed men to tyrannies and conspiracies as Apollodorus did, or that those who robbed their friends of money as Glaucus the son of Epicydes did,[836] never repented, or loathed themselves, or regretted their past misdeeds? For my part, if it is lawful to say so, I do not think evil-doers need any god or man to punish them, for the marring and troubling of all their life by vice is in itself adequate punishment."

§ XII. "But consider now whether I have not spoken too long." Then Timon said, "Perhaps you have, considering what remains and the time it will take. For now I am going to start the last question, as if it were a combatant in reserve, since the other two questions have been debated sufficiently. For as to the charge and bold accusation that Euripides brings against the gods, for visiting the sins of the parents upon the children, consider that even those of us who are silent agree with Euripides. For if the guilty were punished themselves there would be no further need to punish the innocent, for it is not fair to punish even the guilty twice for the same offence, whereas if the gods through easiness remit the punishment of the wicked, and exact it later on from the innocent, they do not well to compensate for their tardiness by injustice. Such conduct resembles the story told of Æsop's coming to this very spot,[837] with money from Croesus, to offer a splendid sacrifice to the god, and to give four minæ to each of the Delphians. And some quarrel or difference belike ensuing between him and the Delphians here, he offered the sacrifice, but sent the money back to Sardis, as though the Delphians were not worthy to receive that benefit, so they fabricated against him a charge of sacrilege, and put him to death by throwing him headlong down yonder rock called Hyampia. And in consequence the god is said to have been wroth with them, and to have brought dearth on their land, and all kinds of strange diseases, so that they went round at the public festivals of the Greeks, and invited by proclamation whoever wished to take satisfaction of them for Æsop's death. And three generations afterwards came Idmon[838] a Samian, no relation of Æsop's, but a descendant of those who had purchased Æsop as a slave at Samos, and by giving him satisfaction the Delphians got rid of their trouble. And it was in consequence of this, they say, that the punishment of those guilty of sacrilege was transferred from Hyampia to Nauplia.[839] And even great lovers of Alexander, as we are, do not praise his destroying the city of the Branchidæ and putting everybody in it to death because their great-grandfathers betrayed the temple at Miletus.[840] And Agathocles, the tyrant of Syracuse, laughing and jeering at the Corcyræans for asking him why he wasted their island, replied, "Because, by Zeus, your forefathers welcomed Odysseus." And when the people of Ithaca likewise complained of his soldiers carrying off their sheep, he said, "Your king came to us, and actually put out the shepherd's eye to boot."[841] And is it not stranger still in Apollo punishing the present inhabitants of Pheneus, by damming up the channel dug to carry off their water,[842] and so flooding the whole of their district, because a thousand years ago, they say, Hercules carried off to Pheneus the oracular tripod? and in telling the Sybarites that the only end of their troubles would be propitiating by their ruin on three occasions the wrath of Leucadian Hera? And indeed it is no long time since the Locrians have ceased sending maidens[843] to Troy,

"Who without upper garments and barefooted, Like slave-girls, in the early morning swept Around Athene's altar all unveiled, Till old age came upon them with its burdens,"

all because Ajax violated Cassandra. Where is the reason or justice in all this? Nor do we praise the Thracians who to this day, in honour of Orpheus, mark their wives;[844] nor the barbarians on the banks of the Eridanus who, they say, wear mourning for Phäethon. And I think it would be still more ridiculous if the people living at the time Phäethon perished had neglected him, and those who lived five or ten generations after his tragic death had begun the practice of wearing mourning and grieving for him. And yet this would be only folly, there would be nothing dreadful or fatal about it, but what should make the anger of the gods subside at once and then afterwards, like some rivers, burst out against others till they completely ruin them?

§ XIII. Directly he left off, fearing that if he began again he would introduce more and greater absurdities, I asked him, "Well, do you believe all this to be true?" And he replied, "If not all, but only some, of it is true, do you not think that the subject presents the same difficulty?" "Perhaps," said I, "it is as with those in a raging fever, whether they have few or many clothes on the bed they are equally hot or nearly so, yet to ease them we shall do well to remove some of the clothes; but let us waive this point, if you don't like the line of argument, though a good deal of what you have said seems myth and fable, and let us recall to our minds the recent festival in honour of Apollo called Theoxenia,[845] and the noble share in it which the heralds expressly reserve for the descendants of Pindar, and how grand and pleasant it seemed to you." "Who could help being pleased," said he, "with such a delightful honour, so Greek and breathing the simple spirit of antiquity, had he not, to use Pindar's own phrase, 'a black heart forged when the flame was cold?'" "I pass over then," said I, "the similar proclamation at Sparta, 'After the Lesbian singer,' in honour and memory of old Terpander, for it is a similar case. But you yourselves certainly lay claim to be better than other Boeotians as descended from Opheltes,[846] and than other Phocians because of your ancestor Daiphantus,[847] and you were the first to give me help and assistance in preserving for the Lycormæ and Satilæi their hereditary privilege of wearing crowns as descendants of Hercules, when I contended that we ought to confirm the honours and favours of the descendants of Hercules more especially because, though he was such a benefactor to the Greeks, he had had himself no adequate favour or return." "You remind me," he said, "of a noble effort, and one well worthy of a philosopher." "Dismiss then," said I, "my dear fellow, your vehement accusation against the gods, and do not be so vexed that some of a bad or evil stock are punished by them, or else do not joy in and approve of the honour paid to descent from a good stock. For it is unreasonable, if we continue to show favour to a virtuous stock, to think punishment wrong in the case of a criminal stock, or that it should not correspond with the adequate reward of merit. And he that is glad to see the descendants of Cimon honoured at Athens, but is displeased and indignant that the descendants of Lachares or Aristo are in exile, is too soft and easy, or rather too fault-finding and peevish with the gods, accusing them if the descendants of a bad and wicked man are fortunate, and accusing them also if the progeny of the bad are wiped off the face of the earth; thus finding fault with the deity alike, whether the descendants of the good or bad father are unfortunate."

§ XIV. "Let these remarks," I continued, "be your bulwarks as it were against those excessively bitter and railing accusations. And taking up again as it were the initial clue to our subject, which as it is about the deity is dark and full of mazes and labyrinths, let us warily and calmly follow the track to what is probable and plausible, for certainty and truth are things very difficult to find even in every-day life. For example, why are the children of those that have died of consumption or dropsy bidden to sit with their feet in water till the dead body is burnt? For that is thought to prevent the disease transferring itself to them. Again, when a she-goat takes a bit of eringo into her mouth, why do the whole herd stand still, till the goatherd comes up and takes it out of her mouth? There are other properties that have connection and communication, and that transfer themselves from one thing to another with incredible[848] quickness and over immense distances. But we marvel more at intervals of time than place. And yet is it more wonderful that Athens should have been smitten with a plague[849] that started in Arabia, and of which Pericles died and Thucydides fell sick, than that, when the Delphians and Sybarites became wicked, vengeance should have fallen on their descendants.[850] For properties have relations and connections between ends and beginnings, and although the reason of them may not be known by us, they silently perform their errand."

§ XV. "Moreover the public punishments of cities by the gods admits of a just defence. For a city is one continuous entity, a sort of creature that never changes from age, or becomes different by time, but is ever sympathetic with and conformable to itself, and is answerable for whatever it does or has done for the public weal, as long as the community by its union and federal bonds preserves its unity. For he that would make several, or rather any quantity of, cities out of one by process of time would be like a person who made one human being several, by regarding him now as an old man, now as a young man, now as a stripling. Or rather this kind of reasoning resembles the arguments of Epicharmus, from whom the sophists borrowed the piled-up method of reasoning,[851] for example, he incurred the debt long ago, so he does not owe it now, being a different person, or, he was invited to dinner yesterday, but he comes uninvited to-day, for he is another person. And yet age produces greater changes in any individual than it does commonly in cities. For any one would recognize Athens again if he had not seen it for thirty years, for the present habits and feelings of the people there, their business, amusements, likes and dislikes, are just what they were long ago; whereas a man's friend or acquaintance meeting him after some time would hardly recognize his appearance, for the change of character easily introduced by every thought and deed, feeling and custom, produce a wonderful strangeness and novelty in the same person. And yet a man is reckoned to be the same person from birth to death, and similarly we think it right for a city always remaining the same to be liable to reproach for the ill deeds of its former inhabitants, on the same principle as it enjoys its ancient glory and power; or shall we, without being aware of it, throw everything into Heraclitus' river, into which he says a person cannot step twice,[852] since nature is ever changing and altering everything?"

§ XVI. "If then a city is one continuous entity, so of course is a race that starts from one beginning, that can trace back intimate union and similarity of faculties, for that which is begot is not, like some production of art, unlike the begetter, for it proceeds from him, and is not merely produced by him, so that it appropriately receives his share, whether that be honour or punishment. And if I should not seem to be trifling, I should say that the bronze statue of Cassander melted down by the Athenians, and the body of Dionysius thrown out of their territory by the Syracusans after his death, were treated more unjustly than punishing their posterity would have been. For there was none of the nature of Cassander in the statue, and the soul of Dionysius had left his dead body before this outrage, whereas Nysæus and Apollocrates,[853] Antipater and Philip,[854] and similarly other sons of wicked parents had innate in them a good deal of their fathers, and that no listless or inactive element, but one by which they lived and were nourished, and by which their ideas were controlled. Nor is it at all strange or absurd that some should have their fathers' characteristics. And to speak generally, as in surgery whatever is useful is also just, and that person would be ridiculous who should say it was unjust to cauterize the thumb when the hip-joints were in pain, and to lance the stomach when the liver was inflamed, or when oxen were tender in their hoofs to anoint the tips of their horns, so he that looks for any other justice in punishment than curing vice, and is dissatisfied if surgery is employed to one part to benefit another, as surgeons open a vein to relieve ophthalmia, can see nothing beyond the evidence of the senses, and does not remember that even a schoolmaster by correcting one lad admonishes others, and that by decimation a general makes his whole army obey. And so not only by one part to another comes benefit, but also to the soul through the soul, even more often than to the body through the body, come certain dispositions, and vices or improvement of character. For just as it is likely in the case of the body that the same feelings and changes will take place, so the soul, being worked upon by fancies, naturally becomes better or worse according as it has more confidence or fear."

§ XVII. While I was thus speaking, Olympicus interposed, and said, "You seem in your argument to assume the important assumption of the permanence of the soul." I replied, "You too concede it, or rather did concede it. For that the deity deals with everyone according to his merit has been the assumption of our argument from the beginning." Then said he, "Do you think that it follows, because the gods notice our actions and deal with us accordingly, that souls are either altogether imperishable, or for some time survive dissolution?" Then said I, "Not exactly so, my good sir, but is the deity so little and so attached to trifles, if we have nothing divine in ourselves, nothing resembling him, nothing lasting or sure, but that we all do fade as a leaf, as Homer[855] says, and die after a brief life, as to take the trouble--like women that tend and cultivate their gardens of Adonis[856] in pots--to create souls to flourish in a delicate body having no stability only for a day, and then to be annihilated at once[857] by any occasion? And if you please, leaving the other gods out of the question, consider the case of our god here.[858] Does it seem likely to you that, if he knew that the souls of the dead perish immediately, and glide out of their bodies like mist or smoke, he would enjoin many propitiatory offerings for the departed and honours for the dead, merely cheating and beguiling those that believed in him? For my own part, I shall never abandon my belief in the permanence of the soul, unless some second Hercules[859] shall come and take away the tripod of the Pythian Priestess, and abolish and destroy the oracle. For as long as many such oracles are still given, as was said to be given to Corax of Naxos formerly, it is impious to declare that the soul dies." Then said Patrocleas, "What oracle do you refer to? Who was this Corax? To me both the occurrence and name are quite strange." "That cannot be," said I, "but I am to blame for using the surname instead of the name. For he that killed Archilochus in battle was called Calondes, it seems, but his surname was Corax. He was first rejected by the Pythian Priestess, as having slain a man sacred to the Muses, but after using many entreaties and prayers, and urging pleas in defence of his act, he was ordered to go to the dwelling of Tettix, and appease the soul of Archilochus. Now this place was Tænarum, for there they say Tettix the Cretan had gone with a fleet and founded a city, and dwelt near the place where departed souls were conjured up. Similarly also, when the Spartans were bidden by the oracle to appease the soul of Pausanias, the necromancers were summoned from Italy, and, after they had offered sacrifice, they got the ghost out of the temple."

§ XVIII. "It is one and the same argument," I continued, "that confirms the providence of the deity and the permanence of the soul of man, so that you cannot leave one if you take away the other. And if the soul survives after death, it makes the probability stronger that rewards or punishments will be assigned to it. For during life the soul struggles, like an athlete, and when the struggle is over, then it gets its deserts. But what rewards or punishments the soul gets when by itself in the unseen world for the deeds done in the body has nothing to do with us that are alive, and is perhaps not credited by us, and certainly unknown to us; whereas those punishments that come on descendants and on the race are evident to all that are alive, and deter and keep back many from wickedness. For there is no more disgraceful or bitter punishment than to see our children in misfortune through our faults, and if the soul of an impious or lawless man could see after death, not his statues or honours taken from him, but his children or friends or race in great adversity owing to him, and paying the penalty for his misdeeds, no one would ever persuade him, could he come to life again, to be unjust and licentious, even for the honours of Zeus. I could tell you a story on this head, which I recently heard, but I hesitate to do so, lest you should regard it only as a myth; I confine myself therefore to probability." "Pray don't," said Olympicus, "let us have your story." And as the others made the same request, I said, "Permit me first to finish my discourse according to probability, and then, if you like, I will set my myth a going, if it is a myth."

§ XIX. Bion says the deity in punishing the children of the wicked for their fathers' crimes is more ridiculous than a doctor administering a potion to a son or grandson for a father's or grandfather's disease. But the cases, though in some respects similar and like, are in others dissimilar. For to cure one person of a disease does not cure another, nor is one any better, when suffering from ophthalmia or fever, by seeing another anointed or poulticed. But the punishments of evil-doers are exhibited to everybody for this reason, that it is the function of justice, when it is carried out as reason dictates, to check some by the punishment of others. So that Bion did not see in what respect his comparison touched our subject. For sometimes, when a man falls into a grievous but not incurable malady, which afterwards by intemperance and negligence ruins his constitution and kills him, is not his son, who is not supposed to be suffering from the same malady but only to have a predisposition for it, enjoined to a careful manner of living by his medical man, or friend, or intelligent trainer in gymnastics, or honest guardian, and recommended to abstain from fish and pastry, wine and women, and to take medicine frequently, and to go in for training in the gymnasiums, and so to dissipate and get rid of the small seeds of what might be a serious malady, if he allowed it to come to a head? Do we not indeed give advice of this kind to the children of diseased fathers or mothers, bidding them take care and be cautious and not to neglect themselves, but at once to arrest the first germ, of the malady, nipping it in the bud while removable, and before it has got a firm footing in the constitution?" "Certainly we do," said all the company. "We are not then," I continued, "acting in a strange or ridiculous but in a necessary and useful way, in arranging their exercise and food and physic for the sons of epileptic or atrabilious or gouty people, not when they are ill, but to prevent their becoming so. For the offspring of a poor constitution does not require punishment, but it does require medical treatment and care, and if any one stigmatizes this, because it curtails pleasure and involves some self-denial and pain, as a punishment inflicted by cowardice and timidity, we care not for his opinion. Can it be right to tend and care for the body that has an hereditary predisposition to some malady, and are we to neglect the growth and spread in the young character of hereditary taint of vice, and to dally with it, and wait till it be plainly mixed up with the feelings, and, to use the language of Pindar, "produce malignant fruit in the heart?"

§ XX. Or is the deity in this respect no wiser than Hesiod, who exhorts and advises, "not to beget children on our return from a sad funeral, but after a banquet with the gods,"[860] as though not vice or virtue only, but sorrow or joy and all other propensities, came from generation, to which the poet bids us come gay and agreeable and sprightly. But it is not Hesiod's function, or the work of human wisdom, but it belongs to the deity, to discern and accurately distinguish similarities and differences of character, before they become obvious by resulting in crime through the influence of the passions. For the young of bears and wolves and apes manifest from their birth the nature innate in them in all its naked simplicity; whereas mankind, under the influence of customs and opinions and laws, frequently conceal their bad qualities and imitate what is good, so as altogether to obliterate and escape from the innate taint of vice, or to be undetected for a long time, throwing the veil of craft round their real nature, so that we are scarce conscious of their villainy till we feel the blow or smart of some unjust action, so that we are in fact only aware that there is such a thing as injustice when men act unjustly, or as vice when men act viciously, or as cowardice when men run away, just as if one were to suppose that scorpions had a sting only when they stung us, or that vipers were venomous only when they bit us, which would be a very silly idea. For every bad man is not bad only when he breaks out into crime, but he has the seeds of vice in his nature, and is only vicious in act when he has opportunity and means, as opportunity makes the thief steal,[861] and the tyrant violate the laws. But the deity is not ignorant of the nature and disposition of every man, inasmuch as by his very nature he can read the soul better than the body, and does not wait to punish violence in the act, or shamelessness in the tongue, or lasciviousness in the members. For he does not retaliate upon the wrong-doer as having been ill-treated by him, nor is he angry with the robber as having been plundered by him, nor does he hate the adulterer as having himself suffered from his licentiousness, but it is to cure him that he often punishes the adulterous or avaricious or unjust man in embryo, before he has had time to work out all his villainy, as we try to stop epileptic fits before they come on.

§ XXI. Just now we were dissatisfied that the wicked were punished late and tardily, whereas at present we find fault with the deity for correcting the character and disposition of same before they commit crime, from our ignoring that the future deed may be worse and more dreadful than the past, and the hidden intention than the overt act; for we are not able fully to understand the reasons why it is better to leave some alone in their ill deeds, and to arrest others in the intention; just as no doubt medicine is not appropriate in the case of some patients, which would be beneficial to others not ill, but yet perhaps in a more dangerous condition still. And so the gods do not visit all the offences of parents on their children, but if a good man is the son of a bad one, as the son of a sickly parent is sometimes of a good constitution, he is exempt from the punishment of his race, as not being a participator in its viciousness. But if a young man imitates his vicious race it is only right that he should inherit the punishment of their ill deeds, as he would their debts. For Antigonus was not punished for Demetrius, nor, of the old heroes,[862] Phyleus for Augeas, or Nestor for Neleus, for though their sires were bad they were good, but those whose nature liked and approved the vices of their ancestors, these justice punished, taking vengeance on their similarity in viciousness. For as the warts and moles and freckles of parents often skip a generation, and reappear in the grandsons and granddaughters, and as a Greek woman, that had a black baby and so was accused of adultery, found out that she was the great granddaughter of an Ethiopian,[863] and as the son of Pytho the Nisibian who recently died, and who was said to trace his descent to the Sparti,[864] had the birthmark on his body of the print of a spear the token of his race, which though long dormant had come up again as out of the deep, so frequently earlier generations conceal and suppress the mental idiosyncrasies and passions of their race, which afterwards nature causes to break out in other members of the family, and so displays the family bent either to vice or virtue."

§ XXII. When I had said thus much I was silent, but Olympicus smiled and said, "We do not praise you, lest we should seem to forget your promised story, as though what you had advanced was adequate proof enough, but we will give our opinion when we have heard it." Then I began as follows. "Thespesius of Soli, an intimate friend of that Protogenes[865] who lived in this city with us for some time, had been very profligate during the early part of his life, and had quickly run through his property, and for some time owing to his straits had given himself up to bad practices, when repenting of his old ways, and following the pursuit of riches, he resembled those profligate husbands that pay no attention to their wives while they live with them, but get rid of them, and then, after they have married other men, do all they can wickedly to seduce them. Abstaining then from nothing dishonourable that could bring either enjoyment or gain, in no long time he got together no great amount of property, but a very great reputation for villainy. But what most damaged his character was the answer he received from the oracle of Amphilochus.[866] For he sent it seems a messenger to consult the god whether he would live the rest of his life better, and the answer was he would do better after his death. And indeed this happened in a sense not long after. For he fell headlong down from a great height, and though he had received no wound nor even a blow, the fall did for him, but three days after (just as he was about to be buried) he recovered. He soon picked up his strength again, and went home, and so changed his manner of life that people would hardly credit it. For the Cilicians say that they know nobody who was in those days more fairdealing in business, or more devout to the deity, or more disagreeable to his enemies, or more faithful to his friends; insomuch that all who had any dealings with him desired to hear the reason of this change, not thinking that so great a reformation of character could have proceeded from chance, and their idea was correct, as his narrative to Protogenes and others of his great friends showed. For he told them that, when his soul left the body, the change he first underwent was as if he were a pilot thrown violently into the sea out of a ship. Then raising himself up a little, he thought he recovered the power of breathing again altogether, and looked round him in every direction, as if one eye of the soul was open. But he saw none of the things he had ever seen before, but stars enormous in size and at immense distance from one another, sending forth a wonderful and intense brightness of colour, so that the soul was borne along and moved about everywhere quickly and easily, like a ship is fair weather. But omitting most of the sights he saw, he said that the souls of the dead mounted into the air, which yielded to them and formed fiery bubbles, and then, when each bubble quietly broke, they assumed human forms, light in weight but with different kinds of motion, for some leapt about with wonderful agility and darted straight upwards, while others like spindles flitted round all together in a circle, some in an upward direction, some in a downward, with mixed and confused motion, hardly stopping at all, or only after a very long time. As to most of these he was ignorant who they were, but he saw two or three that he knew, and tried to approach them and talk with them, but they would not listen to him, and did not seem to be in their right minds, but out of their senses and distraught, avoiding every sight and touch, and at first turned round and round alone, but afterwards meeting many other souls whirling round and in the same condition as themselves, they moved about promiscuously with no particular object in view, and uttered inarticulate sounds, like yells, mixed with wailing and terror. Other souls in the upper part of the air seemed joyful, and frequently approached one another in a friendly way, and avoided those troubled souls, and seemed to mark their displeasure by keeping themselves to themselves, and their joy and delight by extension and expansion. At last he said he saw the soul of a relation, that he thought he knew but was not quite sure, as he died when he was a boy, which came up to him and said to him, "Welcome, Thespesius." And he wondering, and saying that his name was not Thespesius but Aridæus, the soul replied, "That was your old name, but henceforth it will be Thespesius. For assuredly you are not dead, but by the will of the gods are come here with your intellect, for the rest of your soul you have left in the body like an anchor; and as a proof of what I say both now and hereafter notice that the souls of the dead have no shadow and do not move their eyelids." Thespesius, on hearing these words, pulled himself somewhat more together again, and began to use his reason, and looking more closely he noticed that an indistinct and shadow-like line was suspended over him, while the others shone all round and were transparent, but were not all alike; for some were like the full-moon at its brightest, throwing out one smooth even and continuous colour, others had spots or light marks here and there, while others were quite variegated and strange to the sight, with black spots like snakes, while others again had dim scratches.

Then the kinsman of Thespesius (for there is nothing to prevent our calling the souls by the name of the persons), pointed out everything, and told him that Adrastea, the daughter of Necessity and Zeus, was placed in the highest position to punish all crimes, and no criminal was either so great or so small as to be able to escape her either by fraud or violence. But, as there were three kinds of punishment, each had its own officer and administering functionary. "For speedy Vengeance undertakes the punishment of those that are to be corrected at once in the body and through their bodies, and she mildly passes by many offences that only need expiation; but if the cure of vice demands further pains, then the deity hands over such criminals after death to Justice, and those whom Justice rejects as altogether incurable, Erinnys (the third and fiercest of Adrastea's officers), pursues as they are fleeing and wandering about in various directions, and with pitiless severity utterly undoes them all, and thrusts them down to a place not to be seen or spoken about. And, of all these punishments, that which is administered in this life by Vengeance is most like those in use among the barbarians. For as among the Persians they pluck off and scourge the garments and tiaras of those that are to be punished, while the offenders weep and beg them to cease, so most punishments by fine or bodily chastisement have no sharp touch, nor do they reach vice itself, but are only for show and sentiment. And whoever goes from this world to that incorrigible and impure, Justice takes him aside, naked as he is in soul, and unable to veil or hide or conceal his villainy, but descried all round and in all points by everybody, and shows him first to his good parents, if such they were, to let them see what a wretch he is and how unworthy of his ancestors; but if they were wicked too, seeing them punished and himself being seen by them, he is chastised for a long time till he is purged of each of his bad propensities by sufferings and pains, which as much exceed in magnitude and intensity all sufferings in the flesh, as what is real is more vivid than a dream. But the scars and marks of the stripes for each bad propensity are more visible in some than in others. Observe also, he continued, the different and various colours of the souls. That dark dirty-brown colour is the pigment of illiberality and covetousness, and the blood-red the sign of cruelty and savageness, and where the blue is there sensuality and love of pleasure are not easily eradicated, and that violet and livid colour marks malice and envy, like the dark liquid ejected by the cuttle fish. For as during life vice produces these colours by the soul being acted upon by passions and reacting upon the body, so here it is the end of purification and correction when they are toned down, and the soul becomes altogether bright and one colour. But as long as these colours remain, there are relapses of the passions accompanied by palpitation and throbbing of the heart, in some faint and soon suppressed, in others more violent and lasting. And some of these souls by being again and again corrected recover their proper disposition and condition, while others again by their violent ignorance and excessive love of pleasure[867] are carried into the bodies of animals; for one by weakness of reasoning power, and slowness of contemplation, is impelled by the practical element in him to generation, while another, lacking an instrument to satisfy his licentiousness, desires to gratify his passions immediately, and to get that gratification through the medium of the body; for here there is no real fruition, but only an imperfect shadow and dream of incomplete pleasure."

After he had said this, Thespesius' kinsman hurried him at great speed through immense space, as it seemed to him, though he travelled as easily and straight as if he were carried on the wings of the sun's rays. At last he got to an extensive and bottomless abyss, where his strength left him, as he found was the case with the other souls there: for keeping together and making swoops, like birds, they flitted all round the abyss, but did not venture to pass over it. To internal view it resembled the caverns of Bacchus, being beautiful throughout[868] with trees and green foliage and flowers of all kinds, and it breathed a soft and gentle air, laden with scents marvellously pleasant, and producing the effect that wine does on those who are topers; for the souls were elevated by its fragrance, and gay and blithe with one another: and the whole spot was full of mirth and laughter, and such songs as emanate from gaiety and enjoyment. And Thespesius' kinsman told him that this was the way Dionysus went up to heaven by, and by which he afterwards took up Semele, and it was called the place of Oblivion. But he would not let Thespesius stay there, much as he wished, but forcibly dragged him away, instructing and telling him that the intellect was melted and moistened by pleasure, and that the irrational and corporeal element being watered and made flesh stirs up the memory of the body, from which comes a yearning and strong desire for generation, so called from being an inclination to the earth,[869] when the soul is weighed down with moisture.

Next Thespesius travelled as far in another direction, and seemed to see a great crater into which several rivers emptied themselves, one whiter than the foam of the sea or snow, another like the purple of the rainbow, and others of various hues whose brightness was apparent at some distance, but when he got nearer the air became thinner and the colours grew dim, and the crater lost all its gay colours but white. And he saw three genii sitting together in a triangular position, mixing the rivers together in certain proportions. Then the guide of Thespesius' soul told him, that Orpheus got as far as here, when he came in quest of the soul of his wife,[870] and from not exactly remembering what he had seen spread a false report among mankind, that the oracle at Delphi was common to Apollo and Night, though Apollo had no communion with Night: but this, pursued the guide, is an oracle common to Night and the Moon, that utters forth its oracular knowledge in no particular part of the world, nor has it any particular seat, but wanders about everywhere in men's dreams and visions. Hence, as you see, dreams receive and disseminate a mixture[871] of simple truth with deceit and error. But the oracle of Apollo you do not know, nor can you see it, for the earthiness of the soul does not suffer it to soar upwards, but keeps it down in dependence on the body. And taking him nearer his guide tried to show him the light from the tripod, which, as he said, shone as far as Parnassus through the bosom of Themis, but though he desired to see it he could not for its brightness, but as he passed by he heard the shrill voice of a woman speaking in verse several things, among others, he thought, telling the time of his death. That, said the genius, was the voice of the Sibyl, who sang about the future as she was being borne about in the Orb of the moon. Though desirous then to hear more, he was conveyed into another direction by the violent motion of the moon, as if he had been in the eddies of a whirlpool, so that he heard very little more, only a prophecy about Mt. Vesuvius and that Dicæarchia[872] would be destroyed by fire, and a short piece about the Emperor then reigning,[873] that "though he was good he would lose his empire through sickness."

- After this Thespesius and his guide turned to see those that were undergoing punishment. And at first they saw only distressing and pitiable sights, but after that, Thespesius, little expecting it, found himself among his friends and acquaintances and kinsfolk who were being punished, and undergoing dreadful sufferings and hideous and bitter tortures, and who wept and wailed to him. And at last he descried his father coming up out of a certain gulf covered with marks and scars, stretching out his hands, and not allowed to keep silence, but compelled by those that presided over his torture to confess that he had been an accursed wretch and poisoned some strangers that had gold, and during his lifetime had escaped the detection of everybody; but had been found out here, and his guilt brought home to him, for which he had already suffered much, and was being dragged on to suffer more. So great was his consternation and fear that he did not dare to intercede or beg for his father's release, but wishing to turn and flee he could no longer see his gentle and kind guide, but he was thrust forward by some persons horrible to look at, as if some dire necessity compelled him to go through with the business, and saw that the shades of those that had been notorious criminals and punished in their life-time were not so severely tortured here or like the others, but had an incomplete[874] though toilsome punishment for their irrational passions.[875] Whereas those who under the mask and show of virtue had lived all their lives in undetected vice were forced by their torturers with labour and pain to turn their souls inside out, unnaturally wriggling and writhing about, like the sea-scolopendras who, when they have swallowed the hook, turn themselves inside out; but some of them their torturers flayed and crimped so as to show their various inward vices which were only skinned over, which were deep in their soul the principal part of man. And he said he saw other souls, like snakes two or three or even more twined together, devouring one another in malignity and malevolence for what they had suffered or done in life. He said also that there were several lakes running parallel, one of boiling gold, another most cold of lead, another hard of iron, and several demons were standing by, like smiths, who lowered down and drew up by turns with instruments the souls of those whose criminality lay in insatiable cupidity. For when they were red-hot and transparent through their bath in the lake of gold, the demons thrust them into the lake of lead and dipped them in that; and when they got congealed in it and hard as hail, they dipped them into the lake of iron, and there they became wonderfully black, and broken and crushed by the hardness of the iron, and changed their appearance, and after that they were dipped again in the lake of gold, after suffering, he said, dreadful agony in all these changes of torment. But he said those souls suffered most piteously of all that, when they seemed to have escaped justice, were arrested again, and these were those whose crimes had been visited on their children or descendants. For whenever one of these latter happened to come up, he fell into a rage and cried out, and showed the marks of what he had suffered, and upbraided and pursued the soul of the parent, that wished to fly and hide himself but could not. For quickly did the ministers of torture pursue them, and hurry them back again to Justice,[876] wailing all the while on account of their fore-knowledge of what their punishment would be. And to some of them he said many of their posterity clung at once, and just like bees or bats stuck to them, and squeaked and gibbered[877] in their rage at the memory of what they had suffered owing to them. Last of all he saw the souls of those that were to come into the world a second time, forcibly moulded and transformed into various kinds of animals by artificers appointed for the very purpose with instruments and blows, who broke off all the limbs of some, and only wrenched off some of others, and polished others down or annihilated them altogether, to fit them for other habits and modes of life. Among them he saw the soul of Nero tortured in other ways, and pierced with red-hot nails. And the artificers having taken it in hand and converted it into the semblance of a Pindaric viper, which gets its way to life by gnawing through its mother's womb, a great light, he said, suddenly shone, and a voice came out of the light, ordering them to change it into something milder, so they devised of it the animal that croaks about lakes and marshes, for he had been punished sufficiently for his crimes, and now deserved some favour at the hands of the gods, for he had freed Greece, the noblest nation of his subjects and the best-beloved of the gods.[878] So much did Thespesius behold, but as he intended to return a horrible dread came upon him. For a woman, marvellous in appearance and size, took hold of him and said to him, "Come here that you may the better remember everything you have seen." And she was about to strike him with a red-hot iron pin, such as the encaustic painters use,[879] when another woman prevented her; and he was suddenly sucked up, as through[880] a pipe, by a strong and violent wind, and lit upon his own body, and woke up and found that he was close to his tomb.

[806] In the temple at Delphi, the scene of the discussion, as we see later on, §§ vii. xii.

[807] Reading [Greek: edokei] with Reiske.

[808] Euripides, "Orestes," 420. Cf. "Ion," 1615.

[809] Thucydides, iii. 38.

[810] See the circumstances in Pausanias, iv. 17 and 22.

[811] Compare Petronius, "Satyricon," 44: "Dii pedes lanatos habent." Compare also "Tibullus," i. 9. 4: "Sera tamen tacitis Poena venit pedibus."

[812] Reading [Greek: maliota] (for [Greek: molis]) with Wyttenbach.

[813] An allusion to the proverb [Greek: Opse Theôu aleousi myloi, aleousi de lepta]. See Erasmus, "Adagia," p. 1864.

[814] Cf. Plato, "Republic," 472 A.

[815] See Note, "On Abundance of Friends," § ii.

[816] Reading [Greek: ei gar].

[817] Or *a world*.

[818] See above, § ii.

[819] Quoted also in "On restraining Anger," § ii.

[820] It seems necessary to read either [Greek: porizein] with Mez, or [Greek: horizein] with Wyttenbach.

[821] Compare Aristophanes, "Vespæ," 438.

[822] See Pausanias, viii. 27.

[823] Pindar.

[824] Homer, "Iliad," xv. 641, 642.

[825] See Thucydides, i. 127.

[826] See Pausanias, v. 17; viii. 24; ix. 41; x. 29.

[827] Hesiod, "Works and Days," 266.

[828] Ibid. 265. Compare Pausanias, ii. 9; Ovid, A. A. i. 655, 656.

[829] "Significat martyres Christianos, in tunica molesta fumantes."--*Reiske*.

[830] Like the sword of Damocles. See Horace, "Odes," iii. 1. 17, 21.

[831] See also Pausanias, iii. 17.

[832] Surely [Greek: an anatrepoi] must be read.

[833] Compare "On Curiosity," § x.

[834] The reading is very doubtful. I adopt [Greek: hêdonês men euthus kenên charin, elpidos erêmon euriskousi.]

[835] Euripides, "Ino."

[836] See Herodotus, vi. 86; Juvenal, xiii. 199-207.

[837] The company are in the temple at Delphi, be it remembered.

[838] Called Iadmon in Herodotus, ii. 134, where this story is also told.

[839] Wyttenbach suggests Daulis.

[840] To Xerxes.

[841] The allusion is to the well-known story of Odysseus and the Cyclops Polyphemus, who is supposed to have dwelt in the island of Sicily, where Agathocles was tyrant.

[842] See Pausanias, viii. 14.

[843] Two were to be sent for 1,000 continuous years. So the Oracle.

[844] See Pausanias ix. 30; Herodotus, v. 6.

[845] See Pausanias, vii. 27; Athenæus, 372 A.

[846] A former king of Thebes. See Pausanias, ix. 5.

[847] Called Daiphantes, Pausanias, x. 1.

[848] Reading [Greek: apistois] with Xylander.

[849] The famous plague. See Thucydides, ii. 47-54.

[850] The allusion is to the circumstances mentioned in § xii.

[851] "Videtur idem cum *sorita* esse."--*Reiske*.

[852] Compare our author, "De EI a pud Delphos," § xviii. See also Seneca, "Epist.," lviii. p. 483; and Plato, "Cratylus," 402 A.

[853] Sons of Dionysius.

[854] Sons of Cassander.

[855] "Iliad" vi. 146-149.

[856] Compare Plato, "Phædrus," 276 B. These gardens of Adonis were what we might call flowerpot gardens. See Erasmus, "Adagia."

[857] [Greek: euthys] seems the best reading, [Greek: aei] is flat.

[858] Apollo.

[859] See § xii.

[860] Hesiod, "Works and Days," 735, 736.

[861] Compare the French Proverb, "L'occasion fait le larron." And Juvenal's "Nemo repente fuit turpissimus."

[862] So Reiske very ingeniously.

[863] A rather far-fetched pedigree.

[864] See Pansanias, viii. 11; ix. 5, 10. See also Ovid, "Metamorphoses," Book iii. 100-130.

[865] Compare "On Love," § ii.

[866] At Mallus, in Cilicia. See Pausanias, i. 34.

[867] Reading [Greek: philêdonias ischys] with Reiske.

[868] Reading [Greek: diapepoikilmenon on] with Wyttenbach.

[869] A paronomasia on [Greek: genesis] as if [Greek: epi gên neusis]. We cannot English it.

[870] Eurydice.

[871] "[Greek: mignymenon], Turn, et Bong.," *Reiske*. Surely the right reading.

[872] Latin Puteoli.

[873] Vespasian. See Suetonius, "Vespasian," ch. 24, as to the particulars of his death.

[874] The reading is very doubtful. I have followed Wyttenbach in reading [Greek: tribomenên tribên atelê].

[875] Such as that of the Danaides. So Wyttenbach.

[876] Adopting the arrangement of Wyttenbach.

[877] Compare Homer, "Odyssey," xxiv. 5-10.

[878] See Pausanias, vii. 17, for a sneaking kindness for Nero.

[879] See Athenæus, 687 B.

[880] Reading [Greek: dia] with Reiske.

AGAINST BORROWING MONEY.

§ I. Plato in his Laws[881] does not permit neighbours to use one another's water, unless they have first dug for themselves as far as the clay, and reached ground that is unsuitable for a well. For clay, having a rich and compact nature, absorbs the water it receives, and does not let it pass through. But he allows people that cannot make a well of their own to use their neighbour's water, for the law ought to relieve necessity. Ought there not also to be a law about money, that people should not borrow of others, nor go to other people's sources of income, until they have first examined their own resources at home, and collected, as by drops, what is necessary for their use? But nowadays from luxury and effeminacy and lavish expenditure people do not use their own resources, though they have them, but borrow from others at great interest without necessity. And what proves this very clearly is the fact that people do not lend money to the needy, but only to those who, wanting an immediate supply, bring a witness and adequate security for their credit, so that they can be in no actual necessity of borrowing.[882]

§ II. Why pay court to the banker or trader? Borrow from your own table. You have cups, silver dishes, pots and pans. Use them in your need. Beautiful Aulis or Tenedos will furnish you with earthenware instead, purer than silver, for they will not smell strongly and unpleasantly of interest, a kind of rust that daily soils your sumptuousness, nor will they remind you of the calends and the new moon, which, though the most holy of days, the money-lenders make ill-omened and hateful. For those who instead of selling them put their goods out at pawn cannot be saved even by Zeus the Protector of Property: they are ashamed to sell, they are not ashamed to pay interest on their goods when out at pawn. And yet the famous Pericles made the ornament of Athene, which weighed forty talents of fine gold, removable at will, for "so," he said, "we can use the gold in war, and at some other time restore as costly a one." So should we too in our necessities, as in a siege, not receive a garrison imposed on us by a hostile money-lender, nor allow our goods to go into slavery; but stripping our table, our bed, our carriages, and our diet, of superfluities, we should keep ourselves free, intending to restore all those things again, if we have good luck.

§ III. So the Roman matrons offered their gold and ornaments as first-fruits to Pythian Apollo, out of which a golden cup was made and sent to Delphi;[883] and the Carthaginian matrons had their heads shorn, and with the hair cut off made cords for the machines and engines to be used in defence of their country.[884] But we being ashamed of independence enslave ourselves to covenants and conditions, when we ought to restrict and confine ourselves to what is useful, and dock or sell useless superfluities, to build a temple of liberty for ourselves, our wives, and children. The famous Artemis at Ephesus gives asylum and security from their creditors to debtors, when they take refuge in her temple; but the asylum and sanctuary of frugality is everywhere open to the sober-minded, affording them joyful and honourable and ample space for much ease. For as the Pythian Priestess told the Athenians at the time of the Median war that the god had given them wooden walls,[885] and they left the region and city, their goods and houses, and took refuge in their ships for liberty, so the god gives us a wooden table, and earthenware plate, and coarse garments, if we wish to live free. Care not for fine horses or chariots with handsome harness, adorned with gold[886] and silver, which swift interest will catch up and outrun, but mounted on any chance donkey or nag flee from the hostile and tyrannical money-lender, not demanding like the Mede land and water,[887] but interfering with your liberty, and lowering your status. If you pay him not, he duns you; if you offer the money, he won't have it; if you are selling anything, he cheapens the price; if you don't want to sell, he forces you; if you sue him, he comes to terms with you; if you swear, he hectors; if you go to his house, he shuts the door in your face; whereas if you stay at home, he billets himself on you, and is ever rapping at your door.

§ IV. How did Solon benefit the Athenians by ordaining that debtors should no longer have to pay in person? For they are slaves to all money-lenders,[888] and not to them only, what would there be so monstrous in that? but to their slaves, who are insolent and savage barbarians, such as Plato represents the fiery torturers and executioners in Hades who preside over the punishment of the impious. For they make the forum a hell for wretched debtors, and like vultures devour and rend them limb from limb, "piercing into their bowels,"[889] and stand over others and prevent their tasting their own grapes or crops, as if they were so many Tantaluses. And as Darius sent Datis and Artaphernes to Athens with manacles and chains in their hands for their captives, so they bring into Greece boxes full of bonds and agreements, like fetters, and visit the towns and scour the country round, sowing not like Triptolemus harmless corn, but planting the toilsome and prolific and never-ending roots of debts, which grow and spread all round, and ruin and choke cities. They say that hares at once give birth and suckle and conceive again, but the debts of these knaves and barbarians give birth before they conceive; for at the very moment of giving they ask back, and take up what they laid down, and lend what they take for lending.

§ V. It is a saying among the Messenians, that "there is a Pylos before Pylos, and another Pylos too." So it may be said with respect to these money-lenders, "there is interest before interest, and other interest too." Then of course they laugh at those natural philosophers who say that nothing can come of nothing, for they get interest on what neither is nor was; and they think it disgraceful to farm out the taxes, though the law allows it, while they themselves against the law exact tribute for what they lend, or rather, if one is to say the truth, defraud as they lend, for he who receives less than he signs his name for is defrauded. The Persians indeed think lying a secondary crime, but debt a principal one, for lying frequently follows upon debt, but money-lenders tell more lies, for they make fraudulent entries in their account-books, writing down that they have given so-and-so so much, when they have really given less. And the only excuse for their lying is covetousness, not necessity, not utter poverty, but insatiable greediness, the outcome of which is without enjoyment and useless to themselves, and fatal to their victims. For neither do they farm the fields which they rob their debtors of, nor do they inhabit their houses when they have thrust them out, nor use their tables or apparel, but first one is ruined, and then a second is hunted down, for whom the first one serves as a decoy. For the bane spreads and grows like a fire, to the destruction and ruin of all who fall into their clutches, for it consumes one after another; and the money-lender, who fans and feeds this flame to ensnare many, gets no more advantage from it but that some time after he can take his account-book and read how many he has sold up, how many turned out of house and home, and track the sources of his wealth, which is ever growing into a larger pile.

§ VI. And do not think I say this as an enemy proclaiming war against the money-lenders,

"For never did they lift my cows or horses,"[890]

but merely to prove to those who too readily borrow money what disgrace and servitude it brings with it, and what extreme folly and weakness it is. Have you anything? do not borrow, for you are not in a necessitous condition. Have you nothing? do not borrow, for you will never be able to pay back. Let us consider either case separately. Cato said to a certain old man who was a wicked fellow, "My good sir, why do you add the shame that comes from wickedness to old age, that has so many troubles of its own?" So too do you, since poverty has so many troubles of its own, not add the terrible distress that comes from borrowing money and from debt; and do not take away from poverty its only advantage over wealth, its freedom from corroding care. For the proverb that says, "I cannot carry a goat, put an ox on my shoulder," has a ridiculous ring. Unable to bear poverty, are you going to put on your back a money-lender, a weight hard to carry even for a rich man? How then, will you say, am I to maintain myself? Do you ask this, having two hands, two legs, and a tongue, in short, being a man, to love and be loved, to give and receive benefits? Can you not be a schoolmaster or tutor, or porter, or sailor, or make coasting voyages? Any of these ways of getting a livelihood is less disgraceful and difficult than to always have to hear, "Pay me that thou owest."

§ VII. The well-known Rutilius went up to Musonius at Rome, and said to him, "Musonius, Zeus Soter, whom you imitate and emulate, does not borrow money." And Musonius smilingly answered, "Neither does he lend." For you must know Rutilius, himself a lender, was bantering Musonius for being a borrower. What Stoic inflatedness was all this! What need was there to bring in Zeus Soter? For all nature teaches the same lesson. Swallows do not borrow money, nor do ants, although nature has given them no hands, or reason, or profession. But men have intellect in excess, and so ingenious are they that they keep near them horses, and dogs, and partridges, and jackdaws. Why then do you despair, who are as impressible as a jackdaw, have as much voice as a partridge, and are as noble as a dog, of getting some person to befriend you, by looking after him, winning his affections, guarding him, fighting his battles? Do you not see how many opportunities there are both on land and sea? As Crates says,

"Miccylus and his wife, to ward off famine In these bad times, I saw both carding wool."

And King Antigonus asked Cleanthes, when he saw him at Athens after a long interval, "Do you still grind, Cleanthes?" And he replied, "I do, O king, but for my living, yet so as not to desert philosophy." Such was the admirable spirit of the man who, coming from the mill and kneading-trough, wrote with the hand that had baked and ground about the gods, and the moon, and stars, and the sun. But those kinds of labour are in our view servile! And so that we may appear free we borrow money, and flatter and dance attendance on slaves, and give them dinners and presents, and pay taxes as it were to them, not on account of our poverty (for no one lends money to a poor man), but from our love of lavish expenditure. For if we were content with things necessary for subsistence, the race of money-lenders would be as extinct as Centaurs and Gorgons are; it is luxury that has created them as much as goldsmiths, and silversmiths, and perfumers, and dyers in bright colours. For we do not owe money for bread and wine, but for estates, and slaves, and mules, and dining-rooms, and tables, and for our lavish public entertainments, in our unprofitable and thankless ambition. And he that is once involved in debt remains in it all his time, like a horse bitted and bridled that takes one rider after another, and there is no escape to green pastures and meadows, but they wander about like those demons who were driven out of heaven by the gods who are thus described by Empedocles:--

"Into the sea the force of heaven thrusts them, The sea rejects them back upon the land; To the sun's rays th' unresting earth remits them; The sun anon whirls them to heaven again."

So one after another usurer or trader gets hold of the poor wretch, hailing either from Corinth, or Patræ, or Athens, till he gets set on to by them all, and torn to bits, and cut into mince-meat as it were for his interest. For as a person who is fallen into the mire must either get up out of it or remain in it, and if he turns about in it, and wallows in it, and bedabbles his body all over in it, he contracts only the greater defilement, so by borrowing from one person to pay another and changing their money-lenders they contract and incur fresh interest, and get into greater liabilities, and closely resemble sufferers from cholera, whose case does not admit of cure because they evacuate everything they are ordered to take, and so ever add to the disease. So these will not get cleansed from the disease of debt, but at regular times in the year pay their interest with pain and agony, and then immediately another creditor presents his little account, so again their heads swim and ache, when they ought to have got rid of their debts altogether, and regained their freedom.

§ VIII. I now turn my attention to those who are rich and luxurious, and use language like the following, "Am I then to go without slaves and hearth and home?" As if any dropsical person, whose body was greatly swollen and who was very weak, should say to his doctor, "Am I then to become lean and empty?" And why not, to get well? And do you too go without a slave, not to be a slave yourself; and without chattels, not to be another man's chattel. Listen to a story about two vultures; one was vomiting and saying it would bring its inside up, and the other who was by said, "What harm if you do? For it won't be your inside you bring up, but that dead body we devoured lately." And so any debtor does not sell his own estate, or his own house, but his creditor's, for he has made him by law master of them. Nay, but by Zeus, says one, my father left me this field. Yes, and your father also left you liberty and a status in the community, which you ought to value more than you do. And your father begot you with hand and foot, but should either of them mortify, you pay the surgeon to cut it off. Thus Calypso clad and "dressed" Odysseus "in raiment smelling sweet,"[891] like the body of an immortal, as a gift and token of her affection for him; but when his vessel was upset and he himself immersed, and owing to this wet and heavy raiment could hardly keep himself on the top of the waves, he threw it off and stripped himself, and covered his naked breast with Ino's veil,[892] and "swam for it gazing on the distant shore,"[893] and so saved his life, and lacked neither food nor raiment. What then? have not poor debtors storms, when the money-lender stands over them and says, *Pay*?

"Thus spoke Poseidon, and the clouds did gather, And lashed the sea to fury, and at once Eurus and Notus and the stormy Zephyr Blew all together."[894]

Thus interest rolls on interest as wave upon wave, and he that is involved in debt struggles against the load that bears him down, but cannot swim away and escape, but sinks to the bottom, and carries with him to ruin his friends that have gone security for him. But Crates the Theban, though he had neither duns nor debts, and was only disgusted at the distracting cares of housekeeping, gave up a property worth eight talents, and assumed the philosopher's threadbare cloak and wallet, and took refuge in philosophy and poverty. And Anaxagoras left his sheep-farm. But why need I mention these? since the lyric poet Philoxenus, obtaining by lot in a Sicilian colony much substance and a house abounding in every kind of comfort, but finding that luxury and pleasure and absence of refinement was the fashion there, said, "By the gods these comforts shall not undo me, I will give them up," and he left his lot to others, and sailed home again. But debtors have to put up with being dunned, subjected to tribute, suffering slavery, passing debased coin, and like Phineus, feeding certain winged Harpies, who carry off and lay violent hands on their food, not at the proper season, for they get possession of their debtors' corn before it is sown, and they traffic for oil before the olives are ripe; and the money-lender says, "I have wine at such and such a price," and takes a bond for it, when the grapes are yet on the vine waiting for Arcturus to ripen them.

[881] Page 844, A. B. C.

[882] Reading with Wyttenbach [Greek: didousi] and [Greek: echousi].

[883] See Livy, v. 25.

[884] See Appian, lv. 26.

[885] See Herodotus, vii. 141-143; viii. 51.

[886] Reading with Reiske [Greek: katachrusa].

[887] The technical term for submission to an enemy. See Pausanias, iii. 12; x. 20. Herodotus, v. 17, 18; vii. 133.

[888] Reading with Reiske [Greek: daneistais]. Perhaps [Greek: aphanistais] originally came after [Greek: agriois], and got somehow displaced.

[889] See Homer, "Odyssey," xi. 578, 579, and context.

[890] Homer, "Iliad," i. 154.

[891] "Odyssey," v. 264.

[892] "Odyssey," v. 333-375.

[893] "Odyssey," v. 439.

[894] "Odyssey," v. 291-295.

WHETHER "LIVE UNKNOWN" BE A WISE PRECEPT.

§ I. He who uttered this precept[895] certainly did not wish to live unknown, for he uttered it to let all the world know he was a superior thinker, and to get to himself unjust glory by exhorting others to shun glory.

"I hate the wise man for himself not wise."[896]

They say that Philoxenus the son of Eryxis and Gnatho the Sicilian, being exceedingly greedy where good fare was going, would blow their nose in the dishes, to disgust all others at the table, that they alone might take their fill of the choicest dishes. So those that are insatiable pursuers of glory calumniate glory to others who are their rivals, that they may get it without antagonists. In this they resemble rowers, who face the stern of the vessel but propel it ahead, that by the recoil from the stroke of their oars they may reach port, so those that give vent to precepts like this pursue glory with their face turned in the opposite direction. For otherwise what need was there to utter a precept like this, or to write and hand it down to posterity, if he wished to live unknown to his own generation, who did not wish to live unknown to posterity?

§ II. Look at the matter in the following way.[897] Has not that "live unknown" a villainous ring, as though one had broken open graves? Is your life so disgraceful that we must all be ignorant of it? For my part I should say, Even if your life be bad do not live unknown, but be known, reform, repent; if you have virtue, be not utterly useless in life; if you are vicious, do not continue unreformed. Point out then and define to whom you recommend this precept. If to an ignorant or wicked or senseless person, you resemble one who should say to a person in a fever or delirium, "Be unknown. Don't let the doctor know your condition. Go and throw yourself into some dark place, that you and your ailments may be unknown." So you say to a vicious man, "Go off with your vice, and hide your deadly and irremediable disease from your friends, fearful to show your superstitious fears, palpitations as it were, to those who could admonish you and cure you." Our remote ancestors paid public attention to the sick, and if any one had either had or cured a similar complaint, he communicated his experience to the patient, and so they say medical art became great by these contributions from experience. We ought also in the same way to expose to everyone diseased lives and the passions of the soul, and to handle them, and to examine the condition of each,[898] and say, Are you a passionate man? Be on your guard against anger. Are you of a jealous turn? Look to it. Are you in love? I myself was in love once, but I had to repent. But nowadays people deny and conceal and cloak their vices, and so fix them deeper in themselves.

§ III. Moreover if you advise men of worth to live unknown and in obscurity, you say to Epaminondas, Do not be a general; and to Lycurgus, Do not be a legislator; and to Thrasybulus, Do not be a tyrannicide; and to Pythagoras, Do not teach; and to Socrates, Do not discourse; and first and foremost you bid yourself, Epicurus, to refrain from writing letters to your friends in Asia, and from enrolling Egyptian strangers among your disciples, and from dancing attendance on the youths of Lampsacus, and sending books to all quarters to display your wisdom to all men and all women, and leaving directions in your will about your funeral. What is the meaning of those common tables of yours? what that crowd of friends and handsome youths? Why those many thousand lines written and composed so laboriously on Metrodorus, and Aristobulus, and Chæredemus, that they may not be unknown even in death, if[899] you ordain for virtue oblivion, for art inactivity, for philosophy silence, and for success that it should be speedily forgotten?

§ IV. But if you exclude all knowledge about life, like putting the lights out at a supper party, that you may go from pleasure to pleasure undetected,[900] then "live unknown." Certainly if I am going to pass my life with the harlot Hedeia, or my days with Leontium, and spurn at virtue, and put my *summum bonum* in sensual gratifications, these are ends that require darkness and night, on these oblivion and ignorance are rightly cast. But if any one in nature sings the praises of the deity and justice and providence, and in morals upholds the law and society and the constitution, and in the constitution what is honourable and not expedient, why should he "live unknown"? Is it that he should instruct nobody, inspire in nobody an emulation for virtue, and be to nobody a pattern in good?[901] Had Themistocles been unknown at Athens, Greece would not have repelled Xerxes; had Camillus been unknown at Rome, Rome would not have remained a state; had Plato been unknown to Dion, Sicily would not have won its freedom. And as light, I take it, makes us not only visible but useful to one another, so knowledge gives not only glory but impetus to virtue. Epaminondas in obscurity up to his fortieth year was no use to the Thebans, but when his merits became known and he was put into power, he saved his state from ruin, and liberated Greece from slavery, making his abilities efficacious in emergency through his reputation like the bright shining of a light. For Sophocles' words,

"Brightly shines brass in use, but when unused It groweth dull in time, and mars the house,"[902]

are also appropriate to the character of a man, which gets rusty and senile by not mixing in affairs but living in obscurity. For mute inglorious ease, and a sedentary life devoted to leisure, not only injure the body but also the soul: and as hidden waters overshadowed and stagnant get foul because they have no outlet, so the innate powers of unruffled lives, that neither imbibe nor pass on anything, even if they had any useful element in them once, seem to be effete and wasted.

§ V. Have you never noticed how when night comes on a tired languor seizes the body, and inactive torpor overpowers the soul, and reason shrinks within itself like a fire going out, and feeling quite worn out is gently agitated by disordered fancies, only just indicating that the man is alive? But when the sun rises and scares away deceitful dreams, and brings on as it were the everyday world[903] and with its light rouses and stimulates the thoughts and actions of everybody, then, as Democritus says, "men form new ideas for the day," and betake themselves to their various pursuits with mutual impetuosity, as if drawn by a strong impulse.

§ VI. And I think that life itself, and the way we come into the world, is so ordained by the deity that we should know one another. For everyone comes into this great universe obscure and unknown casually and by degrees, but when he mixes with his fellows and grows to maturity he shines forth, and becomes well-known instead of obscure, and conspicuous instead of unknown. For knowledge is not the road to being, as some say, but being to knowledge, for being does not create but only exhibits things, as death is not the reducing of existence to non-existence, but rather the result of dissolution is obscurity. So people considering the Sun as Apollo according to hereditary and ancient institutions, call him Delius[904] and Pythius; whereas the lord of the world of darkness, whether god or demon, they call Hades[905] (for when we die we go into an unseen and invisible place), and the lord of dark night and idle sleep. And I think our ancestors called man himself by a word meaning light,[906] because by their relationship to light all have implanted in them a strong and vehement desire to know and to be known. And some philosophers think that the soul itself is light in its essence, inferring so on other grounds and because it can least endure ignorance about facts, and hates[907] everything obscure, and is disturbed at everything dark, which inspires fear and suspicion in it, whereas light is so dear and welcome to it that it thinks nothing otherwise delightful bearable without it, as indeed light makes every pleasure pastime and enjoyment gay and cheerful, like the application of some sweet and general flavour. But the man who thrusts himself into obscurity, and wraps himself up in darkness and buries himself alive, is like one who is dissatisfied with his birth, and renounces his being.

§ VII. And yet *Pindar* tells us[908] that the abode of the blest is a glorious existence, where the sun shines bright through the entire night in meadows red with roses, an extensive plain full of shady trees ever in bloom never in fruit, watered by gentle purling streams, and there the blest ones pass their time away in thinking and talking about the past and present in social converse....[909] But the third road is of those who have lived unholy and lawless lives, that thrusts their souls to Erebus and the bottomless pit, where sluggish streams of murky night belch forth endless darkness, which receive those that are to be punished and conceal them in forgetfulness and oblivion. For vultures do not always prey on the liver of wicked persons lying on the ground,[910] for it is destroyed by fire or has rolled away; nor does the carrying of heavy burdens press upon and tire out the bodies of those that undergo punishment,

"For their strength has no longer flesh and bones,"[911]

nor have the dead any vestige of body that can receive the infliction of punishment that can make impression; but in reality the only punishment of those who have lived ill is infamy and obscurity and utter annihilation, which hurries them off to the dark river of oblivion,[912] and plunges them into the abyss of a fathomless sea, involving them in uselessness and idleness, ignorance and obscurity.

[895] Probably Epicurus, as we infer from the very personal § iii.

[896] Euripides, Fragm. 930.

[897] Reading with Wyttenbach, [Greek: Alla touto men tautê].

[898] Reading [Greek: ekastou] for [Greek: ekaston]. Reiske proposed [Greek: ekastôn].

[899] Reading [Greek: ei] (for [Greek: hina]) with Xylander and Wyttenbach.

[900] Reading with Wyttenbach.

[901] Adopting the suggestion of Wyttenbach, "Forte [Greek: kalou], at Amiot."

[902] Frag. 742.

[903] "Dormiens quisque in peculiarem abest mumdum, expergefactus in communem redit."--*Xylander*. Compare Herrick's Poem, "*Dreames.*"

[904] Bright.

[905] Invisible.

[906] [Greek: phôs].

[907] Reading with Wyttenbach [Greek: echthairei].

[908] Reading [Greek: phêsin] for [Greek: physin].

[909] Hiatus hic valde deflendus.

[910] As was fabled about Tityus, "Odyssey," xi. 576-579.

[911] "Odyssey," xi. 219.

[912] So Reiske, [Greek: potamin tês lêthês].

ON EXILE.

§ I. They say those discourses, like friends, are best and surest that come to our refuge and aid in adversity, and are useful. For many who come forward do more harm than good in the remarks they make to the unfortunate, as people unable to swim trying to rescue the drowning get entangled with them and sink to the bottom together. Now the discourse that ought to come from friends and people disposed to be helpful should be consolation, and not mere assent with a man's sad feelings. For we do not in adverse circumstances need people to weep and wail with us like choruses in a tragedy, but people to speak plainly to us and instruct us, that grief and dejection of mind are in all cases useless and idle and senseless; and that where the circumstances themselves, when examined by the light of reason, enable a man to say to himself that his trouble is greater in fancy than in reality, it is quite ridiculous not to inquire of the body what it has suffered, nor of the mind if it is any the worse for what has happened, but to employ external sympathizers to teach us what our grief is.

§ II. Therefore let us examine alone by ourselves the weight of our misfortunes, as if they were burdens. For the body is weighed down by the burden of what presses on it, but the soul often adds to the real load a burden of its own. A stone is naturally hard, and ice naturally cold, but they do not receive these properties and impressions from without; whereas with regard to exile and loss of reputation or honours, as also with regard to their opposites, as crowns and office and position, it is not their own intrinsic nature but our opinion of them that is the gauge of their real joy or sorrow, so that each person makes them for himself light or heavy, easy to bear or hard to bear. When Polynices was asked

"What is't to be an exile? Is it grievous?"

he replied to the question,

"Most grievous, and in deed worse than in word."[913]

Compare with this the language of Alcman, as the poet has represented him in the following lines. "Sardis, my father's ancient home, had I had the fortune to be reared in thee, I should have been dressed in gold as a priest of Cybele,[914] and beaten the fine drums; but as it is my name is Alcman, and I am a citizen of Sparta, and I have learned to write Greek poetry, which makes me greater than the tyrants Dascyles or Gyges." Thus the very same thing one man's opinion makes good, like current coin, and another's bad and injurious.

§ III. But let it be granted that exile is, as many say and sing, a grievous thing. So some food is bitter, and sharp, and biting to the taste, yet by an admixture with it of sweet and agreeable food we take away its unpleasantness. There are also some colours unpleasant to look at, that quite confuse and dazzle us by their intensity and excessive force. If then we can relieve this by a mixture of shadow, or by diverting the eye to green or some agreeable colour, so too can we deal with misfortunes, mixing up with them the advantages and pleasant things we still enjoy, as wealth, or friends, or leisure, and no deficiency in what is necessary for our subsistence. For I do not think that there are many natives of Sardis who would not choose your fortune even with exile, and be content to live as you do in a strange land, rather than, like snails who have no other home than their shells, enjoy no other blessing but staying at home in ease.

§ IV. As then he in the comedy that was exhorting an unfortunate friend to take courage and bear up against fortune, when he asked him "how," answered "as a philosopher," so may we also play the philosopher's part and bear up against fortune manfully. How do we do when it rains, or when the North Wind doth blow? We go to the fire, or the baths, or the house, or put on another coat: we don't sit down in the rain and cry. So too can you more than most revive and cheer yourself for the chill of adversity, not standing in need of outward aid, but sensibly using your actual advantages. The surgeon's cupping-glasses extract the worst humours from the body to relieve and preserve the rest of it, whereas the melancholy and querulous by ever dwelling on their worst circumstances, and thinking only of them, and being engrossed by their troubles, make even useful things useless to them, at the very time when the need is most urgent. For as to those two jars, my friend, that Homer[915] says are stored in Heaven, one full of good fortunes, one of bad, it is not Zeus that presides as the dispenser of them, giving to some a gentle and even portion, and to others unmixed streams of evils, but ourselves. For the sensible make their life pleasanter and more endurable by mitigating their sorrows with the consideration of their blessings, while most people, like sieves, let the worst things stick to them while the best pass through.

§ V. And so, if we fall into any real trouble or evil, we ought to get cheerfulness and ease of mind from the consideration of the actual blessings that are still left to us, mitigating outward trouble by private happiness. And as to those things which are not really evil in their nature, but only so from imagination and empty fancy, we must act as we do with children who are afraid of masks: by bringing them near, and putting them in their hands, and turning them about, we accustom them never to heed them at all: and so we by bringing reason to bear on it may discover the rottenness and emptiness and exaggeration of our fancy. As a case in point let us take your present exile from what you deem your country. For in nature no country, or house, or field, or smithy, as Aristo said, or surgery, is peculiarly ours, but all such things exist or rather take their name in connection with the person who dwells in them or possesses them. For man, as Plato says, is not an earthly and immovable but heavenly plant, the head making the body erect as from a root, and turned up to heaven.[916] And so Hercules said well,

"Argive or Theban am I, I vaunt not To be of one town only, every tower That does to Greece belong, that is my country."

But better still said Socrates, that he was not an Athenian or Greek, but a citizen of the world (as a man might say he was a Rhodian or Corinthian), for he did not confine himself to Sunium, or Tænarum, or the Ceraunian mountains.

"See you the boundless reach of sky above, And how it holds the earth in its soft arms?"

These are the boundaries of our country, nor is there either exile or stranger or foreigner in these, where there is the same fire, water and air, the same rulers controllers and presidents, the sun the moon and the morning star, the same laws to all, under one appointment and ordinance the summer and winter solstices, the equinoxes, Pleias and Arcturus, the seasons of sowing and planting; where there is one king and ruler, God, who has under his jurisdiction the beginning and middle and end of everything, and travels round and does everything in a regular way in accordance with nature; and in his wake to punish all transgressions of the divine law follows Justice, whom all men naturally invoke in dealing with one another as fellow citizens.

§ VI. As to your not dwelling at Sardis, that is nothing. Neither do all the Athenians dwell at Colyttus, nor all the Corinthians at Craneum, nor all the Lacedæmonians at Pitane. Do you consider all those Athenians strangers and exiles who removed from Melita to Diomea, where they call the month Metageitnion,[917] and keep the festival Metageitnia to commemorate their migration, and gladly and gaily accept and are content with their neighbourhood with other people? Surely you would not. What part of the inhabited world or of the whole earth is very far distant from another part, seeing that mathematicians teach us that the whole earth is a mere point compared to heaven? But we, like ants or bees, if we get banished from one ant-hill or hive are in sore distress and feel lost, not knowing or having learnt to make and consider all things our own, as indeed they are. And yet we laugh at the stupidity of one who asserts that the moon shines brighter at Athens than at Corinth, though in a sort we are in the same case ourselves, when in a strange land we look on the earth, the sea, the air, the sky, as if we doubted whether or not they were different from those we had been accustomed to. For nature makes us free and unrestrained, but we bind and confine immure and force ourselves into small and scanty space. Then too we laugh at the Persian kings, who, if the story be true, drink only of the water of the Choaspes, thus making the rest of the world waterless as far as they are concerned, but when we migrate to other places, we desire the water of the Cephisus, or we yearn for the Eurotas, or Taygetus, or Parnassus, and so make the whole world for ourselves houseless and homeless.

§ VII. Some Egyptians, who migrated to Ethiopia because of the anger and wrath of their king, to those who begged them to return to their wives and children very immodestly exposed their persons, saying that they would never be in want of wives or children while so provided. It is far more becoming and less low to say that whoever has the good fortune to be provided with the few necessaries of life is nowhere a stranger, nowhere without home and hearth, only he must have besides these prudence and sense, as an anchor and helm, that he may be able to moor himself in any harbour. For a person indeed who has lost his wealth it is not easy quickly to get another fortune, but every city is at once his country to the man who knows how to make it such, and has the roots by which he can live and thrive and get acclimatized in every place, as was the case with Themistocles and Demetrius of Phalerum. The latter after his banishment became a great friend of Ptolemy at Alexandria, and not only passed his days in abundance, but also sent gifts to the Athenians. And Themistocles, who was publicly entertained at the king's expense, is stated to have said to his wife and children, "We should have been ruined, if we had not been ruined." And so Diogenes the Cynic to the person who said to him, "The people of Sinope have condemned you to banishment from Pontus," replied, "And I have condemned them to stay in Pontus, 'by the high cliffs of the inhospitable sea.'"[918] And Stratonicus asked his host at Seriphus, for what offence exile was the appointed punishment, and being told that they punished rogues by exile, said, "Why then are not you a rogue, to escape from this hole of a place?" For the comic poet says they get their crop of figs down there with slings, and that the island is very barely supplied with the necessaries of life.

§ VIII. For if you look at the real facts and shun idle fancy, he that has one city is a stranger and foreigner in all others. For it does not seem to such a one fair and just to leave his own city and dwell in another. "It has been your lot to be a citizen of Sparta, see that you adorn your native city," whether it be inglorious, or unhealthy, or disturbed with factions, or has its affairs in disorder. But the person whom fortune has deprived of his own city, she allows to make his home in any he fancies. That was an excellent precept of Pythagoras, "Choose the best kind of life, custom will make it easy." So too it is wise and profitable to say here, "Choose the best and pleasantest city, time will make it your country, and a country that will not always distract you and trouble you and give you various orders such as, 'Contribute so much money, Go on an embassy to Rome, Entertain the prefect, Perform public duties.'" If a person in his senses and not altogether silly were to think of these things, he would prefer to live in exile in some island, like Gryarus or Cinarus,

"Savage, and fruitless, ill repaying tillage,"

and that not in dejection and wailing, or using the language of those women in Simonides,

"I am shut in by the dark roaring sea That foams all round,"

but he will rather be of the mind of Philip, who when he was thrown in wrestling, and turned round, and noticed the mark his body made in the dust, said, "O Hercules, what a little part of the earth I have by nature, though I desire all the world!"

§ IX. I think also you have seen Naxos, or at any rate Hyria, which is close here. But the former was the home of Ephialtes and Otus, and the latter was the dwelling-place of Orion. And Alcmæon, when fleeing from the Furies, so the poets tell us, dwelt in a place recently formed by the silting of the Achelous;[919] but I think he chose that little spot to dwell in ease and quiet, merely to avoid political disturbances and factions, and those furies informers. And the Emperor Tiberius lived the last seven years of his life in the island of Capreæ, and the sacred governing power of the world enclosed in his breast during all that time never changed its abode. But the incessant and constant cares of empire, coming from all sides, made not that island repose of his pure and complete. But he who can disembark on a small island, and get rid of great troubles, is a miserable man, if he cannot often say and sing to himself those lines of Pindar, "To love the slender cypress, and to leave the Cretan pastures lying near Ida. I have but little land, where I grow strong, and have nothing to do with sorrow or faction,"[920] or the ordinances of princes, or public duties in political emergencies, or state functions hard to get off.

§ X. For if that seems a good saying of Callimachus, "Do not measure wisdom by a Persian rope," much less should we measure happiness by ropes and parasangs, and if we inhabit an island containing 200 furlongs only, and not (like Sicily) four days' sail round, ought we to wail and lament as if we were very unfortunate? For how does plenty of room bring about an easy life? Have you not heard Tantalus saying in the play,[921]

"I sow a field that takes twelve days to travel round, The Berecyntian region,"

but shortly after he says,

"My fortunes, that were once as high as heaven, Now to the ground are fallen, and do say to me, 'Learn not to make too much of earthly things.'"

And Nausithous leaving the spacious Hyperia because of the proximity of the Cyclopes, and migrating to an island "far from all enterprising men,"[922] and living an unsocial life,

"Apart from men beside the stormy sea,"[923]

yet contrived to make the life of his citizens very pleasant. And the Cyclades were first inhabited by the sons of Minos, and afterwards by the sons of Codrus and Neleus, though foolish people now think they are punished if they are exiled to them. And yet what island used as a place of exile is not of larger extent than Scillus, where Xenophon after his military service saw a comfortable old age?[924] And the Academy, a small place bought for only 3,000 drachmæ,[925] was the domicile of Plato and Xenocrates and Polemo, who taught and lived there all their lives, except one day every year, when Xenocrates went to Athens to grace the festival of Dionysus, so they said, and to see the new plays exhibited. And Theocritus of Chios twitted Aristotle with loving to live at the courts of Philip and Alexander, and preferring to dwell at the mouth of the Borborus to dwelling in the Academy. For there is a river near Pella that the Macedonians call Borborus. As to islands Homer seems to sing their praise, and recommend them to us as if on purpose, as

"She came to Lemnos, town of sacred Thoas;"[926]

and,

"What Lesbos has, the seat of the immortals;"[927]

and,

"He captured lofty Scyros, citadel Of Enyeus;"[928]

and,

"And those who from Dulichium came, and from The sacred islands called th' Echinades, That lie across the sea opposite Elis;"[929]

and of the illustrious men that dwelt in islands he mentions Æolus the favourite of the gods, and Odysseus most wise, and Ajax most brave, and Alcinous most kind to strangers.

§ XI. When Zeno learned that the only ship he had left was with all its freight lost at sea, he said, "Fortune, you deal kindly with me, confining me to my threadbare cloak and the life of a philosopher." And a man not altogether silly, or madly in love with crowds, might, I think, not blame fortune for confining him in an island, but might even praise her for relieving him from weariness and anxiety, and wanderings in foreign countries, and perils by sea, and the uproar of the forum, and for giving him truly a secure, quiet, undistracted and private life, putting him as it were inside a circle in which everything necessary for him was contained. For what island has not a house, a promenade, a bath, and fish and hares for those who love fishing and field-sports? And the greatest blessing, quiet, which others frequently pant for, you can freely enjoy.[930] And whereas in the world,[930] when men are playing at dice or otherwise enjoying the privacy of their homes, informers and busybodies hunt them up and pursue them from their houses and gardens in the suburbs, and drag them by force to the forum and court, in an island no one comes to bother one or dun one or to borrow money, or to beg one to be surety for him or canvass for him: only one's best friends and intimates come to visit one out of good will and affection, and the rest of one's life is a sort of holy retirement to whoever wishes or has learnt to live the life of leisure. But he who thinks those happy who are always scouring the country, and pass most of their lives in inns and ferryboats, is like a person who thinks the planets happier than fixed stars. And yet every planet keeps its order, rolling in one sphere, as in an island. For, as Heraclitus says, the sun will never deviate from its bounds, for if it did, the Furies, who are the ministers of Justice, would find it out.

§ XII. Let us use such and similar language, my friend, and harp upon it, to those who are banished to an island, and are debarred all access with others

"By the sea waves, which many keep apart."[931]

But you who are not tied down to one spot, but only forbidden to live in one, have by that prohibition liberty to go to all others. Moreover to the considerations, I am not in office, or a member of the senate, or an umpire in the games, you may oppose these, I do not belong to any faction, I have no large sums to spend, I have not to dance attendance at the doors of the prefect, it is no odds to me who has got by lot the province, whether he is hot-tempered or an objectionable person. But just as Archilochus overlooked the fruitful fields and vineyards of Thasos, and abused that island as rocky and uneven, and said of it,

"It stands like donkey's chine crowned with wild forest,"

so we, fixing our eyes only on one aspect of exile, its inglorious state, overlook its freedom from cares, its leisure, its liberty. And yet people thought the kings of Persia happy, because they passed their winter in Babylon, their summer in Media, and the pleasant season of spring at Susa. So can the exile be present at the Eleusinian mysteries, at the festival of Dionysus at Athens, at the Nemean games at Argos, at the Pythian games at Delphi, and can pass on and be a spectator of the Isthmian and Corinthian games, if he is fond of sight-seeing; and if not, he has leisure, can walk about, read, sleep without being disturbed, and can say like Diogenes, "Aristotle has to dine when Philip thinks fit, Diogenes can dine at any time he himself chooses," having no business, or magistrate, or prefect, to put him out of his general habits of living.

§ XIII. And so it is that you will find few of the wisest and most intelligent men buried in their own countries, but most (even without any compulsion) have themselves weighed anchor, and transferred their course, and removed, some to Athens, some from it. For who ever bestowed such encomium upon his country as Euripides did in the following lines?

"First we are not a race brought in from other parts, But are indigenous, when all other cities Are, draughts-men like, transferred from place to place, And are imported from elsewhere. And, lady, If it is not beside the mark to boast, We have above us a well-tempered sky, A climate not too hot, nor yet too cold. And all the finest things in Greece or Asia We do procure as an attraction here."[932]

And yet the author of these lines went to Macedonia, and lived all the latter part of his life at the court of Archelaus. And of course you have heard the following epitaph;

"Here lies Euphorion's son, Athenian Æschylus, To whom death came in corn-producing Gela."

For he, like Simonides before him, went to Sicily. And many have changed the commencing words of Herodotus, "This is the setting forth of the history of Herodotus of Halicarnassus" into "Herodotus of Thurii." For he migrated to Thurii, and participated in that colony. As to the divine and sacred spirit of the Muses, the poet of the Trojan war, Homer, did not many cities claim him as theirs, because he did not cry up one city only? And Hospitable Zeus has many great honours.

§ XIV. And if anyone shall say that these pursued glory and honour, go to the philosophers, and their schools and lectures, consider those at the Lyceum, the Academy, the Porch, the Palladium, the Odeum. If you admire and prefer the Peripatetic school, Aristotle was a native of Stagira, Theophrastus of Eresus, Strato of Lampsacus, Glyco of Troas, Aristo of Ceos, Critolaus of Phaselis. If you prefer the Stoic school, Zeno was a native of Cittium, Cleanthes of Assus, Chrysippus of Soli, Diogenes of Babylon, Antipater of Tarsus; and the Athenian Archidemus migrated to the country of the Parthians, and left at Babylon a succession of the Stoic school. Who exiled these men? Nobody; it was their own pursuit of quiet, of which no one who is famous or powerful can get much at home, that made them teach us this by their practice, while they taught us other things by their precepts. And even nowadays most excellent and renowned persons live in strange lands, not in consequence of being expelled or banished, but at their own option, to avoid business and distracting cares, and the want of leisure which their own country would bring them. For it seems to me that the Muses aided our old writers to complete their finest and most esteemed works by calling in exile as a fellow-worker. Thus Thucydides the Athenian wrote the history of the war between the Peloponnesians and the Athenians in Thrace near the forest of Scapte, Xenophon wrote at Scillus in Elis, Philistus in Epirus, Timæus of Tauromenium at Athens, Androtion of Athens at Megara, and Bacchylides the poet[933] in Peloponnesus. All these and many more, though exiled from their country, did not despair or give themselves up to dejection, but so happy was their disposition that they considered exile a resource given them by fortune, whereby they obtained universal fame after their deaths, whereas no memorial is left of those who were factious against them and banished them.

§ XV. He therefore is ridiculous who thinks that any ignominy attaches itself to exile. What say you? Was Diogenes without glory, whom Alexander saw basking in the sun, and stopped to ask if he wanted anything, and when he answered, "Nothing, but that you would get a little out of my light," Alexander, astonished at his spirit, said to his friends, "If I were not Alexander, I would be Diogenes." Was Camillus without glory when banished from Rome, of which he is now accounted the second founder? And indeed Themistocles did not lose by his exile the glory he had obtained among the Greeks, but he added to it among the barbarians, and there is no one so without honour, so ignoble, who would prefer to be Leobates who indicted him rather than Themistocles the exile, or Clodius who banished Cicero rather than the banished one, or Aristophon the accuser rather than Timotheus who got driven by him from his country.

§ XVI. But since a good many are moved by the lines of Euripides, who seems to bring a strong indictment against exile, let us see what it is he says in each question and answer about it.

Jocasta. What is't to be an exile? Is it grievous?

Polynices. Most grievous, and in deed worse than in word.

Jocasta. What is its aspect? What is hard for exiles?

Polynices. This is the greatest, that they have no freedom.

Jocasta. This is a slave's life not to speak one's thoughts!

Polynices. Then one must put up with one's masters' follies.[934]

But this is not a right or true estimate.[935] For first of all, not to say out all one thinks is not the action of a slave but of a sensible man, in times and matters that require reticence and silence, as Euripides himself has said elsewhere better,

"Be silent where 'tis meet, speak where 'tis safe."

Then as for the follies of one's masters, one has to put up with them just as much in one's own country as in exile. Indeed, more frequently have the former reason to fear that the powerful in cities will act unjustly to them either through calumny or violence. But his greatest and absurdest error is that he takes away from exiles freedom of speech. It is wonderful, if Theodorus had no freedom of speech, that when Lysimachus the king said to him, "Did not your country cast you out because of your character?" replied, "Yes, as Semele cast out Dionysus, when unable to bear him any longer." And when he showed him Telesphorus in a cage,[936] with his eyes scooped out, and his nose and ears and tongue cut off, and said to him, "This is how I treat those that act ill to me." * *[937] And had not Diogenes freedom of speech, who, when he visited Philip's camp just as he was on the eve of offering battle to the Greeks, and was taken before the king as a spy, told him he had come to see his insatiable folly, who was going shortly to stake his dominions and life on a mere die. And did not Hannibal the Carthaginian use freedom of speech to Antiochus, though he was an exile, and Antiochus a king? For as a favourable occasion presented itself he urged the king to attack the enemy, and when after sacrifice he reported that the entrails forbade it, Hannibal chided him and said, "You listen rather to what flesh tells you than to the instruction of a man of experience." Nor does exile deprive geometricians or grammarians of their freedom of speech, or prevent their discussing what they know and have learnt. Why should it then good and worthy men? It is meanness everywhere that stops a man's speech, ties and gags his tongue, and forces him to be silent. But what are the next lines of Euripides?

Jocasta. Hopes feed the hearts of exiles, so they say.

Polynices. Hopes have a flattering smile, but still delay.[938]

But this is an accusation against folly rather than exile. For it is not those who have learnt and know how to enjoy the present, but those who ever hang on the future, and hope after what they have not, that float as it were on hope as on a raft, though they never get beyond the walls.[939]

Jocasta. But did your father's friends do nothing for you?

Polynices. Be fortunate! Friends are no use in trouble.

Jocasta. Did not your good birth better your condition?

Polynices. 'Tis bad to want. Birth brought no bread to me.[940]

But it was ungrateful in Polynices thus to rail against exile as discrediting his good birth and robbing him of friends, for it was on account of his good birth that he was deemed worthy of a royal bride though an exile, and he came to fight supported by a band of friends and allies, a great force, as he himself admits a little later,

"Many of the princes of the Danai And from Mycenæ are with me, bestowing A sad but necessary kindness on me."[941]

Nor was there any more justice in the lament of his mother:--

"I never lit for you the nuptial torch In marriage customary, nor did Ismenus Furnish you with the usual solemn bath."[942]

She ought to have been pleased and content to hear that her son dwelt in such a palace *as that at Argos*, and in lamenting that the nuptial torch was not lit, and that he had not had the usual bath in the river Ismenus, as though there was no water or fire at Argos for wedded people, she lays on exile the evils really caused by pride and stupidity.

§ XVII. But exile, you will say, is a matter of reproach. It may be among fools, who also jeer at the beggar, the bald man, the dwarf, aye, and even the stranger and resident alien. But those who are not carried away in that manner admire good men, whether they are poor, or strangers or exiles. Do we not see that all men adore the temple of Theseus as well as the Parthenon and Eleusinium? And yet Theseus was an exile from Athens, though it was owing to him that Athens is now inhabited, and he was banished from a city which he did not merely dwell in, but had himself built. And what glory is left to Eleusis, if we are ashamed of Eumolpus, who migrated from Thrace, and taught the Greeks (as he still teaches them) the mysteries? And who was the father of Codrus that reigned at Athens? Was it not Melanthus, an exile from Messene? And do you not praise the answer of Antisthenes to the person who told him that his mother was a Phrygian, "So also is the mother of the gods." If you are twitted then with exile, why do you not answer, "The father of the glorious victor Hercules was an exile." And Cadmus, the grandfather of Dionysus, when he was sent from home to find Europa, and never came back, "though a Phoenician born he changed his country,"[943] and migrated to Thebes, and became[944] the grandfather of "Dionysus, who rejoices in the cry of Evoe, the exciter of women, who delights in frantic honours." As for what Æschylus obscurely hints at in the line,

"Apollo the chaste god, exile from heaven,"

let me keep a religious silence, as Herodotus[945] says. And Empedocles commences his system of philosophy as follows, "It is an ordinance of necessity, an ancient decree of the gods, when anyone stains his hands with crime and murder, the long-lived demons get hold of him, so that he wanders away from the gods for thirty thousand years. Such is my condition now, that of an exile and wanderer from the gods." In these words he not only speaks of himself, but points out that all of us men similarly are strangers and foreigners and exiles in this world. For he says, "O men, it is not blood or a compounded spirit that made the being or beginning of the soul, but it is your earth-born and mortal body that is made up of these." He calls speciously by the mildest of names the birth of the soul that has come from elsewhere a living in a strange country. But the truth is the soul is an exile and wanderer, being driven about by the divine decrees and laws, and then, as in some sea-girt island, gets joined to the body like an oyster to its shell, as Plato says, because it cannot call to mind or remember from what honour and greatness of happiness it migrated, not from Sardis to Athens, nor from Corinth to Lemnos or Scyros, but exchanging heaven and the moon for earth and life upon earth, if it shifts from place to place for ever so short a time it is put out and feels strange, and fades away like a dying plant. But although one soil is more suitable to a plant than another, and it thrives and grows better on such a soil, yet no situation can rob a man of his happiness or virtue or sense. It was in prison that Anaxagoras wrote his squaring of the circle, and that Socrates, even after drinking the hemlock, talked philosophically, and begged his friends to be philosophers, and was esteemed happy by them. On the other hand, Phaëthon and Tantalus, though they got up to heaven, fell into the greatest misfortunes through their folly, as the poets tell us.

[913] Euripides, "Phoenissæ," 388, 389.

[914] Reading [Greek: bakelas]. *Gallus* in Latin.

[915] "Iliad," xxiv. 527-533.

[916] Plato, "Timæus," p. 90 A. Compare Ovid, "Metamorphoses," i. 84-86.

[917] Derived from [Greek: meta, geitôn], because then people flitted and changed their neighbours.

[918] Euripides, "Iphigenia in Tauris," 253.

[919] See also Pausanias, viii. 24.

[920] Pindar, Fragm. 126.

[921] Æschylus, "Niobe," Fragm. 146.

[922] "Odyssey," vi. 8. I read [Greek: andrôn] as Wyttenbach.

[923] "Odyssey," vi. 204.

[924] See Pausanias, v. 6.

[925] In our money about £121 17*s*. 6*d*.

[926] "Iliad," xiv. 230.

[927] "Iliad," xxiv. 544.

[928] "Iliad," ix. 668.

[929] "Iliad," ii. 625, 626.

[930] So Reiske.

[931] "Iliad," xxi. 59.

[932] Euripides, Fragm. 950.

[933] Reiske suggests [Greek: Bakchylidês ho Keios]. A very probable suggestion.

[934] Euripides, "Phoenissæ," 388-393.

[935] Omitting [Greek: prhôtôs], which probably got in from [Greek: prôton] following, and for which Reiske conjectured [Greek: horas hôs].

[936] Such as Cardinal Balue was shut up by Louis XI in for fourteen years.

[937] The answer of Theodorus is wanting.

[938] Euripides, "Phoenissæ," 396, 397.

[939] That is, they never get any further.

[940] Euripides, "Phoenissæ," 402-405.

[941] Euripides, "Phoenissæ," 430-432.

[942] Ibid. 344-346.

[943] Reading [Greek: chthonos]. "Sic mutandum censet Valckenarius."--*Wyttenbach*.

[944] Through his daughter Semele.

[945] Herodotus, ii. 171.

ON FORTUNE.

§ I. "Fortune, not wisdom, rules the affairs of mortals."[946] And does not justice, and fairness, and sobriety, and decorum rule the affairs of mortals? Was it of fortune or owing to fortune that Aristides persevered in his poverty, when he might have been lord of much wealth? And that Scipio after taking Carthage neither saw nor received any of the spoil? Was it of fortune or owing to fortune that Philocrates spent on harlots and fish the money he had received from Philip? And that Lasthenes and Euthycrates lost Olynthus, measuring happiness by their belly and lusts? Was it of fortune that Alexander the son of Philip not only himself abstained from the captive women, but punished others that outraged them? Was it under the influence of an evil genius and fortune that Alexander,[947] the son of Priam, intrigued with the wife of his host and ran away with her, and filled two continents with war and evils? For if all these things are due to fortune, what hinders our saying that cats and goats and apes are under the influence of fortune in respect of greediness, and lust, and ribaldry?

§ II. And if there are such things as sobriety and justice and fortitude, with what reason can we deny the existence of prudence, and if prudence exists, how can we deny the existence of wisdom? For sobriety is a kind of prudence, as people say, and justice also needs the presence of prudence. Nay more, we call the wisdom and prudence that makes people good in regard to pleasure self-control and sobriety, and in dangers and hardships endurance and fortitude, and in dealings between man and man and in public life equity and justice. And so, if we are to ascribe to fortune the acts of wisdom, let us ascribe justice and sobriety to fortune also, aye, and let us put down to fortune stealing, and picking pockets, and lewdness, and let us bid farewell to argument, and throw ourselves entirely on fortune, as if we were, like dust or refuse, borne along and hurried away by a violent wind. For if there be no wisdom, it is not likely that there is any deliberation or investigation of matters, or search for expediency, but Sophocles only talked nonsense when he said,

"Whate'er is sought is found, what is neglected Escapes our notice;"[948]

and again in dividing human affairs,

"What can be taught I learn, what can be found out Duly investigate, and of the gods I ask for what is to be got by prayer."[949]

For what can be found out or learnt by men, if everything is due to fortune? And what deliberative assembly of a state is not annulled, what council of a king is not abrogated, if all things are subject to fortune? whom we abuse as blind because we ourselves are blind in our dealings with her. Indeed, how can it be otherwise, seeing that we repudiate wisdom, which is like plucking out our eyes, and take a blind guide of our lives?

§ III. Supposing any of us were to assert that seeing is a matter of fortune, not of eyesight, nor of the eyes that give light, as Plato says, and that hearing is a matter of fortune, and not the imbibing of a current of air through the ear and brain, it would be well for us then to be on our guard against the evidence of our senses. But indeed nature has given us sight and hearing and taste and smell, and all other parts of the body and their functions, as ministers of wisdom and prudence. For "it is the mind that sees, and the mind that hears, everything else is deaf and blind." And just as, if there were no sun, we should have perpetual night for all the stars, as Heraclitus says, so man for all his senses, if he had no mind or reason, would be little better than the beasts. But as it is, it is not by fortune or chance that we are superior to them and masters of them, but Prometheus, that is reason, is the cause of this,

"Presenting us with bulls, horses, and asses, To ease us of our toil, and serve instead,"

as Æschylus says.[950] For as to fortune and natural condition, most of the beasts are better off than we are. For some are armed with horns and tusks and stings, and as for the hedgehog, as Empedocles says, it has its back all rough with sharp bristles, and some are shod and protected by scales and fur and talons and hoofs worn smooth by use, whereas man alone, as Plato says, is left by nature naked, unarmed, unshod, and uncovered. But by one gift, that of reason and painstaking and forethought, nature compensates for all these deficiencies. "Small indeed is the strength of man, but by the versatility of his intellect he can tame the inhabitants of the sea, earth, and air."[951] Nothing is more agile and swift than horses, yet they run for man; the dog is a courageous and high-spirited creature, yet it guards man; fish is most pleasant to the taste, the pig the fattest of all animals, yet both are food and delicacies for man. What is huger or more formidable in appearance than the elephant? Yet it is man's plaything, and a spectacle at public shows, and learns to dance and kneel. And all these things are not idly introduced, but to the end that they may teach us to what heights reason raises man, and what things it sets him above, and how it makes him master of everything.

"For we are not good boxers, nor good wrestlers, Nor yet swift runners,"[952]

for in all these points we are less fortunate than the beasts. But by our experience and memory and wisdom and cunning, as Anaxagoras says, we make use of them, and get their honey and milk, and catch them, and drive and lead them about at our will. And there is nothing of fortune in this, it is all the result of wisdom and forethought.

§ IV. Moreover the labours of carpenters and coppersmiths and house-builders and statue-makers are affairs of mortals, and we see that no success in such trades is got by fortune or chance. For that fortune plays a very small part in the life of a wise man, whether coppersmith or house-builder, and that the greatest works are wrought by art alone, is shown by the poet in the following lines:--

"All handicraftsmen go into the street, Ye that with fan-shaped baskets worship Ergane, Zeus' fierce-eyed daughter;"[953]

for Ergane[954] and Athene, and not Fortune, do the trades regard as their patrons. They do indeed say that Nealces,[955] on one occasion painting a horse, was quite satisfied with his painting in all other respects, but that some foam on the bridle from the horse's breath did not please him, so that he frequently tried to rub it out; at last in his anger he threw his sponge (just as it was, full of colours) at the picture, and this very wonderfully produced exactly the effect he desired. This is the only fortunate accident in art that history records. Artificers everywhere use rules and weights and measures, that none of their work may be done at random and anyhow. And indeed the arts may be considered as wisdom on a small scale, or rather as emanations from and fragments of wisdom scattered about among the necessities of life; as the fire of Prometheus is riddled to have been divided and scattered about in all quarters of the world. For thus small particles and fragments of wisdom, breaking up as it were and getting divided into pieces, have formed into order.

§ V. It is strange then that the arts do not require fortune to attain to their ends, and yet that the most important and complete of all the arts, the sum total of man's glory and merit, should be so completely powerless. Why, there is a kind of wisdom even in the tightening or slackening of chords, which people call music, and in the dressing of food, which we call the art of cooking, and in cleaning clothes, which we call the art of the fuller, and we teach boys how to put on their shoes and clothes generally, and to take their meat in the right hand and their bread in the left, since none of these things come by fortune, but require attention and care. And are we to suppose that the most important things which make so much for happiness do not call for wisdom, and have nothing to do with reason and forethought? Why, no one ever yet wetted earth with water and then left it, thinking it would become bricks by fortune and spontaneously, or procured wool and leather, and sat down and prayed Fortune that it might become clothes and shoes; nor does anyone getting together much gold and silver and a quantity of slaves, and living in a spacious hall with many doors, and making a display of costly couches and tables, believe that these things will constitute his happiness, and give him a painless happy life secure from changes, unless he be wise also. A certain person asked the general Iphicrates in a scolding way who he was, as he seemed neither a heavy-armed soldier, nor a bowman, nor a targeteer, and he replied, "I am the person who rule and make use of all these."

§ VI. So wisdom is neither gold, nor silver, nor fame, nor wealth, nor health, nor strength, nor beauty. What is it then? It is what can use all these well, and that by means of which each of these things becomes pleasant and esteemed and useful, and without which they are useless; and unprofitable and injurious, and a burden and disgrace to their possessor. So Hesiod's Prometheus gives very good advice to Epimetheus, "not to receive gifts from Olympian Zeus but to send them back,"[956] meaning external things and things of fortune. For as if he urged one who knew nothing of music not to play on the pipe, or one who knew nothing of letters not to read, or one who was not used to horses not to ride, so he advised him not to take office if he were foolish, nor to grow rich if he were illiberal, nor to marry if likely to be ruled by his wife. For success beyond their merit is to foolish persons a cause of folly, as Demosthenes said,[957] and good fortune beyond their merit is to those who are not sensible a cause of misfortune.[958]

Printed in Great Britain
by Amazon